Cooking
by Hand

Cooking
by Hand

Paul Bertolli

Executive Chef & Co-owner
of Oliveto Restaurant

Photographs by
Gail Skoff and Judy Dater

Clarkson Potter/Publishers
New York

Published by Clarkson Potter/Publishers, New York,
New York
Member of the Crown Publishing Group, a division of
Random House, Inc.
www.randomhouse.com

CLARKSON N. POTTER is a trademark and POTTER and
colophon are registered trademarks of Random House, Inc.

Printed in the United States of America

Library of Congress Cataloging-in-Publication Data
Bertolli, Paul
    Cooking by hand / Paul Bertolli.
1. Cookery. 2. Cookery, Italian. 3. Food I. Title
    TX651 .B475   2003
    641.5–dc21   2002152290

ISBN: 0-609-60893-2

10   9   8   7   6   5   4   3   2   1

First Edition

Design by Jack W. Stauffacher of The Greenwood Press,
San Francisco; design assistant, Kina Sullivan. Set in Cycles
type, designed by Sumner Stone.

Photographs on pages i, vi-x, 3, 8, 10, 13, 15, 17, 19, 21, 22, 24,
26, 28, 33, 34, 39, 42, 46, 55, 68, 89, 90, 93, 120, 128, 138, 143,
147, 154, 160, 166, 178, 222, 232, 237, 244, 254, and 263 by Gail
Skoff.
Photographs on pages xviii, 41, 45, 60, 62, 71, 74, 77, 85, 94, 98,
102, 106, 109, 115, 116, 122, 137, 165, 172, 173, 185, 191, 201,
204, 210, 211, 212, 216, and 248 by Judy Dater.
Photograph on page 133 by Gail Skoff and Judy Dater.

Contents

Guide to the Recipes by Chapter

The Whole Hog

Cooking Backward

Acknowledgments

I am sincerely grateful to all who assisted me in the birth of this book and its development along the way: Thanks to my agent, Peter Ginsburg of Curtis Brown Ltd., to Pam Krauss, my editor, who refined the text, and Marysarah Quinn in the design department of Clarkson Potter. Harold Magee generously provided information and explanations that helped me clarify my ideas. Oliveto chef de cuisine Paul Canales, former sous chef Morgon Brownlow, and pastry chef Julie Cookenboo offered vital assistance in developing and testing ideas and recipes while maintaining a full workload at the restaurant. Al and Keith Giusto educated me about flour and Joseph Vanderliet separated the chaff from my sentences on it. Dr. Joseph Sebranek at Iowa State University's meat science department graciously reviewed portions of the chapter on cured meats and Kermit Lynch seeded my thoughts on the organization of the chapter on wine and food. It was great fun to cavort with Gail Skoff and Judy Dater, who were also always game to lug their cameras where an image might be found. I am amazed by what their eyes can see. I am honored to have worked with master printer and book designer Jack Stauffacher, friend and kindred spirit, and his able assistant, Kina Sullivan. I owe a debt of gratitude to my faithful Oliveto partners Bob and Maggie Klein. Maggie researched information in the section Sources and Resources and listened and offered comments on the text; Bob informed me that I was done before *I* knew it. Richard and Kaye Heafey, Francesco Renzi, and Renato Bergonzini helped me to realize my passion years ago for *aceto balsamico.* Heartfelt appreciation to Kate Young, Andy Ross, and Anita Feder-Chernila and all who read and commented on portions of the text: Patty Dinner, Cal Zecca Ferris, Timothy Ferris, Steve Darland, Tom Garrity, Eunice Baek, Ben Fried, Noreen Wu, Suzanne and Chuck Fuery, John Magee, Roger Sender, Ad and June Brugger, Charlie Hass, B.K. Moran, John Harris, Bill Staggs, Fritz Streiff, Josephine Stauffacher, Lynn Carruthers, Jerry and Joan Lubenow, and Nancy Friedman. Linda and Anthony were my immeasurable support. This book is dedicated to you.

Introduction: Good Cooking Is Trouble

So, I am told, said Elizabeth David. And while I have never been able to locate the passage within her writing to see it in context, I am quite sure she wasn't referring to what a diet of delicious meals can do to the waistline. Rather, I take her to mean that good cooking is painstaking—that, as with all things made by hand, cooking well always involves some form of trouble.

The trouble with cooking begins when you decide to take it seriously. This raises the question, "What does seriously good cooking mean I must do?" As long as I have been cooking in earnest, this question has led me down trails full of circles and switchbacks, sometimes taking me directly into the brambles. And the learning never ends. The idea of "mastering" cooking now seems more like an illusion than a goal.

The will to learn anything begins with an awakening. My own education began not in a culinary school but in the gardens and orchards surrounding my family home in California. Before the area was populated with houses, it had been planted with a variety of fruit trees, many of which survived and had grown to noble standing by the time I was old enough to look up at them. My father had himself lined our backyard plot with stone fruit and citrus trees, presided over by a very old English walnut. As a boy I had no inkling that I would eventually become a chef but I knew I loved

Santa Rosa plums. Our two plum trees were the most generous to bear in our backyard tract. The sweetest fruit hung high and heavy in the sun-baked upper branches. Eating my way to the top of the tree was my first experience of the levels and limits of ripeness. At first, I was not particularly discriminating. I liked the sour smack of green plums as much as the sweet spurt of overripe fruit. But as successive summers arrived, I found myself training my eyes somewhere near the top and straining my reach for the fruit that I had come to learn was perfectly ready: plums you could shine on your sleeve without bursting them, heavy in the hand, juicy and sweet and tart with flesh vivid as an open wound. For ripe plums I would risk a ten-foot plunge to the ground, the sting of yellow jackets buzzing after the same prize, and the disappointment of finding the blind half of a seemingly perfect plum blighted by birds. Getting good plums was trouble.

In the same way, I learned to wait patiently for the fruit of our sour orange tree to deliver on the promise of its exquisitely scented spring blossoms. I watched its color change through the summer and autumn from lime green to pale yellow, until the chill of December finally transformed its fruit to a deep persimmon. Tight-skinned and unapproachable for months, the oranges were now easy to peel; their flavor was intensely sweet and tangy at the same time. They seemed to taste of all the light they'd ever absorbed.

I also remember my father sending me out in the yard in the late fall to pick black figs. I had been taught that figs will continue to ripen off the tree and that it was a good idea to pick them while still firm, allowing them to soften further as needed in the house. But I noticed that figs picked this way never quite measured up to those that were left behind to shrivel to "jam bags" on the tree. To have the privilege of tasting these meant trusting that I would be lucky enough to arrive before blue jays and ants that had the same idea.

The neighborhood was full of lessons in lemons, stone fruits, apples, pears, quinces, pineapple-guavas, and our own exotic Rangpur limes. Fruit is unpredictable. Not only are some trees better than others, there are better sides of trees. There are fruits that would rather be left hanging and others that won't ripen until you pick them. But when do you pick them and then how long must they sit before they are ready to eat? A peach might look and feel ripe, but not until you sniff it up close do you really know whether it's truly ready. Supermarket produce such as apples, oranges, and cucumbers are cosmetically enhanced through waxing to brighten their appearance. Lettuce is regularly misted to look as though the dew still clings to it. Piles of corn appeal under flattering lights. In all but farmers' markets, produce is primarily staged to excite the visual sense. The true complexion and/or scent of ripeness needs no improvement. The trouble lies in cultivating a recognition of the qualities of ripeness. Yet even in the most natural setting of a garden, nature withholds ripeness for a particular and limited time. Only by focusing the senses do we know if that time has arrived or if it has passed.

Learning about the finicky nature of fruit also taught me how to associate taste with scent. Wild mushrooms were less for eating than for kicking over in the rough and tumble of play under our hillside oak trees, but I remembered their damp smell rising from a compost of leaves, and I noticed its resemblance to that of the dried porcini mushrooms in my mother's *ragù*. Brushing by leaves of our local bay laurel left its traces on our clothes; and the leaves would lend their scent out to beef stew as well. There was also a whole range of more pervasive scents that belonged umistakably to a season: in the fall, the dense, tobacco-like smoke from burning walnut leaves from our backyard tree, winter's menthol droppings of smashed eucalyptus (the camphor in my cough syrup?); and the first rain after a dry summer releasing a complex of wet asphalt, dry grass, and the trapped exhalations of the earth.

A rich memory for tastes and scents, whether gathered casually or cultivated consciously, lends emotional resonance to cooking. This is as true for the chef whose cooking is guided by such memories as it is for the diner whose subtle or even subliminal recollections of smells are summoned while eating. Scent is like a switch in the memory, triggering old and new sensations, primal associations, and appetites. The surrounding scents of the season and of the particular place associated with a meal can become as much a part of our recollection as the meal itself. I remember eating grilled *bistecca alla fiorentina* on a foggy late autumn day after the grape harvest in Chianti. The smell of burning chestnut wood and composting grape skins will remain forever like a seasoning on that experience. Delicious as the meat was all by itself, had there not been that confluence of aromas in the air, I might well have been eating any old porterhouse steak.

Close proximity to the source affords the best chance of appreciating food as it is born to be. It is no coincidence that fish tastes better near the sea, that wine is at its best when drawn directly from the cellar where it is raised, and tomatoes are the most succulent when pulled from your own backyard vines. When we eat "at the source," we experience food in its most natural setting and the scents surrounding it blend comfortably and unforgettably with the meal itself. Having had these experiences even once sets a standard that later makes us nostalgic for what is missing. For the cook who knows the difference, the trouble lies in both seeking out and preserving the native quality of food.

I have never met a skilled chef who didn't have an acute sense of smell. This heightened sense gives one the ability not merely to perceive and identify aromas and bouquets, but to be *stirred* by the way things smell, for better or worse. I first became interested in learning to cook because I had a strong desire to replicate what I remembered having smelled and tasted. I discovered other worlds beyond my mother's kitchen— restaurants— at a fairly early age. My parents liked to take us to a seafood house on nearby Richardson Bay, a backwater of the Golden Gate, for cocktails of Dungeness crab and bay shrimp, fried sand dabs, and San Francisco *cioppino*. Later, I was part of a group that enjoyed the generosity of my high-school English teacher, a cleric whose rich aunt sent tithes directly to his checkbook. For several years, at nearly every week's end we ate at a different restaurant. I discovered broiled lobster, the seductions of sweet butter and soft-ripened cheese, pasta Alfredo, and French reduction sauces. When we got away with it (who could refuse a priest in collar?), we ordered drinks and I discovered how exciting a meal could be when lubricated with old-fashioneds and red wine.

Later on, I started reading about cooking and experimenting with cookbooks. It didn't take long to discover the disparity between what I remembered having tasted and my own renditions. Even the food I tried that was most familiar to me and more directly accessible, through instructions provided by my mother and grandmothers, never tasted quite the same when I cooked it. Following recipes was frustrating. Trying to match the static words in a book to the leaping events in a saucepan was a clumsy back-and-forth endeavor. Of course, recipes varied in quality, but more often than not, I found them vague, overly general, or outright wrong. Recipes left me with more questions than they answered about the actual process of cooking. I wanted to know why I was being asked to perform a certain step or what to do if things went awry. The reductive efficiency of the recipe offered little clue. It was clear that ingredients could vary across the board, so when instructed to "dice 3 leeks," this raised the question "What size, and in what condition?" Having digested Escoffier's dissertations on the mother sauces and what I could gain of technique from Pellaprat, Pépin, Guérard, Bugialli, Hazan, Ada Boni, and others, I struck out on my own. I substituted ingredients or left them out altogether; I experimented with herbs and oven temperatures, methods and utensils, and levels of reduction. I did my best to correct for deficiencies in flavor or balance, usually by adding *more* of something. In retrospect, some of these meals were abysmal, especially since "more" often resulted in food that no longer resembled itself or the original idea. Nevertheless, occasional successes gave me confidence that following my own nose and instincts would lead me closer to the ideals of my taste memory. I was happiest when improvising.

Later, when I began recording what I had done in the kitchen, I found that I was no more comfortable writing a recipe than following one. Studying my food-stained notes, I was annoyed at having to go back and measure in cups and teaspoons the ingredients that I had originally added according to taste and feel. Any good cook knows how to dose salt in the right proportion to food by the way it feels in the hand. Take that dose, put it into a measuring spoon, and it may come up fractionally short or overfill the brim. When a cook creates a recipe to fit standard weights and measures, the measures themselves creep in to exert control over the cook's better instincts. Precision is lost. Weight rather than volume measurement is the more accurate way to record the amount of any ingredient. But it likewise puts an object foreign to the creative context between the cook and the food. As my friend Richard Olney said, the act of recording a recipe "robs it of the license responsible for its creation." Ultimately it is the reader, the presumed learner, who is left bereft. Subtleties in the way food looks, smells, and behaves are lost when the process of cooking is reduced to a series of simple and efficient steps. Such is the unfortunate legacy of almost all recipe writing.

Still, some measurements are necessary. A cook who fails to provide an ingredients list with a basic guide for quantities would be remiss. But developing a quantified recipe is a long process rich with interesting and informative detail. By moving beyond the rigid confines of the standard recipe format, the writer/cook could add back many subtleties of his own experience that might give the reader a guide for dealing with what happens along the way. This same detail could help the reader understand the "process" well enough to be able to improvise according to his or her own tastes, or in response to the ingredients at hand.

Of course, this thinking about recipes does not apply to all processes in the kitchen. In pastry making and almost all forms of flour confectionery—indeed in any preparation in which the basic ingredients are relatively consistent—precise proportions must be observed in order to achieve good results. It is not a good idea to "wing it" with a cake or with someone's favorite cocktail. Nevertheless, such preparations are not entirely formulaic and call for an equal amount of attention on the part of the cook to the small variables that can make all the difference. It is impossible to communicate in words the precise feel of pasta dough when it is fully kneaded. It's equally troublesome to describe how much moisture and elasticity in the dough will give the eventual noodle its appealing bite. Variations in the manner of incorporating beaten egg white into cake batters can also result in degrees of lightness or heaviness in the finished cake. Regardless of the degree of specificity in any recipe, the difference that makes all the difference lies between the lines. Following a recipe does not absolve the cook from cooking.

While my own early forays into French and Italian cooking had sharpened my mechanical skills, I still felt at a loss for some deeper understanding of what I was doing. Looking around me, apart from a few San Francisco specialties tied to the seasonal availability of certain fish and shellfish, there was no clear food tradition to absorb. America in the thrall of *nouvelle cuisine* and *cuisine minceur*, fast food, and the influences of ethnic cooking was only confusing. In comparison to the Old World, America seemed embarrassingly impressionable. Food writers fascinated with the open restaurant kitchens of the west coast, their grill menus, celebration of local farms, and prophets of the fresh and pure, created the concept of "California cuisine." I am still at a loss to identify a single defining dish that belongs to this "revolution." Professional cooks with credibility either came from northern Europe or looked to it for inspiration. I could only imagine what it might mean to live in a city like Nantes that had a sauce named after it, or in Langhirano, where it took mountain air and a year and a half to age a ham, or in Lyon, where it was considered divine to roast a farm hen in a pig's bladder.

Through a combination of coincidence and fate I began working in restaurants in the late 1970s and after several years of apprenticeship I had the good fortune to land a restaurant job in Italy, the country of my heritage on both sides of my family. I'd grown up on emigrant renditions of Italian food, with no way to judge or question the differences between Italian food in Italy and versions of it made with New World ingredients. By working in Italy, I was able to ground myself in the food with which I was most familiar. I immediately felt drawn to Italy's transparent traditions and the long-established links between the food of a region and nature at its source. I was also intrigued with the intersection of skill and mystery in cooking—the transformations of food initiated through human intervention but only fulfilled by more obscure forces. For how could a mortal man have made this glorious wine, this cheese, and this *aceto balsamico*?

It was through working in Italy and returning time and again over the years to explore the cooking of its various provinces that I discovered what it means to live within a food tradition. I learned to understand the many ways in which simplicity manifests in cooking. Ironically, simplicity represents the trouble that many generations of cooks have taken to arrive at the best expression of their native ingredients. I saw that such simple food lives as much in the most refined dishes of a big-city restaurant as in the rustic menus of an *osteria*. No matter how straightforward or complex the ingredients or the cooking technique, simple food is directly appealing; there is nothing extraneous or fussy about it and the tastes and presentation are clear and unified. I discovered many examples all around me in the homes in which I ate traditional family meals, in markets and restaurants, and in the cellars of vintners, cheese makers, olive oil producers, vinegar makers, and pork butchers. The experience of this simple food was fundamental to my formation as a chef. I learned that olive oil is not just a cooking fat but a culture, that food is determined by place and inseparable from it, and that nourishment around the table is not only a matter of filling one's belly but of taking part in a daily ritual that celebrates and confirms a sense of belonging to the food and to long, recurrent traditions of a place.

Authenticity has its own taste yet its principles are universal. Given that the taste, the process, and the overall effect of particular flavors are bound by place, people and tradition, I do not attempt to duplicate at Oliveto, my restaurant in Oakland, California, the risotto with cuttlefish I ate in Venice, the wild field salads I gathered in Chianti, or the *culatello* I learned to cure in a foggy cellar in Zibello. Instead, I approach my cooking with a similar commitment to present what is grown here, to make food from scratch, to gather in the wild, to maintain my vinegar loft in the quiet of the countryside and my curing cellar in the fog of the Berkeley hills.

Like any active aesthetic practice, cooking is most satisfying when you are creatively involved. Being able to create in the kitchen necessitates learning the language and inner workings of cooking. The painter mixes her color palette to her mind's eye. The musician learns to listen to sound and to play what he hears. Cooks develop an internal memory for scents, tastes, textures, the architecture of flavor, and the path and process toward its consummation. The ever-evolving taste memory is the internal compass that arbitrates the physical steps, maneuvers, and choices a cook makes along the way. When you smell pasta made with fresh wheat you may be impelled to grind your own flour. Your taste for the genuine may temper your impatience at the prospect of waiting six months for your *salame* to ripen. The vivid quality of produce just pulled from the ground may lead you to plant your own radicchio or carrots. With growing curiosity you may find yourself puzzling out the savor missing in a braise you've made a dozen times.

This book aims to bolster your confidence in searching for what is delicious in your cooking and to go to the trouble to get there. I will have succeeded if it also stimulates your own exploration of cooking as an active, creative process. Accordingly, the recipes do

not always specify exact measurements. The reason is to encourage
an open-ended approach that leads you to consider the options
and variables dictated by the moment, to chart your own direction,
to develop a feeling for food, in fact to *cook*. To those accustomed
to cooking more to the letter of a recipe, this approach may appear
annoying or problematic. If I knew of a better or easier path, I
would have recommended it. But experience has shown that the
trouble you take will also be your enduring pleasure.

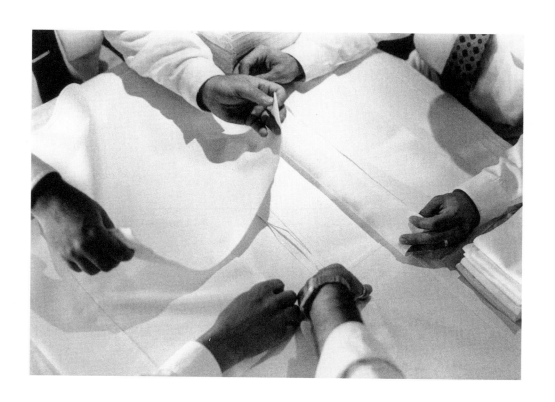

Cleaning the Fresco

Cleaning the Fresco

Some years back I had lunch outside Florence in a restaurant owned by a fellow restaurateur. His *ribollita*, a traditional Tuscan *minestra* of beans, *cavolo nero* (cabbage), vegetables, and bread, was a revelation. Having lived and worked in Florence I had eaten ribollita many times, but never with such a clear sense of the original intention of the dish. My friend explained that he aspired to learn as much as he could about the kitchen wisdom of the old people in the surrounding countryside who kept the local food traditions alive. He was dismayed by what has happened to traditional Tuscan cooking. Ribollita was not the only dish that bore little resemblance to its ancestral form. He likened *cucina Toscana*, as practiced in many of the restaurants of Florence, to the monuments, frescoes, and art treasures of the city that had faded or been covered with dulling layers of soot. Under the constant barrage of so many tourists clamoring for bread soup and *bistecca*, the cuisine had become a tired parody of itself. But in an effort much like restoration, he had attempted to make the original tastes vivid again in his cooking. His ribollita, made from vegetables and legumes from his own garden and perfumed with a thin stream of newly pressed olive oil, was a model of clarity. I felt like I was tasting it for the first time.

The discovery has remained with me as a source of inspiration for my own cooking. Here, with this experience of a tired dish made new again, a thoughtful chef had taken the time to peel back the layers of "innovations" made by generations of cooks, and to cut away what had become deadened by years of mechanical repetition. I now had a metaphor for the type of cooking that made sense to me: food grounded in a tradition, yet enlivened by the act of greeting the process and the ingredients anew. In Italy too I learned that cooking, based on a sensual deference for the essence of food, called for restraint both in mind-set and method; it was a matter of deciding not what to add, but what to allow to be. The spirit of the best of this cooking around the simplest of tables soared beyond the party cry of *cuisine de marché*, manifestos of freshness, or the consoling promises of *antica ricetta della nonna* (grandmother's old recipe), a common qualifier on restaurant menus. It needed no slogan. It spoke for itself. At the same time, my experimentation in the garden and the kitchen left me convinced that a cook must respond to the ingredients, aromas, seasons, and serendipitous events of the moment in order to keep foods tasting alive.

The task of keeping food vibrant and interesting, particularly food that belongs to a long tradition, is the challenge of any cook,

professional or amateur. For those who have a repertoire of their own, the repetitive aspect of cooking and the demands of our relentless need to eat can easily turn cooking into a dull task. Relying upon recipes, no matter how well advised, can turn cooking into drudgery. Food that is both delicious and interesting is always a reflection of an active response to the raw ingredients—one that often turns on its head information found in recipes.

Every cook inherits or chooses to follow a food tradition. Regardless of how distant or blurred the connection, and barring the bizarre concoctions and fusions of different cuisines that attempt novelty for its own sake, food makes reference to the tried and true, to what has been done before. Returning to the roots of a dish or cooking process is never a simple matter, particularly if you live far from the source. There are at least as many renditions of the "authentic" as there are cooks to provide them. Finding the right ingredients is often problematic. Nevertheless, understanding the spirit in which a dish was conceived and the tradition to which it belongs helps make sense of unique variations and personal interpretations, and reveals where one's own version fits in its evolution. Knowing the tradition provides a basis for experimentation and leads to new and sometimes better versions of older dishes. Yet it is often the case that the more primitive version of a dish cannot be improved upon, and a cook can do no better than to attempt to preserve the memory of taste and process associated with it.

I remember stories my grandmother told me about polenta, our habitual family Sunday meal during the years we lived together as an extended family. She talked about the mountains of polenta people used to eat in her town in the Veneto during the war years, and how fully satisfying it was, often served with little else but a bit of stew meat. When I tried milling whole corn myself, I understood why. By comparison, the store-bought, refined polenta to which I had grown accustomed delivered very little of the flavor, texture, or satisfaction of the crude version. No wonder; refined polenta consists of only the starchy endosperm of the corn kernel. The oil and flavor-rich germ and the outer bran that provides fiber are separated away in the milling process. My hand-milled polenta, from midwestern dent corn, has an aroma and texture different from those of Italian varieties of corn, but I believe it more closely recalls the spirit of the original. At Oliveto, we use stone-ground, whole-grist polenta. Our miller uses only certified organic corn that is dried in the field prior to cold milling. Controlling the temperature is critical in maintaining the integrity of corn's constituent parts and its fresh chemistry. The startling difference in flavor is also a matter of the cooking method; this polenta is started in cold water and maintained at a temperature that does not rise above the simmer point rather than whisked into a roiling boil. The reason for the gentler heat is that above a simmer, enzymes in the corn that convert starch to sugar are inactivated. It takes some patience to wait for whole-grist polenta to cook fully at a lower temperature, but the resulting "sweet mill flavor" is very likely to transcend any previous taste impression you had of the more refined form. Our version, enriched with butter and served in cake or porridge form or browned crisp on both sides in olive oil, preserves the simple goodness and fullest flavor of corn polenta in its whole, nutritious form. Either way, this polenta makes a fine, hearty complement to saucy meats.

Fresh Milled Polenta

For 10

Whole-grist polenta is very perishable and once received, should be stored in the freezer. In order to remove some of the excess starch, it is washed in cold water before cooking.

4 cups whole-grist polenta (see Sources and Resources, page 260)

3 quarts cold water for rinsing the polenta

3 quarts plus 1 cup (13 cups) cold water for cooking the polenta

5 teaspoons sea salt

12 tablespoons (1½ sticks) unsalted butter

1 cup hot water (optional, for thinning)

Put the polenta into a large bowl with 3 quarts of the cold water. Stir the polenta for several minutes, then drain it in a colander lined with cheesecloth or a fine-mesh basket strainer. Discard the starchy water.

Pour the remaining 13 cups cold water and the salt into a 6-quart heavy-bottomed pot. Stir to dissolve the salt. Place the pot on medium heat and whisk in the polenta in a fine stream so that none of it forms lumps. Gradually bring the temperature of the polenta to 180°F. Adjust the heat to hold it at that temperature. For the first 20 minutes of cooking, the polenta and water remain separate, though you will notice the top has a yellow milky appearance. While the polenta and water are heating up, stir every 2 to 3 minutes so that the polenta doesn't clump or stick to the bottom of the pot. Once the polenta absorbs the water, continue stirring every 15 minutes. It will thicken as it absorbs water, so it is important to scrape down the sides of the pot so that all the polenta is incorporated and to prevent a crust from developing around the rim. Maintain the heat between 170 and 180°F.; a flame tamer may be useful for this purpose. Cook the polenta for 2½ to 3 hours or until tender and no longer gritty. Stir in the butter. If you desire a smoother, softer texture, add another cup of hot water at this point.

If you're going to cool the polenta for polenta *abbrustollita* (in cake form browned crisp), do not add the extra cup of water. Pour the hot polenta out onto a buttered 8½ by 12-inch sheet pan and cool in the refrigerator for at least an hour. Cut the polenta into rectangles or whatever shape you like. Warm olive oil or clarified butter in a seasoned pan or nonstick pan until a little polenta sizzles when you add it. Allow the polenta to cook at a slow but even rate for 5 to 10 minutes per side or until it forms a deep, golden crust.

Vitello Tonnato

For 8

I have always found this classic summer dish of cold veal in tuna sauce, when well made, irresistible. Unfortunately, because of the expediency of premade mayonnaise, canned tuna, and leftover meats, *vitello tonnato* often does not live up to its promise, even in the best Italian restaurants. The most satisfying vitello tonnato is made from with fresh tuna or dark Italian tuna preserved in oil, mayonnaise made with buttery olive oil, and lean poached veal. Belly of tuna, although not all that common at fish counters, is the cut of choice for making tonnato sauce if you can find a fishmonger willing to save it for you from the trimmings of whole fish. I have also made excellent tonnato sauce from the belly sections of oil-rich swordfish. Mackerel is another option. Of the three, tuna belly has the richest flavor and, when blended with the mayonnaise, yields a voluptuous sauce. In order to reinforce the tuna in the sauce, I also add salt-cured anchovies, garlic, and lemon, giving the sauce a briny sea taste with a slight tang.

Poached veal on its own leaves something to be desired. It is the complement of this sauce and its harmonious blend of ingredients that is largely responsible for the dish's appeal. The key to making the sauce sing is to cook the primary ingredients together in the oil you will use to make the mayonnaise, a feat that is not possible if you are simply blending premade ingredients. Vitello tonnato is best if made the day before to allow meat and sauce to merge.

You will need cheesecloth and kitchen twine for this recipe.

1 piece of boneless veal loin, 1¾ pounds,
   trimmed of all fat and silverskin
4 bay leaves
3 tablespoons salt

Wrap the trimmed loin in the cheesecloth and tie it snugly with the twine at 1-inch intervals. Place the veal in a pot large enough to hold it comfortably. Add enough cold water to cover the loin by an inch. Add the bay leaves and salt. (Starting the veal in cold water enables the slow and gradual transfer of heat to the center of the meat and results in moist and tender slices at the finish.) Place the pot over low heat for approximately 25 minutes, or until the temperature in the center of the thickest part of the loin reaches 120°F. Do not allow the water to exceed 180°F. at any point or the veal will cook too quickly, seize up, and lose its moisture and flavor. Remove the veal from the poaching liquid, transfer it to a cooling rack, and place it in the refrigerator to cool. Discard the cooking water.

Tonnato Sauce
2 cups buttery extra-virgin olive oil
6 garlic cloves, thinly sliced
12 salt-cured anchovies, rinsed, soaked for
   5 minutes in lukewarm water, and peeled
   away from the bone
10 ounces tuna belly, mackerel, or belly cut of
   swordfish, cut into 1-inch pieces
2 egg yolks
½ cup cold water
Juice of ½ lemon
½ cup heavy cream

Warm the olive oil in a small saucepan. Add the garlic and anchovies and place over medium-low heat. Cook slowly for about 10 minutes, or until the anchovies are reduced to a paste. Add the tuna to the pot and cook for an additional 5 minutes. As the tuna cooks, gently mash together the tuna, garlic, and anchovies. Set aside to cool. When the tuna mixture has cooled to room temperature, separate the solids from the oil in a sieve and set aside separately.

In a 1-quart mixing bowl, make a mayonnaise by whisking the reserved cooking olive oil into the egg yolks in a steady, thin stream. After half the oil is incorporated the mayonnaise will become quite stiff. At this point, add the lemon juice to thin it, and continue adding oil until it is all incorporated. Set aside.

Place the tuna, garlic, and anchovy mixture in a food processor. Blend well for approximately 3 minutes, or until the mixture is a very fine paste. Add all of your mayonnaise to this paste and blend for several minutes more to a very smooth consistency. Next add the cream and water and blend for an additional 30 seconds. Correct to taste with salt. Set the tonnato sauce aside.

Garnishing and serving the vitello tonnato
4 tablespoons finely diced celery heart
2 tablespoons capers, rinsed and roughly chopped
¼ cup roughly chopped parsley

Remove the veal loin from the refrigerator and cut away the string and cheesecloth. Slice the meat as thin as possible; you should end up with 30 to 32 slices. Alternately layer the veal slices and sauce in a small baking dish and cover with plastic wrap. Reserve the extra sauce, and refrigerate it and the veal overnight.

Prior to serving, remove the veal and the reserved sauce from the refrigerator and allow it to warm at room temperature for 45 minutes. Vigorously whisk the extra sauce to loosen it, adding a little cold water if the sauce appears overly thick. When ready to serve, distribute the veal slices onto 8 chilled salad plates. Ladle the reserved sauce over the veal slices so that the meat is thinly but completely coated. Finish by garnishing each plate with the diced celery heart, capers, and parsley.

Zucchini Carpaccio

For 6

This dish is a takeoff on traditional carpaccio, a slip of raw veal, beef, or fish pounded to transparent thinness, served on a wide plate, and seasoned with any number of toppings. In order to cut zucchini similarly thin you will need a mandoline, a very useful kitchen tool that makes it possible to slice vegetables paper-thin. The flavor of zucchini, which is almost neutral as a raw vegetable, comes alive with only minimal steaming, and its color is particularly vivid when the skin is left intact. This dish is in every way light, refreshing, and simple to make.

1 medium shallot, finely diced
1 teaspoon salt
¼ cup champagne vinegar
2 very fresh green zucchini, about 1 inch in
    diameter (4 ounces)
2 very fresh golden zucchini, about 1 inch in
    diameter (4 ounces)
1 cup extra-virgin olive oil
12 fresh basil leaves
2 ounces pine nuts, lightly toasted in a 350°F.
    oven for 4 to 5 minutes
Parmigiano-Reggiano, for shaving

Place the shallot, salt, and vinegar in a bowl and allow the shallot to macerate for 5 minutes.

While the shallot is macerating, wash the squash in cold water and trim the tops and bottoms. Using a mandoline, thinly slice the squash lengthwise into ¹⁄₁₆-inch pieces. Discard the first and last slices from each squash, as they are mostly composed of skin. Each squash should yield 9 slices; you'll have 36 slices total. Finish your vinaigrette by beating all but 4 ounces of the olive oil into the shallot and vinegar.

In single-layer batches, steam the squash slices over boiling water for 1½ minutes. Transfer the slices to a sheet pan lined with parchment paper in a single layer. Do not overlap slices, as they are very delicate and will

either tear or overcook. While the squash is still hot, use a pastry brush to moisten the top side only of each slice with vinaigrette. Repeat the process with the remaining squash. Cover the squash with more parchment paper and chill in the refrigerator for at least 20 minutes.

When ready to serve, arrange 6 slices of squash—3 slices of each color—on 6 plates. Next, cut the basil leaves into thin strips. Spoon out 2 tablespoons of vinaigrette onto each serving of carpaccio and sprinkle evenly with pine nuts and basil. Using a vegetable peeler or fine cheese plane, shave Parmigiano in small, thin curls over each plate. Finish by drizzling each with the remaining extra-virgin oil. Serve immediately.

Artichokes

The pure flavor of artichokes is not easy to capture in cooking. One option is to eat them raw. Tender spring bud-chokes, or, if you are lucky enough to find them, the choke-less purple Italian variety, are never better than when sliced very thin and accented with fruity olive oil, salt, a little lemon juice, and fine shards of Parmigiano. In this form artichokes have a nutty flavor and pleasant astringency. Piled atop *bresaola* (air-cured beef) or with a few slices of prosciutto, raw artichokes are in the best possible company. Otherwise, most methods of cooking artichokes are tailored to tenderize them or enhance their flavor. No wonder; breeding has only partially tamed the thistle in their ancestry. Artichokes retain their tough shell of leaves, occasional prickly tips, and inedible furry core. Pared to their pale centers, artichokes seem to plead for the aromatic support of garlic, onions, or other vegetables added during their cooking, or for salty or piquant seasonings like anchovy, olives, or garlic mayonnaise or vinaigrette to rescue them from dullness. While the prize of an artichoke may be its heart, the heart of its flavor lives in the leaves. But only the largest globe chokes offer enough "meat" on their bracts to warrant cooking them whole. Even then only the pale bottom tip of the leaf and, after the extensive cooking necessary to soften the tough shell, the inevitable sodden center are tender enough to eat. Unfortunately, the common methods of cooking large artichokes, by steaming, braising, or boiling, leave the greater portion of an artichoke's essential flavor in the brackish water at the bottom of the pot.

At Oliveto we have developed two methods of treating artichokes that deliver their essential flavor with only minimal additions. I have always felt uncomfortable tossing out the mountain of leaves and trimmings that results from preparing the heart alone. Our first effort to extract the flavor in the leaves resulted in an excessively bitter soup. We learned that allowing the leaves and trimmings plenty of time to stew in a sweet aromatic base of onions, carrots, garlic, and olive oil reduced some of the harshness. But it is the addition of potatoes, simmered and then broken into the swim of the soup, that binds most of the bitterness, leaving only a cleansing dryness in the aftertaste.

ᴑ
Artichoke Soup
For 8
Serve this soup either hot with a sprinkling of Parmigiano-Reggiano or cold with a thin stream of your best extra-virgin olive oil.

2 cups extra-virgin olive oil
1 medium yellow onion, sliced
1 large carrot, sliced
3 garlic cloves, chopped
2 tablespoons salt
Leaves and trimmings (including stems) of
    6 artichokes (4 to 5 pounds), equal to
    approximately 2 gallons by volume
Juice of 1½ lemons
10 cups water
3 russet potatoes, peeled and cut into large dice

Warm the olive oil in a nonreactive pot large enough to hold at least 3 gallons. Add the onion, carrot, garlic, and salt and cook them over medium heat without browning for 15 to 20 minutes, or until soft. Add the artichoke leaves and trimmings to the pot. Turn the heat to high and stir the leaves frequently for 10 minutes. Pour in the lemon juice, reduce the heat to medium low, and cover tightly.

Simmer the leaves until tender at the base, 25 to 30 minutes. Add the water and bring to a boil. Reduce to a simmer and cook for 1 hour, or until all the leaves and trimmings are tender.

Pass the soup in small batches through the medium plate of a sturdy food mill into a clean pot, adding no more than one 6-ounce ladleful at a time. With each batch, rotate the handle of the food mill vigorously until the leaves have rendered all possible pulp. Using a spatula, scrape the residue from the underside of the food mill into the pot. Discard the remains of the leaves from the food mill and repeat the process with each new ladleful. It is important to take the time with this step; otherwise the soup will lack body.

Put the milled soup back on the heat, bring it to a boil, and add the diced potatoes. Reduce the heat to medium low and simmer for 20 minutes, or until the potatoes are very tender. Break up the potatoes into coarse bits with a masher or the back of a slotted spoon. Depending on the amount of artichoke pulp in the soup, you may need to thin the consistency by whisking in a small amount of water. Finally, taste the soup and correct it with salt to your taste.

As for artichoke hearts, a superior method that preserves the clarity of their basic flavor is cooking them slowly in a hot bath of olive oil with nothing else but salt (this technique also works perfectly with meaty summer bell peppers). Submerging in oil is similar to the "confit" process in which duck and pork, among other meats, are first salted and seasoned, then gently simmered, and later stored, in their own fat. Likewise, these artichokes may be held for as long as several months under oil in jars or a covered bowl in a cool place in the kitchen. Small to medium-size artichokes, de-choked and pared to their centers, are most suitable, although the bottoms of the largest "globe" artichokes may be treated similarly. Artichokes are usually sold with a portion of the stem still attached. Don't cut it away! Underneath the fibrous exterior is a tender core and the artichokes look even more handsome with the stem left intact.

You will need a good amount of olive oil to submerge even a small quantity of artichokes.

But over the course of the slow steeping the oil infuses with the artichokes and becomes a fragrant by-product of the process, tasty for dipping bread, for making vinaigrette with a mysterious background note, or for seasoning subtle meat dishes such as veal tartare or grilled fish. Choose a heavy bottomed, non-reactive pan that is taller than it is wide so that the oil can cover the artichokes completely.

Artichokes Braised in Olive Oil
Makes 12

6 very fresh medium-large artichokes
6 cups olive oil
1½ teaspoons salt

Using your hands, tear away the outer leaves of the artichokes until you reach the pale leaves at their center. Pare the fibrous stem down to the tender core and leave it attached. Turn the artichoke on its side. Use a sharp knife to locate the point at which the leaves begin to toughen. Slice them away. Then cut the artichokes in half lengthwise and remove the fuzzy choke with the side of a spoon. If you don't intend to cook the artichokes right away, submerge them in water with the juice of one lemon to prevent browning.

Arrange the artichokes in a 4-quart saucepan in two layers so that they fit snugly. Cover with the 6 cups of olive oil and season with salt. Place the saucepan on low heat. Bring the artichokes to a simmer and reduce the heat to the lowest possible setting or use a flame tamer; the oil should not simmer or bubble. Cook the artichokes for about 25 minutes, or until they are tender at the thickest point of their base. Remove the pan from the heat and allow the artichokes to cool in the olive oil. With a squeeze of lemon these artichokes are good as an antipasto. They can be cut into salads or rewarmed tossed in lemon zest, parsley, and garlic and served as a garnish to roasted meats.

Eggs Cooked in a Bain-Marie
For 6

When I have the time to spare on a lazy morning I like to cook eggs by this slow method—self-contained in a small cup set in hot water. Farmers' markets usually have at least one egg salesman, and the freshness and vibrant color of their eggs call for special treatment. This method sets the white to a custard-like texture, leaving the yolk warmed and thickened but still liquid. The key to cooking eggs in a *bain-marie*, or water bath, is to regulate the temperature of the egg; bear in mind that the white of the egg sets at a lower temperature than the yolk. I use small, thick-walled coffee cups commonly used for cappuccino. These cups moderate the penetration of heat to the center of the egg so that over the course of 10 minutes the white becomes lightly set and the yolk is warmed but still runs at the touch of a fork. It is also important to maintain the temperature of the water bath so that it does not exceed 180°F. These eggs are delicious simply slid out of their cups and sprinkled with coarse sea salt and a grind of pepper. They may also be turned out onto a toasted round of sourdough bread, with a warm salad of bitter greens such as dandelion or curly endive tossed with shallots, young balsamico, olive oil, and Parmigiano-Reggiano, or served together with asparagus spears, brown butter, and sage. During white truffle season in the restaurant we bury the fresh eggs, still in their shells, in truffles before cooking them in the bain-marie and slicing fresh truffles over the top.

3 tablespoons extra-virgin olive oil or melted butter
6 fresh eggs, at room temperature
Salt and freshly ground black pepper

Pour 1½ teaspoons of olive oil into each of six 6-ounce thick-walled coffee cups or custard cups. Crack an egg into each cup. Cover each cup with a small piece of plastic wrap and set them into a pan. Pour enough water into the pan to bring it level with the tops of the eggs. Set the pan over medium heat and bring the water to 180°F. Maintain the eggs at this temperature for 10 minutes.

Remove the cups from the bain-marie and let the eggs stand another 15 minutes in a warm place to complete the cooking. Tilt each cup from side to side to allow the warm oil to cover the yolk and to run down the sides of the white at the edge of the cup. Using the flat tip of a knife or thin flexible spatula, gently loosen the egg from the cup and tip it out. Season with salt and pepper.

Potato Gnocchi with Butter and Parmigiano-Reggiano
Makes about 200 gnocchi or 8 generous portions

For many people, the mention of potato gnocchi brings to mind leaden lumps of flour and potato that blunt the appetite in the middle of a meal. Gnocchi are good only if they are light, a function of the type of potato used, the right proportion of ingredients, and hand working of the dough. I grew up on my mother's gnocchi and her version remains definitive. I remember not only their incomparable lightness, but also the sight of her kneading boiled potatoes, flour, and egg into long strands, nipping them into small pillows, and shaping them one by one. By the time she had finished, the whole counter was covered with plump, ridge-backed dumplings ready to be boiled, then tossed in a long-simmering ragù or simply warmed in butter with Parmigiano.

Large potatoes, often called "baking" potatoes, that are dry, fluffy, and starchy when cooked produce the lightest gnocchi dough. I prefer to use either russets (also known as Idaho) or large Yellow Finn potatoes. Low-starch, "waxy" potatoes are not suitable for making gnocchi. They become especially gluey when added to flour and make ponderous gnocchi. Boiling the potatoes in their jackets, draining them in a colander, and allowing them time to dry in their own steam fluffs the starch and in turn produces the driest, most tender dough.

More than a recipe, gnocchi demand a feeling for the dough, its relative moisture or dryness, and its degree of elasticity. With the confidence that comes from making the dough over and over again, you may enjoy, as I have, the freedom to alter the texture in either direction. Slightly firmer gnocchi stand up to sturdy meat sauces, while delicate gnocchi work well tossed in butter with spring peas. The amount of flour in the dough is crucial to achieving the right texture: Too much makes the gnocchi heavy, and adding

too little causes them to fall apart in the boiling water. For the lightest gnocchi, straddle the line between not enough flour and just enough. Bear in mind that excessive moisture from potatoes that are not thoroughly cooled or from additional egg used to compensate for too much flour will add weight to gnocchi. Remember, too, that over-handling of the dough activates the gluten in the flour, creating stiffness. The dough should feel soft, pliable, and only slightly sticky.

Salt
3 russet potatoes or other high-starch variety
    (about 1½ pounds)
1 egg, whisked
¼ cup heavy cream
Freshly grated nutmeg (about 12 downward
    strokes on the grater) or a generous pinch
    of freshly ground nutmeg
2 cups (9 ounces) all-purpose flour
4 ounces (1 stick) unsalted butter
Parmigiano-Reggiano, for grating

Fill a pot with lightly salted cold water, add the potatoes in their jackets, and simmer them until very tender, about 35 minutes. Drain them into a colander set in the sink and let them rest in their own steam until they are cool enough to handle. Peel the potatoes, and then pass them through the medium plate of a food mill into a large bowl. Add the egg, cream, 1 teaspoon salt, and nutmeg to the potatoes and mix well to combine. Pour the flour onto a large cutting board or work surface and make a well in the center. Add the potato mixture to the well. Using a flat, rigid pastry scraper, cut the flour into the potatoes. Work the dough by cutting, pressing, and turning it over on itself with the pastry scraper. Keep at it until the dough comes together and is soft, supple, and slightly elastic. Roll the mass into a large log and cut the log into four equal parts. Roll the logs into ropes about ¾ inch in diameter, cutting them in half if they are too long to work with. Cut the ropes into ½-inch pieces. If some of the ropes swell as you cut others, roll them back down to the original diameter. Dip the tines of a dinner fork in flour and tap off the excess. Hold a dough piece between your thumb and forefinger, grasping at opposite corners and positioning it so a corner points toward you, diamond-like. Starting at the base of the fork tines, and keeping your thumb perpendicular to the tines, roll the dough over the top of the fork tines, changing from pinching with your thumb and forefinger to pushing gently with your thumb. The point is to create an ovoid shape. Let the gnocchi fall from the fork, flicking it off gently with your thumb if needed. Your thumb will have shaped a dimple on the underside of the dumpling and scored ridges along the back. Flour the fork as before for each dough piece.

Transfer the shaped gnocchi to a well-floured sheet pan. Freeze what you won't cook immediately. Uncooked gnocchi will keep in the refrigerator for up to 12 hours, after which they oxidize and begin to turn a dull gray. (You needn't thaw frozen gnocchi before boiling, but do boil them in batches so as not to bring the temperature of the water down all at once.)

Bring a large pot of lightly salted water to a boil and add the gnocchi. If you have a stove with a high BTU output, add all of the gnocchi at once; otherwise cook them in two batches.

Meanwhile, warm a wide sauté pan and melt the butter. Let the gnocchi simmer in the water for about 5 minutes, or until they float to the surface. Remove the gnocchi with a flat strainer and transfer them directly to the sauté pan. Season with salt and toss lightly over low heat until just coated with butter. Serve immediately in warm bowls with freshly grated Parmigiano-Reggiano.

Cauliflower Soup
For 8

I have never much liked cauliflower. As a raw vegetable, it is dry and gritty in the mouth and resists the improvement of even strong dipping condiments. What little flavor it has is locked up tight in its stiff stems and curd-like florets. Cook it and it is like snails, only as good as the butter, garlic, and parsley you douse them in. I was surprised to find, however, that cauliflower makes an extraordinary puréed soup. When blended, its subtle mustard-like flavor comes into focus. Like celery root or butternut squash, it is utterly transformed as a silky liquid. But unlike the root or the squash, its refined smoothness is due to a rich pectin content rather than to starch. This may explain the fragility of its flavor. While soups of celery root and butternut squash readily absorb and are enhanced by poultry broth, cauliflower is altered if moistened by anything but water. Enrich celery root with a little cream or squash soup with *vin santo* and the flavors of both are toned or accented. But add cream or seasonings such as curry (a common cure) to cauliflower, or add solid garnishes, and you steal from it. Made only with a little stewed onion, water, and salt, this soup is a good example of the austere requirements of certain foods: that the clearest expression of their flavor suggests adding next to nothing. This soup is plain but plainly good.

3 tablespoons olive oil
1 medium onion, 6 ounces, sliced thin
1 pound 6 ounces very fresh cauliflower
Salt
5½ cups hot water
Extra-virgin olive oil
Freshly ground black pepper

Warm the olive oil in a heavy-bottomed pan. Sweat the onion in the olive oil over low heat without letting it brown for 15 minutes. Add the cauliflower, salt to taste, and ½ cup water, raise the heat slightly, and cover the pot tightly. Stew the cauliflower for 15 to 18 minutes, or until tender. Then add another 4½ cups of hot water, bring to a low simmer, and cook an additional 20 minutes. Working in batches, purée the soup in a blender to a very smooth, creamy consistency. Let the soup stand for 20 minutes. In this time it will thicken slightly. Thin the soup with ½ cup water. Reheat the soup. Serve hot, drizzled with a thin stream of extra-virgin olive oil and freshly ground black pepper.

Spring Vegetables

True spring vegetables are by nature a fleeting pleasure. As the days grow longer and warmer, dramatic changes occur in the produce more rapidly than that of any season. Early spring vegetables progress quickly to the point of no return. The brilliant green of fava beans pinched from their skins seems to fade in a matter of weeks, young greens toughen up, the sweet pop of English peas turns dull and starchy, spring onions grow hot, asparagus tips unfold, and garlic swells and looses its leek-like mildness.

The challenge of cooking early spring vegetables rests in preserving their fragile color, texture, and sweetness. My approach is to warm them in only as much water as is required to make them tender and to add any enrichments or enhancements at the end of the cooking. This means judging the water carefully: Too much drowns flavor and causes overcooking. The noticeable advantage, compared to parcooking and rewarming, or boiling, is that none of the flavor is lost to the cooking medium and the vegetables cook to the right point and no further. If butter is the final enrichment, allowing for some moisture assists in holding it in a thin emulsion. If you prefer olive oil, it is better to

allow the water to nearly evaporate. The technique is simple enough but the attention you pay to choosing the right pot relative to the amount of vegetables, the level of the heat, and the length of the cooking makes all the difference. Heat in the right amount is benign but too much or for too long is malevolent to spring vegetables. New peas need nothing more than a little water and the caress of a moderate flame to release their sugars, soften them gently, and tease their color out. Asparagus likes to be nearly covered in a flat pan and left undisturbed until the water disappears. Small carrots want moderate heat and stirring in order to avoid mushiness on the outside and a hard center. Young greens such as chard and spinach will readily release their own water if they are left undried after washing or are allowed to sweat in the steam generated from a splash of water in a hot pan.

Quick stews of spring vegetables are a different matter. When spring vegetables are combined and stewed gently together on a base of onion, garlic, and olive oil, the water they gradually render is sufficient to cook them fully. Olive oil assists in bringing about a melding of the flavors, the goal of such a combination. The cooking proceeds incrementally as vegetables are added to the pot according to their cooking requirements. The added benefit of these timed additions is that the vegetables remain distinct yet also blend like individual voices into a larger chorus of flavor.

Since the cooking time for any of the vegetables below can vary according to their maturity, it is impossible to give precise timing. Observing the order of addition is important so as not to overcook vegetables that are more tender than others. There is no better way to time the additions than by tasting for texture. As a general guideline, add the next vegetable when the previous one has lost some of its crunch but is not softened to the core.

Spring Vegetable Bruschetta
For 8

6 tablespoons extra-virgin olive oil, plus more
    for brushing the bread
1 small shallot, minced fine
8 to 10 spring garlic cloves, sliced thin
6 small artichokes (1⅓ pounds), pared to their
    hearts and sliced thin
8 medium-size asparagus spears (10 ounces),
    peeled, trimmed of woody bottoms, and
    sliced on the bias ½ inch thick
12 spring onions or scallions, roots trimmed
1 pound fresh fava beans, shucked to yield about
    1 cup
1½ pounds peas in the pod, shucked to yield
    ¾ cup
1 heaping tablespoon chopped fresh herbs
    (parsley, chives, chervil, or a small amount
    of tarragon)
6 ½-inch slices sourdough bread, crust removed

Choose a pot that is wide enough (at least 10 inches) to allow heat to penetrate the vegetables evenly and in a shallow layer. Warm the olive oil over medium heat, then add the shallot and garlic. When the scent of both rises from the pan, add the artichokes and cover with a round of parchment paper that is an inch larger than the inside circumference of the pot. Cook the artichokes for 3 to 4 minutes. Next, remove the parchment paper and add the asparagus, followed by the spring onions, then the fava beans. Last, add the peas. Adjust the heat so that the vegetables "sweat"; they should never brown. Replace the parchment paper after each addition. When the vegetables are cooked, stir in the herbs and let stand to cool a bit (the flavors are most vivid when the vegetables are lukewarm). In the meantime, brush the bread slices with olive oil and toast them to a golden brown. Set the toasted bread slices on individual plates and distribute the vegetables on top of each. Serve at once.

Eggplant's taste is diluted in the large amount of water it contains (particularly the globe variety). But after a brief plunge in a boiling bath of lightly acidulated water it can be twisted in a towel to rend its flavor free.

4 very fresh globe eggplant (3¾ pounds), or an equivalent quantity of Italian eggplant
6 quarts water
¾ cup kosher salt, plus more to taste
1 cup champagne vinegar
1 garlic clove, minced
1 fresh cayenne pepper or other small, hot red pepper, sliced thin
1 lemon juiced to yield 1½ tablespoons
3 tablespoons extra-virgin olive oil
6 fresh mint leaves

Cut away the stem portion of the eggplant and using a mandoline, slice it lengthwise into flat sheets about ⅛ inch thick. Assemble a short stack of the eggplant slices and cut them crosswise into strips as thin as possible. Set the eggplant aside.

Combine the water, the salt, and vinegar in a large pot and bring to a boil over high heat. While you are waiting for the water to boil, situate a colander in the sink to receive the eggplant once it is cooked. Add the eggplant to the pot and stir it to disperse the strands evenly in the boiling liquid. After 1 minute test the eggplant for texture by removing a small sample with a slotted spoon. It should be slightly resistant to the bite. If still raw tasting, cook for 1 or 2 minutes more. It is wise to stand over the pot and gauge the cooking; if the eggplant is undercooked it will darken in color; if overcooked it will be mushy.

Drain the eggplant in the colander. Then transfer the drained eggplant to the center of a clean towel or napkin. Roll the towel around the eggplant, then, while holding the towel over the sink, twist the ends in the opposite direction to squeeze out as much of the water as you can. If necessary, squeeze the closed bundle between your hands to release more of its liquid. Transfer the eggplant to a bowl to cool.

☙

Antipasto of Shredded Eggplant
For 6

Eggplant too often suffers in the kitchen from forced compliance, as though it is only through companionship or manipulation that it is delivered from blandness. It is routinely treated with salt to remove its supposed bitterness (I've never had mature eggplant that was bitter) or to leach its water to make it dryer for the fryer, a pointless step since eggplant will, in any case, absorb at least its weight in oil. Or it is treated as faux meat, smothered in tomatoes and cheese, masked with piquancy, made sodden with sauce, or sent to sponge smoke on the grill. More often the lackey or part of the crowd, eggplant is seldom allowed to stand on its own.

When minimally cooked, eggplant has a marvelous slippery texture and its essential flavor comes to the fore. Admittedly, it is a vegetable that invites some seasoning. That suggested below is intended only to support and enhance.

Place the minced garlic, sliced cayenne pepper, and lemon juice in a large mixing bowl. Let the ingredients macerate for a few minutes, then whisk in the olive oil and season with a large pinch of salt. Next, add the eggplant to the mixing bowl. Chop the mint fine, add it to the eggplant, and toss all the ingredients together well. Chill the shredded eggplant until ready to serve. The mild heat of the cayenne pepper and flavor of the mint will emerge as the eggplant sits. Serve alone with crusty bread or as part of a mixed antipasto.

Salad of Parched Summer Vegetables

For 6

Water constitutes the greater part of any vegetable's makeup. Still, depending upon growing conditions and location, the water content of vegetables may vary widely, helping to deliver flavor or causing its dilution. In either case, summer vegetables take particularly well to drying in a slow oven to concentrate and focus their flavors. It is important to cut each of the vegetables to a consistent size so that they will dry evenly.

$1\frac{1}{2}$ pints miniature tomatoes such as Sungold, Sweet 100, Black Plum, or Green Grape
1 cup extra-virgin olive oil
$2\frac{1}{4}$ teaspoons kosher salt
3 yellow summer squash (10 ounces), cut into quarters
3 green zucchini (12 ounces), cut into quarters lengthwise
1 red bell pepper (8 ounces), cut into 6 pieces
1 red onion (8 ounces), cut into wedges
1 globe eggplant (14 ounces), peeled and cut into 12 long wedges

Vinaigrette
1 small shallot, minced
$\frac{1}{4}$ cup red wine vinegar
$\frac{1}{4}$ teaspoon salt
2 tablespoons extra-virgin olive oil
Fresh basil leaves, torn by hand into smallish pieces

Preheat the oven to 400°F.

Stem and wash the tomatoes. Slice the tomatoes in half and set them on a sheet pan coated with a thin stream of olive oil. Season with $\frac{3}{4}$ teaspoon of the salt. Place the tomatoes in the oven on the middle rack and reduce the oven temperature to 300°F. Roast the tomatoes about $2\frac{1}{2}$ to 3 hours, or until they have become shriveled and their flesh appears jammy.

Season each remaining group of vegetables with $\frac{1}{3}$ cup of the olive oil and $\frac{1}{2}$ teaspoon of the salt, grouping summer squash and zucchini, bell pepper and onion, then eggplant. Arrange the vegetables in groups on sheet pans and place them on the bottom rack of the oven. Roast the vegetables for about 1 to $1\frac{1}{2}$ hours. You will notice the vegetables color and reduce in size as they are roasting. The eggplant is done when it has turned a golden brown color and is soft when squeezed. The squash and zucchini finish around the same time as the eggplant but with more caramelized surfaces and a slightly firmer feel. The onion will become translucent and the pepper soft to the touch with browned edges. If one group of vegetables parches sooner than another next to it, transfer it carefully to a serving platter with a spatula and spread out what remains on the pan. Set all the vegetables on a large serving platter to cool.

Make the vinaigrette by macerating the minced shallot in the red wine vinegar for 5 minutes. Season the vinegar with the salt and whisk in the extra-virgin olive oil.

Before serving, place all of the parched vegetables in a large bowl, add the vinaigrette and the torn basil leaves, and mix gently. Place the vegetables on a platter or divide them equally among 6 salad plates.

Strawberry Sorbet

6 to 8 servings

It is hardly possible to improve ripe, in-season fruit. Yet sorbets that aim to capture the essence of fruit in iced form can be equally satisfying. I know of no better way with strawberries than this quick and simple method. You don't need an ice cream machine to make this sorbet, just a little sugar, water, and a food processor. Its intensity is due to the low cutting action of the processor blades; the churning action of ice cream makers leavens the texture, and also the flavor impression, of ices. Rather than sieving away all of the pulp and seeds prior to freezing, use the whole fruit to make this sorbet. The resulting texture and flavor couldn't be truer.

1 quart ripe strawberries, stemmed
5 tablespoons sugar
¼ cup water

Cut any large strawberries in half. Arrange the strawberries on a baking sheet lined with parchment paper and place in the freezer for 2 hours, or until the berries are completely hard frozen. Put the berries in a food processor along with the sugar and pulse the machine on and off until the fruit is broken up. Add the water and continue to run the blades until you achieve a smooth purée. Transfer the sorbet to a quart container and freeze for 2 hours, or until just firm enough to scoop.

Serve in frozen ice cream glasses.

Salmon Baked in a Salt Crust

For 10

Fish never tastes more of itself than when baked in salt. This method is superb when adapted to meaty fish such as salmon and striped bass and large snappers that are by nature rich in oils. Rather than acting as a seasoning, salt is used like earth in clay baking to create a protective shell around the fish that seals in all the flavor. In addition, the fish is cooked in its skin and on the bone, which keeps the surface and the interior of the fish very moist. To make the salt shell, kosher salt is mixed with egg whites to bind it into a hardened, cast-like layer that is easily removed in pieces after baking. This method works very well with whole fish and makes a dramatic presentation for a large gathering. Alternatively, sections may be cut from a whole fish and treated in the same manner. Fish baked in salt may be served hot or in room temperature salads. Salmon in particular is offset nicely by salads of vegetables in vinaigrette, string beans, beets, carrots, favas, and artichokes or lettuces. When served hot, a good match for the fish is a smooth emulsion sauce made with butter, green onions, and sparkling Prosecco wine.

3½ pounds kosher salt
4½-pound head-end section of salmon on the bone with skin
8 egg whites

Salt the fish inside its cavity and lightly over its entire surface. Thoroughly combine the remaining salt and the egg whites. The salt will feel slightly moist. Place a piece of baking parchment on a sheet pan. Make a bed of salt about ½ inch thick on the parchment paper, place the fish on top, and pack the remaining salt around every surface, pressing it against the fish so that it adheres. Bake the fish in a 375°F. oven for about 50 minutes or until a thermometer inserted at its thickest point reads 125°F.

Remove the fish from the oven and let the fish stand in the salt for 15 minutes. In the meantime make the sauce.

Prosecco Sauce
1¼ cups Prosecco wine
4 tablespoons finely minced green onion, white part only
3 tablespoons finely minced tender green onion tops
10 tablespoons cold unsalted butter
Sea salt

Combine the wine and the white of the green onion in a small saucepan. Bring the mixture to a low boil in a saucepan and reduce it until only a small amount of wine remains. Whisk in the butter 2 tablespoons at a time over moderate heat, making sure each addition of butter has melted before adding more. At no point should the sauce boil. Whisk constantly until all the butter is incorporated and the sauce has a smooth, emulsified consistency. Transfer the sauce to a bain-marie and stir in the green onion tops. Season to taste with sea salt.

To serve, insert a knife along the edge of the salt crust. Carefully lift away the salt crust and clean it away from the edges of the fish. Next, pull the skin from the fish. Cut along the top edge of the fish and the line running through the center section to loosen the flesh. Remove any visible bones and transfer portions to a platter or to individual plates. Nap the fish with sauce and serve it right away.

Black Sea Bass al Mattone
For 2

Another way to treat whole fillets of smaller fish to draw out maximum flavor is to cook them under a weight. *Al mattone* (under a brick) is a popular method of cooking chicken in Italy and may be similarly applied to fish such as black sea bass or true snapper, because their oil-rich skin readily crisps in contact with a hot pan. The advantage of this method is that most of the cooking takes place on the skin side so that none of the flavorful juices escape. Since skin-on fillets tend to arch in the center when they touch a hot pan, the weight also serves the purpose of holding the fillets absolutely flat against the pan bottom; as a result, they brown thoroughly and evenly.

Extra-virgin olive oil
2 fillets of black sea bass, skin on and pin bones removed
Salt
1 lemon, cut into wedges

Add enough olive oil to coat a 10- to 12-inch well-seasoned steel or nonstick pan. Season the fish fillets with salt. When the oil is hot, add the fish to the pan skin side down. Immediately place a 2-pound flat brick wrapped in aluminum foil on top of the fillets to press the skin flat against the pan. Adjust the heat so that you hear a sizzling sound. At no point during the cooking process should the pan smoke.

After about 2 minutes you will notice the sides of the flesh have started to turn opaque. When the sides turn totally opaque, remove the brick. Using a spatula, gently turn the fish over onto its flesh side. Lower the heat and allow the fish to finish cooking a minute more. Transfer the fillets onto a serving dish or plate. Serve with a wedge of lemon and a drizzle of your best extra-virgin olive oil.

Chilled Shellfish with Salsa Verde
For 6

Among ocean life, bivalves such as clams, mussels, and oysters convey most directly the primitive scent and taste of the sea. I have always identified the so-called "salt air" more with the heady aroma of seaweed and the mossy smell on rocks as the tide recedes. This and the briny taste of the ocean are the very substance of these two-shelled creatures that live to filter bits of algae floating in their salty surround of seawater.

1¼ pounds small clams
1 pound mussels
1 small shallot, minced
2 bay leaves
¼ cup dry white wine
½ cup extra-virgin olive oil

Wash the clams and mussels in cold water, scrubbing the shells free of sand or seaweed and pulling off the mussels' beards. Put the minced shallot, bay leaves, and wine into a pot at least twice as large in volume as the clams and mussels. Warm the wine and olive oil over medium heat, then add the clams. Turn the heat to high and cover the pot. Cook the clams for about a minute or until they begin to gape, then add the mussels and cook for 2½ minutes more. The goal is to open the clams and mussels but to cook them until tender and no more (there is nothing worse than rubbery shellfish). Pour the mussels and clams into a colander set over a bowl to capture the cooking juices. Transfer the mussels and clams to a wide baking dish. Whisk ½ cup of extra-virgin olive oil into the cooking juices, then pour it back over the shellfish. Allow the shellfish to cool, then cover the dish and chill the mussels and clams in the refrigerator for at least an hour. While the shellfish is cooling make the *salsa verde*.

Salsa Verde
1 large shallot, finely minced
3 tablespoons champagne vinegar
1 tablespoon coarsely chopped fresh oregano
3 tablespoons minced chives
6 tablespoons coarsely chopped fresh flat-leaf parsley
½ teaspoon salt
¾ cup extra-virgin olive oil

Place the minced shallot in a small bowl and cover with the champagne vinegar. Set the shallots aside to macerate. Place the oregano, chives, and parsley in a mortar and add the salt. Pound and grind the herbs to a fine paste with a pestle in a grinding circular motion. Remove the herb paste to a small bowl, and cover with the extra-virgin olive oil. Just before serving combine the shallots in vinegar with the herb paste and stir well.

Distribute the clams and mussels among 6 chilled plates, opening the shells so that the flesh of each is exposed. Over each portion drizzle a tablespoon of the juices. Dab the shellfish on each plate with salsa verde and serve.

Fresh Green Olives

Because I live in an area where there is an abundance of olive trees, the months from late November through January provide the opportunity to cure olives of different types, sizes, and levels of ripeness. When the traditional methods of applying coarse salt or soaking them in salt brine are used, olives can vary in their curing times from a matter of months to the better part of a year. I like to put ripe black olives away in baskets with coarse salt and let them shrivel out their bitterness, which takes a month or two. Then I toss them with oil and dried thyme from the garden. Medium-ripe, straw-colored olives cracked with a smooth stone, soaked in several changes of plain water, then submerged in brine with lemon and garlic are ready four months later. For whole fermented green olives lying under a protective layer of mold in a cool corner of the basement, I have to wait until the following summer.

But just as some fresh cheeses and "new" wines can be enjoyed soon after their harvest, it is possible to cure olives and eat them within their own season; fresh green olives take a matter of one and a half weeks to make. In making olives, I had always avoided the use of lye, which used in the officially recommended amounts for curing strips them of flavor entirely. But an olive-growing friend convinced me that lye used more sparingly results in olives with a firm texture, brilliant green appearance, and buttery flavor that retain a mild bitterness against the pit. The trick is to moderate the amount of lye to leach out the bitterness without denaturing the other elements of flavor in the fruit.

The use of lye is hardly modern. The Romans knew to soak olives in a solution of water and wood ashes, a concentrated source of lye. Having tried this once, I can only say it is a mess and not worth the bother. Flake or household lye can be found in most drug stores. Look for small cans that are marked "100% Lye." Lye should be handled with care as it can cause serious burns. Use latex gloves when mixing the pickling brine and use lemon or vinegar to neutralize the lye if it splashes on your skin. To dispose of lye, pour it down the drain and run cold water to flush it out. Use glass, stoneware, or heavy, light-colored plastic containers. Do not use galvanized or aluminum containers; stirring implements should be made of stainless steel or wood.

To make fresh green olives, use only hand-picked fruit without blemishes or bruises of any sort. Cure the olives directly after picking. Grade the olives so that the batches you cure contain olives of similar dimension. When handling the olives throughout the curing process, treat them carefully. Do not pour the olives into a colander when renewing the lye solution or when rinsing, as this tends to bruise them. Rather, partially cover the top of the container you are using and pour off the liquid. If you are curing a large quantity of olives, remove them by using a wire or perforated skimmer. The amount of lye and the time needed to pickle the olives will depend upon their variety, size, ripeness, and, of course, the quantity of olives to be cured. It is therefore impossible to give precise proportions. Use the following as your guideline.

Lye Cure

Place the olives in a bowl or other container large enough to hold them. Add water to cover by the measured cupful, noting how much was needed to cover them completely, then swish the olives gently to rinse. Partially cover the container with a plate or lid and pour away the water. In a separate container combine the same amount of cold water used above with 2 tablespoons of lye per gallon used. Stir thoroughly to dissolve the lye. Add the olives and keep them submerged under a ceramic plate if making a

small batch; or, if using a larger container, fill a sturdy, clear plastic garbage bag with enough water to keep the olives submerged and place it on top. Soak the olives for 12 hours, stirring occasionally. After this first soak, cut a segment from an olive all the way to the pit to determine how far the lye has penetrated. This will be easily determined by looking at the cut surface from the side; lye will change the flesh to a darker shade of yellow-green when compared to the paler uncured portion. The aim is to remove the olives from the lye solution when the lye has penetrated two thirds of the way to the pit (lye continues to run its course to the pit even after the olives have been removed from the solution). If the lye has not penetrated this distance, soak the olives an additional 12 hours in a fresh lye solution of the same proportions and submerge as before.

Rinsing the Olives

When you have poured off the lye solution, soak the olives for 6 hours in fresh, cold water, again with a plate or water-filled plastic bag on top. Change the water and soak the olives again for 6 hours. Repeat this process changing the water every 12 hours, for 6 to 8 days or until no lye taste remains. After 4 days (the amount of lye remaining is not harmful to consume) the olives are ready to consume.

Brine Cure

Using the same quantity of water you measured for the lye cure, prepare brine in the proportion of $1/4$ cup salt to 1 gallon of water. Add the olives and let them stand 2 days at cool room temperature (65°F.). Then pack the olives in sterilized jars, pour over enough brine to cover them, and refrigerate. The olives are best eaten within a few weeks of pickling. Eat the olives as they are or toss them in fruity olive oil before serving.

A Method with Mushrooms

Autumn is wild mushroom time where I live, as it is in most temperate climates. If I am lucky enough to be free to run to the woods after several downpours of late fall rain, I find *boletus edulis*, the king of mushrooms that the Italians call porcini ("little pigs"). Treading lightly at dawn across a thick-piled carpet of pine needles next to the Pacific coast, I know that I am in the right place at the right time when I see small humps of needles at the base of the bull pines. As I brush the top layer away, what emerges first is the palomino-colored cap of a porcino, then its thick stem, hours out of the ground and struggling to greet the light of day. To beat the competition of rainfall that softens the flesh of porcini, too much growth that makes of them monsters with slimy undersides, or time that invites worms, is to truly strike it rich. Porcini in prime condition are very firm; the youngest are even hard at first grasp. Cool to the touch, they bear the sweet fragrance of rain and the humus scent of seasons of leaf- and needle-drop that have become their dark soil. It is a shame to cook these mushrooms. I slice the firmest to transparent thinness on a mandoline along with the pale green hearts of their companion in-season vegetable, fennel, lay them out on a large white plate, and dress them with a squeeze of lemon, newly pressed oil (the season of which corresponds), and sea salt. Or I slice them thick and sauté them with butter or olive oil in a hot pan with chopped garlic and parsley; the flavor of this simple meal brings back memories of the whole day. Along the way, I may encounter other types of boletus mushrooms. Most hunters avoid the less desirable "slippery jack," which can also be wonderful if captured before its cap turns to jelly. In another habitat, I may even find "pig ears," mushrooms that grow in a purple ruffled clump and offer a pleasantly meaty texture and flavor reminiscent of shiitake. Dainty "yellow foot" mushrooms seem to proliferate in the open spots between tree canopies. Perhaps the subtlest among their cousins on the floor, "yellow foot" mushrooms simply sautéed in butter make an appealing garnish to warm salads, turned with thin egg noodles, or left floating in the blond juices of a roast of veal. Occasionally, I'll come across a lobster mushroom; unlike all others and noticeable from some distance away,

it glows like a nightlight on the side of a dark log. I have to wait for another month to happen upon the so-called "trumpet of death," a jet-black mushroom there to be exhumed at the base of lofty tan oaks. January marks the beginning of chanterelle season. In a privileged spot I share only with my hunting partner, the most extraordinary chanterelles I have ever known push up under majestic live oaks that preside over acres of rolling hills. To come upon their golden caps and elegantly ribbed undersides in the shady bower of the oak's low-hung branches takes my breath away. Even if caught at just the right time, chanterelles from this particular location release a large amount of their woodsy water when sliced and put to the heat. Leaving them in the pan to boil in their own juices violently alters their firm texture and flavor. Instead, I prefer to cook them quickly, remove them from the pan, and reduce the mushroom juice to a near glaze, then add it back to the pan to warm with herbs. When the harvest is plentiful I preserve the mushrooms for use in antipasti to be enjoyed throughout the coming months. This method applies equally to any mushroom that contains a lot of moisture. Most do.

Wash the mushrooms quickly under cold water and, if necessary, use a small knife to scrape away excess dirt on the caps or stems. Slice the mushrooms about ¼ inch thick. Warm a small amount of olive oil in a wide sauté pan. Add enough mushrooms to form a shallow layer, sprinkle with a little salt, and raise the heat to high. In the meantime, place a colander set over a bowl large enough to contain it near the stove. When the mushrooms release their juices and the pan is fairly flooded, taste one of the slices to judge whether the mushrooms may need another moment in the pan; they should be cooked through but retain the memory of their fresh texture and forest flavor. Pour the mush-

rooms into the colander and bowl to capture the juice below. Drain the mushrooms as well as possible and pour them out to cool on a sheet pan or large platter. Proceed in the same manner with the remainder of the mushrooms. When all of the mushrooms are cooked, pour the juices collected in the bowl into the pan, turn the heat to high, and reduce the liquid to a viscous consistency. Taste the reduction for its level of intensity and continue to reduce it if it does not taste strongly of mushroom. Place the mushrooms in a bowl and pour over them all of the reduced juices. Add a little champagne vinegar and extra-virgin olive oil and correct for salt. Pack in sterilized jars, top with olive oil, and refrigerate. These mushrooms will keep well for several months. When you are ready to serve them, allow the mushrooms to return to room temperature, then toss them with finely minced garlic and chopped parsley.

Looking at Pears

For six weeks now I have watched various kinds of pears ripen on my kitchen table. Although the apples that sit among them inspire a kind of admiration, pears capture my attention; they appeal to my heart. Pears are more beautiful than handsome. Where the flavor of the apple is robust, the pear is subtle. Bite into an apple and you meet resistance. The pear is soft and yielding. Add to this the exceptionally smooth skin of many varieties, the fairness and occasional blush of its cheek, and the graceful curve of its form. A pear sheds no tear like the fig, to signal its peak, nor is its perfume or suppleness a reliable indication of its readiness to be eaten. In the words of one English epicure, Edward Bunyard, in *Anatomy of Desserts*, "The pear must be approached, as its feminine nature indicates, with discretion and reverence; it withholds its secrets from the merely hungry."

Ripening pears can be frustrating. Patient waiting, sometimes for weeks, often produces no observable change, whereas it is also common to return, after what seems like a matter of hours, to find fruit that has transformed to a musky mess. This behavior on the part of the pear leads to the opinion that it is an inscrutable and uncooperative fruit. This is not an altogether fair assessment. Ripening proceeds at different rates among different varieties of pears. The Winter Nellis doesn't ripen like the Bartlett or the Bosc; nor does the same measure that one uses to judge the progress of one apply to the other. Bartlett ripens much faster, develops a noticeably rich perfume, softens dramatically, and lightens in color. Such transformations in the Winter Nellis and the Bosc are muted and occur more slowly. Senescence follows ripening and is marked by the deterioration of the fruit and the cessation of its functions. Like all living things the fruit is "mortal," although the seed survives.

The pear is one of the most ephemeral fruits. Once it has reached its culmination, it makes fast toward decay. But unlike other fruit, it prefers to exhibit no shame and rots from the inside out. The virtue of the pear's subtlety is not without its cost. One must reach for the full flavor of the pear and, as with all subtle things, imperfections are more noticeable. Pears can be profoundly disappointing. When captured at the elusive moment of ripeness, however, a pear is nothing less than a consummation.

Planning to enjoy a perfectly luscious pear depends on choosing suitable fruit, the right environment for ripening, and understanding the behavior and particular indications of certain varieties. Generally speaking, the optimum condition for storing pears is a room temperature of about 65°F. and a relative humidity of 80 to 85 percent (which rules out the refrigerator as an option). Pears ripen when set out in layers in a dark or shaded place. At higher temperatures or in sunny spaces, pears tend to ripen too quickly. Gauging ripeness is a matter of being on the lookout for color shifts, changes in firmness and fragrance, and weight in the hand. While no increase in actual weight accompanies ripening, ripe fruit nevertheless possesses a gravity that must be felt to be understood.

Ultimately, it is the act of attending to the course of ripening that matters the most. In this, pears have taught me much about restraint and the rewards of patience. Most of all, I've learned that the art of cooking consists largely of "watching" with all the senses. Fruit "intends" nothing as it relates to human consumption. Its ripening is fundamentally a biological imperative rather than a wish to please human taste. Other foods are even more passive in this regard. The flesh of animals or fish couldn't care less. The ripening of cheese runs its own course. Yet all food offers the promise of an answer to human needs and desires, from basic sustenance to aesthetic and sensory pleasure. It is therefore up to us not only to notice food but also to nurture it to this end. To neglect a pear on the table and then return to find it ripe days later is merely a lucky coincidence. But to keep a pear in mind as it ripens is to practice cooking in its simplest form. It is through such observance of any food from the point of purchase throughout its preparation and later in the act of eating itself, that cooking is purged of lapses of attention, imposed formula, impatience, or expediency. Like a fresco restored to its former clarity, food reveals what we wish for or remember it to be.

Ripeness

Ripeness

If the garden is a metaphor for the cycle of life, then ripeness is its most poignant symbol of mortality. We are planted; we grow, ripen, and return. Ripeness is the point upon which living things poise. Relative to the long, intricate process by which it arrives, ripeness is tragically short-lived. The state of ripeness may amount to only minutes, hours, or days in the garden, or a few years in a human life, yielding to the winding down of function, decay, and eventual dissolution.

Yet, despite these temporal limitations, the actual experience of ripeness seems momentarily to cheat time. Ripeness embodies all something has ever been, and the most it ever will be. Yet in its brief and glowing completeness, the moment of ripeness seems timeless. No wonder that harvest is an ecstatic season tinged with melancholy. The contrast could never be starker. Fields that seem endlessly laden with fruit in the abundance of summer are afterward cut to the quick and abandoned to the barrenness of winter. Death is a reaper.

Intensity is the hallmark of ripeness, the culmination of growth and experience. But ripeness is not simply a reward for waiting nor is it necessarily guaranteed. The precondition of ripeness is maturity, which in turn can only come about through the right kind of development along the way. Ripeness, then, is one of the naturally fortunate outcomes of life. Tomatoes, cheese, and the new vintage ripen, but so do the moon, careers, and stock markets. Judgment, if it is any good, is ripe: We choose the ripe moment to act; we grow to a ripe old age. In many large and small ways life swells and recedes.

My fascination with food has led me to learn to recognize and cultivate ripeness as the very basis of my approach in the kitchen. Great cooking requires skill but is built on two basic abilities: to observe ingredients and to respond to them. This runs altogether contrary to the idea that good cooking comes from recipes, adroit culinary manipulation, or novel flights of imagination. Good cooks learn to look at and "listen to" their ingredients. Ripeness in the garden beckons an observant cook, telling him what to pick and when. And it does so by appealing directly to his sense of desire and pleasure. What better way to begin cooking than with the irresistible? I'm convinced that if all cooks were afforded the luxury of a garden, half of the effort of conceiving a menu would be eliminated. A garden can also teach cooks how to shop as it trains the senses to look for ripeness, aliveness, and seasonality in all foods.

Once taken from the garden, ripe fruit and vegetables enjoy a finite span of time in which their qualities of ripeness and aliveness

remain vivid. This is expressed in the amalgam of fragrance, texture, flavor, and "complexion." I am thinking about young salad
greens, for instance, that smell like newly mown grass, the warm
exhalation of ripe tomatoes, the way summer melons split open
under the tension of ripeness, the close-up, candy aroma of ripe
strawberries, the sugary tear on the ripe fig. Scratch a fully mature
lemon just pulled from the tree and compare it with one that has
sat on the shelf for three days. To the responsive cook, that
difference is everything.

Plants, just like people, thrive under conditions most appropriate to their individual development. Any product of the soil, be it
wine, fruit, or vegetables, is ultimately wedded to *terroir* for its
general well-being and the nuance of its characteristics. It follows
that qualities of ripeness of certain varieties of fruits and vegetables may be more fully realized in one plot of earth than another.

It has become clear to me, for example, after years of buying cooking greens and radicchio from a variety of sources, that a particular cool-weather farm a mile from the ocean with soils rich in clay produces leaf cabbage, kale, and chicory with greater flavor, depth of color, and overall vitality than that produced in other inland locations. The same is true of other terroirs and varieties of tomatoes, asparagus, sweet peppers, and turnips.

Ripeness in some fruits and vegetables can hardly be improved upon. The job of a responsive cook is to preserve these native qualities, recognize the point beyond which they fade, and exercise restraint in the way of any additions. In such an instance, the act of cooking may be as simple as waiting patiently for a persimmon to ripen or anointing a tomato with a little olive oil and sea salt.

But of course, not all ripe food is palatable if so simply presented. The raw quality of zucchini, eggplant, mustard greens, or beets must be transformed by cooking; their latent flavors and textures are revealed by means of heat, seasoning, and other manipulation. Constant trial and error is the only way to understand the culinary path toward making delicious food that is also true to itself. Eggplant may be cut into chunks, lightly salted, and fried in olive oil to reveal its soufflé-like texture, or it may be sliced extra thin and seared on a hot charcoal grill to show off its good looks. Julienned and parboiled in a vinegary water bath, tossed with olive oil, mint, garlic, and hot pepper, it reveals its unique ability to embrace flavors alongside its own. All of these treatments are valid, but in order to bring a ripe process to a ripe food might there be a way to show all the facets that eggplant possesses at once? This is the cook's challenge as well as his secret as it is born of his unique and accumulated experience.

The skill of a cook is most called upon in judging quantities, supporting elements, and seasonings in long-cooked stews and ragùs whose success depends on the maturing of flavors and textures under the private lid of the braising pot. In order to bring about such a synthesis, the cook has to be able to foretaste the effect of any number of culinary judgments: which and how many aromatic vegetables to add, the effects of various degrees of caramelizing, the level of reduction of the liquid used as moistener, whether or

not to use wine, herbs, or spices. The skill comes again from a developed sense of the composition of ripe flavors.

When a food has become all that it can be, whether this is the result of a given natural process or the skill of a chef, it is at its peak of quality and fulfillment. Like any other ideal, however, the appreciation of ripeness requires experience and understanding, intellect, and emotion in order to perceive it. This, I believe, is the fundamental work of being a cook, a process itself that ripens with time.

Twelve Ways of Looking at Tomatoes

Introduction

". . . on the table, in the belt of summer, the tomato,
luminary of earth, repeated and fertile star, shows us
its convolutions, its canals, the illustrious plenitude
and the abundance . . ."

– Pablo Neruda

I never feel that I have fully experienced summer until my tomatoes ripen. Living in a climate where proximity to the ocean means
cool blanketings of fog until late in the morning and temperatures
that swing too widely for the likes of tomatoes, ripening comes
late and is often unpredictable. Every year as the air begins to
thin and I watch the light descend toward its low autumn angle,
I worry whether my tomatoes will ripen at all. But usually I am
encouraged by a reprise of heat and dryness in the last days of
summer and early fall. By then I have cut the water off, the ground
has stiffened, and my tomato plants wither alongside the leaves of
the buckeye trees that arch overhead. Fortunately, tomatoes, like
grapes, benefit from such suffering, as though depriving them of
what they seem to need most provokes a deeper search through
their own rooted resources. Water, I have learned, is the enemy
of tomatoes. What the plants lose in yield, they gain in fruit with
fully saturated color and a profound concentration of flavor. If
tomatoes are good only in season, they are truly only superb at the
end of it.

I first started growing tomatoes years ago because I couldn't find
a decent one to buy. Having eaten vine-ripened tomatoes as a child
and later in the heartland of Italy, I longed for their full taste and
perfume. Ripe tomatoes directly off the vine smell like the viney
tangle that surrounds them. They weigh heavy on the nose, grassy,
pungent, sour, almost skunky. We know that most Europeans
shunned them for centuries for this reason and because they associated them with their poisonous cousins in the nightshade family.
But as is the case when the pleasure a food provides causes one to
entirely reconsider any negative first impression, ripe tomatoes
have for many become the stuff of a summer dream.

In the early 1990s, the tomato began to emerge from what had
been a long, dark age when the presence of the dismal mass-market
tomato in markets everywhere nearly usurped the possibility of
any other choice. Their later hydroponic, hot-housed, and trans-
genic relatives had improved looks and aroma but fell flat in terms
of taste. Mercifully, these are no longer the only choices available.
The tomato resurgence was due in large part to the efforts of small

organic farmers and their discovery of older heirloom varieties via seed-saving exchanges. Through markets and restaurants that championed them on their menus, tomatoes literally burst into color, displaying a range of shape and size and wide diversity in skin and flesh quality and acid and sugar content. Their given names were equally appealing. Who, after all, could resist Daydream, Sulia's Heart, or Korean Love? Abe Lincoln, Grandpa's Cock's Plume, Amish Paste, Arkansas Traveler, Box Car Willie, and Mortgage Lifter spoke of people, places, and other times. Many of the heirlooms tasted as good, or at least as unique, as they looked. Derived from seeds handed down through families, traded throughout the world, grown for flavor, and harvested ripe by human hands, tomatoes became as they had once been born and bred, a personal pleasure.

At first I was astounded by the sheer number of tomato varieties on the market. In 1994, Oliveto hosted a tasting of more than 100 varieties of heirloom and hybrid tomatoes. Sizes ranged from the minuscule Currant to Giantissimo. Colors ran the gamut from white to pastel pink to ochre to winy purple. There were tomatoes with stripes, tomatoes with peach-like fuzz, and those that impersonated other fruits altogether, such as Red Plum, Lemon Boy, and Banana Legs. In an attempt to make sense of all this abundance I circulated a rating sheet that encouraged tasters to consider the tomato's fundamental characteristics: its sugar-to-acid balance, color, flesh quality, and ratio of flesh to "gel"—the glassy liquid holding the seeds in the pockets of cross-sectioned fruit. Their proud parent-farmers were present to tell stories of their origins and slice samples, and we followed with a dinner featuring those tomatoes that were rated the highest.

We experimented wildly. We made "meatballs" bound with bread, tomato pulp, cheese, and herbs; we tried fricassees of cherry tomatoes, gratins, soufflés and timbales, and ravioli with tomato filling. There was *pasticcio* of tomato and lamb, chicken stuffed under the skin with green tomatoes, pork cutlets *al diavolo* with tomato sauce and hot pepper, tomato terrine, green tomato pickles, and fried rice croquettes with peas, mozzarella, and tomatoes. We even tried granita, upside-down tomato tarts, and tomato ice cream. Not all of these dishes were worth repeating. We took stock of all of our attempts and some patterns emerged. This led to Oliveto's first tomato event, entitled Twelve Ways of Looking at Tomatoes, and to a menu devoted entirely to them from antipasto through dessert.

Through this extensive first tasting and dinner I began to think of the tomato as perhaps the most multifaceted of all summer produce. Having selected those varieties that best represented some singular aspect—color, acid–sugar balance, suitability to stuffing, sauce-making, and so on—we prepared dishes that revealed their unique attributes. Every year since, the "Twelve Ways" structure has served as the menu template for introducing new tomato varieties and novel ways to use them in the kitchen. Our most recent menu featured thirty-six dishes, which were organized more like a flow chart than the usual progression from first course to dessert. This organization of tomato dishes by particular use seemed to better suit the exploratory theme of the dinner. It also encouraged diners to invent their meals more freely.

I begin the process of making a tomato menu by talking to growers, visiting markets when the first tomatoes appear, and tasting with the Oliveto chefs as many tomatoes as we can get our hands on. In this way, I am brought up to date on the new varieties, and I get a feel for the timing of the season. I also have a chance to understand a little more each year about the way in which geography, farming practice, climate, and other factors can influence the taste of tomatoes. As the market has matured and with it our farmers' understanding of what grows successfully on their land, it has become possible to recognize what makes tomatoes distinctive beyond their inherent varietal character. And since many heirloom varieties are grown by farms in different areas, it is possible to compare them directly.

Sometimes regional variations are subtle, sometimes dramatic. In the process of tasting, I notice for instance that one farm's tomatoes have a distinct mineral character, that another's develop deeper color and softer flesh because the farmer picks them at the limit of ripeness, and that I far prefer the small, tough-skinned dry-farmed version of a popular hybrid over its irrigated alternative. I keep a tasting log and in addition to judging levels of sugar and acid I jot down notes that help me later to determine their treatment in the menu. For instance, I sampled two versions of Marvel Stripe, one of the more spectacularly bi-colored heirlooms, with flesh a deep, red-stained orange. The first version from a hot inland farm was huge in size, picked on the underside of ripe, and paler than its desert-grown counterpart. The desert tomato was half its size, suggesting less water in the diet; it was juicy, compact, and as intensely colored as an autumn liquid amber tree. Normally, I would have opted for the latter version, but I reasoned that the first, because of its drier, meatier flesh and bright acidity, could stand up well in the *fritto misto* of tomatoes I had planned. I reserved the second for the tasting platter on which I presented unadorned slices of the newest and most unusual examples.

Tasting the current crop's Lemon Boy, I am disappointed by its overall blandness. It rates low in acid and sugar and has a soft,

pasty flesh quality that nearly leads me to discard it. But I like its pastel yellow color so much I decide to concentrate it for several hours in a slow oven to bring it into sharper focus. I find later that it makes a subtle sauce for poached sole. Odoriko, a Japanese heirloom, is a thin-skinned delicacy, soft fleshed and plummy tasting. Since it would be a shame to cook it in any way, I decide to use it as a raw stuffer. I pass over Tangerine, a showy tomato with insipid flesh and empty gel pockets. Evergreen, with a wonderful leaf and mineral taste, seems most naturally suited to dessert; because it is very high in acid and nearly devoid of sweetness, I decide to enhance it with sugar and spice. After tasting hundreds of tomatoes, I know the possibilities for new ways of considering the tomato's use are infinite. But my current list provides the most essential ways tomatoes can be used.

Color

The splashy hues of heirloom tomatoes are the most immediate reason for their appeal. The simplest way to exhibit the season's best new varieties and their dazzling colors is to slice and arrange them on a large white platter, then dress them simply with your best olive oil and sea salt. Vinegar or any other form of acidic condiment is redundant; ripe tomatoes, even the more gentle varieties, have plenty of natural acidity. Furthermore, if you have taken the pains to grow your own tomatoes or to find them in peak season in farmers' markets, you will find that adding further acidity only interferes with their flavor.

A more dramatic option for showcasing color is to present puréed soups made from two or more variously colored tomatoes side by side in a large white bowl. Not only is the contrast of colors spectacular but also it affords the most direct opportunity to compare their flavor differences. If you choose tomatoes with different aromas and different acid and sugar profiles, the soups will be as appealing to taste as they are to look at.

Tricolor Gazpacho

Allow 1 medium-size 3- to 4-ounce tomato per person for each of the three soups. This amount will leave you enough soup for seconds should anyone want them. Core and quarter the three types of tomatoes and place them, one type at a time, in an electric mixer fitted with a paddle. Add a little salt and turn the mixer to moderately low speed. Allow it to turn until the tomatoes are thoroughly broken and reduced to a pulpy slush. (Do not use a blender or food processor to purée the tomatoes. Doing so introduces air and you will end up with foam as rigid as cotton candy.) Transfer the mixer's contents directly to a food mill fitted with a plate that is sized smaller than the tomato seeds, and set it over a bowl. Load the mixer with the second

batch of tomatoes quartered and salted as before, and paddle as with the first. While the mixer turns, return to the food mill and pass the juice and pulp into the bowl. Set the first batch of puréed soup aside, transfer the second batch to the food mill over a clean bowl, and quarter, salt, and paddle the third variety.

When all three types are puréed, check their consistency. Tomatoes of different types will inevitably produce thicker or thinner purées relative to one another. In order that the soups greet, rather than invade, each other in the bowl, you may need to adjust them with a little cold water so as to achieve a liquid that is easily pourable without being runny.

To start, season each soup with salt only. If you find the flavor of the soups to be satisfying as is, refrigerate them until fully chilled, at least 4 hours (or hasten the chilling by setting the soups over crushed ice). If you would like to augment their flavor and texture, welcome additions include a small amount of finely diced sweet red onion, cucumber, and bell or gypsy pepper; or green herbs such as tarragon, basil, chervil, parsley, or chive. Add this garnish before you chill the soups so that their flavors have a chance to harmonize.

To serve the soups, use two ladles and scoop up about ⅓ cup of two of the purées. Pour the soups simultaneously into the backside of the bowl and allow them to flow forward toward you. Ladle an equal amount of the third soup to the front of the bowl and at the line where the first two meet.

Juice

Rendered in the manner above, tomato juice can also be used to make lively apéritifs with a fresh, viney taste not found in the usual Bloody Mary mixers or in commercially pasteurized juice. To make cocktails from fresh juice, I prefer to use ripe, juicy tomatoes with a bright acidity and intense spicy tomato flavor. Here are the proportions for Oliveto's most popular tomato-time cocktail.

Sanguinaccio Cocktail
Makes 8 cocktails

Wash and core 5 to 7 large tomatoes. Choose large, deep-colored tomato varieties such as Big Beef, Purple Cherokee, or Mortgage Lifter. The tomatoes should be as ripe and juicy as possible. Cut them into a coarse dice and pass them through a food mill fitted with a fine plate. This should yield 4 cups of juice. As noted above, do not use a blender or food processor as a substitute for the food mill. Transfer the juice to a pitcher and add ½ teaspoon Tabasco sauce, 1 teaspoon Worcestershire sauce, 4 teaspoons of freshly grated horseradish, and 2½ tablespoons of condiment-grade balsamic vinegar. Grate 2 to 3 stalks of celery on the finest grater possible—a microplane cheese grater works best—and add it to the juice with ½ cup fresh lime juice and 2 cups of your favorite vodka. Stir to blend all of the ingredients well, and serve over ice.

Essence

Unlike the soups above, which are a blended purée of the whole tomato—pulp, juice, gel, and what can be pushed from the skin— "tomato water" is the essence of tomato flavor. After crushing the fruit, it is wrapped in cheesecloth and suspended over a catch pan. What drips free is the delicately tinted blood of the fruit. It makes a very refreshing soup with the limpid appearance of a consommé.

Four pounds of ripe, very juicy tomatoes will yield about 1 quart of essence. Add a little salt and paddle them in a mixer until you achieve a runny slurry of pulp and juice. To ensure that the essence runs clear, you will need to pass it through multiple layers of cheesecloth. Line a colander or basket sieve with five double layers, pour in the crushed tomatoes, and bring the four corners of the cloth to the center. Tie two opposite corners together, then the two others, and insert the handle end of a wooden spoon

under the knots, hobo-style. Suspend the tomato bundle over a nonreactive pot deep enough to allow the tomato sack to hang free of the juice it exudes and refrigerate it overnight. (The pulp and skin left inside the cheesecloth may be reserved for a second rendering for use in a quick sauce, or as the aromatic basis of a broth or braise.)

To make chilled soup from tomato water, simply correct it for salt and add a few garnishes. My preference, in keeping with the clean transparency of tomato water, is for paper-thin slices of cucumber (the small Japanese or Armenian varieties look and fit best in the bowl), thin sliced green onion or thin spikes of chive, and a scattering of fragrant green herbs such as chervil, tarragon, or basil. One quart makes 6 portions.

One outstanding use of tomato water is for crystalline aspics. It is of course possible to make a natural jelly of tomato using veal bones in the classic method, but this would necessitate cooking it for an extended period of time. The point of tomato water is that it is a raw essence. Instead, use 1 level tablespoon of powdered gelatin for every pint of tomato water. (If you prefer an entirely vegetal aspic, use a small amount of agar, which is a seaweed-based gelatin.) To incorporate the gelatin, ladle off about 1 cup of tomato water, pour it into a bowl, and sprinkle the gelatin over the surface. If you are making a large quantity you will need more liquid in which to dissolve the gelatin; maintain roughly the same proportion as given above. Allow the gelatin to soften. Pour it into a saucepan and warm it slightly while stirring slowly and constantly with a spoon so as not to introduce air bubbles until all the gelatin dissolves. Pour the dissolved gelatin back into the remaining tomato water, then pour the mixture into a glass baking dish and chill it until it sets. Without any other addition, this aspic makes an elegant garnish to shellfish salads such as lobster, sea scallop and crab. Its bright flavor also adds shimmer to plates of vegetables such as cold green beans, heart lettuces, and avocado. In the proportions given, this aspic is more tender than firm in consistency and better presented scrambled than cut. Drag a fork through the layer, first in one direction then the other, until it pleases your eye. Then spoon it over and around the elements of the dish.

Tomato-water aspic may also be used to knit together terrines (increase the amount of gelatin to 1 tablespoon plus 2 teaspoons per pint) and other molded forms of summer vegetables or to compound the flavor of tomatoes themselves. One of the more stunning dishes we have presented at Oliveto is Tomatoes "Under Glass." Chill thick slices of a colorful variety such as Persimmon, Marvel Stripe, or Purple Cherokee in a baking dish. Spoon over each slice some barely set aspic of tomato water flecked with herbs and edible blossoms. Chill for at least 4 hours, then lift the tomato out of the dish so that the edges are ragged. Present on a white plate surrounded with a drizzle of champagne vinaigrette.

Heirloom tomatoes come in a range of sizes but the miniature varieties exhibit the most variation in form. The once solitary variety of red cherry tomato has now been joined by a number of so-called "toy-box" tomatoes, each with its own flavor profile. Black plum, a plump oval, is a soft, mild variety, as are yellow and red pear, aptly named for their pyriform shapes. Green grape, a small round variety, is spicy and sweet. Currant tomatoes commonly sold on the branch, only slightly larger than pyracantha berries, are attractive but to my taste are better used as table decoration. Less commonly found are the mildly citric Plum Lemon, Galina, and Riesentrabe, whose German name means giant bunch of grapes. One of my favorites is Principessa Borghese, a pendulous Sicilian variety, whose shape is, well, deliciously feminine, sourced several years ago by farmers who specialize in growing miniatures. Principessa is the common variety grown for sauce and bruschetta, and bunches are hung on rungs over the thresholds of Sicilian homes to shrivel in the sun. Sweet 100 and Sungold are the most commonly available hybrid cherry tomatoes. Perfect orbs, they are irresistible for their incomparable sweetness.

ᔶ
Peeled Miniature Tomatoes

Because miniature tomatoes have a higher ratio of skin to flesh, I prefer to peel them. This may sound fussy and time-consuming, but it can actually be accomplished quickly. It makes for an impressive presentation (your guests will gasp at the pains they think you have taken!) and greatly enhances the eating. To peel miniature tomatoes, choose firm but ripe tomatoes; the fresher they are, the easier they peel. Score the stem end with the point of a sharp paring knife. If you are working with several different varieties, boil each separately (the skins of some slip off more easily than others). Plunge the tomatoes into boiling water for 5 to 10 seconds and refresh them immediately in a bath of ice water. Use the tip of a knife to catch the loosened skin at the point where each tomato was scored; the flesh will slip free easily.

Simply dressing a variety of peeled miniatures and nesting them in a tangle of frisée dressed in an olive oil and tomato dressing makes a simple and stunning presentation. To make the dressing, mix together finely minced shallot with salt, pepper, and about 2 tablespoons extra-virgin olive oil. Push a ripe tomato through a sieve fine enough to capture the seeds and add the juice to the mixture. Your vinaigrette should be red-stained and slightly thickened, and it should taste distinctly, if subtly, of tomato. If the dressing lacks acidity, spike it with a little red wine vinegar.

Miniature tomatoes are also delicious enrobed in aspic of tomato water. Pour the aspic into a glass baking dish and densely scatter as many shapes and colors of peeled tomatoes as you can find over the aspic before it sets. Make sure the tomatoes are fully covered. Chill the aspic for 4 hours. Use a spatula to cut the aspic into rough shapes and serve with young lettuces, tomato dressing, and herb mayonnaise.

Sauce

My reference for the best and simplest tomato sauce, called *salsa di pomodoro* or *pomarola*, is south and central Italy, where the tomato with its fiery complexion seems the very embodiment of the region—both the heat of summer and the temperament of its people. Salsa di pomodoro is the soul of hundreds of pasta dishes and of ragù, the celebrated meal in two courses (see page 143). Many households put away gallons of tomato sauce in the summer months to use throughout the year in order to recall something of the bright taste of summer. At Oliveto, tomato sauce provides the foundation for numerous preparations throughout the year.

No doubt, the taste of good tomato sauce has much to do with a long tradition of sauce making and the established affinities of particular tomato varieties to the places where they are grown in southern Italy. Tomato sauce also varies from one family to the next and each is proud of its own proprietary or communal version. Still, most are made in a similar fashion. A large quantity of coarsely chopped ripe tomatoes is put to cook over a gas or wood fire (the latter is preferable for the subtle smokiness it lends) with onion, salt, olive oil, and basil branches. Garlic and black pepper are also added at will. When the tomatoes are soft enough to be puréed, they are passed through a food mill, then returned to clean pots and further reduced to a thickened consistency and bottled. Many southern Italian families also make a concentration of tomato called *estratto*, the ancestor of tomato paste. Unfortunately, commercial paste is a weak tribute to the real thing. The process of making estratto is initially the same as for salsa di pomodoro, except no onion or basil is added, and just a little salt and olive oil are used. After the sauce has been passed, it is poured into platters and set out in the hot sun. Once the sauce has evaporated to a less liquid consistency it is spread onto wide

wooden boards. Over the course of four to six days and with frequent overturning, the paste contracts to a fraction of its original volume, and deepens to an intense brick red. Packed away in oil-topped jars, it is used throughout the year to fortify thinner tomato sauces, as a primary element in the mingled flavors of braises, and wherever the underlying depth and sweetness of tomato is desirable. Estratto, as the Italians say, is seasoned "only by the sun," a description that is not merely poetic. While the heat of the sun of the *Meridione* can be torrid, it offers a comparatively gentle means of concentrating the tomato. Just as sun tea is far less tannic than that left to steep in boiling water, true sun-dried estratto is a pure distillation of tomato flavor with none of the altered effects of a harsher heat treatment.

My own tomato sauce is a hybrid blend of rapidly cooked sauce fortified with my own version of estratto, which we call "Conserva" at Oliveto. Into this mixture I introduce a small amount of tomato leaves and stems, an optional step but one that preserves the fresh, vivid taste of tomatoes that is lost through the reduction process traditionally carried out after the cooked fruit is puréed. There is a common mis-

understanding that tomato leaves are poisonous. They are in fact harmless and may be even beneficial (see additional information on the alkaloid tomatine on page 263). The addition of conserva compensates for the more watery consistency of the rapid sauce and it thickens, sweetens, and strengthens its flavor; the leaves and stems make the sauce evoke the pleasures of eating a ripe tomato right off the vine.

Unfortunately, my local weather is unpredictable and rarely seems to cooperate long enough to provide for the kind of intense sun needed to make true estratto. But the next best thing may be made using a very slow oven.

Traditionally, tomato sauce and conserva are made with tomato varieties that are fleshy and mildly acidic. The denser, less liquid flesh of these "paste" tomato types allows for sauces that do not require extensive cooking. The most evolved thinking about tomato sauce is that it should be cooked as quickly as possible to avoid the transformation of its fresh chemistry and to keep its volatile aromas intact. In the case of estratto, where acid is concentrated when moisture is evaporated, the resulting paste is not excessively tangy. If you can locate the Amish Paste tomato, you will be very happy with your results, but any tomato matching these characteristics will work. The important thing to understand when making tomato sauce for pasta and when blending sauce with conserva is that the sauce must be thick enough to coat the noodle. Depending on the moisture content of the tomato, this inevitably means making some adjustments, such as preparing a stiffer conserva or sieving away some of the liquid that exudes from the fresh sauce. You may also need to add a little sugar to correct for tartness.

Conserva

Whatever quantity of tomatoes you decide to make into Conserva, bear in mind that after the tomatoes have been concentrated you will end up with about one tenth of their raw weight. Five pounds of tomatoes make between 8 and 10 ounces of Conserva. The work is simple. All it takes is time.

Cut 5 pounds of ripe tomatoes into small dice; this promotes the most rapid cooking. Warm a little olive oil in a wide skillet or casserole, add the tomatoes, salt them lightly, and bring them to a rapid boil. Cook the tomatoes for about 2 minutes, or until they are very soft. Immediately pass them through the finest plate of a food mill, pushing as much of the tomato pulp through the sieve as you can. The purée should be devoid of seeds.

Lightly oil a half sheet pan with olive oil. Place the tomatoes in a 300°F. convection oven for 3 hours. If you don't have a convection oven, another hour or two will be necessary to evaporate the water from the paste. Use a spatula to turn the paste over on itself periodically as water evaporates and you notice the surface darken. Reduce the heat to 250°F. and continue to evaporate the paste for another 2½ to 3 hours, or until it is thick, shiny, and brick-colored. Tomato Conserva holds for a long time at room temperature if stored in a glass canning jar and topped with ½ inch of olive oil. As you use it,

make certain you maintain this level of olive oil on top; otherwise it will likely be attacked by mold. If your kitchen tends to be quite warm, store Conserva in the refrigerator.

Around-the-Clock Tomatoes

Small round or oblong tomato varieties (those that weigh in at about 1 ounce) may be concentrated similarly and used whole as a garnish to grilled meats. At the restaurant we call these tomatoes "cooked around the clock," since we concentrate them overnight in the dying heat of the wood oven. Over the course of the period they spend in the oven the tomatoes achieve a reduced, jammy consistency and pick up traces of wood smoke. You can achieve a similar effect by drying them in a standard oven. "Around-the-clock" tomatoes are delicious as an accompaniment to grilled meat and poultry. One of my most interesting recent discoveries was a new heirloom tomato called Juliette, a small torpedo-shaped tomato whose flavor transforms to sour cherry in the process of concentration. I serve them with grilled pigeons marinated in a little dry maraschino liqueur (look for Luxardo, Perla Dry) to further carry the cherry flavor into the flesh of the bird.

Wash the tomatoes and cut them in half perpendicular to their stems. Cut elongated varieties in half lengthwise so as to expose the widest possible surface to the heat of the oven. It is not necessary to core the tomatoes. Place them on a lightly but completely oiled baking sheet, salt them very sparingly, and place them in a very slow oven (180 to 200°F.) for 5 to 6 hours or as long as it takes to reduce them to a jammy consistency. Using a convection oven will speed the process by at least half. The tomatoes should have a pungent intensity, concentrated sweetness, and about one quarter of their original moisture. Pass the tomatoes through the fine plate of a food mill and scrape away as much of the dense purée as you can push through.

A small spoonful of tomato Conserva makes for a surprising outburst of flavor when placed in the relatively neutral backdrop of *risotto bianco* perfumed with leeks, moistened with a full-flavored blond poultry broth, and finished with butter and Parmigiano.

Tomato Noodles

Conserva also lends gentle acidity and sweetness as well as a red or ochre color to the dough of fresh egg pasta. To make tomato noodles, allow 5 ounces of flour for each person eating. Mix in 1/4 cup plus a heaping teaspoon of Conserva and 1 egg yolk per portion. Knead the dough for 8 to 10 minutes by hand. The dough should be shiny and elastic, and should spring back when depressed with a finger. Wrap the dough in plastic and let it stand at room temperature for 1 hour. Roll it into thin ribbons, about 3/16 inch wide (taglioline), using a pasta machine and cut it by hand.

Keep the quality of the sauce used with this pasta transparent. Tomato noodles dressed with basil-infused oil are satisfying in an understated way. To make basil oil, crush fresh leaves of basil in a mortar with a little salt and a clove of garlic. Add your best extra-virgin olive oil to make a thin, herb-infused slurry. Let stand for several hours to flavor the oil before dressing the noodles. Similarly, tomato pasta cut into tagliolini (flat egg noodles cut slightly less than 1/4 inch wide) is a good foil to a quick sauté of little shrimp, olive oil, garlic, parsley, and a squeeze of lemon.

For a richer effect, tomato may also be the basis for a butter sauce. The intensity of the tomato flavor and the final color of the sauce depend upon the use of Conserva or a less concentrated purée. I make one type of foamy butter sauce based on the method used for *beurre blanc* with a combination of tomato juice and sparkling wine such as Prosecco. The greater proportion of liquid to butter in the emulsion makes this far less rich than a traditional beurre blanc. I deepen the flavor to taste with tomato Conserva. Generally, I do not plan butter sauces to accompany foods that are rich by themselves, but there are exceptions. Salmon, for instance, is sublime with tomato butter.

Sauce with Conserva

Wash and core tomatoes and cut them into a small dice. Next cut a fine dice of yellow onion and a little chopped garlic: 1 small onion and 2 cloves of garlic for each 5 pounds of tomatoes are sufficient. First soften the onions in olive oil over moderate heat in a wide, shallow skillet large enough to contain the tomatoes in a layer not deeper than an inch; do not let the onions brown. Add the garlic and cook, stirring constantly. When the garlic aroma hits your nose, add the tomatoes and raise the heat as high as it will go. Cook the tomatoes until they release their juice and their pulp is soft. Then immediately pass them through a food mill fitted with a plate that is small enough to catch the seeds. Whisk enough Conserva into the fresh sauce to achieve a moderately thickened sauce. Finally, if you have access to fresh tomato leaves and stems, add a few of these to the sauce while it is still warm. Let them steep for 10 minutes, then discard. Serve with semolina noodles such as fusilli or penne, and a sprinkling of Parmigiano-Reggiano, *ricotta salata*, or dry Monterey Jack.

Complement

The role of sauces is myriad and nuanced. When a sauce is successful the effect is harmonious and integrated. This can be achieved when the sauce lends the right degree of contrast or when it strikes a balance based more on similarity of tone to the food it accompanies. In either case, the taste impression of food and sauce is like the fairest kind of agreement where both sides are happier by virtue of the negotiated result. Some food that is bland in nature or would be monotonous on its own calls out for such a complement. Pasta and rice, for instance, are justified by sauce. Rich dishes are balanced by a lean contrast, dry foods beg for the moistening that a sauce provides, and simple base ingredients that would be lackluster on their own benefit from the underscoring of their elemental flavors.

The function of the right sauce can often answer to several demands at once. Take the case of *sformatino* of Gorgonzola with tomato coulis. Coulis is a simple purée, either raw or cooked, of any fruit or vegetable. In the case of tomato, the purée is made by passing cooked tomatoes through the fine plate of a food mill.

Sformatino is the Italian word for soufflé, although Italian soufflés seldom resemble their airy French counterparts. In practice they are made like soufflés with béchamel bound with eggs, enriched with butter, and leavened with beaten egg white. However, sformatini are proportioned so as to settle into a pudding-like form and texture. They can be a medium for carrying the flavor of any number of additions, savory or sweet, and are a particularly transparent vehicle for cheese. In most cases, sformatini are usually accompanied by a sauce. In this dish, tomato coulis counteracts the potent strength of the cheese, whose aromas are even more volatile when warmed. The sauce also counterpoints the pudding's richness.

ᔐ

Sformatino of Gorgonzola

Makes 8 sformatini

2 ounces (½ stick) unsalted butter
½ cup all-purpose flour
4 cups milk
5 ounces aged Italian Gorgonzola
Salt and freshly ground black pepper
7 egg yolks
2 egg whites
1 pound ripe, moderately acid tomatoes
½ teaspoons potato starch

Preheat the oven to 350°F. Melt the butter in a saucepot. Add the flour and stir over low heat. Add the milk all at once and whisk over moderate heat until the béchamel thickens and is smooth without lumps. Crumble the Gorgonzola into the warm béchamel, stir to combine, and season to taste with salt and pepper. Allow the mixture to cool, then add the egg yolks. In a separate bowl, beat the egg whites to stiff peaks. Fold them into the cheese béchamel.

Butter eight 4-ounce ramekins well on all sides and fill them to just under the brim. Place the sformatini in a baking dish and fill the dish with warm water. Bake for 1 hour or until the tops are gently browned and a probe comes out clean.

While the sformatini are cooking, cut the tomatoes into a small, coarse dice. Place them in a pan and cook them quickly, only to soften them. Pass them immediately through the fine plate of a food mill to create a smooth and pourable purée. Season to taste with salt and pepper. Mix the potato starch with a little cold water to a thin slurry and whisk it into the hot sauce. This will keep the tomato's liquid and pulp in emulsion and prevent it from separating at its pooled edges. Run the edge of a sharp paring knife around the sides of the puddings. Holding the ramekin in one hand, carefully turn the sformatino out onto your other hand, and then place it browned side up on a warm plate. Spoon a little sauce around each portion.

Braise

Like most food plants, tomatoes are mostly made of water. The percentage of water a tomato contains varies depending on the manner in which it is farmed. Tomatoes that have been dry-farmed (a process by which water is cut off when the fruit sets, or even earlier where moisture-retaining soils allow it) contain much less water than tomatoes farmed under continual irrigation. Still, when I made my own paste with tomatoes raised in both ways and it became apparent that at least 90 percent of the moisture content had evaporated, I realized that a tomato is essentially a floating world held in a tenuous structure of pulp and skin.

Tomatoes have always played an important role in certain of Oliveto's braised dishes, where their depth of color and acidity blend well with the meat and its renderings. But I had never before used tomatoes as the sole means of moistening the pot. I was surprised to learn that tomatoes combined with braising cuts of meat and poultry could form very savory sauces, lending a pleasant fruitiness and underlying acidity to counteract the weighty effect of these rich cuts.

Rotolo of Chicken Smothered in Tomatoes

For 8

Serve these chicken bundles with soft polenta, smashed potatoes, or your favorite root purée.

Salt and freshly ground black pepper
8 chicken legs, thigh included, boned
8 slices prosciutto di Parma
Extra-virgin olive oil
6 to 8 ripe tomatoes to yield 1 quart diced
1 medium-size onion, diced
8 garlic cloves, finely chopped
3 to 4 sprigs of fresh thyme
Handful of fresh flat-leaf parsley

Salt and pepper the cut side of the chicken, and lay a thin slice of prosciutto over the meat. Roll the leg lengthwise and tie it with kitchen twine so that it maintains a roughly uniform cylinder. Salt and pepper the skin side of the chicken. Warm a little olive oil in a skillet large enough to contain the chicken, and brown it fully on all sides. Remove the chicken from the pan and transfer it to a baking dish large enough to hold all 8 pieces comfortably.

Core the tomatoes, then plunge them in boiling water for 15 seconds to loosen the skin. Seed the tomatoes over a sieve to catch and retain any of the flavorful gel and liquid. Push the gel and liquid through the sieve mesh, then dice them coarsely.

Preheat the oven to 350°F.

Pour off any excess fat from the pan used to brown the chicken, leaving just enough to coat the pan bottom. Combine the onion, garlic, and herbs in the pan and cook until softened without browning. Add the tomatoes and the reserved juices to the pan, bring to 1 boil, then pour the tomato mixture over the chicken. Bake the chicken for 50 minutes or until tender in the center.

Remove the chicken from the dish, allow it to cool somewhat, and remove the strings. In the meantime, transfer the tomato mixture to a wide sauté pan and reduce it to just about half its volume. It should have a slightly coarse texture and a deep, savory flavor, and it should be sufficiently reduced so that the sauce does not bleed any clear liquid at the edges. Return the chicken to the sauce and warm it gently. To serve, place one chicken bundle on each of 8 warm plates. Make a final correction to the sauce: Taste it for salt, reduce it further, or add a little water if it appears overly thick.

Tomatoes also act to mollify the pungent aromas of certain foods. My mother used to cook sauerkraut with tomatoes; her version was meltingly soft, appealingly tinted, and more savory/sweet than purely sour, and it had none of the gassy cabbage fumes of less sensitive treatments. Similarly, tomatoes tame the visceral aromas of beef and pork tripe.

Beef Tripe Braised in Tomatoes

For 8

2½ pounds honeycomb beef tripe
1 quart (6 to 8) ripe tomatoes
Extra-virgin olive oil
1 celery stalk, leaves included, diced
2 medium carrots, diced
1 medium yellow onion, diced
¼ pound pancetta, sliced and cut into small pieces
6 to 8 sage leaves
Large pinch of red pepper flakes
Salt
2 ounces (½ stick) unsalted butter
¾ cup grated Parmigiano-Reggiano
1 tablespoon chopped fresh flat-leaf parsley
Freshly ground black pepper

Cut the tripe into thin strands about ⅛ inch thick and 3 inches long. Core the tomatoes, then plunge them in boiling water for 15 seconds to loosen the skin. Peel the tomatoes, halve them, then seed them over a sieve to catch and retain any of the flavorful gel and liquid. Push the gel and liquid through the sieve mesh, then dice the tomatoes fine.

Warm a little olive oil in a heavy-bottomed pot and add the vegetables, the pancetta, sage leaves, and red pepper flakes. Soften the vegetables and herbs over moderate heat. Add the tomatoes and their sieved juices and bring to the boil. Add the tripe to the tomatoes and aromatics and mix them together. Add a little salt, cover the pot, and simmer the tripe for 1½ hours. Uncover the pot and simmer 1 hour longer. The tripe should be tender but not overly soft. Before serving, stir in the butter, Parmigiano, and parsley. Correct it as necessary for salt and finish with freshly ground black pepper.

Container

Voided of most of its fleshy interior and juicy gel pockets, a tomato becomes a vessel ready to receive cold fillings or to be stuffed and baked. The possibilities for such fillings are endless. Tomatoes invite a range and combination of ingredients from humble to extravagant and are as much at home on the menu of an elegant dinner party as they are on a picnic blanket.

Hollowed-out tomatoes are an excellent means of accommodating leftovers. They can house last night's garlic mashed potatoes remoistened with a little cream, topped with Parmigiano, and gratinéed. They can dress up remaindered ratatouille, salt cod, or small shell or elbow macaroni. Rice mixed with remnants of ragù and small amounts of fresh legumes such as peas perfumed with garden herbs make another savory stuffing. And tomatoes can hold yesterday's roasted meats and poultry (diced or torn) or shards of poached or baked fish, dressed in vinaigrette. I always keep olives, capers, and anchovies on hand, all of which enhance cold meats, fish, and, of course, tomatoes. Minced onion or shallot, garlic if you wish, a small amount of celery heart, and ripe tomatoes are all you need to transform bits of chicken, lamb, or salmon into a meal by itself.

In more planned preparations, raw tomato containers not only make an attractive presentation but also provide contrast to the richness of mayonnaise-bound shellfish salads such as crab, shrimp, sea scallops, and lobster. Their acidity offsets the suave flavor and texture of avocados, diced, perfumed with lime and olive oil, and mixed with summer peppers and sweet onions.

A number of heirloom tomatoes are bred specifically for stuffing. My favorite is Yellow Ruffles, a tomato of variable size with fluted sides and an open interior more reminiscent of a bell pepper than a tomato. Its added benefit is a flesh and skin sturdy enough to hold fillings without breaking when exposed to heat. For the same reason, Yellow Ruffles and other thick-skinned, firm-fleshed tomatoes are not as well suited to being served raw and stuffed. For cold fillings in raw tomatoes, choose tomato varieties that are thin-skinned, ripe, and soft-fleshed, such as Odoriko, Lemon Boy, or medium-size Purple Cherokee. Cutting into raw, stuffed tomatoes with loose fillings always means that they will fall apart on the plate unless the tomato flesh yields easily to knife and fork.

Simple Stuffed Tomatoes

The ideal weight of tomatoes for stuffing, whether they are to be baked or filled raw, is 6 to 7 ounces. This size provides for an ample portion as a course in itself, although it can be sized down if served as part of a varied antipasto or multicourse meal. Core a tomato, then cut a conical section out of the center of the tomato, leaving about ¼ inch of flesh at the sides so that the tomato does not collapse when it is heated. Chop the tomato pulp you removed and combine it with minced garlic, chopped parsley, sturdy sourdough bread crumbs tossed in olive oil and browned in the oven, salt, and pepper. Reserve some of the bread crumbs for the top of the tomato. Salt and pepper the cavity of the tomato shell and fill it with the tomato–bread mixture. Top with grated Parmigiano-Reggiano cheese. Warm the tomato through in a 350°F. oven, then put the tomato under the broiler to brown the crumbs.

As an antipasto at this year's Oliveto tomato dinners we featured three different stuffings. Each complemented the others as well as the small (4 ounces on average), thick-skinned Early Girl tomatoes we received from a local coastal farm.

Zucchini Frittata Filling

Makes about 3 cups
(enough to stuff twelve 6- to 7-ounce tomatoes)

You will need cheesecloth to wring the moisture from the zucchini.

12 ounces zucchini
1¼ teaspoons salt
1 tablespoon olive oil
2 small shallots, minced
6 whole eggs
5 tablespoons heavy cream
¾ cup grated Danish Havarti cheese (also called Dofino)
1½ cups grated Parmigiano-Reggiano
20 basil leaves, coarsely chopped
Freshly ground black pepper
Twelve 6- to 7-ounce thick-skinned tomatoes

Wash and trim the ends of the zucchini and grate them coarsely. Add ½ teaspoon of the salt and mix well. Cut a piece of cheesecloth large enough to hold the zucchini and wrap it tightly. Squeeze as much of the water out of the zucchini as you can.

Warm the olive oil in a small pan, add the shallots, and cook them over medium heat for several minutes to soften them. Whisk the eggs together with the cream, then add both cheeses, the shallots, and the basil. Season with the remaining ¾ teaspoon of salt and a little freshly ground pepper and mix all the ingredients very well.

Preheat the oven to 375°F.

Core the tomatoes, scoop the flesh out, then salt the shells (retain the flesh of the tomatoes for soup or sauce). Spoon about ¼ cup of the frittata filling into each tomato shell. Bake on the top shelf of the oven for 20 minutes. Raise the heat to 400°F. and bake the tomatoes for another 6 to 10 minutes, or until the filling is set and the tops are nicely browned.

Ricotta Filling

Makes 2 cups filling
(enough to stuff eight 6- to 7-ounce tomatoes)
The ricotta should be as dry as possible. If it is moist, wrap it in cheesecloth and hang it over a bowl in the refrigerator overnight.

2 cups ricotta (preferably sheep's milk)
2 eggs
Salt and freshly ground black pepper
Eight 6- to 7-ounce thick-skinned tomatoes

Preheat the oven to 375° F.

Using a whisk, mix the ricotta and the eggs together well. Season the mixture to taste with salt and pepper. Divide the mixture evenly among the tomatoes. Bake on the top shelf of the oven for about 15 to 18 minutes, or until the cheese browns lightly and is firm to the touch.

Saffron Rice and Shellfish Filling

Makes 4 cups
(enough to stuff twelve 6- to 7-ounce tomatoes)
Twelve 6- to 7-ounce thick-skinned tomatoes
1 quart water
1½ teaspoons salt
1 pinch of saffron threads
1 cup risotto such as Arborio or Canaroli
2 tablespoons extra-virgin olive oil
2 bay leaves
1 small shallot, sliced
¼ cup white wine
1 pound small clams, scrubbed
8 ounces mussels, cleaned, "beards" removed
2 teaspoons tomato Conserva (see page 46) or tomato paste
8 ounces fresh shrimp, peeled and chopped
¼ teaspoon Spanish paprika
¾ teaspoon salt
Freshly ground black pepper

Core the tomatoes, then scoop them out. Dice the tomato flesh and pulp you've removed and measure 1 cup. Reserve the rest for another use. Bring the water to a boil in a saucepan, add the salt and saffron, and stir in the rice. Reduce the heat to a simmer and cook the rice for 15 to 18 minutes, or until it softens but still retains some of its bite. Drain the rice in a colander, then immediately spread it on a platter. Stir in the olive oil, mix it well, and allow the rice to cool.

Combine the bay leaves, shallot, and wine in a 12-inch sauté pan. Turn the heat to high, add the clams, and cover the pot. After about 1 minute, shake the pan. When the clams begin to gape, add the mussels. Cover and steam the shellfish for several minutes more until fully opened. Pour the shellfish into a colander set over a bowl to capture the cooking juices.

Preheat the oven to 375°F.

Transfer the cooking juices to a small pan and reduce them by half, then stir in the tomato Conserva. Shuck the clams and mussels and chop them coarsely. Add the clams, mussels, raw shrimp, reduced shellfish juices, and Conserva to the rice. Mix in the diced tomato pulp. Season the rice with paprika and salt and pepper to taste. Salt the tomato shells and divide the rice and shellfish filling among them equally. Bake for 25 minutes. Serve warm.

Condiment

Certain meats and poultry have a classic affinity for fruit and sweet condiments or sauces. Pork with apples or prunes; game birds with grapes; foie gras with raisins; and lamb with chutney, pungent fruit purées, or herb jelly are familiar dishes in the repertory of northern European cooking. In Italy the tradition of preparations in *dolce forte* and the taste for *agrodolce* (sweet and sour) sauces allude to days when the savory and the sweet were not so clearly segregated in the menu or within its individual courses. This was not the only recollection that prompted me to apply similar preparations to the use of tomatoes. Some years ago I had late-planted a crop of fruit that hung on my vines well into the end of the season. Fully formed but green as grass, these tomatoes held little hope of ripening further in the chilly air of fall. Green tomatoes are solid from skin to core, mildly sour, and otherwise uninteresting in flavor. But I learned that prolonged simmering can transform their latent tomato flavor into something agreeably fruity, ideal for sweetening and enhancing with vinegar and spice.

Green Tomato Condiment
Makes 2 quarts

5 pounds underripe green tomatoes
2 cups light brown sugar
2 large yellow onions, finely diced
1 cup red wine vinegar
1 ounce sliced peeled fresh ginger
One 2-inch cinnamon stick
1 cup dry currants
1 cup golden raisins
2 teaspoons mustard seed
1 teaspoon celery seed
12 whole cloves
8 to 10 whole allspice berries
1 teaspoon salt

Cut the tomatoes into quarters, then slice the quarters into small pieces about ⅛ inch thick. Place the tomatoes in a heavy-bottomed pot. Add the brown sugar, onions, vinegar, ginger, cinnamon, currants, raisins, mustard seed, and celery seed. Using cheesecloth, make a little spice sack containing the cloves and allspice and add it to the pot along with the salt. Bring the mixture to a boil, reduce to a low simmer, and cook for about 2¾ hours, or until the mixture has reduced to a glossy, jam-like consistency and all of the liquid has evaporated. Remove the cinnamon stick, ginger slices, and spice bag, then ladle the condiment into sterilized mason jars. Cover the jars and submerge them in a boiling water bath for 15 minutes. Cool, then store in the refrigerator or a cool cellar.

Side Dish

Our nightly Oliveto menu keeps with the Italian tradition of offering *contorni*—an array of vegetable side dishes designed to accompany relatively unadorned meat, poultry, and fish dishes following a soup or pasta course. The idea of contorni has always made sense to me. There are a number of options for pairing vegetables with roasts from the spit, grilled dishes, braises, and sautés, and it is gracious to allow guests to choose what best suits their taste and appetite. Beyond this, offering contorni also leads the cook to regard vegetables as an end in themselves rather than as a subservient garnish. Oliveto's side-dish menu allows us to present whatever bright possibility presents itself in our daily markets or what our local farmers have pulled from the soil just that morning. The challenge of a menu devoted entirely to tomatoes is to come up with side dishes that are different enough from one another and partner well with many dishes in the menu.

Broiled Tomatoes

If there were to be an "all-purpose" tomato accompaniment it would be the following simple treatment. Choose ripe, fleshy beefsteak varieties with good acidity and sturdy skin. Cut the tomatoes evenly in half perpendicular to the stem. Set the tomato halves on a baking sheet and salt and pepper their cut surfaces. When salting the tomato imagine you are salting not just its surface but the entire orb as the tomatoes should absorb the salt for 1 hour before cooking. After an hour, heat them for 20 minutes in a moderate oven or until they are hot all the way through but not slumping. Prepare a mixture of chopped fresh garlic, flat-leaf parsley, and, if you wish, freshly grated Parmigiano-Reggiano moistened with a little fruity olive oil. Alternatively any fresh green herb such as basil, tarragon, mint, or fresh coriander may be used. Consider the main dish your tomatoes will accompany and select your herbs accordingly. For a clean, simple effect chop the herbs; if you want a more concentrated burst of flavor make an herb pesto in a mortar.

Turn the oven to broil and place the tomatoes on a low rack at least 4 to 5 inches below the oven flames or coils. When the tomatoes are very hot, apply the herbs liberally to the cut surface of each tomato and return them to the broiler momentarily. When the garlic is fragrant but not browned, remove the tomatoes. Allow the tomatoes to cool slightly. Serve with grilled meat, poultry, or fish.

Fried Tomatoes

Tomatoes, from green to firm ripe, may be sliced, breaded, and fried. Several varieties, or at least several levels of ripeness, make for an interesting fritto misto of tomatoes; their tart-to-sweet flavors and varying textures under the crust mingle well both with the juices of roasted meats and with fish. Because of their pungent sourness and firm consistency, unripe tomatoes should be sliced about ⅛ inch thick; eating them reminds me of the tart bite of deep-fried lemon slices. Ripe tomatoes can be cut thicker but should not exceed ⅜ an inch or they won't cook through to the center by the time the breading has fully browned.

Because we have so many tomatoes on hand during the course of our weekly tomato event and we can make use of their interiors for sauces and stuffings, we often serve just the "cheeks"— oval sections removed from each of four sides of the tomatoes. The advantage of frying the whole cheek lies in its solid integrity. It is pure tomato flesh. Such is not the case with a sliced cross-section, which, in the case of ripe tomatoes, is more apt to exude juice and gel from its open pockets. This interferes with the breading and makes for a far less crisp sealed result. If you want to fry tomato slices, choose fruit that is firm ripe and more tightly held together.

For the breading, arrange flour, a whole beaten egg, and coarse sourdough bread crumbs in three separate bowls. First dip the tomato slice or cheek into the flour so that it is lightly coated, then coat the tomato similarly in the egg, allowing any excess to drip back into the bowl. Finally, place the tomato into the bread crumbs and pack them lightly around all sides. If you are breading a lot of tomato slices, hold half of the crumbs in another bowl, as they tend to get soggy and resist adhering over the course of the breading.

Pour about 2 inches of olive oil into a heavy-bottomed skillet. Bring the oil to 375°F. (or until a crumb quickly sizzles) and fry the tomato slices 4 to 5 at a time in order to maintain the frying temperature of the oil. In order to assure a crisp, crusty exterior it is important to maintain the high temperature. Turn the tomatoes once as they cook to brown them on both sides. Transfer the tomatoes to a tray lined with absorbent paper and sprinkle them lightly with sea salt. Hold in a warm oven as you fry successive batches.

Fruit

Though to most people tomatoes might seem like a remote option as a dessert ingredient, the idea is not altogether far-fetched. Botanically speaking, the tomato is a fruit. But the tomato's resemblance to other fruits seems not to progress much past the fact that it can be quite sweet.

Even though I am convinced that tomatoes can be every bit as satisfying as other dessert fruits, my approach is to use them in ways that are familiar to most people and have been proven successful with other fruits. The pleasing associations that people make with eating crostata, puff pastry, steamed puddings, jam tarts, and cakes make it a little easier for them to swallow the idea that they are about to eat tomatoes in their dessert. They are more often than not pleasantly surprised.

The challenge in working with the tomato as a dessert ingredient is to reconcile and balance its vegetal taste. This task falls each year to our pastry chef, Julie Cookenboo, who says she goes to battle with tomatoes over this very problem. Seldom does she think of masking flavor in her fruit desserts, but in the case of the tomato, it is necessary in order to translate it from the savory domain to the sweet. The most obvious answer is to add sugar. Tomatoes accept it gladly, either in granulated or caramelized form. Tomato desserts tend to be sweeter than most but their counteracting acidity mollifies the sweetness. The judicious use of spices, nuts, and raisins also works to transform tomatoes in dessert preparations.

One of the most striking tomato desserts is an open-faced crostata. It consists of a large single slice of tomato baked in either a puff pastry or *pâte brisée* free-form shell. We make this dessert in individual hand-shaped forms with large, deep yellow-orange tomato varieties such as Valencia and Persimmon. Both of these tomatoes are tangy and have a compact flesh and brilliant color that glistens under a raisin glaze.

Tomato Crostata
Makes 1 large crostata (for 8)

Cut 6 ounces cold, unsalted butter into small cubes of roughly 1 inch. In a mixing bowl combine 2 cups flour, the butter, ½ teaspoon salt, and 1 tablespoon sugar. Toss the ingredients together so that all the butter is coated. Add ¼ cup ice water. Using two knives, cut through the mixture to disperse the water and reduce the size of the butter cubes to roughly ½ inch pieces. Add another 6 tablespoons ice water, pouring it over the dry portions of the dough, and continue to cut until all the flour is damp. Gather the dough together by hand, knead it very briefly to make certain the butter is well coated with flour, and press it into a disk. Wrap the dough in plastic and refrigerate it for at least 1 hour.

Preheat the oven to 400°F.

Roll the dough into a rough circular shape about 13 inches in diameter and transfer it to a baking sheet. Sprinkle with a tablespoon of flour over the center of the dough, leaving a border all around of about 1½ inches. Slice 3 large medium-ripe yellow tomatoes, preferably Valencia, ¼ inch thick. Arrange the tomato slices on the pastry circle, leaving about 1 inch at the edges. Fold the border up and over the tomatoes, pinching pleats as needed.

Brush 1 tablespoon melted butter over the folded pastry border and sprinkle 2½ tablespoons sugar over it and the tomatoes. Bake the crostata for 50 to 60 minutes, or until the pastry is deeply browned. Allow the crostata to cool on the sheet.

To make the glaze, combine ½ cup yellow raisins, ¼ cup sugar, and ½ cup water in a saucepan. Bring to a boil. Reduce the heat to a simmer and continue cooking the mixture for 5 to 7 minutes, or until syrupy. Strain. Allow to cool. Brush the tart all over its surface with the glaze just before plating. Serve the tart with a dollop of mascarpone.

Spiced Tomato Pudding
For 8

Cooking a tomato, either by concentrating it in the oven beforehand or by reducing its purée, makes for a more mellow tomato presence in any dessert. Like persimmons, tomatoes also act as a moisture retainer in batter cakes and puddings. This pudding is dark and fragrant and bears a faint but unmistakable trace of the tomato's sunny flavor.

4 large tomatoes such as Brandywine,
    Red Slicer, or Marvel Stripe
1½ cups sugar
1¼ cups all-purpose flour
¼ teaspoon salt
1 teaspoon ground cinnamon
¼ teaspoon ground cloves
¼ teaspoon freshly grated nutmeg
2 teaspoons baking soda
2 teaspoons hot water
2 eggs
4 ounces (1 stick) unsalted butter, melted
¾ cup chopped walnuts
⅔ cup currants
Lightly sweetened whipped cream, for serving

Core the tomatoes, then plunge them into boiling water for 15 seconds to loosen the skins.

Peel the tomatoes, then purée them in a food processor. Combine the purée and ½ cup of the sugar in a saucepan, bring to a boil, and reduce to 1 cup. Set aside.

Sift together the flour, salt, and spices. Mix the baking soda and hot water in a small cup. In a large bowl, beat the eggs and the remaining cup of sugar until smooth. Whisk in the butter, then the tomato purée and finally, the soda and water. Add the sifted dry ingredients and mix until completely smooth. Fold in the walnuts and currants.

Heavily butter a 2-quart tube-shaped pudding mold. Pour the pudding batter into the mold, secure the top, and place it in a large pot. Make a bain-marie by pouring hot water around the mold to half the level of the mold. Cover the bain-marie with a tight-fitting lid or aluminum foil. Bring to a boil, reduce to a simmer, and steam for approximately 1½ hours. The pudding is done when a skewer stuck in the middle comes out clean. Remove the pudding from the pot, allow it to cool for 10 minutes, then invert it onto a plate and remove the mold. The outside of the pudding will be sticky and wet but it will dry out and become firm as it cools. Serve the pudding warm with lightly sweetened whipped cream.

Tomatoes may also be cooked into rich jams and clear jellies. Their tartness is offset with sugar, enhanced with lemon, and perfumed with ginger and clove. Each year we make preserves out of various types and colors of miniature tomatoes and use them in a trio of tartlets that resemble miniature linzertortes.

Tomato Jam Tartlets
Makes six 4-inch tartlets

Tart Dough
Place 3⅓ cups all-purpose flour, ⅓ cup granulated sugar, and ⅓ teaspoon salt in the bowl of an electric mixer fitted with a paddle. Cut 12 ounces (3 sticks) unsalted butter into 1-inch cubes. Add the butter to the flour mixture and mix on lowest speed until the dough barely starts to come together in the middle of the bowl. Stop the mixer, add 1 egg yolk, and continue to mix until the dough and butter are well incorporated. Divide the dough into two pieces, one twice as big as the other. Wrap both pieces in plastic and refrigerate them overnight.

Green Tomato Jam
Combine 2 cups chopped green underripe tomatoes, 1 cup water, and a heaping ¾ cup sugar in a saucepan. Bring to a boil and simmer until the tomatoes are tender and translucent, about 15 minutes. Raise the heat to high and, stirring constantly, cook until the mixture is thick and jam-like and no liquid seeps out.

Cherry Tomato Preserves
Combine 1 quart washed, stemmed cherry tomatoes such as Sweet 100, 1 cup brown sugar, 1 cup granulated sugar, 1 lemon halved lengthwise and sliced thin, 1½ cups water, a 1-inch piece of cinnamon stick, and 2 tablespoons peeled, chopped fresh ginger in a stainless-steel saucepan. Simmer the mixture for 30 minutes, then raise the heat to high and reduce the mixture to a thick consistency while stirring constantly.

Yellow Tomato Preserves

Combine 1 quart Yellow Pear tomatoes, 1 lemon halved lengthwise and sliced thin, ¾ cup brown sugar, ¾ cup granulated sugar, and ½ cup water in a stainless-steel saucepan. Simmer for 30 minutes. Raise the heat to high and reduce the mixture to a thick consistency while stirring constantly.

Assembly

You will need six 4-inch tart pans. Remove the tart dough from the refrigerator and allow it to soften to a workable consistency (the dough should remain firm but be malleable enough to roll). Roll the larger piece of dough into a rectangle measuring 11 by 16 inches.

Place the tartlet pans on top of the dough and cut the dough into 6 squares at least 1 inch larger on all sides than the edge of the tartlet pans. Fit the dough into each pan, pushing the dough into the corners of the pans, and trim the excess. Save the excess for other tarts; it freezes well for up to 1 month.

Roll the smaller piece of dough into a 10 by 10-inch square. Use a sharp knife to cut ¼-inch strips. Fill two of the tart pans with the green tomato jam, two with the cherry tomato preserves, and the last two with the yellow tomato preserves, using approximately 3 tablespoons for each tartlet.

Place 3 of the dough strips on top of each tartlet. Mix 1 egg and 1 tablespoon cream together and brush the strips lightly with the mixture. Place 3 more strips on top of the first 3 strips, on the diagonal. Brush these with the egg and cream mixture as well.

Bake the tartlets at 375°F. for approximately 25 minutes, or until nicely brown all over. Serve at room temperature.

Tomato Upside-Down Cake

Makes one 9-inch cake (for 8 to 10)

Incorporating an intense tomato preserve as described above is the most effective way to reveal the tomato's flavor in batter cakes. The flavor of more watery purées of tomato, even those that have been reduced, is lost in the enveloping medium of flour and eggs.

In a saucepan melt ½ cup dark brown sugar together with 5 ounces of butter. Pour it into a 9-inch round cake pan. Slice one firm ripe tomato such as Brandywine or Marvel Stripe about ⅛ inch thick. Place the slices in the cake pan, allowing them to touch but not overlap. Spread 1½ cups of plum tomato preserves (recipe follows) over the tomato slices, taking care not to disturb the slices.

Sift together 1 cup all-purpose flour, 1 teaspoon baking powder, and ¼ teaspoon salt. Using a mixer fitted with a paddle, cream together 4 ounces unsalted, room-temperature butter and ½ cup sugar on medium speed until light and fluffy, about 5 minutes. Add 2 large eggs one at a time and beat briefly (the mixture will not be completely smooth at this time). Add the sifted dry ingredients and beat only until smooth. Scrape the bowl thoroughly with a rubber spatula and beat briefly until the batter is completely smooth. Spread the batter in the pan evenly.

Bake in a 350°F. oven for approximately 30 minutes, or until a skewer stuck in the middle of the cake comes out clean. Remove the cake from the oven and allow it to cool for 10 minutes, then flip the cake over onto a large plate to remove it from the pan. Be sure to unmold the cake while still quite warm, otherwise the tomatoes may stick to the pan. Serve warm with a dollop of whipped cream.

Plum Tomato Preserves

1 quart Black Plum or cherry tomatoes
1 lemon, halved lengthwise and sliced thin
¾ cup brown sugar
¾ cup granulated sugar
½ cup water

Combine all ingredients in a stainless-steel saucepan and simmer for 30 minutes. Raise the heat to high and reduce the mixture to a thick consistency while stirring constantly.

Captured in syrups and caramels, tomatoes can be used as topping or sauce for ice cream that carries their flavor clearly. Vanilla ice cream is the most transparent vehicle, but the sharp zing of fresh ginger marries with tomato syrup beautifully.

Ginger Ice Cream with Tomato Syrup

Makes 4½ cups or 6 to 8 portions

3 ounces peeled fresh ginger
2¼ cups whole milk
2¼ cups heavy cream
1 cup sugar
7 large egg yolks

Slice the peeled ginger and blanch it in boiling water for 2 to 3 minutes. Drain, then chop the ginger fine in a food processor. Combine the milk, cream, and ½ cup of the sugar in a saucepan and bring it to just under a boil. Turn off the heat, add the chopped ginger, and allow it to steep for 1 hour. Reheat the mixture to just under a boil. Whisk together the egg yolks and the remaining ½ cup of sugar. Pour about half of the hot milk and cream into the yolks, whisking all the while, then pour the yolk mixture back into the pan. Cook the mixture, stirring constantly, until steam rises from the surface, then strain it immediately through a fine conical sieve. Chill the ice cream base, then freeze it in an ice cream maker according to manufacturer's directions.

Tomato Syrup

Makes 1¼ cups

6 small tomatoes to yield 1 cup tomato purée, about 1½ pounds
1 cup sugar
½ cup water

Quarter the tomatoes and place them in a small pot. Bring to a boil, reduce the heat, and simmer for 5 minutes. Pass the tomatoes through a food mill fitted with the finest strainer, then pass them again through a fine conical sieve.

Combine the purée, sugar, and water in a saucepan. Boil the mixture for 12 to 15 minutes to reduce it by about one third, or until the syrup is slightly thickened and translucent.

Tomato Sugarplums

Makes about sixty 1-inch round candies

Each year's tomato dessert menu at Oliveto features a plate of mixed confections. This year the offerings included miniature tomatoes in a glassy shell of crack caramel, tomato jam cookies, and these "sugarplums," a dried tomato candy bound with nuts, honey, citrus, and spices.

1¼ pounds Juliette or small plum tomatoes
2 tablespoons granulated sugar, plus more for
   sprinkling
1 cup whole almonds
2 tablespoons honey
1 teaspoon grated orange zest
¾ teaspoon ground cinnamon
¼ teaspoon ground ginger
½ cup confectioners' sugar

Preheat the oven to 300°F.

Cut the tomatoes in half lengthwise. Place the halves cut-side up on a greased rack set atop a sheet pan and sprinkle the tomatoes with granulated sugar. Roast them until quite dry but still soft and pliable, about 40 minutes to 1 hour or until their texture resembles that of dried fruit. Halfway through the roasting period, sprinkle again with granulated sugar. The tomatoes should be nearly leathery; if the tomatoes are not dry enough the sugarplums will not hold their shape.

Increase the oven temperature to 350°f. Spread the almonds on a sheet pan and toast until well browned, 10 to 15 minutes. Allow them to cool, then chop them fine in a food processor. Chop the tomatoes fine by hand with the 2 tablespoons of granulated sugar, tossing them a few times to coat. Combine the honey, orange zest, cinnamon, and ginger in a medium bowl. Add the almonds and tomatoes and mix well.

Roll the mixture into small balls approximately ½ inch in diameter. Keep a bowl of water beside your work space. With a dry hand take up some of the mixture and squeeze it tight to compress the ingredients. Moisten your other hand with water and "cup" it around the mixture to form it into a round shape. Roll the balls in confectioners' sugar. Store the sugarplums in an airtight container in the refrigerator. Their flavor improves after several days.

For a list of sources where you can purchase heirloom varieties of tomatoes and other vegetable seeds, see page 263.

Aceto Balsamico

Letter to My Newborn Son

Dear Anthony,

It is two months now that you have been alive and I have decided not to wait to tell you about a special gift we have received in honor of your birth. Your gift came in six separate boxes from our friends in Italy, Francesco, an artisan barrel maker, and his wife, Maura, whom you will soon meet and visit. Francesco has built for you six beautiful casks, Antonio's *batteria* he calls it, for making aceto balsamico, no ordinary vinegar, as you will see. When Francesco's sons were born he built barrels for them as well and if you were to climb to the very top floor of his house, there under the roof you would see them lined up in rows, one slightly bigger than the next, his sons' names, Roberto and Matteo, burned into the head of each. Next to these are casks that Francesco's father filled for him nearly 50 years ago! You would also smell something extraordinary as you approach the low door that leads to this room, called the *acetaia*, the place where vinegar ages—an aroma that is dense and pungent and like no other that has passed under your nose. The keeping of family vinegar casks is a very old tradition in that part of Italy and if you were to visit the homes of people who live there, you would eventually be led to the quiet attic spaces where balsamico has rested in casks for generations. Why all this fuss over vinegar? When you enter the acetaias, hear the proud history of the family, and taste the legacy of the vinegar left there, you will understand. Balsamico is a way of perpetuating the memory of family descendants and future generations. It is a living symbol rather than a static reminder, a gift given forward, growing ever more valuable as it grows older, that binds distant generations to one another. What makes it all the more unique is that it commemorates the family through its taste and aroma, a vividly tangible way to pass along memories. In it you taste another time, you are reminded of people who were optimistic enough to imagine an heir, and you feel the affection of those present now who have prepared its way to you. So you see, Francesco has given not only to you, but also to our family, a rare gift and the wish of continuity.

By the time you are old enough to read this, the vinegar that I will soon start for you will have aged enough to draw. In it you will taste the years it has marked since you were born. It will grow sappy as you move into your teens, then deepen and thicken as you become a man. In your twenties its dark obscurity will mirror the complexities of life that dawn on you; in middle age balsamico may help you remember who you are and with whom you have belonged. When you grow old, it will be the nectar that you have waited all your life to sip, by then a kind of magic elixir. Like you, it will have become everything it has ever been for better or worse, an embrace of the "sweet and sour" that is life, a family keepsake to pass along to loved ones of your own. Long after you outgrow the gifts of your first toys, your books, beyond your childhood, and throughout your life in fact, these barrels and their precious contents will remain.

Among balsamico makers in Italy, there is a saying. To make balsamico you need three essential things, the cooked juice of grapes, wooden barrels, and time. This sounds easy enough, but as you will see, there is a lot to it. Let this serve then as your introduction, words that will become our work together for as long as we both remember and promise not to forget.

Your father

The Tradition

Everyone who loves to eat has experienced a private moment of awe over some particular food or drink. Such moments refuse description; it's impossible to reduce to words a perfectly ripe pear, the luscious synthesis of a slow-cooked braise, or vintage wine that has found its way to fullness. Our attention is first riveted by the utter simplicity of what we sense and is then caught afterward in the complex architecture of taste. We praise the gardener, cook, or wine maker, and justifiably so, but what caused our reaction can really only occur at the hands of Mother Nature, under the closed lid of the braising pot, or through the secret alchemy of time.

The first time I had the privilege to taste aged balsamic vinegar from the family casks of my friend, the cooper Francesco Renzi, I felt awe. He taught me to extend my hand and to turn my thumb upward to form a small well just below my wrist. Reaching with a small wooden spoon into the black abyss of an old juniper cask with a small wooden spoon, he poured several drops of a shiny dark syrup, as thick as molasses, into the hollow in my hand and stood back in silence, smiling. Our mutual friend Renato, who was also there for my introduction, explained that a rare old balsamico should be savored directly from the wood without ever touching glass or metal. He went on to say that it should be drawn into the mouth slowly from the hand as a baby might suckle the breast. Renato is never short of poetic advice. But, tasting balsamico this way also makes physical sense. Focusing first with the tip of your tongue and the inside of your lips, rather than drinking it back, slowly reveals balsamico's dimension. My first taste was both sweet and sour, balanced in such a way that neither was more prominent. There is an Italian word for this seamless blending of opposites—agrodolce—and the taste for it runs through Italian cooking back to Roman times. Next I noticed that its thick texture opened to layers of aromatic wood and a raisin-like grapiness. As I held it in my mouth, it took my mind on a wild-goose chase for descriptors: my mother's old cedar chest, stewed cherries, the incensed aisles of churches, tobacco, but also some hint of a taste that resisted description. I must have looked perplexed. Renzi nodded and said, *"Sa del tempo."* It tastes of time.

No one knows this better than Renzi, who comes from a long line of coopers and whose skill applies equally to the construction of new casks and to the renovation of ancient ones. Such experience has put him in touch with the vinegar of old casks handed down through generations. Renzi's "manufacture" is both a place and a method, where casks are "made by hand," each one a measured size but visually unique. During the season of production,

Renzi and his two sons can produce three or four barrels per day, but making them begins long before. In the yard surrounding the workshop there is stack upon stack of wood, long, rough slabs of oak, cherry, chestnut, acacia, ash, juniper, and mulberry. Renzi insists that the wood must dry naturally in the air rather than by the more expedient method of kiln drying. Allowing the wood time to dry naturally preserves its perfume, an essential component of balsamico's complex bouquet. Once the wood has dried enough, straight staves are cut from the planks. Only the densest heartwood with the most compact grain is useful for making a stave. Most barrel staves are bent by fire; Renzi instead dips his in a large vat of boiling water fueled by the discard from the cutting of the staves. This hot soak makes the wood pliable enough to form under racks that force the edges into a curve. The staves are massively thicker and much shorter than those of a common wine barrel; to achieve the bulging shape that will form the belly of the barrel seems almost miraculous.

After several weeks of cooling and drying, the staves are again set out in the yard to finish drying for another several months. Then begins the rough assembly, the cutting of a groove in the end of each stave to hold the head of the cask, and adjustment of the staves so that they fit snugly together. Having made so many barrels in his life, Renzi hardly needs use of a measure. Working more like a sculptor on the age-old symmetry of the barrel, he does most of the cutting entirely by eye, an impressive skill considering the number of cuts and the different sizes of the casks. Temporary steel bands hold the barrel together in early assembly. Then heads are dropped in and Matteo, Renzi's younger son, works on the rough and finish sanding and the replacement of the steel binding with bright stainless-steel rings. The last step is to burn the Renzi name on the head of the cask; mark its volume, wood type, and year of construction; and apply a thin coat of varnish that will protect the outside of the barrel from staining when it is filled.

Renzi makes casks in ten sizes that diminish in volume by about 25 percent from 75 liters to 10 liters. The diminutive size of the casks as compared to wine barrels encourages a more intimate association between vinegar and wood and faster evaporation, the key to arriving at balsamico's rich density. The word *balsamico*, by the way, has nothing to do with balsam wood. Rather, because of its putative effects—protective, curative, tonic, aphrodisiacal— and its long, pleasant aftertaste, balsamico conveys the sense of a balm, both soothing and stimulating.

A battery of casks can vary in number from a minimum of three to ten, each constructed of different woods. There is no hard and fast rule about the progression of woods in a battery although

common wisdom advises that the softer, more porous woods that admit more oxygen and hasten evaporation fall at the larger volume end of the series. The hardest woods with the most compact grain, such as oak and ash, are best suited to the smallest casks as they are more capable of holding old vinegar whose sugars have concentrated to heavy syrup. Balsamico casks are more than a mere container for the vinegar or the "seasoning" it provides. Each cask expresses a unique "personality": chestnut is dark and brooding; cherry, fresh and fetching; ash is austere; oak is refined; juniper is spicy, resinous, and most persistent. In the first years, the aroma of the wood lays on top of the flavor of the vinegar. After 4 or 5 years, wood and vinegar begin to integrate as the vinegar's color darkens. After 10 to 15 years, the wood aromas recede and give way to a mellowing of the vinegar and a deepening of its perfume. In old age, the smell of the cask and the vinegar inside seem to be entirely joined to a singular bouquet with a complex underpinning. This merging of opposites, solid and liquid, happens by itself in its own good time.

I watched with interest one day as Renzi greeted an elderly *signora* who had brought to him a very old cask that had been in her family for three generations. It was in disrepair and blackened from the old vinegar that had seeped to the outside of the stave wood. Inside, it was as though the staves were completely covered in pitch, but the aroma was otherworldly. I fully expected him to tell her that it was time to retire the cask. Instead he looked at it as though he had come upon some rare archeological find. He assured her that he would rescue the barrel and its contents not by rebuilding it, but by constructing another larger barrel around its failing staves. In the tradition of balsamico, an old barrel such as this one is not only considered a precious family heirloom but the "patrimony" of the vinegar—the wealth and intricacy of its aromas, so long nurtured and accrued, there to enrich succeeding generations of vinegar that would pass through it.

The fundamental difference between balsamic vinegar and wine vinegar is that rather than beginning as wine, balsamic vinegar is made from cooked, concentrated grape juice called *mosto cotto*. This sweet, tawny liquid is balsamico's *prima materia* and ranges in flavor and weight from delicate to rich and viscous, depending on the extent to which it is concentrated. In the region of Italy where balsamico is made, the grape most commonly used to make mosto cotto is Trebbiano, a white variety that grows abundantly in the hills and plains surrounding the provinces of Modena and Reggio Emilia in the region of the Emilia-Romagna. There Trebbiano makes a thin wine but is ideal for balsamico because its flavor is fairly neutral, an asset given the concentration of the vinegar over time and the aromatic seasoning it receives from the different woods in which it takes up residence. Trebbiano is also high in natural acids that supply the underlying nerve of balsamico. While Trebbiano is widely used, many other local red and white varieties and mixed lots fall into the vats. Here in California, I use French Colombard because it most resembles the cooked musts I tasted in Italy. I have also tried a range of grape varieties—Chardonnay, Chenin Blanc, Cabernet, and Zinfandel—and learned the important lesson that it isn't necessary to purchase expensive wine grapes to make mosto cotto. The lengthy cooking process irretrievably alters the fresh varietal character of any grape.

How Balsamico Is Made

Balsamico is a creature of the seasons, and harvest marks the beginning of its annual cycle. It is the most ecstatic time. To walk through a vineyard in the cool fire of autumn is to feel a part of a timeless cycle and the promise of the earlier seasons fulfilled in trails of vines burdening under the weight of ripeness. Among my family and friends, it is also a time of celebration, of legs stained purple to the knees and a long table of friends gathered for the purpose of enjoying an annual excess—too much wine, loud talk, late hours, followed by a bleary night of trading the watch over pots simmering the new blood of the grape.

We gather early in the morning in the vineyard. Once the grapes are hauled in, for the sheer romp of it, we jump into the bins to crush them underfoot, then pour them into a basket press where the best juice runs free for everyone to slurp. After measuring the sugar in order to gauge how much to concentrate the must, we pour the juice through a coarse filter to catch any bits of skins, seeds, or stems. In the old days, copper cauldrons would be set over a live wood fire in an open space. While most of the copper has been traded in for stainless steel and the less controllable wood fire for natural gas, Italian producers of traditional aceto balsamico still insist upon the importance of the open flame, responsible, they say, for the *sapore del cotto,* the fire-cooked taste and amber color that develop as the grape juice cooks gently. The practice of cooking down grape juice has very old roots in Roman farming practices and it is not hard to imagine that primitive forms of balsamico might reach back that far. Grape juice concentrated by half was called *sapa* and provided a less expensive and more abundant alternative to honey for sweetening dishes. Because highly concentrated grape juice is less prone to spoilage and offers a sweet medium in which to temper astringent fruits such as quince, wild pears, and underripe figs, cooked grape juice was also used in preserved fruit condiments. These "fruit mustards" (the root of *mustard* coming from the word for grape "must") still survive today in the cooking of northern Italy. There *mostarda* based primarily on a dense reduction of grape juice cooked together with autumn fruits and hazelnuts and spiked with vinegar is still offered as a condiment to boiled meats or for spreading on the morning toast. The addition of mustard-seed oil in the Cremona version is its only resemblance to what we know of the seed paste more commonly recognized as mustard today.

Making balsamic vinegar involves two fundamental transformations. First, a portion of the sugar in the cooked juice is converted to alcohol by special yeast. Once alcohol is present in the mosto

cotto, the job is handed off to tiny rod-shaped organisms—aceto-bacteria—that convert the alcohol in the mosto cotto to the acid that is vinegar. Italians refer to the cooking of the must as *la bollitura del mosto* (the boiling of the must), a misleading description. In practice, the temperature is maintained well below the boiling point, high enough that water can evaporate but low enough to prevent the sugars in the juice from burning. Mosto cotto that has been scorched is unusable as the sugars in it become unfermentable.

The cauldrons that I use in California are nearly 60 gallons each and we set them in an outdoor enclosure on sturdy stoves over a powerful flame. After about an hour, as the juice approaches the boil, a mocha-colored froth, *la schiuma,* rises to the surface, carrying with it suspended solids and murky impurities. I use a wide skimmer to draw the froth away repeatedly until the juice below appears clear. At this point, I lower the heat and maintain it just below the simmer point so that there is no movement other than wispy breaths of steam that swirl around the surface. Thus the pots sit for some 40 hours, or until the juice has reduced by about half and the sugar concentration has nearly doubled. The mosto is then left to cool and settle.

The degree of concentration is a judgment that I must make each year with a view to developing the harmonious agrodolce taste of balsamico that only occurs over the course of successive vintages. In the first years of balsamico's development my primary goal is to build the acid foundation of the juice. Accordingly, when new casks are initiated, I prepare mosto cotto with a lower percentage of sugar so as to put less stress on the tiny organisms that will transform it to vinegar. Once the acid foundation is vigorously established, I can then focus on building sugar by concentrating the mosto cotto to higher levels of sweetness.

Unlike fresh grape juice that readily begins to ferment naturally or with the addition of wine yeast, mosto cotto presents a challenge. Because it is too sweet for wine yeasts to tolerate, I must rely upon a tough-celled bug that can withstand the pressure of the weight of sugar against its cell walls. This yeast, called zygosaccromyces, is nature's clever adaptation to the excesses of sweetness. Considered a nuisance when it visits food manufacturers who rely upon concentrates and other sweeteners in their products, it is balsamico's best ally. I once walked under a grove of apricot trees whose pickers had arrived too late. The air was rich with the scent of overripe fruit, at once sweet, yeasty, and slightly sour. I imagined this yeast and its companion acetobacteria having a feast in the field. This experience offered a clue to balsamico's primal origins. As the agent of balsamico's transformation, I have invited the same bugs to the banquet that nature would have attend the rotting floor of a fruit orchard.

The fermentation of the mosto cotto proceeds at a languid pace, usually completing in 6 to 8 months. I could hurry it by warming the juice (zygosaccromyces multiply rapidly at temperatures that mimic a hot summer day), but I prefer to ferment at cooler temperatures that yield more complex aromas and better clarity. A favorable peculiarity of this yeast is that its fermentation slows to a near standstill once it has produced alcohol in the range of 9 percent, leaving the greater portion of its sugars intact. It is as though it knew to prepare the way for acetobacteria that thrive in moderately alcoholic liquids. Acetobacteria in turn produce acid in near direct proportion to the amount of available alcohol and provide a level of sharpness to the mosto that is neither weak nor harsh. It is this elegant natural sequence that determines balsamico's pleasing sweet–sour contrast. Once it is fermented and inoculated with acetobacteria, I lay away the fermented mosto cotto in large oak barrels, left open to the air. There it will slowly develop an optimal acidity before it is transferred to casks.

Left entirely to the devices of nature, wine ultimately turns to vinegar. It is accurate to speak of vinegar as "wine gone bad." For vinegar makers, on the other hand, it is equally true to say that wine is an arrested form of vinegar. It is the presence of air that makes all the difference. Very much the opposite of wine, whose fermentation and aging are conducted in the absence of oxygen, acetobacteria actually *require* oxygen to make vinegar.

Accordingly, balsamico casks have a wide square bung opening on their top surfaces that allows the casks to "breathe" through their covering of porous cloth. Also, the casks are filled to 80 percent of their capacity. Because of the expanding belly of the cask, lowering the level of the liquid inside increases its surface area, providing ready access to the air for oxygen-hungry acetobacteria. The wide bung also permits for inspection of the vinegar and its "mother," a formation at the surface of the vinegar that varies widely in appearance and quality. So named because it is used and traded by vinegar makers to beget new batches, "mother" is the by-product of the acetic fermentation. Louis Pasteur, who recorded some of the first in-depth studies on the biology of vinegar, thought of the mother as an adaptive mechanism on the part of acetobacteria, the cellulose raft they build to float and feed on the oxygen-rich surface. Depending upon the species of bacteria, the "mother" can appear lacy or powdery; it can resemble a landmass seen from a high altitude or an isolated cloud formation. One species expands over the entire surface to the outer edges of the staves. There it forms a gelatinous stratum that must be removed before it overtakes the cask and chokes the vinegar or else "drowns" at the bottom and spoils the lot. At the end of the warm season, I often find myself literally up to my elbows in vinegar fishing for "mothers."

In addition to preparing and fermenting mosto cotto, there are other important tasks at harvest time. Each year, I must make dry red wine to add to my cultures of acetobacter, which depend upon its alcohol as a nutrient. If there are new casks to initiate, these must also be seasoned with dry-wine-and-vinegar culture. This tempers the raw qualities of the new wood and builds up a dominant population of acetobacter and a sharp acidic environment that protects the casks from molds and other microorganisms that might compete and create off flavors.

In Italy, the roomy attic space of the family dwelling has traditionally been the preferred location of the acetaia, the place where balsamico is left to perfect itself. There are aesthetic as well as practical reasons for this choice. The attic is the least disturbed place in the house, located as it is far away from the loud traffic of family life and the mundane affairs of the street. It is also, fittingly, where one goes to visit memories. The uninsulated condition of the attic means that balsamico is subject to wide fluctuations in seasonal temperature. In the Emilia-Romagna, torridly hot summers alternate with frigid cold in the dark months of the year. Because it is a living substance, balsamico is naturally responsive to these seasonal changes, which in turn determine its progress within the yearly cycle. The gradual warming trend of spring followed by summer heat stimulates the busywork of acetobacteria

and with it the further development of acidity in the vinegar. At the same time, hot and dry conditions in the acetaia encourage the evaporation of water (as well as some of its volatile alcohol and acidity) through the open bungs at the top of the casks.

Seasonal variations in temperature can affect the timing and the extent of balsamico's development from year to year. A late spring, for instance, and a cool start to summer foreshorten the period in which the casks have the opportunity to "work" hardest, that is, develop acidity and evaporate. Particularly hot, dry summers often necessitate a more substantial topping later in the year due to a dramatic drop in the levels of the casks. On a more localized level, even the position of the cask within the acetaia, its mini-microclimate, can affect the performance of the casks. Add to this the variability of acetobacteria, which readily assume new shapes and habits, and the differences in size and porosity of the various woods, and it is no wonder that traditional producers speak of the mystery and unpredictability of the process. Balsamico is as much allowed to happen as it is made.

If autumn harvest is a time of initiation, winter is the season of balsamico's renewal and fulfillment. As the air grows crisp, aceto-bacteria that have remained vigorous through the last warm days of the fall grow sleepy. December's chill forces them into dormancy altogether. At the same time the cold causes fine particles left in suspension by the activity of acetobacteria to precipitate, giving the balsamico a brilliant clarity. This is the time for the drawing of the vinegar and the *rincalzo,* the annual refilling of the casks, whose levels have dipped by nearly half over the long hot months. To accommodate the topping, the series of casks that constitute a battery is organized in descending volume; if each cask were not larger than the one next to it, at a certain point there would be no vinegar remaining to pass forward. Starting with the smallest barrel, as much vinegar as is necessary to restore the previous year's level is taken from the larger adjacent cask. The level of this cask is in turn restored by the larger cask next to it and so forth down the line. The largest cask at the head of the series is topped with fermented and partially acidified mosto cotto from the previous vintage. With the passing of vinegar from cask to cask over the course of the years, balsamico grows ever more dark and viscous while the various woods in the battery perfume its passage toward the terminal cask.

When the vinegar is judged to be mature enough to draw, a small amount of what remains before the topping is taken from the smallest cask so as to perpetuate a portion of the first and each subsequent year's vinegar. This restraint is in keeping with the ethos of balsamic vinegar, focused as it is in the awareness that those who make it do so for future generations. No wonder then that aged balsamico has always been a rare gift; the offering of what little can be drawn from what has been so long nurtured constitutes a genuine act of generosity that demonstrates the esteem in which one holds a friend.

With the drawing of vinegar, so ends balsamico's cycle. What remains behind continues indefinitely, as old vinegar is continually refreshed with the new in a process that knows no necessary end point. Only a few things—wine, cured meat, and certain cheeses— improve with age. Even among these, balsamico stands apart in that it does not inevitably succumb to a descent in quality, the loss of a former vitality, or the tragedy that follows ripeness. Rather, the older it grows, the higher it ascends. In the lore surrounding it, balsamico is often personified. Like an old philosopher contemplating the stars, balsamico sits in its lofty attic, defiant of time and the vicissitudes of life. However, as long as balsamico is tended by human hands and enjoyed in any particular present, it will be firmly planted on the ground from which it arose. And if it outlives human lives, its longevity is a testament to mortality and all those spirits whose time-bound acts of faith, loyalty, and preservation are distilled in its essence.

Types of Balsamico

Before it was introduced to foreign markets in the late 1970s, balsamic vinegar was known only to those who might have had the chance to hear of it or taste it on their travels through the city of Modena or Reggio Emilia and the surrounding countryside. Up to that point, balsamico remained a guarded family tradition that existed well outside of commerce. Avid commercial interest in balsamico spawned the production of quick-process vinegars that varied widely in their approximation of the real thing. In order to protect the reputation and authenticity of balsamico, councils or consortia were established in Modena and in Reggio Emilia, the epicenters of balsamico production. These councils developed legal standards that govern every aspect of how the vinegar is made, beginning with the grape varieties and including methods of crushing and concentrating the must, fermentation, and aging. To qualify as *Aceto Balsamico Tradizionale* the vinegar must be aged for a minimum of 12 years in wooden casks, and be approved by a board of master tasters. Strict standards apply to packaging as well. The councils control the shape of the bottles, their labels, and even the foil that covers the cap. There are currently three categories of balsamico produced in Italy. Authentic balsamic vinegar has the words *Aceto Balsamico Tradizionale di Modena* or *Reggio Emilia* on the label. The important word to note is *tradizionale,* the standard-bearer that is in a class by itself. Aside from tradizionale, there is *Aceto Balsamico di Modena.* Also governed by Italian law, Aceto Balsamico di Modena is produced in large vinegar plants according to more lenient standards and is, for all intents and purposes, a poor imitation of tradizionale. Little more than concentrated grape juice mixed with strong vinegar and darkened with caramel coloring, imitation balsamico may or may not be aged in wood, nor does it undergo fermentation or the lengthy aging that dignifies the real thing. It is always less viscous and often unbalanced with respect to sweetness and acidity. While tradizionale has a round, integrated effect, the imitations tend to separate on the palate: Sweetness up front gives way to an acid bite and lingering pharmacy aroma. The greater share of the balsamic vinegar available in the market falls into this category, and the packaging that includes fancy bottle shapes, sealing wax, claims of age, and images of dusty dukes often promises more than it delivers. In fairness, not all of these vinegars are bad. Some do a decent job of delivering an honestly balanced product, but none measures up to genuine tradizionale. Unfortunately, there is no easy way to judge the quality of these vinegars by their bottles or the claims they carry. Tasting is the only true test.

Recently, various producers from the province of Modena and Reggio Emilia grouped together to create the *Consorzio Produttori Condimento Alimentare Balsamico,* a third category of balsamic vinegar (see page 77). Balsamico made in near accordance with the traditional method but released prior to the obligatory twelve years falls into this category. Condimento may also apply to vinegar that meets or exceeds the minimum aging period of tradizionale but is released without the approval of the Reggio Emilia or Modena councils. In effect, it allows balsamico producers to expand their line, making it possible to release vinegar earlier and at more accessible prices than the tradizionale, which is always more costly and in limited supply.

Balsamico in the Kitchen

Having spent many happy hours around the tables of friends and restaurants in Modena and the surrounding region of the Emilia-Romagna, I've learned that few foods are not enhanced by aged balsamico. Nevertheless, there is a prevailing way of thinking about balsamico in the kitchen that honors its age and degree of complexity. Cooks often speak of three general ages of condimento grade and tradizionale: young, middle-aged, and very old.

Young Balsamico

Condimento balsamico, three to six years in process with the most pronounced acidity, is *da insalata*—vinegar to be used in combination with oil to dress salads, to enliven cooked vegetables, or for *pinzimonio,* a vinaigrette improvised at the table and used as a dipping sauce for raw vegetables. Cold sauces such as mayonnaise and salsa verde (chopped fresh herbs with capers and minced shallots) may also be seasoned with young balsamico. Either of these makes a fine condiment to leftover roasts of beef, lamb, or pork. Young balsamico also mingles agreeably with pan renderings of quick sautéed meats that welcome its dark perfume and acid spike.

Because of its sweet–sour aspect, balsamico offsets and balances salads of bitter or pungent greens such as dandelion, green chicory, arugula (the wild type if you can find it), curly endive, and radicchio. Young lettuces, with the exceptions of radicchio, are the most appealing visually and are not overwhelmingly bitter. This salad, a favorite at Oliveto, is a lively interplay of ingredients including cured fresh bacon, walnuts, and Parmigiano that harmonize naturally with young balsamico.

Salad of Bitter Greens, Tesa, Walnuts, and Parmigiano

For 8

4 tablespoons young condimento balsamico
1 ounce shallots, finely diced
1 teaspoon kosher salt
8 ounces *Tesa* (page 202) or Italian pancetta, sliced thin and cut into 1-inch pieces
½ cup extra-virgin olive oil
8 to 10 ounces mixed bitter greens (dandelion, radicchio, green chicory, arugula, young escarole, or blanched frisée)
4 ounces walnuts, toasted and roughly chopped
Chunk of Parmigiano-Reggiano for cutting into shards

To make the vinaigrette, combine the vinegar, shallots, and salt in a bowl and allow the shallots to macerate for at least 5 minutes. Meanwhile warm a sauté pan, add the Tesa or pancetta, and render it over medium heat for a few minutes so that it remains soft and only slightly browned at its edges. Transfer the Tesa to a warm plate lined with a paper towel, and reserve a few spoonfuls of the renderings. Whisk the extra-virgin olive oil and the renderings into the vinaigrette.

Place the salad greens in a large bowl. Add the Tesa and the walnuts and dress with the vinaigrette. Toss gently until the greens are well coated. Divide the salad among 8 room-temperature plates, distributing Tesa and walnuts equally. Using a microplane grater with a wide blade or a vegetable peeler, shave Parmigiano as thin as possible directly onto each portion so that each is well covered.

Boiled Chicken with Vinegar Sauce

For 4

This sauce is a sharper version of *pevra*, a peppery bread sauce that is one of the four traditional condiments that accompany *bollito misto*, the grand array of boiled meats served throughout Italy's northern regions. Spiked with young balsamico, it is a perfect match to boiled chicken, my comfort dish for a cold evening. In order to avoid overcooking the breast before the legs are done, water is added to the level of the top of the thigh joint, leaving the breast exposed. When the legs are tender the chicken is inverted to finish the cooking of the breast. The flavorful broth that results is used to moisten the sauce.

1 very fresh chicken, about 4 pounds
1 medium carrot
1 celery stalk
1 small yellow onion
Bouquet of fresh thyme and flat-leaf parsley
Salt

Place the chicken on a work surface breast side up with the legs toward you. Turn the wing tips over the top of the breast and secure them against the underside of the bird. Using both hands, tension a piece of kitchen twine, slide it under the front of the cavity, and tie a loose knot around the ends of the drumsticks. Place the chicken backside down in a deep pan that holds it comfortably with several inches of space all around. Add the vegetables and herbs and only enough water to reach the top of the drumstick, leaving most of the breast exposed. Lightly salt the water, bring to a boil, skim away the froth that rises to the surface, then reduce it immediately to a bare simmer. Cook the chicken for 30 to 35 minutes. Test the thigh and legs for tenderness with the tip of a knife. Carefully invert the chicken breast side down. Simmer the chicken for an additional 15 minutes, then turn the chicken backside down again, turn off the heat, and cover the pot. Make the vinegar sauce:

2 cups (4 ounces) fresh sourdough bread
   crumbs
4 tablespoons (½ stick) unsalted butter, melted
2½ cups cooking liquid from the chicken
½ teaspoon freshly ground black pepper
¾ teaspoon salt
5 teaspoons young condimento balsamico

Combine the bread crumbs with the melted
butter in a pie pan and toast them to golden
brown in a moderate oven. Add the chicken
cooking liquid to the toasted bread. Pass the
bread and broth through the finest sieve of the
food mill. If the sauce is coarse, pass it again
until you achieve a smooth consistency. Stir in
the pepper, salt, and balsamico. Keep warm over
warm water.

   Cut the chicken into serving pieces and remove
its skin. Divide the chicken among 4 plates and
nap each piece with the vinegar sauce. Serve with
buttered peas or carrots.

Balsamico's fundamental ingredient—cooked
concentrated grape juice—in combination with
young balsamico and meat broth is an ideal
medium for braising cuts such as pork hocks
or beef short ribs and cheeks that have a pronounced flavor. Where vinegar alone would be
too forceful (not to mention expensive!), the
blending of these ingredients makes it possible
to concoct a deep, nearly black, agrodolce sauce
that stands up to the rich sumptuousness of
these cuts. Concentrated grape juice goes by
the name *vin cotto* or *saba*, after the old Roman
word *sapa*, which referred to grape juice that
had been reduced by half. Whether modern
producers follow this guideline or not, saba is
always quite sweet, mildly tart, deep-toned, and
syrupy in consistency. On its own it makes an
excellent topping for baked quinces, apples, and
pears, or for fig ice cream with young balsamico
in its base.

Short Ribs Agrodolce
Hearty portions for 6

Short ribs can vary widely according to size and
specification and may be cut to include the bone
or not. Choose meaty short ribs with ample fat
marbling that contain the bones (these will contribute to the richness of the sauce). One whole
rib, measuring 8 inches in length and weighing
in at about a pound, looks ungainly. Bear in
mind that short ribs, a rich cut, shrink considerably over the course of braising and the bones
easily pull away from the meat so that they can
be comfortably accommodated on a plate or
platter. The option, of course, is to purchase ribs
that have been cut to 3- to 4-inch lengths or to
divide the ribs off the bone after braising if you
prefer to serve a more modest portion. Because
an adequate amount of liquid is required to
cover the ribs so that they don't dry out during
braising, you will end up with more sauce than
you need. The remaining sauce is a tasty medium in which to cook little onions and mushrooms; or it can be reserved to fortify pan
sauces or the juices of beef roasts or to form the
savory basis of another braise.

6 beef short ribs, 6 pounds, trimmed of excess
   surface fat
2 tablespoons salt
Freshly ground black pepper
½ cup olive oil
3 ounces prosciutto, diced coarse
1 celery stalk, diced fine
2 medium carrots, diced fine
12 medium yellow onions, diced fine
10 fresh sage leaves
1 small sprig of fresh rosemary
1 ounce dried porcini mushrooms
¼ cup tomato paste
2 cups full-bodied red wine
1 cup saba (see Sources and Resources,
   page 260)
½ cup young condimento balsamico
1½ quarts Meat Broth (page 135)

Preheat the oven to 350°F.

Season the short ribs with the salt and pepper. Do this over a bowl to catch any salt or pepper that may fall, and then use the fallen salt and pepper to continue seasoning the rest of the ribs.

Select a heavy-bottomed pot, at least 13 inches wide by 5 inches deep, that will hold all the ribs and allow them to be submerged while they are braising. Place the pot on the burner, turn the heat to high, and add the olive oil. When the oil is hot but not smoking, place the short ribs into the pot, one by one, bone side up. Thoroughly brown the ribs on their three meaty sides but do not brown the bone side or the meat will release prematurely during braising. Be careful when turning the ribs; the oil has a tendency to spatter. Transfer the short ribs from the pan to a platter, and turn off the heat. There should be about 1 cup of oil in the pot. Pour off half of the oil, then return the pot to the stove and turn the heat again to high. Add the prosciutto and let it sizzle for about 1 minute. Stir in the celery, carrots, and onions. The moisture from the vegetables will loosen the residues from the bottom of the pan. Add the sage leaves, rosemary, and dried porcini and stir frequently for about 10 minutes or until you notice that the vegetables have caramelized and the brown residues have reformed on the bottom of the pan. Stir in the tomato paste, reduce the heat to medium, and let it cook until it develops a dark red color, about 5 minutes. Add the red wine, saba, and balsamico. Reduce this mixture of liquids by half or until thick and bubbly, then add the meat broth and bring to a simmer.

Using tongs, place the short ribs on their sides in the pot. Cover the pot tightly and place it in the oven. Braise the short ribs for 2 to 2¼ hours. The meat should feel slightly firm but tender to the point of a knife at its thickest point. Transfer the short ribs to a warm serving platter.

Pass the vegetables and the braising juices through the medium plate of a food mill. You will end up with about 6 cups of sauce. Skim all of the fat off the top of the sauce. Place the sauce on the stove in a saucepan and reduce it over medium heat until it thickens and small bubbles begin to form over the surface. Then whisk in 1 teaspoon pepper.

Remove the bones from the short ribs and return them to the pot. Pour the reduced sauce back over the short ribs and warm them gently. To serve, plate the short ribs and coat each with a generous amount of sauce. Accompany with a dollop of puréed potatoes.

Fig and Balsamico Ice Cream with Saba

Makes approximately 1 quart

5 tablespoons cold water
½ teaspoon powdered gelatin
1⅓ cups whole milk
3 tablespoons light corn syrup
½ cup plus 3 tablespoons sugar
½ cup cold heavy cream
1 pound very ripe black Mission figs
2 tablespoons plus 2 teaspoons young condi-
    mento balsamico
Saba, for drizzling (see Sources and Resources,
    page 260)

Pour 2 tablespoons of the cold water into a small bowl. Carefully sprinkle the gelatin on the water in an even layer, and let sit until softened, about 5 minutes. Put the milk, corn syrup, and ½ cup of the sugar in a saucepan and heat gently to just below the simmer point. Place the cold cream in a large bowl. When the milk is hot, pour about ½ cup of it into the gelatin, and whisk until the gelatin is dissolved. Pour the gelatin and milk mixture and the rest of the hot milk through a fine-mesh sieve into the cold cream. Stir to combine all the ingredients well.

Remove the stems from the figs and cut each fig into quarters. Put the figs, the remaining 3 tablespoons of water, and the remaining 3 tablespoons of sugar into a small pot and bring to a boil. Reduce to a simmer and cook until the figs are tender, about 10 minutes. Remove the figs from the heat and chop them coarse in a food processor. Stir the figs into the milk and cream and refrigerate the mixture until very cold, at least 4 hours. When the mixture is chilled, add the balsamic vinegar.

Transfer the chilled mixture to an ice cream maker and freeze according to the manufacturer's directions. Pour a thin stream of saba over each serving.

Medium-Bodied Balsamico (Medio Corpo)

As balsamico ages, its flavor mellows and its texture thickens. *Medio corpo*, medium-bodied vinegar, which applies to condiment grade and tradizionale alike, is aged twelve to twenty years. Rather than playing a supporting role, as younger vinegar does, it is better suited as a stand-alone condiment to be drizzled on pasta and risotto or used as a final accent to omelets and antipasti or steamed, butter-tossed root vegetables. If it is mixed with other ingredients in a dish, medio corpo is added at the last minute and in a proportion that does not mask its complex aroma. Otherwise, it is paired with foods that share a similar intensity of flavor or richness that balance the weight of this more mature vinegar. Veal Carpaccio is one of the best ways to allow this vinegar to sing out clearly above the other flavors.

Veal Carpaccio
For 6

Extra-virgin olive oil
12 ounces (12 thin slices) veal scallopine
    free of any connective tissue
Sea salt
Freshly ground black pepper
Parmigiano-Reggiano in one piece for slicing
Medium-bodied balsamico

Cut twelve 6 × 6-inch squares of kitchen parchment paper. Brush one sheet lightly with olive oil and place 2 slices of the veal in the middle. Brush the veal with olive oil, then cover with another piece of parchment paper. Using a flat metal meat mallet, gently pound the veal to an even thickness of approximately $\frac{1}{16}$ of an inch (when you hold it to the light it should appear translucent). Repeat this process with the remaining veal slices. Refrigerate for at least 1 hour.

Remove the top layer of parchment paper and invert the pounded veal slices onto a chilled plate. Press down gently on the paper so that the entire surface of the veal below makes contact with the plate. Carefully peel away the bottom layer of parchment. Repeat this process with the remaining scallopine.

Season each serving with $\frac{1}{2}$ teaspoon extra-virgin olive oil, then lightly spread the olive oil with the back of a spoon. Sprinkle each carpaccio with sea salt and a twist or two of pepper. Finally, using a microplane or vegetable peeler, shave thin slices of Parmigiano directly over each serving. At the table, drizzle each serving liberally with medium-bodied balsamico.

Risotto of Leeks with Balsamico
For 4

Your risotto will be as good as the broth you use to moisten it. This recipe calls for poultry broth; turkey carcasses, necks, giblets, and other trimmings make a superb broth but any unbrowned poultry stock will do. The flavor of the broth is further enhanced by the addition of dry porcini mushrooms that are first rehydrated quickly in the broth and then added directly to the rice. Take care not to let the dry porcini stand in the hot broth for more than 10 minutes or they will render their entire flavor and will taste bland in the rice. This rice is an outstanding foil to a medium-bodied, slightly syrupy balsamico.

$\frac{1}{2}$ ounce dry porcini mushrooms
1 quart rich, blond poultry stock
3 tablespoons unsalted butter
$\frac{1}{2}$ cup diced white of leek
1 small pinch of saffron (about 15 threads)
1 cup risotto, preferably Canaroli or Arborio
    superfino
$\frac{1}{2}$ cup dry white wine
6 tablespoons freshly grated Parmigiano-
    Reggiano
Salt and freshly ground black pepper
Medium-bodied balsamico

Combine the dry porcini mushrooms and the poultry stock. In a saucepan, bring gently to a simmer and let stand for 8 to 10 minutes, or until the porcini are tender and rehydrated. Strain the broth, and reserve both the mushrooms and the broth separately. Return the broth to the saucepan and heat it to a low simmer.

Place a heavy-bottomed casserole over medium heat. Melt 1 tablespoon of the butter in the pot, then add the diced leeks and saffron and cook them for about 4 minutes, until softened. Raise the heat slightly and add the rice, stirring often to prevent it from sticking to the bottom and to make sure it is coated well with hot butter. "Toast" the rice for about 5 minutes. When you notice the rice has turned from opaque to shiny and translucent, add the wine. Cook until the wine has evaporated entirely, then add the rehydrated porcini and about 1½ cups hot broth, just enough to barely cover the rice. As the rice absorbs the broth, add more broth in small increments, keeping the heat at a constant simmer. When adding broth, it is important to limit the amount so as to maintain the emulsion it forms with the starch released through the initial toasting of the rice kernels. Frequent stirring will also encourage a creamy final consistency. You may need to adjust the heat up so that the rice and broth continue to bubble lazily. Rice that cooks too fast will bloat and go soft; cooking the rice too slowly will result in a mushy texture.

After about 15 minutes the rice will have lost most of its hard-kernel quality but will still be firm in the middle. Continue to cook the rice for 3 to 5 minutes more. Taste the rice for texture; when it is still slightly chewy but yielding, add the remaining 2 tablespoons of butter and the Parmigiano. Season the rice with salt and pepper to taste.

Correct the consistency of the rice and surrounding liquid by adjusting the heat. The goal is to bring about a marriage of rice, broth, and the final addition of butter and cheese. The rice should be nearly pourable and cooked to the point that there is no separation between broth and rice. Spoon the risotto into 4 warm, wide-brimmed bowls. Tilt the bowls from side to side to distribute the risotto across the bottom of each.

Drizzle balsamico liberally in a circular pattern over each portion at the table.

Risotto with Sausages
For 8

This risotto is modeled after *risotto alla pilota*—the celebrated rice dish of Montova—and represents a wholly different method of making risotto. Rather than encouraging the breakdown of starch to yield a creamy integrated consistency, the rice is first boiled, then sautéed with fresh and cured sausage. Besides its mildly spicy savor and tang, the rice has an appealing lightness that preserves the lively texture of rice kernels that are unburdened of their starch. It is complemented dramatically, both in color and flavor, by medium-bodied balsamico.

At Oliveto we prefer to pack the rice into warmed ramekins and then invert them onto individual warm plates (the rice will easily release from the ramekins, so there is no need to butter them). Forming the rice improves the presentation and keeps the rice warm as it is eaten. Alternatively, the rice may be turned out on a warm platter.

6 cups water
2 tablespoons plus 1 teaspoon salt
2 cups risotto such as Arborio or Vialone Nano
8 tablespoons unsalted butter
24 ounces Fresh Italian Sausage (see page 189), removed from its casing
8 ounces coarse-grained cured Italian salame, sliced thin, then coarsely diced
1 teaspoon freshly ground black pepper
Parmigiano-Reggiano, for grating
Medium-bodied balsamico

Pour the water into a 2-quart sauce pot, add 2 tablespoons of salt, and bring to a boil. Sprinkle the rice into the water, stirring all the while so that the rice does not clump together. When the water returns to a boil, reduce the heat to a slow simmer and cook for 15 minutes, stirring occasionally. At the 15-minute point the rice will be nearly done. Remove the pot from the heat and set aside.

Next melt the butter in a 12-inch sauté pan. Add the sausage and salame, adjust the heat to medium, and use a wooden spoon to break up the sausage into small pieces as it cooks. When the sausage is cooked through but not browned, about 4 minutes, drain the rice through a basket strainer or fine mesh colander and add it to the pan. Add the remaining teaspoon of salt and the black pepper and stir the rice and sausage mixture to ensure that the ingredients are well incorporated and the rice is nicely coated with the butter and sausage drippings. Grate Parmigiano generously over the top of each serving and pour a stream of balsamico around the edge of the rice.

Fillet of Sole al Balsamico

For 2

Balsamico's dark intensity is a ravishing counterpoint to delicate fish such as sole. This dish is very quick to make but requires some forethought. In order to fully wed the flavors of the fish with the vinegar, it is necessary to make a small amount of fish broth from the bones of the sole. This broth is used to deglaze the pan renderings, then is reduced and enriched with balsamico just before serving. Be sure to request that your fishmonger include the bones with your fillets.

2 whole petrale sole, skinned and filleted, bones reserved
1 cup water
1 teaspoon salt
4 tablespoons (½ stick) unsalted butter
2 tablespoons medium-bodied balsamic vinegar

Break the sole bones into 4-inch pieces and place them in a 2-quart sauce pot with the water. Bring to a boil over high heat, then reduce the heat and simmer for 15 minutes. Strain the fish broth into a bowl and set aside. You should have 1 cup.

Pat the surface of the sole dry with paper towels and season each side with salt. Place a 12-inch sauté pan over medium heat and add the butter. When the butter has melted and begins to foam, gently lay the sole fillets in the pan. Sauté the fillets on the first side for 2 minutes, then flip them over with a spatula and cook for an additional minute. When the fillets have finished cooking, transfer them to 2 warm dinner plates.

To make the balsamico sauce, pour off the butter remaining in the sauté pan. Return the pan to the stove and increase the heat to high. Add the fish broth and scrape up the residue from the bottom of the pan. Reduce the pan juices by three quarters to about ¼ cup and add the balsamic vinegar. Continue cooking for an additional minute to marry the flavors, then spoon the sauce over the sole fillets.

Old Balsamico
(Balsamico Extra Vecchio)

Extra vecchio, the oldest vinegar in the acetaia, is balsamico that has aged at least twenty-five years. Due to the nuances of its flavor, its dense texture, and its lingering aftertaste, it is reserved for sparing use as a condiment, dosed in droplets onto unadorned prime cuts of beef, fish, poultry, or veal. It is delicious on sautéed liver; foie gras and old balsamico is a decadent glory, but calf's liver or sautés of duck or even chicken liver are equally welcoming. Unmarinated wild game is also particularly suited to a few drops of old balsamico; try loin of venison, pigeon roasted pink and served in its natural juices, wild duck, as well as choice cuts of fish such as tuna, halibut, or sole. Certain fruits in their prime of ripeness also deserve balsamico's benediction: Pears, wild strawberries, and white peaches are exquisite, as are mild creamy cheeses such as ricotta. The ice cream that goes by the name of crema in Italy is marvelous with balsamico extra vecchio. The version that follows is less rich than the Italian model but equally satisfying. But the best way of all to enjoy old balsamico may be in a thimble glass all by itself after dinner.

Returning from the various regions I have visited in Italy, I am always haunted by the unique smells in the air that stay with me as a kind of vivid sensory emblem of the place. In Chianti, it is the grassy aroma of new olive oil, stews of white beans, meat cooking in the fireplace. I cannot think of the port towns of the northern Mediterranean without imagining the distinctive smell of that sea and its fish. In and around Modena it is the scent of balsamico that wafts from its high attic to the greeting place of family homes on the ground floor and the barnyard aroma of Parmigiano that literally blows through the streets. It is no wonder that balsamico and Parmigiano share a special affinity, born as they are of the same soil and such long use in the kitchen. Young, pale Parmigiano that is broken into soft and crumbly shards, rather than the harder and more granular aged cheese, is considered the ideal match for mature vinegar. It is no doubt the most direct way to enjoy both. But I often find that the cheese usually ends up overtaking the vinegar. This sformatino, a type of sunken soufflé, tones down the sharpness of the cheese so that these two kindred flavors come into balance.

Sformatino of Parmigiano

For 10

1 quart whole milk
5 tablespoons unsalted butter
Heaping ½ cup (3 ounces) flour
1⅛ cups (4 ounces) freshly grated
    Parmigiano-Reggiano
8 egg yolks
½ teaspoon salt
1 egg white
Balsamico extra vecchio, for drizzling

Preheat the oven to 350°F.

Combine the milk and 4 tablespoons of the butter in a saucepan and heat them to the simmer point. Add the flour in a thin stream, whisking constantly to prevent lumping. When the mixture thickens, cook it for 1½ minutes more. Remove from the heat and whisk in the Parmigiano. Allow the mixture to cool to lukewarm, add the egg yolks and salt, and mix well. Using a rubber spatula, press the mixture through a fine sieve.

Use the remaining tablespoon of butter to grease ten 4-ounce ramekins.

Beat the egg white to stiff peaks. Fold half of the whites into the yolk mixture, then follow with the other half. Incorporate the egg white quickly so as to not to deflate it, but make sure that no lumps of white float in the mixture.

Divide the mixture among the buttered ramekins. Put the ramekins in a baking pan that holds them comfortably and pour warm water around them to the level of the cheese mixture. Bake without a cover for 25 minutes on the oven's top rack. If you notice that the sformatini in the back are browning first, rotate the pan to move the darker ones forward. Bake for an additional 15 minutes to evenly brown the tops and until the point of a knife exits cleanly from the center. Allow the sformatini to cool for about 20 minutes. Run a knife around the edge of each and invert each one onto a warm plate. Drizzle the balsamico around each sformatino and serve at once.

Timbales of Braised Oxtails, Onions, and Turnips

For 6

3½ pounds meaty oxtails
2 teaspoons salt
1 teaspoon freshly ground black pepper
¼ cup olive oil
1 small yellow onion (4 ounces), cut in 4 pieces
1 small carrot (2 ounces), cut in 4 pieces
1 celery stalk (2 ounces), cut in 4 pieces
1 bay leaf
6 sprigs of fresh thyme
1 quart Meat Broth (page 135)
12 small white turnips (7 ounces), trimmed, washed, and quartered
2 small yellow onions (8 ounces), cut into small segments
2 tablespoons olive oil
½ teaspoon salt
½ cup water
Balsamico extra vecchio, for drizzling

Season the oxtails with all of the salt and pepper. Warm the olive oil in a heavy-bottomed pot of at least six-quart capacity over medium heat. Add the seasoned oxtails and begin browning the meat, turning the oxtails about every 5 minutes for a total of 20 minutes. The oxtails should develop a deep brown color on all sides. At this point, place a cover on the pan and tilt it to pour off the fat. Add the onion, carrot, celery, bay leaf, and thyme sprigs. Continue cooking the meat with the vegetables for an additional 10 minutes. Add the meat broth, bring to a boil, then reduce to a low simmer, and cover. Braise the oxtails for approximately 2 hours and 15 minutes, or until the meat is tender enough to fall easily from the bone.

While the oxtails are cooking, place the turnips and onions in a pan and add the olive oil, salt, and water. Bring the water to a boil, reduce the heat to a simmer, and cook for 5 minutes, or until just tender.

Transfer the oxtails to a plate to cool and

reserve the cooking liquid. When the oxtails are cool enough to handle, pull the meat free from the bones. You should end up with about 1 pound of meat; discard the bones. Combine the meat in a bowl with the onions and turnips and cover loosely with plastic wrap.

Carefully spoon away and discard the fat on top of the cooking liquid. Next, strain the vegetables. You should have about 1¼ cups of clear braising juices. Pour the cooking juices into a sauté pan and boil until reduced by half. Pour half of the reduced juices over the oxtail mixture and reserve the remainder for spooning onto each plated portion.

To assemble the timbales, line six 6-ounce ramekins with plastic wrap, allowing enough to hang over at the edges to completely cover the top of the ramekin. Spoon the oxtail mixture into the ramekins.

When half filled, gently pull up the sides of the plastic wrap and firmly tap the bottom of the ramekins on a towel-lined countertop to settle the mixture in the bottom of the timbale. Fill the ramekins, press the top with the back of a spoon, and tap them one more time. Fold the edges of the plastic wrap over the ramekins to cover the filling.

Warm six 9-inch plates.

Place the ramekins in a wide, shallow pot or flame-proof baking dish that holds them side by side and pour enough hot water around the molds to reach the level of the meat. Place the pot over medium heat, bring to a simmer, and warm the timbales for 5 minutes. Remove the ramekins from the pot using a pair of tongs in one hand and a towel to catch them in the other.

Warm the remaining braising juices in a small sauce pot. Unfold the plastic wrap at the top of each timbale. Invert the timbales onto the plates; gently remove the ramekin and then the plastic wrap. Finish each portion by drizzling a spoonful of the reduced cooking juices over the top. Pour balsamico extra vecchio around each portion at the table.

⌾

Avocado and Lobster Salad with Old Balsamico

For 4

On its own, ripe avocado, simply dressed with extra-virgin olive oil and salt, is a natural foil for old balsamico. The addition of lobster, however, is exquisite; the vinegar echoes the sweetness of the lobster at the same time it provides a mildly tart contrast.

2 live lobsters, 1½ pounds each
2 tablespoons extra-virgin olive oil
1 carrot, sliced
1 small celery rib, sliced
1 shallot, sliced
3 sprigs of fresh flat-leaf parsley
1 bay leaf
5 cups water
Salt

Twist off the claws and tails from the lobsters and set aside. Split the bodies, remove the viscera, and rinse well under cold water. Cut the lobster bodies into pieces. Warm the olive oil in a wide pan. Raise the heat to medium high, and sauté the lobster bodies, stirring often, until the shells redden. Add the carrot, celery, shallot, parsley, and bay leaf and stir together. When you notice a crust forming on the bottom of the pan, deglaze the pan with 1 cup of water, scraping up the residue on the bottom of the pan. Then add 4 cups more water. Lower the heat and simmer the broth for 25 minutes. Strain the broth, discarding the shell pieces.

In the meantime, bring a pot of lightly salted water to a boil. Add the reserved claws and tails and boil them for 5 minutes. Drain the claws and tails and plunge them immediately into ice water for several minutes to stop the cooking and to chill them.

Remove the claw and tail meat from the shells. Slice the tail vertically in half and remove the vein (digestive tract) and any dark or orange matter at the edge of the cut. Slice the tail sections into diagonal pieces. Slice the claw meat lengthwise and pull out the hard structure inside. Crack the knucklebones and remove the meat. Cover the lobster meat and set it in the refrigerator to chill.

Lobster Sauce
Reduced lobster broth
1 teaspoon minced shallot
1 teaspoon lemon juice
3/8 cup extra-virgin olive oil

Pour the lobster broth in a clean pan with wide surface area. Reduce the broth over high heat to about 1/8 cup. Put the reduced lobster broth in a small bowl. Add the shallot and lemon juice and whisk in the olive oil. If the mixture is thick and not easily pourable, whisk in a little cold water.

2 Hass avocados
2 small handfuls of tender, pale curly endive (frisée)
Balsamico extra vecchio

Halve the avocados, remove the pit, and peel the fruit. Cut a thin slice from the rounded bottom of each avocado half to stabilize them, and place one in the center of each of four plates. Chop the slices and add them to the hole in the center of the avocado. Sprinkle salt over each avocado. Place the lobster in a bowl with the lettuces, add a little salt, and dress with lobster sauce. Nap each avocado with the remaining lobster sauce. Pile the lettuces on the avocado, then some of the lobster. Spoon the remaining lobster over and around the plate. Finally, drizzle balsamico extra vecchio over each portion and serve.

Crema
For 4
1/3 cup cold water
1/2 teaspoon powdered gelatin
2 cups whole milk
1/4 cup light corn syrup
2/3 cup sugar
3/4 cup cold heavy cream
Balsamico extra vecchio, for pouring

Place the cold water in a small bowl, sprinkle the gelatin on the water in an even layer, and let sit for 5 minutes or until softened. Put the milk, corn syrup, and sugar in a saucepan and warm it to just below the simmer point. Place the cold cream in a large bowl. When the milk mixture is hot, pour 1/2 cup of it into the gelatin, and whisk it until the gelatin is dissolved. Pour the rest of the hot milk mixture, and the gelatin and milk mixture, through a fine-mesh sieve into the cold cream. Stir the mixture to combine all the ingredients well. Refrigerate until thoroughly chilled, and then transfer to an ice cream maker and freeze according to the manufacturer's directions. Serve in chilled ice cream bowls and pour balsamico extra vecchio over each portion.

Baked Pears with Ricotta, Walnuts, and Old Balsamico

For 4

To buy condiment-grade balsamico and aceto balsamico tradizionale, see Sources and Resources, page 260.

4 very ripe Bosc or Winter Nellis pears
Unsalted butter
½ cup very fresh ricotta (preferably
    sheep's milk)
¼ cup toasted walnuts, chopped
Balsamico extra vecchio, for drizzling

Preheat the oven to 375°F. Peel and core the pears and arrange them cored side up in a buttered baking dish. Bake the pears for 15 to 20 minutes, or until tender to the tip of a sharp knife.

Serve the pears while still blood warm with a dollop of fresh ricotta and a scattering of walnuts. Spoon any juices remaining in the baking dish over and around the pears. Drizzle balsamico extra vecchio over each portion at the table.

Pasta Primer

Introduction

Many years ago I had a conversation with an Italian friend who is a passionate connoisseur of pasta. He said that a plate of *al dente* spaghetti with a drizzling of olive oil and sea salt was one of his favorite ways to eat pasta, and while occasionally he would permit a little grated Parmigiano, he really preferred pasta dressed with nothing at all. At the time, I took this as an indication of the austerity of his Tuscan temperament but also as an exaggeration calculated to impress upon me the difference between the Italian appreciation for the pleasure of pure noodles and the American habit of burying them in sauce. Following this conversation, I began to question my own disappointment at being presented with linguine or tagliatelle in Italian *trattorie* with a meager dab of pesto or scant spoonful of ragù left sadly unmixed on the top of the bowl. In assuming this was kitchen stinginess, was I missing the point? The experience of eating pasta in Italy has taught me to consider the unadorned noodle in an altogether different light. Although not all Italians would consider it sufficient by itself, sensitivity is high to the basic qualities of well-made pasta as well as the importance of the complementary role of sauce. While it is common to think of pasta as a vehicle for sauce, under the best of circumstances, pasta and sauce are equal partners in a harmonized interplay of texture and flavor.

The conversation with my friend also jogged a memory of my mother's handmade fettuccine. As a child, I liked them buttered and salted and found them even more satisfying than ice cream. Beyond their taste and texture, I loved the steamy scent of wheat that wafted up from the colander just after the pasta was drained from its boiling bath. Yet, as my culinary career progressed, I came to feel the pleasure of pasta derived more from the sauce than the noodle, since it appeared that beyond a certain point there was little I could do about the quality of the pasta. The dried pasta I bought from bulk bins in Italian delicatessens or as a standard grocery item in cellophane wrapping varied little from one brand to the next. Making my own egg noodles gave me some control over the variables that affect the finished quality of pasta and was certainly an improvement over store-bought versions. However, after years spent bent over the crank of my rolling machine, it dawned on me that my pasta, though good, was not getting better. Since I was certain that making the pasta from scratch and by hand was critical to achieving fine noodles, it became evident that focusing my attention on their fundamental ingredient, flour, must be the next step. Experimentation soon showed me the ways in which different types of flour could fundamentally affect the bite and consistency of pasta and how a choice of flour could influence or alter, for better or worse, its partnership with a sauce. After I bought a small mill I discovered I could bring further dimensions of aroma and texture by grinding select grains that were not available as flour or producing whole-grain flour that was comparatively much fresher than I could buy.

This chapter is devoted to discovering the successful partnership of pasta and sauce. As the cook, you may wish to think of yourself as the arbiter of a dialogue. Viewing pasta and sauce as equal players compounds the variable to consider. When you depart from the recipes you will no doubt find yourself reaching for options among types of flour, altering the sauce, or reconceiving the sauce to bring accord. The information that follows is the fruit of my own investigations, which I hope will entice you to try the pleasures of pasta making. Experimenting with different flours or grinding your own will help you to understand their basic properties and behaviors.

The Importance of Flour

Pasta in its simplest form is grain moistened with water. Water, added directly or contributed by eggs, has little effect on the flavor of flour other than to help convey it, and eggs, which are themselves composed of water, play an understated if noticeable role in the taste of pasta made from them. Flour is the essence of pasta, all the more reason to consider its selection seriously.

Flour used very soon after milling produces the best, most fragrant pasta. Unfortunately, most flour is packaged without an expiration date so it is impossible to ascertain its age. The best option is to buy it directly from a mill or from a well-frequented market where flour bins are regularly rotated. The perishability of whole-grain flour is one reason for the wide availability of manual and electric grain mills designed for home use or low-volume flour production in restaurants. At Oliveto we use two different mills, one manual, the other electric. The manual mill grinds flour by means of two opposing steel plates that can be adjusted to vary the fineness or coarseness. Our plate mill also accepts whole corn for making corn flour and polenta. But cranking its flywheel, particularly to make very fine flour, requires a good deal of elbow grease and amounts to an aerobic workout. Rather than wearing out our crew, I recently installed a motor-driven stone mill that converts grain to flour from extra fine to coarse at the rate of 30 pounds per hour. Our stone mill is not much larger than a domestic blender and produces far more flour than we would ever need to make a day's worth of pasta. If you decide to purchase your own grain mill, grind only as much flour as is needed and store it cold. See page 260 for resources.

While it may appear from the meager selection in most markets that flour is limited to a few uniform types judged to be suitable to a wide spectrum of purposes, the world of grain and flour is vast, and the options for their use in

pasta making are myriad and nuanced. Learning about flour means developing a sensual appreciation for the variables among different types of flour and manipulating them to achieve the flavor and textural results you most desire.

Grain into Flour

All grain has three fundamental parts: bran, germ, and endosperm. This division is important insofar as the classification and grading of flour are concerned. The bran is the tough outer coat. The germ at the base of a kernel of grain will grow a new plant if planted as seed. The endosperm is the storage center of protein and starch that acts as a nutrient source for growing the plant. Grain may be milled whole or may have its parts separated, resulting in flour that varies in flavor, color, texture, granulation, consistency, and behavior when turned into dough. White flour from wheat is just milled endosperm, the bran and germ that carry the bulk of the nutrients and fiber having been removed.

Most mills that sell flour, unless they indicate a single variety, blend grain from a diverse network of farms across a wide geographical area according to a specification for protein, color, flavor, and performance. Such blending is necessary given the variations in character among varieties within the major wheat classes and because of the differences that manifest in wheat types grown in different locations. Millers are much like winemakers whose job begins in the vineyard with the careful selection of fruit. As winemakers produce blends from different grapes, so millers combine wheat types to obtain consistent flour and the characteristics that fulfill its intended use. Although there is a sophisticated technology for scrutinizing the physical properties and behavior of flour, to the conscientious miller, the proof also rests in its taste, color, fragrance, and feel.

There are two seasons for growing wheat. "Spring" wheat, planted in spring, is grown in colder, northern climates. "Winter" wheat, planted in the fall, is grown in milder climates. Both mature by mid to late summer. Wheat contains more or less protein depending upon variety and growing environment. Bakers often use the terms *protein* and *gluten* interchangeably. Although protein in flour comprises substances other than gluten alone, protein content, expressed as a percentage by weight, is at least a preliminary indication of the flour's "strength." Strength is a measure of the extensibility of gluten and its resistance to shearing when stretched. In general, the higher the protein in flour, the "harder"—or stronger— it is and the less starch it contains. The higher the starch content, the "softer" the flour. In the United States whole-wheat flour contains 13.5 to 15 percent protein; bread flour, 11 to 13 percent; all-purpose flour, 10 to 11 percent; and cake flour, 7 to 9 percent. Hardness is also used in a different sense to describe varieties of wheat such as durum or hard red winter wheat that are literally, physically hard. Since most wheat is destined to become bread, protein quality is evaluated with a view to its loaf-making potential. Yet some of the functional differences of flour that are relevant to bread bakers also manifest in pasta making. Flour milled from "hard" durum wheat is used primarily for pasta. The amount and quality of protein in the flour and its interaction with water affects the firmness of the dough, its extensibility and elasticity, and, consequently, the texture of the noodle.

Learning about Flour

Color

In order to evaluate the wealth of flour options, I combine what I can learn about its type or blended makeup, protein content, and quality with how it looks, smells, behaves, and tastes when made into pasta. When working with an unfamiliar grain or flour, I first put it on a darker surface to look closely at its color. (I find it helpful to place different types of flour next to one another in order to have a means of comparison.) Although color is an incidental attribute of flour, it nevertheless influences my thinking about sauce; a fine yellow hue enhances the visual appeal of pasta when joined with olive oil- or cream-based sauces where its color stands out. I use more yellow flour when making classic pasta dishes such as tajarin alla Piemontese or tagliatelle Bolognese, both of which utilize profoundly yellow Italian wheat and deep orange egg yolks. Flour's various shades, from lily white to pale blond, bright yellow to golden, buff to dark flecked, can also mirror the intensity of sauce and reinforce the mood of a dish or underscore its seasonal appropriateness.

Fragrance and Flavor

Wheat has a characteristically clean aroma ranging from mild and dusty to various intensities of dry grass, to toasty or nutty. The aroma flour has in its raw state becomes clearer and stronger when trapped in dough and when eventually cooked. When I encounter very fragrant flour, or blend for this quality, I often prefer to toss it in sweet butter and sea salt alone. But pasta made from fragrant whole-grain flour is also suited to savory ragùs of game, poultry, and mushrooms and stands firm against weighty additions such as cabbage, bacon, or the pungent brininess of salted anchovy. White flour, on the other hand, makes pasta with a more subtle wheat scent that is best suited to more delicate sauces based on vegetables, cheese, certain shellfish, and white poultry meats.

The Feel of Flour

After having looked at and smelled a flour, I rub it between my fingers to get a sense of its moisture and granulation. These first impressions give me an idea of how much moisture must be added in order to make dough. Because whole-grain flour contains bran, which ruptures the gluten fabric, it must be "cut" with white flour to improve the integrity of the dough. Feeling the bran helps me to determine how much will be needed.

Once I have a clear sense of the color, fragrance and feel of the flour, I make test batches of dough and pasta. Mixing and kneading indicate the strength of the flour; some dough is very resistant to kneading, other yields easily. If necessary I adjust as I go along, adding a little more water either in the mixing stage or by spraying the dough as I knead it. I err on the side of adding less rather than more water, the reason being that flour absorbs water during kneading and afterward when the dough is allowed to rest. What looks like dough that will never cohere at first comes together nicely after an hour's relaxation.

The last and most telling step is to roll or extrude the dough, cut the pasta, cook it, and taste it. At this point I note anything I might have done differently. Sometimes, for instance, I discover a noodle is too grainy and decide to reduce the proportion of whole-grain flour in the blend. Or, I might find that I could have used less water or more egg to make dough with better consistency. If I want the pasta to have more bite or better color, I plan to blend in stronger durum flour or a more yellow variety next time.

Choosing Flour

Matching pasta with sauce is a back-and-forth process; the quality of pasta I make from particular wheat or a blend of flour determines the nature of the sauce to be used with it and vice versa. As noted above, flour from "hard" wheat is the most suitable for making pasta. At Oliveto, a roster of fifteen flour and grain selections affords us unlimited options for partnership with sauce and allows us to fine-tune these combinations even further. These fall into five classes: Durum wheat semolina and whole-wheat durum flour; unbleached white flour; whole red winter wheat; whole spelt flour; and specialty flour made from other grains, seeds, or nuts. With the exception of the flours listed below that go by the names Extra Fancy semolina (the milling designation for the finest granulation of semolina) and Baker's Choice and Artisan, names conferred by our local mill, the types described below are commonly available from natural or health food stores, from some well-supplied supermarkets, or by mail order (see page 260).

Durum

Durum is the hardest wheat available and has traditionally been used in Italy and the United States to make extruded, shaped pasta as well as flat noodles. Semolina is the endosperm of durum wheat and may be milled more or less coarse. Whole-wheat durum flour is also available. Both, when mixed with water alone, make a very stiff pasta dough and a sturdy noodle, ideal for holding the shape of extruded pasta and for standing up to hearty sauces. Semolina also makes a superb machine-rolled—also called laminated—noodle. Unlike some refined flours, semolina is never bleached; the yellow color of the durum grain has historically been a matter of aesthetic importance to those who make and consume it. I purchase organic durum semolina in two standard granulations that go by the names Number 1 and Extra Fancy, both of which are suited to the making of laminated pasta. But Extra Fancy is more easily extruded through the small openings of the dies. I also use whole durum flour to improve the strength of certain pastas. Semolina pasta is well suited to sauces that are richly flavored or intense in character. Because of the stiffness and thickness of semolina pasta, sauce and pasta should be tossed repeatedly in the pan following cooking. As the pasta absorbs flavor, the sauce, through gradual reduction, clings to the surfaces of the noodle.

Unbleached White Flour

See page 260 for a source of the specific flours listed below or purchase flour with similar characteristics from your local source.

Our basic white flour is called Baker's Choice Milled from selected premium hard red wheat. It contains 11.75 percent protein. It is stronger than most "all-purpose" flour I have tested but not as strong as bread flour. I use this flour to make delicate flat egg noodles and combine it with vegetable purées to make flavored pasta, as well as to improve the structure of dough made with whole-grain flour.

To make flat pasta with a very firm bite and superb flavor I use Artisan flour, the proprietary name of a single variety of wheat called Promotory. Promotory wheat is a hard, red winter variety that thrives on dry land in Utah. It is nearly as yellow as some Italian durum wheat. With it I make tajarin and tagliatelle with egg yolk alone and whole egg noodles with an unmatched flavor and texture.

Whole-Grain and Specialty Flour

Flours made from whole grains, which contain the germ, are the most perishable. To be assured of the freshest whole-grain flour, I prefer to grind it myself in small quantities when needed rather than purchase it pre-milled. To this end, I keep on hand hard red winter wheat, durum wheat, rye, spelt, and Italian farro. Hard red winter wheat makes very fragrant, coarse flour that must be blended with at least an equal amount of white flour in order to make pasta that does not fracture when extended and when cooked. By adding more white flour, you can alter the color, texture, and flavor of pasta and tune it finely to the pitch of the sauce. Whole-wheat pasta matches well with wild mushrooms, with gorgonzola and walnut sauce, and with dark meat braises of game, oxtail, or beef cheeks, to name a few. Whole wheat is also the basis of traditional Venetian *bigoli*, a coarse-textured, thick, spaghetti-like noodle dressed with salt-cured anchovies, garlic, and olive oil. American spelt (*Triticum aestivum spelta*) is something of a sleeper among grains, escaping the notice of chefs and home cooks. Spelt closely resembles wheat (*Triticum aestivum*) and has been grown in North America for close to two hundred years, having first been introduced to eastern Ohio by Swiss immigrants. Although it spread across grain-growing regions of the

United States in earlier times, spelt was nearly abandoned in favor of modern wheat varieties. It makes superb pasta with a light coffee-stain color, a mild wheat flavor, and an intriguing floral aroma that rises from the steam after it is cooked. For the best texture and aroma, I prefer to mill my own spelt and blend it with finer separated spelt flour that I purchase. Our local mill produces two types of spelt flour that differ from one another in how much fine bran they contain. Spelt offers a special advantage in that some individuals intolerant of wheat can eat spelt products with no ill effects. Spelt pasta marries well with sauces made from braised poultry such as rabbit, pigeon, chicken, and duck.

Italian farro (*Triticum dicoccum*) is often referred to as spelt but is actually a distinct species properly called emmer. Farro was the favored cereal of the ancient Romans, who boiled it whole in water and combined it with legumes. Farro makes fine, mild-flavored flour that is low in gluten and must be blended with stronger flour to produce pasta with good consistency. In a nod to the tradition, we make farro pasta with a sauce of fresh shell beans, tomato, prosciutto, and herbs. It is likewise delicious with sautéed wild mushrooms and lean poultry such as rabbit and quail.

Buckwheat

Botanically, buckwheat is neither a grain nor a form of wheat but a seed from a plant in the same family as sorrel and rhubarb. Buckwheat is a hardy plant that has traditionally been grown in mountainous regions otherwise inhospitable to cereals. Buckwheat makes flour with a pocked appearance. Like farro, it is very low in gluten content and has a forceful taste all its own, though the necessity of mixing it with a greater proportion of white flour to strengthen the dough structure also serves to tone down its flavor. When I discovered that a local farmer

was growing buckwheat as a cover crop, I asked him to send us the tender leaves. Combined with Italian bacon and new onions, their flavor fused perfectly with buckwheat tagliatelle.

Corn

Corn is another option for use in pasta making. Corn flour is available pre-milled but has a much more pronounced flavor and perfume if ground fresh. Bear in mind that corn flour contains mostly waxy starch and must rely entirely on stronger flour for its structure. Chestnut flour, called *farina di castagne* or *farina dolce,* is indeed sweet and is used primarily in desserts in Tuscany. However, it makes unusual pasta that finds an agreeable match in braised duck or pigeon. The best chestnut flour comes from the Garfagnana area in Italy, north of Lucca. Chestnuts gathered from high-altitude forests are placed in drying rooms on straw mats and undergo a smoking-drying process for some forty days. Afterward, the dry chestnuts are stone-ground to a very fine consistency that resembles talcum powder. Chestnut flour is very perishable and not available at all times of the year. Look for it in the fall and winter in specialty groceries or Italian delicatessens (see Sources and Resources, page 260). When you receive it, store it in the freezer.

Tools and Equipment

With the basic tools and equipment list below you will be able to make a wide range of pastas, both rolled and extruded.

Flour mill
Bread bowl or freestanding mixer
Straight rolling pin
Scale that measures in ounces
Sharp, thin-bladed 12-inch knife
Pasta machine (for laminated pasta)
Electric extruder (for hard wheat pasta),
   optional attachments
Atomizer
Special cutting or shaping tools: round pastry
   cutters, fluted wheel cutter, *chitarra*, *torchio*
   or *bigolaro*

Making Pasta: Seven Steps

Once you have decided on the flour there are seven basic steps to making pasta: weighing the ingredients, moistening and mixing the flour, kneading, hydrating, extruding or laminating, cutting or shaping the dough, and finally, cooking it.

Water makes flour functional by binding its singular granules at first into a shaggy mass. With additional mixing, flour and water coalesce to form a tight matrix of dough. Water also mixes with gliaden and glutenin, two insoluble proteins that capture water and bond to each other to form gluten, the sticky, stretchable substance that gives dough its structure. When kneaded, the gluten fabric of dough elongates and becomes plastic and elastic, capable of changing its shape and holding it under tension. It is this property of gluten that begets the large number of cuts and sizes of pasta. Compression makes it possible to extrude dough through a die to form distinct shapes or, by means of opposing rollers, to laminate the dough, flattening and stretching it to a transparently thin, uni-

form sheet. In either case, the principle of elasticity works in both directions: Once dough has become stretched through mixing and kneading and then further extended or extruded, its tendency is to relax. Surprisingly, the relaxation of pasta that has been rolled and cut hours before has little effect on the finished texture of the noodle; relaxed noodles don't loose their toothsome texture. This is because when pasta is cooked, the bonding of proteins is stronger than the forces that create elasticity. If you don't intend to cook fresh pasta the day you make it, it is wise to dry it under the slow breeze of a fan before storing it in order to avoid discoloration (oxidation) of the dough.

Weighing Ingredients

Volume measurements of flour are unreliable, their accuracy affected by the type of flour and its degree of compaction and granulation. Likewise, eggs come in different sizes. It is therefore best to weigh all ingredients, including water, when formulating your own flour blends and dough. Should you decide to make larger batches of dough, weighing the ingredients also assures the right proportions.

Moistening and Mixing Flour

Achieving the proper ratio of flour to water, whether in its pure form or in eggs or vegetable purée, is critical in pasta making. Different flour types absorb more or less water and at different rates. Too much water results in soft pasta that sticks together when cut into strands or shapes. The right amount of water yields pasta that maintains its integrity and has a lively bite. Although the functional contribution of eggs is primarily water, they also affect the binding of flour. Pasta made with coarse flour whose bran interrupts the continuity of dough particularly benefits from the addition of eggs rather than pure water alone (except in the case of durum semolina, which binds with water alone). You will notice that dough made with whole eggs or egg yolks feels different from dough made with water alone. This is because egg proteins are sticky and so lend cohesiveness to raw dough. Dough made with insufficient water will prove difficult to extrude or roll and will produce pasta that tears apart. The amount of added water also affects the workability of the dough. Overly wet dough sticks to the die or the roller and makes limp pasta. Pasta dough is also affected by the temperature and humidity of the workspace. In general, high-protein and whole-grain flour require a little more water to lubricate dough sufficiently to stretch it. On dry, hot days, a little more water may be needed to compensate for that which is lost to the air. In practice, given the variability of flour, and different ambient conditions, it is possible to give only an approximate idea of the amount of water necessary to make dough with the right consistency. Making pasta is more a matter of feel that can easily be developed with a little patience and experience. Very finely milled flour with a silky feeling requires less water and absorbs it quickly. Drier or more coarsely milled flour requires some faith that water, in what appears a hopelessly disintegrated dough mass at first, will eventually come together when wrapped and allowed time to disperse.

Bear in mind that pasta contains 25 to 30 percent water as a proportion of the total dough weight, depending on the flour used. In general, for every 10 ounces of flour, begin by adding 3½ to 4 ounces of water or 2 large eggs (eggs contain approximately 75 percent of their weight in water), then adjust by adding more if necessary. The quality of the starch and protein in semolina binds well with water only. The addition of whole eggs helps to bind dough with whole flour containing bran, or with other solid ingredients that interfere with the fabric of the dough such as herbs. For enriched dough that yields pasta with a strong bite, add egg yolks

alone; avoid the use of egg in dough that you wish to carry a single flavor transparently, such as nettle or spinach, tomato or saffron, or the whole-grain flour itself. Cut flour with no or low gluten strength with strong flour. If dough feels dry after mixing it with the primary liquid, add a small amount of water, mix again, and test the dough for coherence by squeezing it between your fingers. Dough that contains enough moisture adheres at first, and then with kneading comes together in a stiff mass.

Machines that make extruded pasta from semolina are self-mixing. Flour and water are combined in the machine, kneaded, and then extruded directly. Laminated pasta made with a rolling machine must be mixed by hand or in a freestanding mixer. When making laminated noodles by hand, I prefer to mix and knead flour and liquid in a large bowl rather than directly on the work surface. Keeping the flour and liquid contained in the limited space of the bowl makes it easier to incorporate all of the flour and liquid and means less cleanup afterward.

To mix the dough, pour the flour into the bowl, make a well, and add the water or whisked eggs. Using a large fork, stir the liquid into the flour with a circular motion that radiates outward to drag the liquid into the dry edges. When the dough begins to clump, feel it for moisture by taking up some in your hand and pressing it together. If it is somewhat sticky, begin squeezing and compressing the flour to form a solid mass of dough; alternately grasp it with your fingers and press down with the back of your palm. If the flour resists integration, add a little more water; an atomizer is handy for this purpose since only a small amount of water is usually necessary. Misting the dough also distributes water more evenly than sprinkling it. Continue to knead the dough in the bowl, forcing its floury surface into the wetter center. As you knead, you will notice that the dough stiffens at first, then after several minutes becomes more smooth and elastic. The color of the flour also emerges as it absorbs water. Turn the dough onto a lightly floured surface and continue to knead the dough until it losses its tackiness, its solid color reveals itself without dry flour particles, and it rebounds when depressed.

Hydrating the Dough

When making laminated pasta, wrap the dough tightly in plastic wrap and let it sit at room temperature for 1 hour. This permits the flour to fully absorb the water. During this time the dough also relaxes and returns to a less elastic state that makes it easier to compress and extend.

Extruding and Laminating

With a small, affordable home extruder machine (see Sources and Resources, page 262) it is possible to make fresh macaroni from hard durum semolina in a wide variety of shapes. If you are accustomed to packaged dry pasta you are likely to find the process rewarding. Packaged pasta is not generally considered perishable; on the contrary, dry pasta loses aroma and flavor and becomes brittle over time or in contact with air.

Regardless of the brand, the principle of an extruder machine is the same. Flour is placed in a hopper at the top of the machine, the mixing gear is engaged, and water is added slowly until the dough begins to come together. After a period of kneading, a chute at the bottom of the hopper is opened where a worm drive pushes the dough to the head of the machine and through the openings of a die. As the pasta exits the die, it is cut to size by hand, or in the case of larger, commercial machines by a rotating blade mounted on the front of the die. While the machine does all the work of mixing and kneading the dough, it is important to assure that the dough is well amalgamated, slightly tacky (but never wet), and resilient to the touch before opening the chute. The manufacturer of your extruder machine will recommend the general proportions of flour, water, or eggs according to the machine's capabilities. These will encompass limited flour choices; once you get a feeling for the dough and the requirements of the machine, however, you can experiment with other flours.

You have more choices when it comes to purchasing a machine for making laminated pasta, but even the smallest machines are quite durable and adequate for regular use at home. Large or small, pasta machines have an opposing set of rollers that compress and extend the dough to gradually wider, thinner ribbons. It is important that the dough be sufficiently dry to make clean passes through the rollers. Knead the rested, hydrated dough to a roughly rectangular shape about two thirds of the width of the rollers. (If you have made a large batch of dough, it will be necessary to divide it into smaller, more manageable pieces.) Then flatten it further with a rolling pin to ease passage through the widest setting of the rollers. Pass the dough through the pasta machine, cranking with one hand and keeping the dough parallel to the edges of the rollers with the other. If it feels tacky, dust the entire sheet on both sides with flour. If it feels dry and resists the rollers, use the atomizer to finely mist the surfaces. Fold the ends of the dough into the center so that they overlap like a package and its width does not exceed the width of the rollers. If the pasta emerges with holes or seems somewhat ragged in consistency, as can be the case with doughs having a high proportion of bran, fold it over on itself and pass it through the widest setting several more times. Once the dough forms a uniform ribbon, proceed to the next setting. Judging pasta thickness is a matter of taste as well as an accommodation to flour strength and the character of the sauce it will be paired with. For most sauces and in order to maintain the bite of the noodle, I prefer to roll pasta once or twice through the next to last setting. The finer and more delicate the sauce, the harder the wheat I use and the thinner I roll the pasta.

Cutting and Shaping

Pasta machines are outfitted with two standard attachments: rolling blades turned by a separate crank that cut tagliarini (⅛ inch) and fettuccine (¼ inch) from a band of extended dough. But pasta has a more attractive, slightly irregular character if you cut it by hand. To make wider noodles, hand cutting is a necessity unless you purchase additional cutting attachments. Before cutting the pasta to width, consider its interaction with sauce. In general, the finer the consistency or the elements of a sauce are, the less wide the noodle need be. Julienne vegetables, minced shellfish, herb pesto, sugo, or finely ground meat ragù marry well with thin widths such as fettuccine, tagliolini, spaghetti, tagliarini, or chitarra. Pair medium-wide noodles such as tagliatelle with more coarsely ground or chopped meat ragù and broad noodles such as lasagnette and pappardelle with sauces that coat well or those with chunked or sliced ingredients.

Once you have extended the pasta to the right thickness, cut the sheets into 10- to 12-inch lengths. To prevent sticking, rub a bit of the flour you used to make the dough into each sheet on both sides. Place one sheet on top of another and beginning at the end closest to you, roll the sheets into a loose cylinder stopping an inch short of the end. Use a very sharp 10- to 12-inch knife with a thin blade (Global stainless-steel knives are excellent for the purpose) to cut the pasta to width and lift it by its loose ends to unfurl the strands. Fluff the pasta with your fingers to separate the strands and transfer it to a floured sheet pan or platter.

As noted above, the job of shaping macaroni is taken care of by the die of the extruding machine. At Oliveto we keep eight different dies on hand to make bucatini, a thick tubular pasta about 3/16 inch in diameter; penne rigate (tubular pasta with ridges for trapping sauce); creste di gallo (cock's combs); spaghetti and spaghettini; cappellini (angel hair); radiatori (a shape that mimics the grill of a radiator); strozzapreti (literally "priest stranglers," a twisted shape); and conchiglie (shell pasta). In addition we extrude whole-wheat pasta through a bigolaro for making traditional Venetian bigoli, a thick, spaghetti-like noodle. A bigolaro is a threaded bronze cylinder with a die in the bottom through which dough is forced by a plate on the end of a handle that settles against the dough and with a turning motion, screws down tight against and through the die. The roughness of whole wheat emerges from the bigolaro with a ragged surface that gives this pasta its characteristic texture.

Wide noodles such as lasagne, quadrucci (3-inch squares), and stradette ("little streets"—1½-inch strips) must be stacked and cut to size or wheel-cut strand by strand. Pici, farfalle, and stuffed pasta are formed individually. Making such pasta is not as time-consuming as it sounds once you establish a rhythm. Specific directions for hand-shaped pasta follow in the recipes below.

Cooking Pasta

Cooking pasta causes the proteins in the flour as well as those in eggs, if they are present, to stiffen and coagulate. The phenomenon is similar to what happens when meat emulsions are heated or when proteins in sausages "gel" when cooked. Likewise, the gluten in pasta sets and its color changes to a paler tone (in the case of dough made with finely separated flour) or darker tone (whole or partially whole-grain flour). The gluten in pasta coagulates in a matter of minutes, then charts a fast course toward flaccidity. Properly cooked pasta is firm yet yielding to the bite, if to a degree that is somewhat subjective. It should be removed from the pot at the point when heat has altered the gluten from hard (uncooked) to very firm (tightly coagulated) to al dente, which means toothsome.

To cook pasta, use a large pot and an abundant amount of water. For every 12 ounces of noodles (the approximate amount in the standard dough formulas given below) bring to a rolling boil one gallon of water and 5 teaspoons salt. I prefer to use a coarse sea salt that is 83 percent sodium chloride, the balance being made up of potassium, iodine, and minerals, which to me has the best, purest flavor. Ideally, the water should boil throughout the cooking. However, most stoves need a few minutes to recover the boil once the pasta has been added. If your stove is weak, it is better to use several burners and pots rather than allow the pasta to dwell too long in water that is slow to the boil; the texture of pasta quickly degrades under such circumstances.

Pasta made with hard or whole-grain flour requires at least two times as long as that made with softer flour. In general, freshly made pasta takes 3 to 7 minutes to cook. Pasta made from white flour, when cooked properly, is actually tensile and stretches like a rubber band when pulled gently. To monitor the cooking of pasta it is wise to taste it several times before draining it. Keep a small plate and a pair of tongs next to the stove and test the pasta several times over the course of the cooking. Have a colander ready before you add the pasta to the boiling water; last-minute confusion spent hunting it down can lead to pasta that is overcooked.

Pasta Types and Sauces to Match

My own experiments with pasta over the years have revealed compatibilities between types of flour and sauce. I use whole-egg dough for making fine-textured flat noodles and as a reliable casing for filled pasta. Egg-yolk dough has a distinct bite and intense yellow color that most resembles the traditional flat noodles of the Northern provinces of Italy, at home equally with meaty ragùs, spring vegetables, or simply butter and sage. Eggless semolina makes extruded, shaped pasta and firm, flat noodles and provides the structure to best support fresh herbs, vegetables pastes, or purées. Whole-wheat, spelt, buckwheat, corn, and chestnut flour make pastas with more pronounced flavors and distinct textures. Their pairing with sauce requires special consideration. When you set out to make your own pasta, you may wish to think in these terms and use the recipes below as your examples.

The following recipes are based on the distinct flour products of our local mill. (To purchase this flour see page 260.) Otherwise, seek out flours with characteristics similar to those described above.

Whole-Egg Pasta

Makes 4 ample portions

10 ounces Artisan flour
4 ounces whole eggs (2 eggs), lightly beaten
½ ounce water

Place the flour in a bread bowl and make a well in the center. Add the eggs to the well and stir with a fork to combine. Drizzle the water over the mixture and stir again until it begins to form a shaggy mass. With your stronger hand, reach into the bowl and alternately squeeze and push down on the dough with your palm to gather it together. Press any loose bits of flour into the mass. When the dough feels tacky and fully incorporated, transfer it to a clean, lightly floured surface and knead it for 4 to 5 minutes, or until it loses its surface moisture, is a uniform color, and springs back when depressed. Wrap the dough in plastic and allow it to hydrate for at least 1 hour before rolling.

Pappardelle with Rabbit

For 12

Pappardelle is a Tuscan dialect word for long, rectangular noodles about 1¼ inch wide most often served with wild hare (*lepre*) or boar. Pappardelle are well adapted to braises or wine-laced game sauces, whose richness and intensity are evenly distributed over the wide surface area of the noodle. For such weighty sauces, I recommend making laminated pappardelle with semolina and water (see recipe below). With braises of domestic rabbit and chicken, a softer pasta made with whole eggs is in keeping with the more delicate flavors of the sauce.

1 fresh rabbit (3 pounds), with kidneys and liver, cut into 12 pieces
1 tablespoon plus 1 teaspoon salt
1 tablespoon freshly ground black pepper
2 tablespoons olive oil
1 medium onion (12 ounces), diced
8 garlic cloves (2 ounces), sliced
5 ounces pancetta or Tesa, thinly sliced and then cut in large dice
1 sprig of rosemary, finely chopped
6 sprigs of sage, roughly chopped
½ ounce dry porcini mushrooms
1 tablespoon tomato Conserva (see page 46) or tomato paste
½ cup white wine
1 quart Meat Broth (page 135)
1 recipe Whole-Egg Pasta (see left)
Parmigiano-Reggiano, for grating

Season the rabbit pieces with the salt and the pepper. Warm the olive oil in a 6-quart heavy-bottomed pot over medium heat. Add the rabbit pieces (except the kidneys and liver), turn up the heat, and brown the rabbit, turning it frequently, for 15 minutes or until well browned on both sides. Add the onion, garlic, pancetta, rosemary, sage, porcini, and rabbit kidneys to the pot and stew them with the rabbit for 15 minutes. Dissolve the tomato conserva in the white wine, add it to the pot, and simmer for an additional 5 minutes. Add the meat broth and bring to a boil over high heat, then reduce to a bare simmer and cover with a tight-fitting lid. Braise the rabbit for 1 hour and 20 minutes, or until tender. Five minutes before you remove the rabbit from the stove, add the liver. Set aside to cool slightly.

When the rabbit pieces are cool enough to handle, remove them from the pot and carefully separate the meat from the bones. Discard the bones and pick through the meat again to ensure there are no bone fragments remaining. Roughly chop the rabbit meat and add it back to the sauce. Then, finely chop the kidneys and the liver and add them as well.

Using a pasta rolling machine, extend the dough to a make a substantial noodle (one pass through the number 5 setting). Dust the sheets well with flour on both sides, roll the sheets lengthwise leaving an inch unrolled at the end, and cut the rolls into 1¼-inch-wide strands. Unfurl the pasta and transfer it to a plate.

To serve, heat the rabbit ragù in a large sauté pan (12-inch diameter with 4-inch sides is ideal). Cook the pasta in a generous amount of salted, boiling water until al dente, drain the pasta, and add it directly to the warm sauce. Toss for several minutes until it is evenly coated with the sauce. Serve in warm, wide-brimmed bowls with freshly grated Parmigiano-Reggiano.

Tagliolini with Crab
For 4

1 recipe Whole-Egg Pasta (page 104)
5 tablespoons sea salt
1 live Dungeness crab (approximately 1½ to
     2 pounds) or 2 or 3 live blue crabs
¼ cup extra-virgin olive oil
2 garlic cloves, finely chopped
¼ teaspoon red pepper flakes
2 tablespoons finely chopped flat-leaf parsley

Extend the pasta dough to setting number 5, roll it up, and cut it into ⅛-inch-wide noodles.

In a 6-quart pot, bring 1 gallon of water to a roiling boil. Set up a large bowl filled with water and ice nearby. Add the sea salt to the water. Cook the crab for 12 minutes, then submerge it in the ice bath for 5 minutes to cool. Pull the legs from the crab, then working over a bowl, remove the carapace and allow the tomalley (internal organs and unformed shell) to drain into the bowl. Using a small spoon, scrape any tomalley remaining in the shell into the bowl and set it aside. Use a fine kitchen shears to cut through the shell of the leg pieces and pick out the meat. Pull off and discard the gills from the body, and section it by cutting vertically through the middle and then through the natural divisions where the legs formerly attached. Pick the meat from the body. Discard the shells and sort through the crabmeat to remove any remaining shell fragments.

Place the olive oil, garlic, and red pepper flakes in a 12-inch sauté pan and set it over medium heat. When you smell the garlic, and before it browns, add the reserved tomalley and cook it for 3 minutes. Reduce the heat to *very* low, add the crabmeat and parsley, and toss gently just to warm.

Meanwhile, cook the pasta in a generous amount of salted boiling water until al dente, drain it, and add it to the pan with the crab. Toss well over medium heat. Divide the tagliolini among 4 warm bowls and serve immediately.

Tagliatelle with Fresh White Truffle

For three days in the month of November Oliveto's dining room is taken over by the heady scent of Italian white truffles. Our truffle dinners culminate not only a year of waiting for the return of this celebration but also an annual trip abroad to hunt for them ourselves. The Piedmont region and Alba in particular is the reputed Mecca of the truffle; Alba's narrow streets are crowded with pilgrims undeterred by the fabulous price of fungus clad in dirt. We have learned to steer clear of Alba, where, despite the local broker's claims of strictly local truffles, an arrangement may deliver truffles of dubious origin and quality or, at worst, a shell filled with mud. No matter; there are treasures to be found elsewhere. Our friend Giorgio, a truffle hunter, and his avid dogs work the fine clay soils of the forested outskirts of Siena in Tuscany. Although the harvest is unpredictable from year to year and gathering enough to sup-

ply a menu devoted entirely to truffles can be nerve-wracking, there hasn't been a season in the last four when we didn't return with the full bounty. In order to pass United States customs inspection, we stay up half the night before departure washing soil from the fungi's knobby surfaces. After paying a punitive tariff, we rush them back to the restaurant just in time for full perfume to emerge.

The potency of white truffles varies greatly and is influenced by such factors as the soil and plants that surround them, their maturity, and their state of freshness. This is one of the reasons why truffles are offered *a piacere* (as it pleases) in Italian restaurants and at Oliveto. The other reason is of course the hefty price. When buttered pasta arrives, the waiter weighs the truffle while the customer weighs his wallet. Once begun, the shaving ends with the approving nod of the guest.

Given the brevity of the season and the fragility of white truffles, my own philosophy is to seize the moment and splurge on one meal rather than spreading them thin over the course of several. I know of no other partnership as mutually flattering as egg pasta with truffle, good, fresh butter, a little Parmigiano, and sea salt. No recipe is required; simply dress freshly made egg noodles with as much butter as you can stand and as much shaved white truffle as you can afford. Begin by examining the truffle. If it has soil clinging to it, use a vegetable brush dipped in cold water to remove the dirt and the point of a knife to dig mud out of the crevices. Rinse the truffle and set it out to allow its surface to dry. Meanwhile, make fresh egg pasta, roll it out, finish it with several passes through the next to last setting of the rolling machine, and cut the pasta into tagliatelle about 3/8 inch wide. Toss the pasta with sweet butter and sea salt to your taste, grate a little Parmigiano-Reggiano over the top, and use a truffle cutter (a small handheld mandoline) to shave white truffle as thin as you can over the pasta. The rest is even easier.

Italian soil also yields a marvelous black autumn truffle called *lo scorzone* (*Tuber brumale*) that commonly grows to the size of a small orange. Our friend Giorgio describes white truffles as olfactory and the black scorzone as gustatory, by which he means that the white truffle appeals directly to our sense of smell while the black scorzone must be tasted before it releases its flavor and perfume. The scorzone's flavor is more like mushroom than truffle and lends a woodsy perfume when steeped in sauces and ragùs. When very fresh they are also striking sliced raw atop veal carpaccio or roast chicken. Scorzoni are cloaked in a rather thick, hard skin that must be pared away before they are sliced. The peelings in turn may be pounded fine in a mortar and included as a last-minute addition to sugo or sauce.

Black winter truffles (*Tuber melanosporum*) bloom later in winter and reach their peak of quality and fragrance around the New Year in Italy and a month later in France. When cooked, the aroma of black truffles is as potent as that of white truffles, but their raw fragrance is decidedly more guarded. The aroma of white truffles is generous and effusive and evokes descriptions that are earthy and sensuous. Each demands different treatment in the kitchen. White truffles need only the gentlest heat that an underpinning of pasta, melted cheese, or creamy risotto provides in order for their effusive perfume to nearly cloud the senses; black truffles must be teased out with time, or trapped with food with which their scent commingles. A basket of farm eggs closed up tight with truffles, a roasting hen stuffed with truffles under the skin, or a beef roast studded with black truffles becomes infused after a day or two together. Black truffles are also compatible with spirits such as Cognac and Armagnac and the sweet botrytised wines of Sauternes, which both amplify and focus their elegant scent.

Tagliatelle with Black Truffle
For 4

50 grams fresh black winter truffle
Sea salt
6 tablespoons (¾ stick) fresh unsalted butter
¼ cup Sauternes
1 tablespoon Armagnac
1 recipe Whole-Egg Pasta (page 104), rolled and cut into tagliatelle

Wash the truffles and peel them over a bowl to capture the trimmings. Place the trimmings in a mortar and pestle and pound them to a fine paste. Add a little sea salt and 4 tablespoons of the butter. Pound the butter with the truffle trimmings to soften and integrate it. Set aside. Cut the peeled truffles into paper-thin rounds on a truffle slicer or sharp mandoline. Warm the Sauternes, the Armagnac, and the remaining 2 tablespoons of butter in a sauté pan over low heat. Add the truffle slices and allow them to soften and steep for about 10 minutes off the heat. Cook the tagliatelle in a generous amount of boiling salted water until al dente, drain it, and add it to a wide sauté pan. Pour over the truffle slices and wine mixture. Toss the pasta over low heat until most of the wine mixture has been absorbed, then stir in the truffle butter. Serve at once.

Pasta alla Chitarra with Shrimp, Basil, and Peas

For 4

Pasta alla chitarra ("guitar-style" pasta) is named for the rectangular stringed tool (see page 260 for source) used in the Abruzzi to form its characteristic shape. A sheet of dough is placed on top of the taut strings and the dough is cut into a sort of square-sided spaghetti by rolling a wooden pin over the strings.

1 pound fresh shrimp in the shell
2 tablespoons extra-virgin olive oil
1 garlic clove, smashed
15 basil leaves
3 cups water
½ teaspoon sea salt
8 tablespoons (1 stick) unsalted butter
½ cup small, fresh shelled peas
1 recipe Whole-Egg Pasta (page 104), rolled and cut alla chitarra

Peel the shrimp, reserving the shells. Devein the shrimp and cut in half lengthwise. Place a 2-quart saucepan on the stove over medium-high heat. Add 1 tablespoon of the olive oil and the shrimp shells and cook the shells, stirring frequently, for 5 minutes, or until they brown slightly. Add the garlic, 3 or 4 of the basil leaves, and the water. Bring to a boil, reduce the heat, and simmer for 15 minutes, or until about 1 cup remains. Strain the shrimp broth through a fine sieve and discard the shells.

Warm a wide sauté pan or skillet. Add the remaining tablespoon of olive oil and raise the heat to high. Season the shrimp with the salt. Quickly brown the shrimp, cooking them only about 50 percent. Remove the shrimp from the pan. Deglaze the hot pan with the shrimp broth and cook over high heat until reduced by half. Add the butter and continue to reduce the sauce until it thickens to a viscous consistency and small bubbles appear on the surface. Add the peas and simmer the sauce 1 minute more. Turn off the heat and return the shrimp to the sauce. Cook the pasta in a generous amount of boiling salted water until al dente, drain it, and toss it with the shrimp sauce and peas. Chop the remaining basil coarse and stir it into the pasta. Serve in warm bowls.

Egg-Yolk Pasta

For 6

6 ounces Artisan flour
4 ounces Baker's Choice flour
8½ ounces egg yolks (about 14 large egg yolks)
½ ounce water

Place the flour in a bread bowl and make a well in the center. Whisk the eggs, add them to the well, and stir with a fork to combine. Drizzle the water over the mixture and stir again until it begins to form a shaggy mass. With your stronger hand, reach into the bowl and alternately squeeze and push down on the dough with your palm to gather it together. Press any loose bits of flour into the mass. When the dough feels tacky and fully incorporated with the eggs, transfer it to a clean surface and knead it for 4 or 5 minutes, or until it loses its surface moisture, is a uniform color, and springs back when depressed. Wrap the dough in plastic and allow it to hydrate for at least 1 hour before rolling.

Tajarin

Tajarin are very thin hand-cut pasta that resemble tagliarini and are made with egg yolks alone. Because of their emphatic bite, tajarin are most commonly tossed in sage butter so as not to interfere with the pure pleasure of their texture.

Roll the pasta dough as thin as possible and cut it into 8-inch lengths. Rub flour into both sides of the sheets. Stacking 3 sheets at a time, use a sharp, thin blade to slice the pasta into strands about 1/16 inch wide. Fluff the tajarin with your fingers and transfer them to a platter or sheet pan.

For every portion of pasta add 2 tablespoons of butter and 3 or 4 four fresh sage leaves to a pan. Cook the sage leaves over medium heat for 3 to 4 minutes, adjusting the heat down if necessary so that the butter does not color. Cook the tajarin al dente and toss them with the sage butter. Correct the pasta with sea salt and serve with fresh grated Parmigiano-Reggiano.

For a more nutty taste, the butter may be first browned.

Farfalle with Gorgonzola and Walnuts
For 4

Egg yolks give pasta dough added structure and a drier consistency that are an advantage when making farfalle ("butterfly" pasta). The wide wings of farfalle, and the strength of the dough, carry cream sauces buoyantly.

1 recipe Egg-Yolk Pasta (page 108)
4 tablespoons chopped walnuts
1 cup heavy cream
3 tablespoons aged Gorgonzola
Freshly ground black pepper

Roll the pasta into a 4½-inch-wide band two times through the next to last setting of the pasta machine. Using a fluted wheel cutter, trim both ends of the band, then cut 1½-inch ribbons of dough along its length. Cut across the strips to yield rectangular pieces 3½ inches long. Place a small bowl of water next to your workspace. Take up a rectangle of dough in one hand.

Moisten the forefinger of your other hand and dab a small amount of water across the center of the dough. Using both hands, fold the long sides of the dough up partially in a U shape. Pinch the bottom center, then fold down the sides ("wings") away from the pinch. Transfer the farfalle to a sheet pan and allow them to dry in the air or under a fan.

Toast the walnuts at 350°F. for 7 to 10 minutes, or until they smell good, and then chop them coarse. Pour the cream into a wide sauté pan or skillet and reduce it by about half over high heat. Remove from the heat and whisk in the Gorgonzola. Cook the farfalle in a generous amount of boiling salted water until al dente, drain them, and add them and the walnuts to the cream in the sauté pan. Turn the heat back on to medium high and stir the farfalle and sauce together. If the sauce appears too thick, add a little hot water. The sauce should coat the pasta but not cling heavily. Serve the farfalle in warm bowls with freshly ground black pepper.

Tagliarini with Mussels and Clams
For 4

Tagliarini are ideal for carrying the saltwater taste of mussels and clams, here chopped to match the slender dimension of the noodle.

¼ cup extra-virgin olive oil
1 cup thinly sliced shallots
6 garlic cloves, thinly sliced
¼ teaspoon red pepper flakes
1 bay leaf
1 pound 6 ounces small live clams, washed
14 ounces live mussels, washed and debearded
¼ cup dry white wine
1 cup heavy cream
1 recipe Egg-Yolk Pasta (page 108)
1½ tablespoons chopped flat-leaf parsley

Place a wide 6- to 8-quart casserole over medium heat. Warm the olive oil, then add the shallots, garlic, red pepper flakes, and bay leaf and sweat them in the oil until softened, about 5 minutes. Add the shellfish and the white wine. Increase the heat to high and cover the pan. Cook the shellfish until the shells open, 3 to 4 minutes.

Remove the pot from the heat, pour the contents into a large baking dish, and set aside for a few minutes. Once the shellfish is cool enough to handle, pull the meat and discard the shells, reserving the garlic, shallots, and juices in the dish. Strain the juice from the mixture and set it aside. Turn the shellfish mixture onto a board and chop it coarse. Transfer the chopped shellfish to a wide sauté pan and strain the juice back over the shellfish through a very fine sieve to catch any possible sand particles. Add the heavy cream.

Turn the heat to medium high and reduce the sauce to a rich, viscous consistency, about 4 to 5 minutes. Cook the pasta in a generous amount of boiling salted water until al dente, drain it, and add it to the pan with the sauce. Toss over low heat until the sauce coats the pasta. If the pasta feels heavy, loosen it by stirring in a little hot water. Finally, add the chopped parsley, mix well, and serve immediately in warm pasta bowls.

Durum Semolina Pasta

The possibilities for shapes and cuts of pasta made from hard-wheat durum flour are limitless; its enjoyment rests in its texture and the way particular shapes carry or trap sauce. Unlike pasta made from softer wheat, which absorbs sauce much more quickly, pasta made of durum semolina takes time to accept sauce. The Italian word *strascinare* means "to drag" and is often used to describe the action of merging pasta with sauce. Dragging the pasta through the sauce is generally carried out over moderate heat to encourage the simultaneous reduction and absorption of the sauce. If the sauce is of a consistency or intensity that would force it out of balance through further reduction, small amounts of water are added incrementally to encourage pasta and sauce to mingle in the pan. The sauce is then reduced again to the desirable intensity before the pasta is dished.

Refer to the manufacturer's instructions that come with your extruder machine for proportions of flour and water. For the best results, purchase Extra Fancy semolina.

Amatriciana Sauce
For 4

This classic sauce from Amatrice in Lazio is traditionally served with bucatini, a sort of fat tubular spaghetti, which carries its bold flavors. (See pages 101-102 for information on making spaghetti or bucatini with an extruder.) Special cured bacon made from the cheek and jowl of the pig called *guanciale* (see page 202) gives the sauce its unique savor. Pancetta or Tesa (page 202) is a close substitute.

2 tablespoons olive oil
8 ounces guanciale, pancetta, or Tesa, sliced thin into small flat squares
1 medium red onion, finely diced to yield ½ cup
1 cup fresh chopped tomato
2 teaspoons tomato Conserva (see page 46) or tomato paste
1 small fresh red chile or ¼ teaspoon red pepper flakes
Bucatini or spaghetti from semolina dough for 4
½ cup Parmigiano-Reggiano, grated
½ cup Pecorino Romano, grated

Place a wide sauté pan or skillet over medium-high heat. Add the olive oil and the guanciale. Cook to render its fat, stirring frequently with a wooden spoon. When the guanciale begins to take on color after several minutes, add the onion. Continue cooking over high heat and shaking the pan to develop even color. After a few minutes the guanciale will crisp and you will notice a brown residue on the bottom of the pan. Add the chopped tomato, conserva or tomato paste, and the chile. Cook the sauce until the water in the tomato evaporates and the sauce develops a rich brick-red color. Set the sauce off the heat.

Cook the pasta in a generous amount of boiling salted water until al dente. Drain it, add it to the sauce, and toss over medium heat until the noodles are fully coated. As you continue to toss the sauce and the pasta, add small amounts of pasta water to thin it, and then reduce again to a smooth emulsified consistency. Remove the pan from the heat. Correct the consistency of the sauce; it should appear creamy and emulsified. Serve at once in warm pasta bowls and pass the grated cheeses.

Arrabbiata Sauce
For 8

This sauce is *arrabbiata* (angry) because it is made with hot fresh chile pepper. Rather than subjecting guests to my own tolerance for hot food by adding chile directly, I send out a small bowl of sliced, vinegared peppers for each to add as they wish in addition to the moderate amount added in the recipe. At the peak of pepper season I buy fresh cayenne peppers in bunches (other small hot red peppers will do), slice them into thin rings, and put them covered with vinegar and sealed with a layer of olive oil in glass jars—about ¼ cup champagne vinegar for every 8 peppers. Let stand for 1 day before using. This hot red pepper condiment keeps well for several months.

One freedom permitted by the extruder is that you can cut pasta to any length you wish. Penne is considered a type of *pasta corta,* that is, pasta cut to short lengths. With this sauce I prefer to cut the penne to 4 or 5 inches, which extenuates the appeal of its shape and ridged surfaces. Most extruders include a standard die for making penne. See pages 101-102 for information on extruders. For this recipe you will need semolina dough for 8 portions.

¼ cup extra-virgin olive oil
1 small onion, thinly sliced
6 garlic cloves, thinly sliced
1 fresh cayenne pepper, chopped
1½ teaspoons sea salt
2 pounds small, ripe red tomatoes
Semolina penne for 8
Ricotta salata, for grating
Cayenne pepper condiment (see head note)

Place a large casserole on the stove. Warm the olive oil and add the onions, garlic and cayenne pepper. Season them with the salt and turn the burner to medium low. Cook until the onion and garlic begin to turn translucent, about 5 minutes. Add the tomatoes. Increase the heat to medium high. When the tomatoes begin to bubble, reduce the heat and simmer the sauce for 20 to 25 minutes, or until the sauce develops a thick consistency. Pass the sauce through the medium sieve of a food mill.

Transfer the sauce to a 14-inch sauté pan and bring to a simmer on medium heat. Cook until reduced, about 10 minutes. Cook the penne in a generous amount of boiling salted water until al dente, drain it, and toss with the sauce over medium heat until the sauce clings to the noodles. Serve in warm bowls with grated ricotta salata. Let your guests intensify the heat of their pasta with the cayenne pepper condiment.

Semolina Dough for Flat Pasta
For 4

Serve with a simple tomato sauce (page 44) or with meat, poultry, or game sugo, the depth of flavor of which is best carried by pasta with a substantial bite and sturdiness.

10 ounces Extra Fancy semolina
4 ounces cool water

Pour the flour into a bread bowl or the bowl of a freestanding electric mixer. While mixing with a fork or the mixer's paddle attachment, pour the water into the center of the dough. When the flour begins to clump, start gathering and kneading the dough by hand. Continue to knead the dough until it loses its stiffness, is well incorporated with the water, feels smooth on the surface, and springs back when depressed. Wrap the dough in plastic and set it aside to hydrate for 1½ hours. Roll the pasta once through the next to last setting of a pasta machine and cut it to a width of your choosing.

Semolina Fettuccine with Italian Sausage
For 8

2 teaspoons extra-virgin olive oil
4 sweet Italian sausages (approximately 6 ounces each), pricked with a pin at ½-inch intervals
1 medium red onion (8 ounces), thinly sliced
6 garlic cloves (1 ounce), sliced
4 ounces pancetta or Tesa, thinly sliced and cut in large dice
½ teaspoon red pepper flakes
6 fresh sage leaves, roughly chopped
1 teaspoon fresh rosemary leaves, chopped
3 tablespoons tomato Conserva (page 46) or tomato paste
¼ cup red wine
½ cup Meat Broth (page 135)
2 cups fresh tomatoes, roughly chopped
2 recipes Semolina Dough for Flat Pasta (see left), rolled and cut into fettuccine
8 tablespoons grated Pecorino Romano cheese
2 tablespoons chopped flat-leaf parsley

Warm the olive oil over low heat in a 4-quart casserole. Raise the heat to medium, add the sausages, and brown them on all sides. Transfer the sausages to a plate. Add the onions, garlic, pancetta, red pepper flakes, sage, and rosemary to the pan and cook for about 15 minutes, until the onions are softened. Add the tomato conserva, red wine, and meat broth and cook for 5 minutes. Add the chopped tomatoes and cook an additional 5 minutes. Slice the sausages lengthwise, then cut them crosswise into half-moons. Return the sausages to the pot, as well as any juices left on the cutting board. To serve, heat the sauce in a large sauté pan (12-inch diameter with 4-inch sides is ideal). Cook the pasta in a generous amount of boiling salted water until al dente, drain it, and toss it well with the sauce over medium high heat. Add the Pecorino and the parsley, and divide the pasta equally among 8 warm bowls.

Basic "Wet" Dough for Filled Pasta

Dough intended for filled pasta that is shaped by hand, such as agnolotti, tortelli, and ravioli, benefits from an increased percentage of water. Slightly wetter dough is easier to stretch around the filling and to join in tight edges, and it is less apt to dry out in the course of filling. When making filled pasta, it is wise to roll all of the dough to within two settings of the final thickness and keep it under a kitchen towel, then finish rolling only as much as you can fill before the dough dries. Dry dough does not seal well and cracks when stretched around the filling.

5 ounces Artisan flour
5 ounces Baker's Choice flour
4 ounces eggs (2 whole eggs)
1 ounce cool water

Place the flour in a bread bowl and make a well in the center. Whisk the eggs, add them to the well, and stir with a fork to combine. Drizzle the water over the mixture and stir again until it begins to form a shaggy mass. With your stronger hand, reach into the bowl and alternately squeeze and push down on the dough with your palm. Press any loose bits of flour into the mass. Transfer it to a clean, lightly floured surface and knead it for 4 or 5 minutes, or until it loses its surface moisture, is a uniform color, and springs back when depressed. Wrap the dough in plastic and allow it to hydrate for 1 hour before rolling.

Tortelli of Pigeon

For 10 to 12 (180 tortelli)

2 whole fresh pigeons, with giblets
1½ teaspoons salt
½ teaspoon freshly ground black pepper
2 tablespoons olive oil
4 medium garlic cloves, whole and unpeeled
1 sprig of rosemary, finely chopped
¼ cup vin santo
3 ounces Parmigiano-Reggiano cheese, grated, plus more for garnish
3 recipes Basic "Wet" Dough for Filled Pasta (see left)

Season both the cavity and the skin of the pigeons with salt and pepper. Warm the olive oil in a heavy-bottomed, ovenproof pot that holds the pigeons comfortably. Place the pigeons in the pot breast side down with the giblets and brown them thoroughly on all sides. Adjust the heat if necessary so that the skin develops a deep brown color. This will take about 40 minutes. In the last 10 minutes, add the garlic and rosemary and preheat the oven to 350°F. Place the pot in the oven and roast for 30 minutes. Remove the pigeons from the oven and transfer them with all solid contents of the pot to a platter to cool. Return the pot to the stove and deglaze the residues (do not discard the fat in the pot) with vin santo, scraping free any bits with a wooden spoon.

When the pigeons are cool enough to handle, pick the meat from the bones, reserving the skin. Next, lay the skins on a baking sheet and crisp them in the oven for 10 to 15 minutes. On a cutting board, combine the pigeon meat, skin, and giblets and finely chop them. Alternatively, chop the meat in a food processor or pass it through the finest die of your meat grinder. Place the finely chopped or ground meat in a bowl and add the Parmigiano-Reggiano and the deglazed juices and fat from the pot. Squeeze the garlic from the roasting pan from its skin and thoroughly mix it with the pigeon. Season the filling with salt and pepper to your taste. If you like, transfer the filling mixture to a pastry bag with a plain ½-inch tip.

To form the tortelli, roll a thin sheet of dough and use a 3-inch round pastry cutter to stamp out individual circles. Cut only about a dozen circles at a time and hold the unrolled dough under a towel to keep it moist. Spoon or pipe about ½ teaspoon of filling just below the center line of the dough circle. Fold the top edge over the filling to meet the bottom edge and using your down-turned thumbs, compress the edges all around the filling. Then, bring the corners of the half-moon together, folding one corner over the other, and pinch them tight. Turn the edges up around the filling. Keep the finished tortelli under a towel while you work. Cook them as soon as possible after filling. If you decide to make the tortelli ahead of time, lay them on a sheet pan, cover with foil, and freeze them. They will hold for up to a week.

Cook the tortelli in a generous amount of boiling salted water. When they rise to the top of the pot, test one for doneness—the pasta should be al dente and the filling hot all the way through. Toss in melted butter and divide among individual warm bowls. Sprinkle grated Parmigiano-Reggiano over each serving at the table.

Agnolotti
For 16

Agnolotti are very small pasta bundles that traditionally encase a filling of leftover roasted, boiled, or braised meats. At Oliveto we commonly use the flavorful meats and poultry remaindered from the making of sugo augmented by the ends of cured meat such as salame or mortadella and occasionally Swiss chard or spinach. Rice cooked in milk is often included for a lighter texture. Agnolotti may be served in a fine meat broth, tossed in melted butter, or lavished with truffle or pan drippings

from a roast. In the recipe for Basic Meat Sugo (page 136), two thirds of the meat used to make it will be left over for transforming into filling. Otherwise, a simple recipe for agnolotti filling follows. Given the diminutive size of agnolotti, it takes about 100 to make a portion for one. Agnolotti freeze well for up to a week.

1½ teaspoons extra-virgin olive oil
½ pound boneless veal shoulder, trimmed
    of excess fat, cut in 1-inch pieces
4 ounces boneless, skin-on chicken leg,
    cut in 1-inch pieces
2 ounces pancetta or Tesa, cut in ½-inch dice
1 teaspoon salt
¼ teaspoon freshly ground black pepper
½ small onion (1¾ ounces), thinly sliced
4 fresh sage leaves, coarsely chopped
½ ounce dry salame, diced
1¼ cups Meat Broth (page 135)
1½ ounces grated Parmigiano-Reggiano
1 recipe Basic "Wet" Dough for Filled Pasta
    (page 114)

Pour the olive oil into a small, heavy-bottomed braising pot and place it over medium heat. Add the veal, the chicken meat, the pancetta or Tesa, and the salt and pepper to the pot. Raise the heat and begin browning. Stir the pot regularly and adjust the heat up or down as needed to encourage a deep caramelization of the meat and the formation of a residue on the bottom of the pot. This will take about 20 minutes. When the meat is well browned, add the onion, sage, and salame to the pot and continue browning for about 5 minutes more. Add ¼ cup of the meat broth and scrape up the pan residue. Allow the pan juices to reduce until the residue reforms, then add an additional ¼ cup of broth. Repeat this process one more time, again adding ¼ cup of broth. Then add the final ½ cup of broth, release the residue, cover with a tight-fitting lid, and reduce the heat to the lowest possible simmer. Cook for 1½ hours, or until the meat is tender, stirring intermittently to ensure that it does not stick to the bottom of the pot or burn.

Transfer the solids from the pan to a cutting board using a slotted spoon. Reserve the pan juices. Finely chop meat to a very fine paste. Alternatively, chop the meat in a food processor pulsing it on and off to achieve a fine consistency. Transfer the filling to a bowl; add the Parmigiano and 2 tablespoons of the reserved pan juices. Mix thoroughly until incorporated.

To form the agnolotti, roll the dough very thin and use a sharp knife or pizza wheel to cut rectangular ribbons about 16 inches long and 1½ inches wide. Place one of the ribbons in front of you on the work surface and cover the others under a kitchen towel. Using a pastry tube fitted with a small round tip, pipe small knobs (⅟₁₆ teaspoon) of filling just below the center line every ½ inch. Using an atomizer, spray the strip lightly with water. Fold the bottom edge up and over the filling, leaving a small border of unlapped dough at the top edge. Pinch the dough between the fillings, then fold the pinch to the top edge, compress it lightly so that it sticks, and cut over the fold with a fluted wheel. Proceed along the length of the dough and filling, making about 800 agnolotti. Use the remaining dough and filling to form additional agnolotti.

Alternate filling from leftover sugo meat

12 ounces sugo meat (see page 136)
1 ounce cured Italian salame, *mortadella*, or Tesa
1½ ounces Parmigiano-Reggiano, grated
2 tablespoons unsalted butter, softened
¼ teaspoon freshly grated nutmeg
Salt and freshly ground black pepper to taste

Pick through the braised meat to remove any bones or cartilage. Combine the sugo meat and the cured meat. Grind it through the finest plate of a meat grinder or chop in a food processor to a fine consistency. Transfer the meat to a bowl and add the Parmigiano, the butter, and the nutmeg. Stir all the ingredients together. Correct the mixture to your taste for salt and pepper.

Raviolini of Spinach and Ricotta
For 8

3 tablespoons extra-virgin olive oil
8 ounces spinach leaves, washed
1 garlic clove, minced
¾ cup fresh ricotta, drained of excess whey
¼ cup Parmigiano-Reggiano, grated
1½ teaspoons salt
1 recipe Basic "Wet" Dough for Filled Pasta
    (page 114)

Warm 1 tablespoon of the olive oil in a wide sauté pan. Raise the heat to high, add the spinach, and cook it until it wilts and releases its water. Turn off the heat and transfer the spinach from the pan to a plate and let it cool. When the spinach is cool, bind it in a clean towel or cheesecloth and squeeze it tight to remove the water it contains. Add the remaining 2 tablespoons of olive oil to the pan, warm it, add the minced garlic, and soften it gently over low heat. Chop the spinach fine to a smooth paste. Transfer the spinach to a mixing bowl and add the garlic, the ricotta, the Parmigiano, and salt. Blend well.

To form the raviolini, use a fluted pastry wheel to cut a 4-inch-wide ribbon of dough about 16 inches long. Place about a teaspoon of filling just below the center line. Starting at the top edge of the dough, fold it over the filling so that it meets the bottom edge. Do not seal the bottom. This allows any trapped air around the filling to escape. With both hands splayed, use your forefingers to compress the dough on either side of the filling. Proceed in the same way along the length of the strip. Use your fingertips to press the bottom edges together to seal them. Trim the folded edge with a fluted wheel. Then form individual raviolini by cutting with the fluted wheel through the center of the space between each teaspoon of filling.

Cannelloni of Chicken and Fontina
For 12 (Makes 24 cannelloni)

4 tablespoons unsalted butter
2 medium leeks (10 ounces), trimmed to their
    pale green tops, finely diced
10 garlic cloves, finely chopped
1 tablespoon salt
1 teaspoon freshly ground black pepper
1 tablespoon plus 1 teaspoon all-purpose flour
¼ cup whole milk
3½ pounds chicken legs, boned, skinned, and
    chopped medium fine or ground through a
    ³⁄₁₆-inch plate
8 ounces fontina Valdostana cheese, grated
1¾ cups grated Parmigiano-Reggiano
1 recipe Whole-Egg Pasta (page 104)
1 cup heavy cream
2 cups chicken sugo or 4 cups chicken broth,
    reduced by half

Melt the butter in a heavy-bottomed sauce pot. Add the leeks, garlic, salt, and pepper and stew over medium-low heat until softened. Slowly stir in the flour and cook it for 5 minutes. Whisk in the milk and simmer, whisking constantly, until thickened and then 3 minutes more. Next, add the ground chicken, raise the heat to medium, and cook for 5 minutes, stirring often. Spread the filling on a sheet pan lined with parchment paper and cool in the refrigerator for 20 minutes. When the chicken filling is cool, mix in the fontina and ¾ cup of the Parmigiano and set it aside.

Extend the pasta to approximately 4-inch-wide sheets through a pasta machine. Pass the sheets once through the machine on the next to last setting. Cut the sheets of pasta into 4-inch squares.

Preheat the oven to 500°F.

To cook the pasta for the cannelloni, you will need a large pot of boiling salted water, a large bowl of ice water near the stove for cooling the pasta, and a table lined with an absorbent towel or cloth to dry the pasta once it has cooled. Cook the pasta until it is al dente (2 to 3 minutes), 2 or

3 sheets at a time. Using a flat strainer, transfer the pasta immediately from the boiling pot to the ice water, then to the absorbent cloth. Repeat the process with the remaining pasta sheets. Divide the filling among the 24 sheets, making each roll about 1 inch in diameter. Place the filling closer to the edge facing you and dab the other edge with water. Roll the cannelloni against the moistened edge to seal them. Pour the cream into a rimmed sheet pan. Roll each of the cannelloni in the cream and place them evenly on the sheet pan. Sprinkle the remaining cup of the Parmigiano over the cannelloni and bake them for 7 minutes. Place two cannelloni on each of 12 warm plates. Thin the cream left on the sheet pan with the reduced chicken broth and spoon a little around each serving.

Spelt Pasta

For 4

5 ounces whole spelt berries, milled fine
5 ounces spelt flour
4 ounces eggs (2 whole large eggs)
½ ounce cool water

Place the spelt and flour in a bread bowl and make a well in the center. Add the eggs to the well and stir with a fork to combine. Drizzle the water over the mixture and stir again until it begins to form a shaggy mass. With your stronger hand, reach into the bowl and alternately squeeze and push down on the dough with your palm. Press any loose bits of flour into the mass. When the dough feels tacky and fully incorporated, transfer it to a clean, lightly floured surface and knead it for 4 to 5 minutes, or until it loses its surface moisture, is a uniform color, and springs back when depressed. Wrap the dough in plastic and allow it to hydrate for at least 1 hour before rolling.

Spelt Pasta with Chanterelles

For 4

1 recipe Spelt Pasta (see left)
8 tablespoons (1 stick) unsalted butter
8 ounces chanterelle mushrooms, thinly sliced
1 teaspoon sea salt
½ cup water (optional)
1 tablespoon chopped fresh flat-leaf parsley

Roll the pasta on the next to last setting of the pasta machine. Cut the strips into ⅜–inch noodles with a sharp knife.

Warm the butter in a wide sauté pan or casserole. Add the chanterelles, season them with the salt, and sauté the mushrooms over medium-high heat without browning until cooked through. If the mushrooms exude a lot of water, raise the heat and allow the liquid to reduce to a little more than ½ cup. If the mushrooms are small, firm, and dry, add the ½ cup of water. Cook the mushrooms just until the sauce surrounding them develops a creamy emulsified consistency.

While the mushrooms cook, bring a large pot of salted water to the boil. Cook the pasta al dente, drain it, and add to the pan with the mushrooms. Toss the pasta over medium-high heat until the sauce reduces somewhat around the noodles, all the while adding splashes of pasta water to maintain the creamy sauce. Before serving, toss in the parsley and divide the pasta, mushrooms, and sauce among 4 warm bowls.

Farro Flour Pasta

For 4

5 ounces whole farro, freshly milled
5 ounces Extra Fancy semolina
4 ounces cool water

Place the farro and semolina flour in a bread
bowl and make a well in the center. Add water to
the well and stir with a fork to combine. When
the dough begins to form a shaggy mass, reach
into the bowl with your stronger hand and alternately squeeze and push down on the dough
with your palm. Press any loose bits of flour into
the mass. When the dough feels tacky and fully
incorporated, transfer it to a clean, lightly
floured surface and knead it for 4 to 5 minutes,
or until it loses its surface moisture, is a uniform
color, and springs back when depressed. Wrap
the dough in plastic and allow it to hydrate for
at least 1 hour before rolling.

   If you own a grain mill, you may wish to grind
your own farro flour, which presently is available only in whole form. Farro makes pasta the
color of caffè latte with a subtle wheat taste.

Farro Pasta with Fresh Cranberry Beans

For 4

1 recipe Farro Flour Pasta (see left)
10 ounces fresh cranberry beans or flageolet
   in the pod, shucked to yield 5 ounces
1 ounce prosciutto, minced
1 garlic clove, sliced
2 fresh sage leaves
Sea salt
3 whole salt-cured anchovies
¼ cup plus 2 tablespoons extra-virgin olive oil
2 ounces pancetta or Tesa, sliced thin, then
   diced
1 small red onion, diced
1 teaspoon red pepper flakes
2 teaspoons tomato Conserva (page 46) or
   tomato paste
2 tomatoes (9 ounces,) peeled, seeded, and
   diced, liquid passed through a sieve and
   reserved
2 tablespoons chopped fresh flat-leaf parsley
½ cup Parmigiano-Reggiano, plus more for
   serving

Roll the pasta thin on the next to last setting of
the pasta machine and cut by hand into ¼-inch-
wide noodles. Place the beans in a 4-quart
saucepan with the prosciutto, garlic, and sage
leaves. Cover the beans with 3 cups cold water,
add 1 teaspoon of sea salt, and place the pan
over high heat. Turn the heat down to low when
the beans come to a simmer, about 5 minutes
later, and simmer for 25 to 30 minutes or until
tender. Remove the beans from the heat and
allow them to cool in their cooking liquid.

   Meanwhile, prepare the other ingredients.
Soak the anchovies in cold water for 5 minutes
to soften them and remove the salt. Peel the
fillets from the bones and mince them into
small pieces; set aside.

   Place a wide sauté pan or casserole on medium-
high heat. Add ¼ cup plus 1 tablespoon of the
olive oil and the pancetta. When the pancetta
develops color after about 5 minutes, add the

onion. Stir the two together and continue to cook them until the onion softens. Add the anchovy and red pepper flakes. Cook until the anchovy breaks down, a minute or two, then add the tomato Conserva and cook it for several minutes until it develops a brick-red color. Stir in the diced fresh tomatoes and the reserved tomato juice and simmer the mixture until most of the liquid has evaporated.

Drain the beans, reserve their cooking liquid, and add them to the pot. Using a wooden spoon, crush a portion of the beans to spread the bean flavor into the sauce. Continue to cook the sauce over medium-high heat and when the sauce reduces and concentrates again, add 1 cup of the bean-cooking juices to the pan with the chopped parsley. Reduce the sauce again to an emulsified consistency.

Bring a large pot of salted water to a boil, cook the pasta al dente, drain it, and combine it with the sauce. Add the remaining tablespoon of olive oil and ½ cup grated Parmigiano-Reggiano and continue to toss the pasta together with the sauce. Add little splashes of the bean water to correct the sauce if it appears dry. Serve in 4 warm pasta bowls and pass additional grated cheese at the table.

Chestnut Flour Pasta

For 4

5 ounces chestnut flour
5 ounces Extra Fancy semolina
3½ ounces cool water

Place the chestnut flour and semolina in a bread bowl and make a well in the center. Add the water to the well and stir with a fork to combine. When the dough begins to form a shaggy mass, reach into the bowl with your stronger hand and alternately squeeze and push down on the dough with your palm. Press any loose bits of flour into the mass. When the dough feels tacky and fully incorporated, transfer it to a clean, lightly floured surface and knead it for 4 to 5 minutes, or until it loses its surface moisture, is a uniform color, and springs back when depressed. Wrap the dough in plastic and allow it to hydrate for at least 1 hour before rolling. Roll the pasta on the next to last setting of the pasta machine and cut by hand into ³⁄₈-inch-wide noodles.

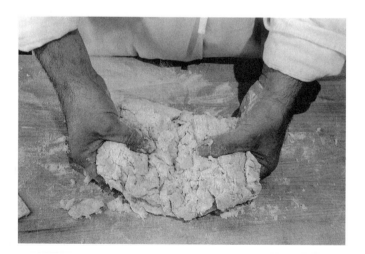

Chestnut Flour Tagliatelle with Duck Braised in Red Wine and Vinegar

For 8

1 whole white Peking duck, head and feet included, 3½ pounds
Salt and freshly ground black pepper
1 carrot, diced
1 small celery stalk, diced
1 medium onion, diced
4 or 5 fresh sage leaves
½ ounce dried porcini mushrooms
⅛ teaspoon ground cinnamon
⅛ teaspoon ground cloves
¼ teaspoon ground ginger
Pinch of freshly grated or ground nutmeg
3 cups dry red wine
½ cup red wine vinegar
2 recipes Chestnut Flour Pasta (see left), rolled and cut into tagliatelle
2 tablespoons unsalted butter

Trim the neck and feet from the duck and cut the carcass into 10 pieces: separate the legs from the thighs, split the breast and cut each half in thirds. Trim any excess fat away from the neck and stomach cavity of the duck and around the legs. Salt and pepper the duck pieces and place them along with the skinned neck and the feet into a heated 14-inch casserole. Brown the duck well on both sides for about 20 minutes over medium heat, then pour off the fat. Add the diced vegetables, sage leaves, and porcini mushrooms. Allow the vegetables to soften for about 5 minutes. Stir in the cinnamon, cloves, ginger, and nutmeg, then deglaze the pan with 1 cup of the wine. Allow the wine to evaporate entirely, and then add the remaining 2 cups of wine and the vinegar. Reduce the heat to a simmer, cover the pan, and braise the duck for 1 hour and 10 minutes over very low heat. Allow the duck to cool in its braising juices, and then transfer the duck pieces to a separate plate. Pass the liquid and solid contents of the pot through the medium-fine plate of a food mill. Pick the meat and skin from the duck, discarding any fat, and shred the meat with your fingers. Add the shredded meat back to the sugo. When you are ready to serve the pasta, warm the sauce in a large casserole. Cook the chestnut pasta al dente, drain it, and toss it together well with the sauce. Stir in the butter and thin it if necessary with a little warm water. Serve in 8 warm bowls.

Spinach or Nettle Pasta

For 4

Spinach pasta may be substituted for whole-egg pasta and marries well with oysters or braised rabbit. If you can locate a source of young, fresh nettles, all you will need is extra-virgin olive oil, preferably one very recently pressed (see Sources and Resources, page 261) in early winter.

8 ounces fresh spinach or young fresh nettle leaves
10 ounces Extra Fancy semolina
½ ounce water

Wash the spinach or nettles. Bring a sauce pot of water to a boil. Submerge the leaves for 10 seconds or until just wilted; drain in a colander and rinse with cold water. Gather the spinach or nettles into a ball and weigh them. Squeeze water out until you end up with 4 ounces of greens. Pound the par-cooked greens to a fine purée in a mortar and pestle or purée them in a food processor. Combine the purée and the flour in a bread bowl or the bowl of a freestanding mixer and stir or paddle the two together. Drizzle ½ ounce water over the surface of the dough and stir again. When the dough begins to clump, squeeze it together in a rough shape, turn it out onto a work surface, and knead it for 4 to 5 minutes. Wrap the dough in plastic and let it hydrate for 1 hour before rolling.

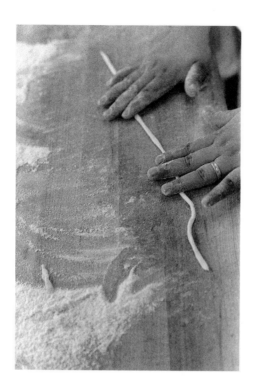

Pici Noodles

For 8

Pici are a type of fat, hand-formed spaghetti from the countryside surrounding Siena. The dough has a higher percentage of water and will feel quite slack compared to other dough. The wetter dough facilitates the hand shaping of the noodles and olive oil lubricates against sticking. Pici are typically served with mushrooms; with a sauce of onions, tomatoes, and Tuscan pancetta (rigatino); or with ragù of lamb.

12 ounces Baker's Choice flour
7 ounces cool water
3½ teaspoons olive oil

Place the flour in a bowl, make a well in the center, and pour in the water and olive oil. Use a fork to stir the flour and liquids together. Flour your hands and knead the dough briefly to amalgamate the dough, then cover it with a kitchen towel and allow it to relax for 30 minutes.

Dust the dough with flour, knead it into a uniform shape, and cut it into 5 roughly equal pieces. Cut each piece into about 12 smaller pieces. To shape pici, take up a piece of dough in your hands and, with fingers outstretched, rub the dough between your palms lightly at first then with slightly more pressure to elongate the strand to about 8 inches. Transfer the strand to an unfloured work surface and roll the dough under your fingers from the center outward to an even length of about 16 inches. Move the pici aside on the work surface as you form them and keep them lined up parallel to one another; otherwise they have a tendency to adhere to one another. When finished forming the pici, transfer them likewise to a well-floured sheet pan.

Pici with Lamb Sugo

For 8

2 tablespoons extra-virgin olive oil
2 pounds lamb shoulder, trimmed of excess fat
  and cut into 1-inch pieces
2 teaspoons salt
½ teaspoon freshly ground black pepper
1 small yellow onion, sliced
1 celery stalk, sliced
1 medium carrot, sliced
6 garlic cloves, sliced
2 sprigs of fresh rosemary
¼ teaspoon red pepper flakes
½ cup dry white wine
3 tablespoons tomato Conserva (page 46)
  or tomato paste
2 quarts plus ½ cup lamb broth or Meat Broth
  (page 135)
1 recipe Pici Noodles (see left)

Pour the olive oil into a 6-quart heavy-bottomed pot and place it over medium heat. Season the lamb pieces with the salt and black pepper and add them to the pot. Brown the meat well on all sides, turning it frequently, for 20 minutes. Add the onion, celery, carrot, garlic, rosemary, and red pepper flakes and stew for about 15 minutes, or until the vegetables are tender. Add the white wine and the tomato Conserva and cook for an additional 3 minutes. Add 1½ cups of the broth and scrape up the residue on the bottom of the pot. Reduce the pan juices until a new residue forms, then add another 1½ cups of broth. Repeat this process one more time. When you have completed the third reduction, add the remaining 4 cups of the broth and bring to a boil. Reduce the heat to a low simmer, and then cover the pot with a tight-fitting lid. Braise the lamb for 2 hours. When the lamb is very tender, pass it through the medium plate of a food mill and return to the pot with the braising liquid.

To serve, heat the lamb sugo in a large sauté pan (12-inch diameter with 4-inch sides is ideal).

Cook the pasta al dente, approximately 7 minutes, drain it in a colander, and toss it with the sugo over medium heat until the sauce reduces around the pasta and clings well to it. Divide the pasta among 8 warm bowls.

Herb Noodles

For 4

An alternative to seasoning pasta by the usual method of letting herbs loose in sauce or finished pasta is to trap them in the pasta dough itself. Sauce can then assume the role of support to the herb that becomes the governing flavor of every bite. Herb noodles may be enhanced, for instance, with the pan renderings of roast chicken, beef, or lamb, or with foods that share special reciprocity (such as tomatoes with basil noodles, goat cheese with oregano, parsley and thyme noodles, or poultry giblets with rosemary noodles). The strength of herb flavor in pasta should nevertheless be calibrated to what it partners. Herbs that have relatively mild or fragile flavors that can be eaten directly— parsley, chervil, tarragon, basil, chives— are better suited to milder accompaniments. Those pungent herbs that are stronger and less palatable in the raw state (rosemary, sage) stand more comfortably next to more forceful sauces.

5 ounces Artisan flour
5 ounces Baker's Choice flour
4 ounces eggs (2 whole eggs)
½ ounce cool water
1 ounce (½ cup) chopped mixed herbs

Place the flour in a bread bowl and make a well in the center and add the eggs, the water, and the herbs to the well. Use a fork to stir the flour, eggs, water, and herbs together. When the dough begins to form a shaggy mass, reach into the bowl with your stronger hand and alternately squeeze and push down on the dough with your palm. Press any loose bits of flour into the mass. When the dough feels tacky and fully incorporated, transfer it to a clean, lightly floured surface and knead it for 4 to 5 minutes, or until it loses its surface moisture, is a uniform color, and springs back when depressed. Wrap the dough in plastic and allow it to hydrate for at least 1 hour before rolling. Roll the pasta on the next to last setting of the pasta machine and cut by hand into ¼-inch-wide noodles.

Herb Noodles with Chicken Breast

For 4

8 tablespoons unsalted butter
¼ cup water
12 ounces boneless, skinless chicken breast, cut into thin strips
1 teaspoon sea salt
¼ teaspoon freshly ground black pepper
Parmigiano-Reggiano, for grating
1 recipe Herb Noodles (page 123)

Combine the butter and water in a wide sauté pan. Season the chicken with the salt and pepper. Bring the butter and water to a slow boil over medium heat. When the butter and water emulsify, turn off the heat and add the chicken strips, tossing to coat the pieces. In a large pot of boiling, salted water cook the herb noodles al dente, 3 to 4 minutes. Drain them in a colander, add them to the chicken in the pan, and toss again. Turn the heat to medium high and cook the chicken with the pasta for about 1 minute more, until the sauce appears creamy. Add small amounts of pasta water if necessary to maintain the sauce consistency. Divide the pasta evenly among 4 warm bowls. Grate fresh Parmigiano liberally over each portion and grind a little fresh black pepper over each serving.

Corn Flour Pasta

For 4

Pasta made with corn flour has a warm, buttery flavor that matches well with sauces made from crustaceans such as crab and lobster, with sugo of pork, and with stewed leeks or summer peppers.

4 ounces fresh milled corn flour
6 ounces Extra Fancy semolina
4 ounces eggs (2 whole large eggs)
½ ounce cool water

Place the corn flour and semolina in a bowl and make a well in the center. Add the eggs and water. Use a fork to stir the mixture together. When the dough begins to form a shaggy mass, reach into the bowl with your stronger hand and alternately squeeze and push down on the dough with your palm. Press any loose bits of flour into the mass. When the dough feels tacky and fully incorporated, transfer it to a clean, lightly floured surface and knead it for 4 to 5 minutes, or until it loses its surface moisture, is a uniform color, and springs back when depressed. Wrap the dough in plastic and allow it to hydrate for at least 1 hour before rolling.

Roll the pasta on the next to last setting of the pasta machine. Cut 8-inch lengths from the rolled sheets. Use a fluted pasta wheel to cut individual strands about ¾-inch-wide.

Stradette ("Little Streets") with Summer Peppers

For 4

¼ cup extra-virgin olive oil
4 garlic cloves, thinly sliced
4 sweet red peppers, gypsy or bell, cored, seeded, and thinly sliced
1 teaspoon salt
½ cup heavy cream
1 recipe Corn Flour Pasta (see left), cut into stradette
Parmigiano-Reggiano, for grating

Add the olive oil, garlic, peppers, and salt to a 12-inch sauté pan and place over medium heat. Sauté the peppers until tender, about 5 to 7 minutes, add the cream, then cook for 2 minutes more to blend the flavors. Cook the stradette al dente and drain them in a colander. Toss the pasta with the pepper mixture over high heat for a minute or so until the sauce coats the pasta, but does not become thick and sticky. Divide among 4 warm bowls. Serve with grated Parmigiano-Reggiano.

Rye Flour Pasta

For 4

When made into pasta, rye has a subtle but unmistakable flavor that marries well with salmon, smoked or fresh, or a simple sauce of smoked prosciutto (speck), leeks, and cream.

5 ounces rye flour
5 ounces Extra Fancy semolina
2 ounces egg (1 whole large egg)
2½ ounces cool water

Place the rye flour and semolina in a bread bowl and make a well in the center. Whisk the egg, add it to the well, and stir with a fork to combine. Drizzle the water over the mixture and stir again until it begins to form a shaggy mass. With your stronger hand, reach into the bowl and alternately squeeze and press the dough with your palm to gather it together into a rough shape. Press any loose bits of flour into the mass. When the dough feels tacky and fully incorporated, transfer it to a clean surface and knead it for 4 or 5 minutes, or until it loses its surface moisture, is a uniform color, and springs back when depressed. Wrap the dough in plastic and allow it to hydrate for at least 1 hour before rolling.

Rye Pasta with Fresh Salmon and Tarragon

For 4

6 tablespoons unsalted butter
1 large shallot, minced very fine
Sea salt
8 ounces fresh salmon, cut into thin strips
1 tablespoon dry white wine
1 recipe Rye Flour Pasta (page 125), rolled on the next to last setting of the pasta machine, cut into ¼-inch-wide noodles
1 teaspoon chopped fresh tarragon leaves
1 teaspoon chopped fresh flat-leaf parsley

Melt the butter in a wide sauté pan. Add the shallot and soften it over low heat. Salt the salmon lightly and add it to the pan. Raise the heat slightly, add the wine, and poach the salmon in the butter for only about 20 seconds, just enough to leave it half cooked (the heat from the pasta will complete the cooking). Turn off the heat. Cook the pasta al dente, drain it in a colander, and add it to the salmon. Scatter the herbs in the pan and toss the pasta gently with the sauce so as not to break up the fish. Dish the pasta among 4 warm bowls, arranging salmon pieces equally over each portion.

Buckwheat Flour Pasta

For 4

3 ounces buckwheat flour
7 ounces Extra Fancy semolina
4 ounces eggs (2 whole large eggs)
½ ounce cool water

Place the buckwheat flour and semolina in a bowl and make a well in the center. Add the eggs and water. Use a fork to stir the mixture together. When the dough begins to form a shaggy mass, reach into the bowl with your stronger hand and alternately squeeze and press the dough with your palm. Press any loose bits of flour into the mass. When the dough feels tacky and fully incorporated, transfer it to a clean, lightly floured surface and knead it for 4 or 5 minutes, or until it loses its surface moisture, is a uniform color, and springs back when depressed. Wrap the dough in plastic and allow it to hydrate for at least 1 hour before rolling.

Pizzocheri

For 4

Buckwheat pasta with butter and caviar is a rare treat. Another favorite is *pizzocheri*—wide buckwheat noodles tossed with cabbage, potatoes, sage, butter, and fontina cheese—a specialty of the mountain cuisine of the Valtellina.

1 recipe Buckwheat Flour Pasta (see above), cut into 8-inch lengths from the rolled sheets
5 teaspoons sea salt
8 ounces new potatoes, peeled and sliced ⅛ inch thick on a mandoline
7 ounces Savoy cabbage, separated and torn into rough pieces
7 tablespoons unsalted butter
8 to 10 fresh sage leaves
1 garlic clove, chopped fine
1 cup fontina Valdostana cheese, grated
1 cup Parmigiano-Reggiano, grated

Roll the pasta until quite thin, then use a fluted pastry wheel to cut into strips ¾ inch wide and 6 inches long.

Preheat the broiler.

Bring 1 gallon of water to a boil and add the sea salt. Toss the potatoes into the boiling water, then after 2 minutes, add the cabbage. Boil the vegetables for about 5 minutes total or until the potatoes are cooked through and the cabbage is tender but not soft. Remove to a plate with a slotted spoon and keep the water boiling. Meanwhile, place a wide sauté pan on medium heat; add the butter, sage leaves, and garlic. Lower the heat so that the garlic does not brown. Cook the pasta in the same water as the vegetables, drain it in a colander, and add it to the sauté pan. Butter a 10-inch gratin dish or similar baking dish and assemble 3 layers each of pasta, vegetables, and cheese. Finish by sprinkling the remaining cheese on top. Place the gratin under the broiler for 4 to 5 minutes, until the cheese is melted and slightly browned. Serve at once.

Squid Ink Pasta

For 4

Make this dough in an electric mixer to avoid staining your hands with squid ink.

1½ tablespoons squid ink (see Sources and Resources, page 263)
2 ounces white wine
1 ounce cool water
10 ounces Extra Fancy semolina

Combine the squid ink, the wine, and the water in a small bowl and whisk it well to distribute the ink. Add the ink mixture to the semolina and allow the machine to run for 3 to 4 minutes on medium low. Then knead the dough and wrap in plastic. Allow the dough to rest for 1 hour before rolling.

Chitarra Nera with Squid Braised in Red Wine

For 8

This pasta is somewhat shocking in appearance because of the addition of squid ink; I cannot think of another food in any cuisine that is so purely black. But the color intensity is no indication of the subtlety of flavor that it envelops. Although this sauce may be served to good effect with basic durum pasta, the addition of squid ink draws the sauce into perfect union.

3 tablespoons extra-virgin olive oil
1 leek, finely diced (8 ounces)
8 garlic cloves, sliced
1 teaspoon finely chopped fresh thyme leaves
1¾ teaspoons red pepper flakes
1¾ teaspoons salt
½ teaspoon freshly ground black pepper
3 tablespoons tomato paste
4½ pounds uncleaned fresh squid to yield 3⅓ pounds cleaned, bodies cut in rings and tentacles left whole
3¾ cups dry red wine
2 recipes Squid Ink Pasta (see left), rolled and cut alla Chitarra

Warm the olive oil a heavy-bottomed 6-quart pot. Add the leeks, garlic, thyme, red pepper flakes, salt, and pepper and stew over medium heat for 15 minutes without browning the garlic. Stir in the tomato paste and cook for an additional 5 minutes. At this point, the vegetables will be tender and the paste will have turned from bright red to red-orange. Add the squid and the wine to the pot, stir well, bring to a boil, and reduce the heat to a slow simmer. Cook until the squid is tender, approximately 1 hour. To serve, heat the sauce in a large sauté pan (12-inch diameter with 4-inch sides is ideal). Boil the chitarra al dente and toss well with the sauce over medium-high heat until the noodles are well coated. Divide the pasta and sauce equally among 8 warm bowls.

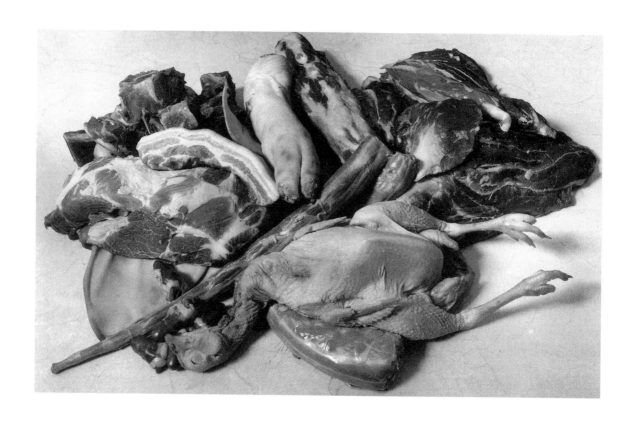

Bottom-Up Cooking

Bottom-Up Cooking

Some years back my wife and I took a vacation that began in Naples and ended at what I have come to regard as its cultural antipode, Paris. I was relieved to get away from the hectic whirl of the restaurant, she the jarring back and forth of her city job. In the days before leaving we imagined lazy hours pacing the ruins of Paestum, shuffling to the quiet corners of museums, surrendering to sleep in the middle of the day and wandering no particular map of the towns and inlets of the *costa Amalfitana*. We were guests at a marvelous old *palazzo* and were favored with a spacious room with a pair of arching doors onto an airy balcony overlooking the Tyrrhenian Sea. Considering our fatigue and the desire for a change of pace, we decided we would keep to a lean diet of relaxation and simple food tailored more to sustaining these easy visits than to pursuing restaurant research and meals for meals' sake. But after several outings and days of staring at the sea we began to think less about the allure of frescoed churches, ancient statues dragged from the deep, and the buried tragedies of Pompeii. A brief stroll through the redolent alleys of Naples one Sunday morning reminded us that we were once again simply starving. Immediately, I was back in chef's mode, thinking about options for the menu, where to eat lunch—and what about dinner?

Up to that point, I had only read about the mythic ragù of the south. Now I was in hot pursuit. Ragù, I had come to understand, is a matter of heart. It is a symbol, not merely a pasta condiment, that evokes the ritual Sunday family meal and a collective nostalgia for what is good, generous, and comforting. Through our host we were directed to a country *agriturismo* (a farm open to the public for meals and lodging) near Battipaglia that habitually prepared ragù at the week's end. After a tour of a local water buffalo farm and *caseficio* (cheese factory) specializing in *mozzarella di bufala*, we formed part of a long, disorderly queue to buy *bocconcini* ("little mouthfuls"), a near kilo of which we finished before we even arrived at our lunch destination. According to locals and true connoisseurs, we were told, mozzarella must be eaten by noon of the day it is made; otherwise it loses its tensile, milk-erupting structure and faint aftertaste of hazelnut.

We sat down at a long, outdoor table in front of a sunny field of eggplant. Cold antipasti were first to arrive—terra-cotta bowls of artichoke hearts, small and tender enough to have been pickled raw with salt, white vinegar, and olive oil; and on a simple plate, thick slices of a coarse-grained salame were laid out next to giant green olives stuffed with salted tuna and anchovies. The farm's eggplant, cut into fine shreds, briefly scalded in vinegar-spiked water, and squeezed nearly dry, were tossed with garlic, peperoncino, mint, and olive oil. A half-kilo of mozzarella that had been embalmed in smoldering hay was mounded on a long platter. Next came a generous bowl of hand-made fusilli. I had earlier watched our perspiring host twist the noodles, one by one, around a long knitting needle with jerking forward motions of her large, hairy arms. Coincidentally, today's ragù had been made with a joint of water buffalo—a cousin of the same horned beast we had seen earlier lolling in a muddy pond at the mozzarella manufacture.

The day was already developing its own organic theme, a phenomenon that I have noticed is typical of excursions to the heart of Italy's food culture. Where food is alive and long-ingrained, it confirms the nexus of people and earth and the familiar refrains of season and soil. Its cross-referencing of aromas waft everywhere from kitchen windows, restaurants, wine cellars, and any common table. The food of such a place is like a dialect, utterly distinctive and commonly shared by its locals. Just as language indelibly colors the character of a people, traditional food nourishes an inseparable relation to place. "You are what you eat," the saying goes. "And *where* you eat," I would add. Wandering in as an outsider, it is not so much by accident or coincidence but by simply *being there* that you meet the shepherd and then the sheep whose meat and cheese you later share with the coarse bread and proud wine of a village in a room that smells congruently like a barnyard stall.

We finished our fusilli and its mahagony-sheened sauce reluctantly. Culled from the bottom of the braising pot, it was remarkable for its integrated intensity—a brawny rendering married to a mellow background of *soffritto* (fine-diced onion and garlic sweated in olive oil), wine, and sun-dried estratto (sun-dried tomato paste). The meat followed, fragrant from its exchange with the sauce and tender enough to eat with a spoon.

Several days later, we left bustling Naples for a quiet hotel off the Boulevard Saint-Germain in Paris. On our way out of the city, our cabbie seemed to negotiate the traffic less with the wheel of his car than with outraged glares of disbelief at the invading foot traffic, exasperated gestures, and a ready onslaught of obscenities on the theme of pork and the Virgin. We arrived late that evening in Paris, and since the flight had precluded the possibility of dinner, we wandered out for a light meal before calling it a day. As we walked, we were both struck by the quiet mood of the city—such a dramatic contrast to the screaming, bumper-car town we had just left. After two weeks of southern Italian hospitality that might be characterized as effusive, even raucous, where people talk and laugh with their whole bodies and where public tables and their surrounding spaces are enjoyed as though they were the front room of an extended family home, we found ourselves, within a space of hours, in the discreet gentility of a low-lit Parisian café. Our waiter brushed by like an apparition and quietly took our order for an omelet and a steak *demi-glace* that arrived with quiet ceremony.

My steak had been placed in the center of a stark white plate. Without bone, neatly trimmed, and garnished with a single sprig of watercress, it was a model of restraint. Its measured pool of brown sauce had a refined tawny taste set in delicious juxtaposition. It struck me that this steak, and in particular, this sauce—the product of hours of reduction—was somehow consistent with the understated exchanges going on all around us.

I looked over the well-behaved room, its solitary readers lost in their books, locals, lovers, and liaisons locked tête-à-tête. It seemed not too elaborate a conceit to suggest that sauce mirrors culture. Like the surface of a simmering stockpot, the room held itself at a low murmur. Muted laughter would occasionally bubble up to break the even hum of hushed voices. A couple at a table nearby was bending in and out of a tortured exchange that was still being traded hours later, apparently only slightly reduced to any meatier terms. I couldn't help but recall the easy humanity of the Italian table, its bumptious waiters, overflows of enthusiasm, joke-telling, and communal arguments that usually resolved in hysterics, but also, sauce, the savory heart of Italian cooking, that seemed to come from some other place closer to the ground.

When I first began cooking I read much about Italian food and, in particular, about its distinctive method of extracting liquid flavor. I had tasted it in my mother's and grandmother's cooking. The seductive aroma of fresh meat browning in the early hours before dinner used to drive me crazy with appetite. It was there too in the pan juices and in the scrapings from a resting roast that I mopped with bread when my mother's back was turned. Later I found it in dishes I ate all over Italy: Tuscany's *arrosto morto* (meats first roasted then braised) and game in dolce forte (sweet and sour sauce); the wide menu of braised dishes that fall under the general class of *gli umidi* (moist-cooked dishes), Piedmont's *brassato;* Bolognese ragù, *stufato, stracotto, spezzatino, salmi,* and *civet*—the numerous variations on *intingolo* (dense sauce) and sugo (essential rendering) for pasta and rice.

The direct and natural flavor of the best Italian sauces is due to the fact that they are rendered directly from the meat, fish, or poultry they accompany and by no extraneous procedure. An Italian version of my café steak would likely have been grilled over wood embers and served with no other sauce than its own bleeding juices. While modern French cooking, heir to the classic methods systemized by Carême and later Escoffier, has evolved less lengthy

methods for making sauce with lighter results, it is still based on
the relatively long reduction of previously made stocks, carried
out separately from the meat, poultry, or fish to which it is later
applied. The French sauces were developed first for the aristocracy
and later, the international hotel set, who expected them to taste
the same whether in London or New York. But the Italian model,
made in a single pot and based on the essential renderings settled
in the bottom, has retained its humble roots in the home kitchen.
It is no exaggeration then to state that Italian sauces as an echo of
home and hearth are deeply satisfying, with a character that is
nothing less than personal.

When Italians refer to sauce of this sort, they use the word *sugo*
or, in more technical terms, *fondo di cottura* (literally "the bottom
of the cooking") rather than the direct translation of the word for
sauce, *salsa*. *Salsa* is reserved for semi-liquid condiments or emulsions such as green herb sauce (salsa verde), *salsa pevra* (a peppery
sauce built with bread and broth), *salsa alle noci* (walnut sauce),
salsa agresto (unripe grape juice mixed with aromatic herbs and
spice), and cold emulsions based on olive oil and egg yolk (*salsa
maionnese*). It also includes the flavored reductions that are clearly
imported from France or influenced by the French reduction
method. Sugo or *sughetto*, its diminutive, refers to the essential
renderings of meat, fowl, fish, and shellfish and even vegetables.
In Italian *il succo del discorso* is the essence of the matter.

Sugo has the same root as *succulent* and it is synonymous with *succo,* the word for freshly squeezed fruit or vegetable juice. The term *sugo* applies equally to the simple pan drippings of roasted meat, braised fish, or vegetables, and to the more complex liquid amalgam that results from the long, moist cooking of meat or fowl with or without aromatic components. Whoever invented the poultry press—a medieval kitchen torque that manually expresses the juice and marrow from the carcasses of roasted birds—had the right idea. But to render meats that are heavier and denser in order to collect their sugo requires a more indirect process.

Oliveto's sugo is the mother of all of our sauce preparations. It can stand alone as one of the most savory and fulfilling marriages to pasta, risotto, and gnocchi or be used, as described above, to fortify thin deglazing from rapidly cooked sautés. Similarly we use it to lend structure and background support to braised dishes or to amplify the natural renderings of roasted or braised meats. Using it as the sole means of moistening a braise compounds its flavor to the most satisfying pitch of intensity. A braise, moistened or bolstered at the finish with premade sugo, has a generous, even ecstatic quality. People don't merely smile when they eat it; they beam! The added advantage of a ready store of sugo is that, relative to the use of lengthy stock reductions, it cuts down drastically on the amount of time necessary to develop flavor. What's more, its flavor is truer.

The best meat sugo begins with the making of a flavorful meat broth. The process of making meat broth and sugo may seem involved and is, in fact, time-consuming. But because of the wide utility of both sugo and meat broth and the convenience and economy of maintaining such flavorful resources at hand, it is well worth the initial expense and trouble. A little bit goes a long way. Furthermore, what stands to be gained in terms of understanding how to extract flavor (which is, after all, what makes any cook worth his salt) is indispensable. Learning and repeating the process also reveals the variables that account for final differences in taste, texture, and the degree of flavor. Knowing how to manipulate these variables is important in wedding sugo to the food it accompanies. While the overall principle of making sugo is the same for all meat, fish, poultry, and vegetables, the process and ingredients vary in keeping with the character and quality of each. A sugo rich enough for mature beef or wild game is overwhelming to spring lamb. Likewise, young veal, "white" poultry like quail or rabbit, and fish call for gentler sughi in keeping with their more understated flavor.

Meat Broth

Makes about 1 gallon

Apart from the fundamental role it plays in sugo, meat broth is vital to the making of risotti; it can form the basis of hearty soups, the medium for deglazing flavorful pan residues from the browning process, or the liquid fundament of a braise. Our own Oliveto meat broth is a mixture of beef cuts, poultry, and other remnants that changes according to the availability of bones and trimmings from other kitchen operations. Though the elements of our broth change, we nevertheless maintain the rough proportion of 65 to 70 percent beef (a combination of meat and meaty bones), 20 percent poultry, and 10 percent gelatinous pork. Beef and beef bones contribute color and the primary meaty taste. The addition of poultry backs, necks, and carcasses adds a soft and homey dimension of flavor. Pork trotters, ears, or trimmings of the head-end of the pig add body in the form of the protein collagen. You will notice that after your meat broth has been refrigerated for a day; it will have jelled to a semi-firm consistency.

It is important that the meat and poultry you use be impeccably fresh. The broth pot is not the place for old or "high" meats, as their off aromas do not cook away. The general rule regardless of the size of your stockpot is to fill it to half full with meat parts in the above-given proportions and the remainder, to the brim, with cold water. You will note that our broth contains no aromatic vegetables. Since the broth cooks for an extended period of time, I have found that the vegetables lose their force and I prefer the pure flavor of the meat extraction. Furthermore, the broth will inevitably be used to moisten preparations that eventually contain aromatic vegetables. Adding them sooner is unnecessary.

12 ounces oxtails
2 pounds meaty beef neck bones, or short ribs trimmed of fat
3 pounds boneless shin meat, beef shoulder chuck, beef skirt, or brisket
1 pound 8 ounces chicken carcasses (including neck and feet), or turkey backs and necks
12 ounces pork trotters, or combination of pork skin, pork ears, and split pork tail
1½ gallons water

Coat the surface of a heavy-bottomed stockpot with olive oil, warm the pot, and brown the beef in batches over medium-high heat until they are well colored all over and smell deliciously meaty. It is not necessary to brown the meat to the point that its surface develops a crust. Pour off the fat and oil and discard it. Loosen any residues on the bottom of the pot with hot water. Pour off and reserve the residues and proceed with the next batch of beef. Repeat the process until you have browned all the beef. Then add the poultry carcasses and the pork. Pour in the water and the reserved residues and bring to a boil. As the broth approaches the boil, skim and discard the foamy impurities that rise to the surface. When the broth reaches the boil, reduce the heat to a bare simmer, and continue to skim the surface for the next 15 minutes. Replace the volume of liquid you have skimmed away with an equal volume of water and cook the broth for 4½ hours, or until the meat is very tender to the point of a knife. Strain the broth, discarding the meat and bones, and allow it to cool. Refrigerate the broth overnight. When you return to use the cold broth it will have a layer of congealed fat at the surface, which should be spooned away and discarded. The meat broth should be clear, golden brown, and lightly jelled. The broth may be frozen and will remain fresh tasting for up to a month.

Basic Meat Sugo

Makes about 1½ quarts

The savory flavor of sugo is due to the preliminary browning of the meat and the resulting residues that are released in the process and concentrated to a browned, sticky essence on the bottom of the pot. These residues are then repeatedly loosened with broth, wine, or simply water in a process called deglazing. Sugo can be the pure extraction of a single meat or of several in combination.

The raw materials for making sugo are nearly identical to those used for meat broth. Turkey necks, backs, and giblets and/or other poultry carcasses, wings, necks, and feet give the sugo a marvelous suave texture and homemade aroma; oxtails, beef shin meat, and beef skirt, brisket, or shoulder chuck contribute a dense meatiness; pork meat adds sweetness, and the presence of pork trotters or gelatinous trimmings such as ears, tails, or defatted pork skin lends weight, sheen, and a background richness to finished sugo.

The degree of depth of flavor, color, and texture in sugo is directly related to the extent to which the meat is browned and the amount of residue that develops on the bottom of the pot. The most intense sugo depends upon the formation of a heavy layer of browned residues. The residues are deglazed with a small amount of meat broth or other liquid, quickly reduced, and allowed to reattach. This procedure is then repeated three to four times. The value of multiple deglazing is the compounding of flavor that results from the reduction of the liquid used and its fusion with the residues. For this reason it is important to use meat broth as described above; it is also possible to use wine, the liquid portion of a marinade, vinegar in combination with broth, or any liquid capable of contributing additional flavor or enhancement through concentration. In the event that any of these liquids are not available, water is an acceptable alternative; bear in mind, however, that concentrating with water results in nothing more substantial

and that your water-deglazed sugo will be less rich in flavor. Fish is the exception to the use of water for deglazing. Water keeps the flavor of fish pure.

To make sugo you will need a lidded, heavy-bottomed pot with a wide diameter and sides at least 4 inches high. My favorite restaurant pot is a casserole of laminated construction with stainless steel on either side of an aluminum core. It is 14 inches wide and 9 inches deep. When I am at home I use a heavy, pounded copper sautoir to make sugo and other braises. Casseroles made of a combination of cast iron lined with enamel, such as those made by Le Creuset, work very well. The heavy bottom enables the residues formed in the browning process to attach to the pot gradually without burning.

An added benefit of extracting sugo from the ingredients below is the leftover meat that may be reserved for ravioli filling.

You will need a nutmeg grater or grinder and cooking parchment for the sugo.

4 ounces belly of pork (also called side pork) or
    cured Italian pancetta, sliced thin
1 pound chicken thighs, wings, and feet or
    equivalent quantity of turkey necks, gizzards,
    and meaty backs
1¼ pounds boneless beef shank (also called shin
    meat), sliced roughly into ¾-inch-thick
    pieces
14 ounces meaty oxtails or short ribs, trimmed
    of outer fat
6 ounces pork shoulder, sliced into roughly
    ¾-inch-thick pieces
1 tablespoon unsalted butter
½ medium-sized yellow onion
1 small carrot
½ stalk celery
1½ teaspoons salt
1 small bay leaf
2 quarts Meat Broth (page 135)
Fresh nutmeg
⅛ teaspoon ground clove
Salt and freshly ground black pepper to taste

Place the fresh pork belly slices or pancetta in the braising pot so that the bottom of the pot is almost entirely covered. Turn the heat on medium high to begin rendering the meat. In the meantime, using a cleaver, break the chicken wings, and chop the thighs and legs into 1-inch pieces. Distribute the chicken parts on top of the sliced pork all around the bottom of the pot. Do the same with the rest of the meats. Dot the surface with small pieces of butter. Raise the heat and maintain it at a high enough level so that you hear a consistent sizzling. Attending to this level of heat beneath the pot is critical. Care should be taken to adjust the flame up or down to assure that the meat browns but does not fry and that the residues form without burning. This process takes 30 to 40 minutes, as often the meat will first release its juice and these juices must reduce before they attach and begin to take color. When you notice a residue forming, add the onion, carrot, celery, and bay leaf and turn the meat over with a wooden spoon to expose any unbrowned surfaces to the bottom of the pot. Continue turning the meat until it is well colored and the pot is coated with a solidly attached residue. In the event that you notice unevenness in the browning, adjust the pot in relation to the flame to redistribute the heat to bald areas of the pot bottom.

Next, set a colander over a bowl and pour the meat and vegetables into it so that the fat drips free of the meat. If you wish to use some of the meat to make pasta filling, reserve the fat separately. Return the pot to the stove and set it over high heat. Add a few ladles of meat broth; it will sputter violently. Loosen the residue with a wooden spatula. Add a little more meat broth if necessary to facilitate detachment of the residues. Allow the meat broth and residue to reduce to a dark glaze and when it begins to reattach to the bottom, add several more ladles of meat broth. Reduce again as above, and then repeat this process two more times.

Add the meat and aromatic vegetables back to the pot, grate 20 single strokes of fresh nut-

meg over the meat, add the ground cloves, and pour the remaining broth over the meat. Bring the broth to a boil and immediately reduce to the barest simmer. Cover the meat and broth with cooking parchment cut slightly wider than the inner circumference of the pot and presses it closely against the surface of the meat. Cover the pot with a tight-fitting lid. Simmer the meat very gently (use a flame tamer if necessary) for about 2 hours, or until it is tender to the point of a knife. Remove any meat still attached to bone from the pot with a pair of tongs and transfer it to a plate to cool. When the meat is cool, pick it from the bones and place about one third of it back in the pot with the sugo and the rest of the browned trimmings. Discard the bones. Reserve the remainder of the picked meat for stuffing agnolotti or raviolini (see pages 115 and 117).

Using a sturdy food mill fitted with the medium plate, pass the meat and all the liquid through the mill in batches to extract as much juice and meat as you can. If your food mill is small, it may be necessary to chop the meat first. It is not necessary to push every bit of the meat through the sieve: the goal is to obtain a semi-thick, yet easily pourable suspension of dark liquid and meaty bits. If the sugo is too coarse for your liking, pass it through the mill with a finer plate a second time. Correct the sugo to your taste with salt and freshly ground black pepper.

As it first comes out of the pot, this sugo is delicious with semolina-based pasta: small maccheroni such as tubetti, conchiglie, pennette rigate, creste di gallo, or any other shape specially formed to trap sauce. It also works wonderfully with filled pasta such as agnolotti or ravioli stuffed with the leftover braising meats, or with potato gnocchi or tagliatelle made with egg yolks alone (page 107). It is important to use enough of the sugo to coat the pasta thoroughly. Bear in mind, however, that because of the richness of its flavor, a little bit goes a long way. Cook the pasta al dente, drain it well, and combine it with the sugo in a pan. Toss the pasta in the sugo over moderate heat until the pasta has absorbed the flavor and color of the sugo. You may wish to add a small amount of sweet butter to smooth the flavors. Serve with freshly grated Parmigiano-Reggiano. Meat sugo can also be used to flavor risotto that has been moistened with meat broth. Add it two thirds of the way through the cooking process. Sugo is best eaten within the hour of its making, but it will keep fresh for up to 3 or 4 days in the refrigerator and several months in the freezer.

Extending the Natural Juices of a Roast

Sugo derived solely from a single meat or vegetable and by means of a single cooking process is as precious in quantity as it is in purity of flavor (the "essence" of anything is always in short supply!). It is obvious to anyone who has cooked a large roast that there are never sufficient pan drippings to moisten the numerous plates it fills. Similarly, one often comes up short on sugo with braises properly moistened with a minimum amount of liquid during the cooking process. The problem also arises with quick sautés where deglazing and rapid reduction of the pan juices to the right intensity yields an inadequate amount of sauce. At Oliveto and at home, my challenge has been to devise a way to expand the quantities of a sugo from roasts, braises, and sautés so that there is enough to go around without diluting its spontaneous flavor. Admittedly, it is impossible to duplicate by any practical means the purity of a natural jus from roasted meat or the reduced savor of a long-cooked braise. Often this predicament gives me cause to consider whether a roast that I know will be short on its own pan drippings, such as

loin of pork, veal, poultry, or beef sirloin, might be cooked and presented in a way that better suits it. I would much rather eat a juicy chop seared on both sides than a few dry slices of the same meat cooked as a roast. Otherwise, the solution requires an adjacent process of extraction from the roast's trimmings or from additional meat to obtain a flavor and intensity similar to natural pan drippings.

In order to ensure a source of scraps and trimmings, it is wise to buy roasts untrimmed or partially trimmed. In the case of cuts that have limited trimmings, such as leg of lamb or sirloin tip roast, it is necessary to buy a little extra meat for extending the natural juices. Stewing meat from the shoulders of animals is always a good, economical choice but I often utilize other odd cuts such as lamb riblets, pieces of beef flank, or other trimmings that the butcher himself has removed to improve the appearance of a roast.

⏺

Roast Shoulder End Loin of Pork

Bone-in pork loin is a cut that affords a roast and trimmings all in one. My preference is the shoulder-end pork loin cut 10 ribs down from the head-end of the loin. The meat from this part of the pig is darker, more tender, and very moist, especially when turned on the spit. The cut weighs approximately 6½ to 7 pounds. Have your butcher remove the blade bone, chine, and featherbones (making sure these are included in your purchase), and cut the rib bones so that they protrude 2 inches from the end of the meat lying against the bone all along the length of the roast. To further prepare the roast for the oven or the spit, start from one end of the "eye" (the exposed lean when the roast is viewed at either end) and make a long cut against the rib bones to the end of the opposing eye. Cut under this first incision against the bones to remove the "strap" of belly meat and cut it into 1-inch pieces. Reserve all the bones and trimmings and use a cleaver if necessary to chop them down to

small sizes that will fit easily in a pan. Trim any excess fat from the top surface of the roast, leaving about ⅛ inch of cover. You will notice that the shoulder blade end of the loin is more bulky. Trim the roast at this point to an even cylindrical form that mimics the other end of the loin in shape and thickness. This assures that the roast cooks evenly. Finally, using a small, sharp boning knife, cut away the meat between each rib that protrudes from the eye.

Warm a little olive oil in a 6-quart saucepan (mine measures 11 inches across by 4 inches deep), add the scraps and bones, and brown them well over moderate heat, stirring often. Add a small handful of sage leaves. This is the only aromatic ingredient added, the reason being that the intention is to approximate as closely as possible the flavor of the natural sugo that exudes from the roast when it rests after cooking. Adjust the heat higher if necessary in order to encourage the formation of a residue on the bottom of the pot. Pour away any excess fat or the meat and bones will fry instead of render, reducing the amount of residue. Brown the meat and bones for 30 minutes, then raise the heat to high and deglaze the residue with 1 cup of hot meat broth. Scrape up all the residues clinging to the bottom and sides of the pan and reduce rapidly until the residue begins to form again. Repeat this process two times more. Add 3 cups of meat broth, bring to a boil, reduce immediately to a simmer, cover with a tight lid or parchment paper, and cook for 45 minutes.

Remove the lid, take out the bones in the pot, and discard them. Pass the remaining meat and its rendered juices through the medium plate of a food mill, extracting as much of the juice as possible. Prior to joining this flavorful rendering to the natural juices that pool around the rested roast, heat it gently to just above warm. Add the roasting juices to the pan juices and do not reheat them again; otherwise the blood from the roast will coagulate and the pure flavor of the meat juices will be altered. You will now have enough pork sugo for 10 to 12 portions.

Fortifying Quick Pan Sauces

Sugo's meaty flavor also extends and gives substance to the deglazing of the light residues of sautés of thinly sliced or pounded meat and poultry, cuts that require only moments in a hot pan to cook them to the right point. Similarly, thicker, tender slices such as mignonettes of beef tenderloin, and cuts such as boneless breasts of poultry, lamb loin, and chops, reach the right internal temperature without extended browning or a prolonged stay in the pan. Adding sugo produces a far richer sauce than might otherwise be obtained by the common practice of deglazing the pan residues and enriching and/or thickening them with butter and starch. Also, the sugo mingles with yet another meat essence, further compounding its flavor and focusing it on its partnered meat.

The most important requisites of obtaining a residue in sautéing are a very hot pan and the right amount of oil or fat added just beforehand. A hot pan assures that the watery fraction of the meat juices evaporates nearly on contact with the pan, allowing the surface of the meat to caramelize and residues to form on the pan bottom. Caramelization enhances the flavor of both the meat and the sugo. If the pan is not hot enough, browning does not occur and the meat overcooks in the juices that flood the pan. The right amount of oil brings the surfaces of the meat into even contact with the pan bottom and prevents them from adhering too stubbornly Add too much oil and you run the risk of frying the meat. In the case of thick slices this results in the development of a heavy crust because of the extended period of time it takes to brown them; thin slices quickly overcook in too much oil. Maintaining the high temperature necessary for sautéing on a standard home stove with limited BTU output can be problematic, but it is not impossible. In this case, it is wise to avoid using a heavy-bottomed sauté pan or skillet that demands "recovery time" when cooled by the addition of raw meat. Your pan should also be sized to maintain the high heat needed for browning relative to your stove's output. For most home stoves, excluding those with commercial output, a 9-inch pan will best ensure successful sautéing. By far the best sauté pans for home use are cold-rolled steel pans that are thin-gauged and strongly heat conductive. Crowding the pan will also cause it to lose temperature quickly no matter how powerful the heat source. Often this necessitates sautéing in progressive batches.

Cooking pork and veal cutlets, thin beef steaks, escalopes of chicken or turkey, or breasts of pigeon all follow the same basic approach: First, sauté the meat over high heat in a pan large enough to fit it comfortably (an overcrowded pan or insufficient heat will cause the meat to steam rather than brown) and so as to develop a browned residue in the bottom of the pan. Transfer the meat to a warm platter or to individual plates. For each portion you are making, add about 1 ounce of sugo to the pan, scrape up the residues on the bottom of the pan, and quickly reduce by half. Add a small knob of butter to enrich the sugo and continue to reduce it until it develops a slightly thickened consistency. If you prefer a leaner sauce, reduce it first, then enrich it with a little of your best extra-virgin olive oil. Spoon the sauce over the meat and serve at once.

Ragù alla Bolognese

Other than the ragù of southern Italy, that grand two-course meal common to Naples and the surrounding regions, there are a great number of dishes given the same name throughout Italy. In its pure form, ragù is a braised meat sauce. Those based on vegetables, mushrooms, fish, or poultry are ragùs by association. The most well-known meat ragù is found in the north in the cities of the Emilia-Romagna. Despite the fierce controversies that abound in Italy over the rightful claim of origin and authenticity of many dishes, Italians seem to agree that Bologna is the source of a particular type of chopped-meat ragù.

Ragù alla Bolognese has traveled far and wide. In America, it is the progenitor of many home and commercially prepared versions of meat sauce. When most Americans think of spaghetti, unless otherwise qualified, some version of this simmered sauce is understood to partner with it. Ragù alla Bolognese can be either sublime or rather dull. Beyond the proportioning of all its other elements, the difference lies in the choice of beef cut and, most important, whether the cook has taken the time to "build a bottom" to the sauce. Many renditions favor very little browning at all, with no residue development on the bottom of the pot. The sauce made by this method tends to be on the bland end of the flavor scale. I prefer to brown the meat thoroughly and to deglaze the pot at least three times in order to build a foundation of flavor. Milk or cream, an element of every authentic Bolognese ragù, is added very near the end of the process to soften the meat flavors and to smooth its texture.

Various cuts of beef may be used to make Ragù alla Bolognese. Ground "chuck," from the shoulder, is a very suitable choice; it contains approximately 18 to 22 percent fat and makes very good ragù with a mellow intensity. The most sublime, deeply flavored Bolognese, however, is made from the hanger steak or hanging tenderloin, a special-order item from your butcher. It is the only asymmetrical muscle on the cow (meaning there is only one of them), a roughly rectangular muscle that hangs from the diaphragm of the animal and weighs 2 to 2½ pounds. It is very dark and well marbled, and when cooked, it has a sumptuous aroma and persistent flavor akin to oxtail. Nearly as aromatic and deeply beefy in flavor is the beef "skirt." Beef skirt also produces a buttery ragù with a softer, more consistent texture than that made from chuck or hanging tenderloin. It is also the richest of the three because it contains the most fat. Because the hanging tenderloin and the skirt contain more fat that exudes in the process of braising and is eventually skimmed away, both of these cuts yield as much as 20 to 40 percent less than chuck. Hanger also requires 2½ to 3 times as long to cook as chuck and skirt, respectively. Both hanger and skirt are more tenacious than chuck, which tends to break down in the braising process, resulting in a texture that is a mixture of coarse and fine-grained bits. This is by no means a flaw.

Because of the differences in fat content of chuck, hanging tenderloin, and skirt, the cooked yield for equal weights of raw meat varies. Three pounds of each yields 6½ cups, 5¼ cups, and 5 cups, respectively.

Whatever cut of meat you choose, the process for making Ragù alla Bolognese is the same. I favor ragù that is coarsely ground but meltingly soft, allowing it to combine harmoniously in texture with wide-cut egg tagliatelle. For this I grind the meat through a ⅜-inch plate. Most small butchers who grind their own beef should be able to accommodate this request.

There are five steps to the making of Ragù alla Bolognese:

Step 1: Sweating the meat

Warm 3 tablespoons of olive oil in a 6-quart, heavy-bottomed pot. Add 3 pounds of very fresh ground beef and 3½ ounces of coarsely diced pancetta. (As an alternative or addition to pancetta, I often add fine-diced ends of salame, mortadella, or prosciutto.) Turn the heat to high and stir in 2 teaspoons of salt. The meat will rapidly begin to release its liquid. Depending on the cut there will be more or less juice and more or less fat. Maintain the heat on high until the meat juices evaporate and you begin to hear the meat sizzle, indicating that it is beginning to brown. Lower the heat a little to slow the browning. If the meat is not leaving a residue there is probably too much fat in the pan; pour some of the fat away. In this case, the meat is likely to fry, causing it to toughen up rather than to gently brown.

Step 2: Residue formation

Break up 2 tablespoons of sweet butter and distribute the pieces over the surface of the meat. This will aid in the browning process. Stir the pot frequently to expose the unbrowned sides of the ground meat to the bottom of the pot. If you notice that the browning is occurring unevenly, move the pot relative to the flame in order to encourage an even development of residues. Raise or lower the heat if necessary to encourage the development of color (a deep chestnut) or to discourage too much color (blackening). While the residue is forming, cut and set aside a ¼-inch dice of 1 celery stalk, 1 carrot, and 1 small onion. After about 30 minutes you should notice a solidly stuck layer of brown residue covering the bottom of the pot.

Step 3: Add aromatic vegetables

Add the diced vegetables along with 10 to 12 fresh sage leaves and ½ ounce of dry porcini mushrooms broken into small pieces. Lower the heat and allow the vegetables to sweat with the meat for about 15 minutes. Then add ⅜ cup of tomato Conserva (see page 46) or good tomato paste. Stir in the Conserva well to distribute it evenly among the meat and vegetables. Maintain moderate heat and cook the meat and vegetables for 5 minutes more.

Step 4: Deglazing with meat broth

You will notice that the addition of the vegetables (which contain a fair amount of water) and the stirring of the pot have caused most of the residue to loosen. Raise the heat to high and add 1 cup of hot Meat Broth (page 135). Using a wooden spoon, scrape up any residues still clinging to the bottom and low sides of the pot. In addition to loosening the residues, the broth will wash back to the bottom of the pot residues clinging to the solid elements. Allow the broth to evaporate. When the meat appears nearly dry and you notice some re-formation of residue, add another cup of broth. Repeat this process one more time, for 3 cups of broth in all. With progressive additions of broth, the meat will begin to swell as it reabsorbs liquid. Consequently the evaporation process takes a little longer with each broth addition. After the third and final addition and evaporation of broth, add another 3 cups of broth to the pot, make certain that all residues are free of the bottom, reduce to a bare simmer, and cover the pot tightly.

Cook the ragù until it is meltingly tender—approximately 1½ hours for beef chuck and skirt, and 4 hours for hanging tenderloin. Whichever cut you choose, and particularly if you use hanging tenderloin, look in on the pot every 30 minutes and add a little more broth if necessary so that the meat does not go dry.

Step 5: Finishing the ragù: Adding cream
Because I view Ragù alla Bolognese as an indulgence, I don't spare the rich addition of cream. When the ragù is tender, remove it from the heat. If there is an excessive amount of fat (skirt will render the most) skim most but not all of it away. Stir in ½ cup of heavy cream and simmer the meat over very low heat for 5 minutes. Finally, season the ragù to your taste with salt and freshly ground black pepper. Ragù alla Bolognese refrigerates well for several days but is never better than when eaten an hour after it is made with fresh egg tagliatelle.

Southern-Style Ragù: Two Courses, One Preparation

In southern Italy, ragù is traditionally enjoyed as a full meal and eaten in two courses. First comes pasta served with a sugo rendered from the slow braising of meat, then comes the *secondo*, the meat itself, which has become fragrant from its exchange with the sugo and tender over the course of its slow simmering. The savoriness of ragù, like all great braises, results from a languid cooking process during which the meat, aromatic vegetables, and the always-present tomato meld into one harmonious surge of flavor. You can use just about any kind of meat to make ragù—beef, veal, lamb, goat, or pork. Whatever meat you choose, select a braising cut such as the shoulder, the most reliable and generous to yield. Shoulder also allows for the meat to be presented in one piece. Ragù can also be made from beef short ribs, oxtails, or shank. All of these cuts have a great deal of intrinsic flavor relative to the other cuts, and braising breaks down their sturdy texture. I like to use beef shoulder meat, commonly precut and sold as bone-in chuck, a thick slab of marbled beef.

To make ragù you will need a heavy-based casserole or a large sauce pot with a wide surface area and sides that are at least 4 to 5 inches high. The pot should be large enough to contain the meat comfortably. Never use a nonstick pot; its surface prevents a residue from forming. You will also need a food mill to pass the rendering and vegetables for the pasta sugo.

There are four basic steps to ragù. Begin by browning the meat and the vegetables; then deglaze the pan and reduce the liquid several times. Next, set the meat to braise. Finally, when the meat is fully cooked, pass the braising liquid through the food mill to make the pasta sauce.

Ragù
For 6 to 8

Step 1

Heat 2 tablespoons of olive oil in a large pot. Season a 5-pound blade-in beef chuck steak, 2½ inches thick, with salt and pepper on both sides and put it in the pot. Adjust the heat so that the meat sizzles gently. Brown the meat thoroughly on both sides, turning it over every so often as its juices rise to the surface. This will encourage the formation of a residue on the bottom of the pan. Monitor the heat carefully so that the meat and the residue don't burn. This browning process should take about 40 minutes.

Add 4 ounces of thick-sliced pancetta and an equal amount of fresh pork skin or a small pork trotter and set these elements to brown for another 10 minutes. Pork skin or trotter gives the sugo body and sheen. Remove the meat from the pot and transfer it to a platter. Add to the pot a carrot, a rib of celery, and a medium onion, all diced fine, plus ¾ cup of tomato Conserva (see page 46) or good tomato paste. Allow the vegetables to soften and the tomato to lightly brown for about 15 minutes over low heat. Add ½ ounce dried porcini mushrooms broken into small pieces and 4 chopped garlic cloves.

Step 2

When the smell of garlic rises up from the pot, raise the heat to high and add about 1 cup of Meat Broth (page 135). Immediately begin scraping up any residues still clinging to the bottom of the pot. Allow the brown juice to reduce entirely and the residue to form again. Add another cup of broth, stir, reduce, and deglaze again. Repeat this step until you have used about 4 cups of broth. Then stir in 3 cups of chopped stewed tomatoes. Ease the meat back into the pot and pour in another 4 cups of meat broth so that the meat is submerged.

Step 3

Bring the liquid to a very gentle simmer and let the ragù bubble pensively for 2½ to 3 hours, or until it is tender to the tip of a sharp knife. Halfway through the cooking, turn the meat over. If the sugo thickens too much, add a little more broth or water. The meat should remain submerged through most of the cooking. Transfer the meat to an ovenproof platter and spoon enough sugo over it to cover its surface and keep it moist. Cover the platter tightly with foil and keep it in a warm oven.

Pass the sugo through the coarse plate of a food mill. Work vigorously to push through the entire solid content of the sugo. Spoon away and discard any excess fat that rises to the surface of the sugo. You will have enough sugo for at least two meals (12 to 16 portions) and meat enough for one meal. The extra sauce will keep for about 5 days in the refrigerator.

Keeping true to its origins, this sugo is best served with a durum semolina-based pasta such as penne rigate or rigatoni, which has more bite and substance than egg noodles. Figure about ¼ pound of pasta per person. Cook the pasta al dente, drain it, and toss it with half of the passed sugo until well coated. Traditionally, thin-sliced fresh hot peppers, salted and held in vinegar, are offered as a zingy condiment, as well as grated ricotta salata.

Serve the meat with a vegetable that is fresh and in season. Lightly sautéed or steamed vegetables provide a pleasing contrast to the long-cooked meat. Slowly braised vegetables such as fennel, cabbage, or mature green beans work equally well because of their compatibly soft textures and long-cooked flavors.

Varying the Liquid in a Braise

Varying the liquid with which meat residues are deglazed and in which meat is cooked can dramatically change the fundamental flavor of braised dishes. Red wine is a common choice for meat, fowl, and especially wild game because it contributes not only a vinous quality and underlying acidity to balance the richness or gaminess of red meat, but also adds color to enrich the meat's sugo. Red-wine braises are seasonal at Oliveto and echo the darkness of the cooler seasons.

By far the best way to incorporate wine as a flavor in braised dishes is to marinate the meat ahead of time and later use the marinade to moisten the pot. I prefer to apply the marinade hot to a fresh cut of meat; I find that the heat helps the marinade to penetrate the flesh more thoroughly and I do not have to wait days for this to happen. Heating the marinade also tones downs the vegetables and any added spices so that they play their proper role as background support in the finished braise. Wines most suitable for braising are bright and fruity without excessive tannin or acidity. It is of course possible to use big, structured wines; classic Stracotto al Barolo is a case in point. But with such a wine some compensation may be necessary for the tannin and acidity that concentrates in the meat renderings. You can mitigate this buildup by selecting a cut of meat richer in connective tissue and fat and so able to stand up to the wine. If using a leaner cut of meat, elements such as pork trotter or skin or cured meat such as pancetta or prosciutto can be combined in the base with a higher percentage of sweet vegetables such as carrot to help counter harsh characteristics of the wine.

✑ Stracotto

In Italian, the word *stracotto* has two related usages. The first refers to any food that has been overcooked. Stracotto also describes a dish of braised meat that is moistened with wine and meltingly tender but still intact. The tradition of stracotto is to use mature animals, particularly beef but also horsemeat and donkey in certain regions, that require a very lengthy stay, 6 to 8 hours, in the braising pot. Even by Italian standards, this is a long cooking time, earning the prefix "stra-," which always connotes excess of some sort. I make stracotto with a dense cut of meat, the flat bottom round that comes from the larger outside round of beef hind leg. The flat bottom round, a working muscle, is one of the leanest of the entire hindquarter of beef, containing virtually no intermuscular fat. As such, it is best suited to moist, slow cooking at moderate temperature and to a marinade that further tenderizes it. I also find it necessary to lard this cut with fat in order to keep it moist and to add a small amount of gelatinous pork to improve the quality of the sugo. When purchasing the beef, ask for approximately 6 pounds cut to yield two roughly uniform roasts, approximately 4 inches thick with a thin fat cover on one side. The even 4-inch thickness ensures that the meat cooks at the same rate throughout and allows for portioned slices that fit attractively on the plate.

Begin with a 3-pound roast and tie it tight with kitchen twine every inch along its length. To lard the roast, cut strips of fresh pork back fat an inch longer than the length of the roast. The strips should be about ⅜ inch square. Using a larding needle, insert the strips roughly 1 inch apart from each other and from the outside edge of the roast. To lard a 4-inch-thick roast, you will need 5 to 6 strips of fat. Lard the other roast similarly. Next, cut one fresh pork trotter into 4 to 5 pieces. Repeat the process with the other roast.

To make the marinade, finely dice 1 carrot, 1 celery stalk, and 1 small onion. Put the vegetables in a pot and add 1 bottle of red wine along with a small sprig of rosemary, a very small piece of cinnamon stick, 3 whole cloves, 2 sliced garlic cloves, and 2 or 3 crushed juniper berries.

Turn the heat to high and bring the marinade to a boil. Transfer the roasts and the pork trotter pieces to a container that will allow both roasts to be nearly entirely submerged. Immediately pour the marinade over the roasts. Let cool to room temperature, then cover and store in the refrigerator for 48 hours. After the first day, turn the roasts over to allow the exposed side to be submerged for the second day.

Remove both roasts and pork trotter from the marinade, push any vegetables clinging to them back into the marinade, and pat them dry with paper towels. Choose a wide pot that is at least 4 inches deep and that will contain the meat with a minimum of empty space around it at the bottom. Brown the roasts and pork trotter over moderate heat for 30 minutes turning them over often and exposing their surfaces to all parts of the bottom of the pan. The goal is to brown the surfaces of the meat and at the same time build a residue across the bottom of the pot. Move the pot on the flame if you notice cool spots where residues are not forming. After browning the meat and allowing the residue to form, remove the meat from the pan and transfer it to a plate off the heat. Pour the marinade through a sieve with a bowl beneath to capture the vegetables and spices. Add the vegetables and spices from the marinade to the pot and sweat them over moderate heat for 10 minutes. This will cause the residue to lift off the bottom. Thoroughly stir in 1 tablespoon of flour. Add 2 tablespoons of saba or vin cotto (concentrated grape juice, see Sources and Resources, page 260) and the wine from the marinade. Place the meat and pork trotter back in the pot and bring to a slow boil. Remove the pot from the heat and cover it tightly. Place the pot in a 300°F. oven for approximately 3½ hours, or until a skewer inserted to the center of the meat yields easily. If your roast is slightly thicker or thinner than specified above, the cooking time will vary. It is wise to check a 4-inch-thick roast at the 3-hour mark in case of oven irregularity or some other factor that may affect cooking time. The goal of cooking stracotto of beef is to arrive at the point where the meat is fully tender and moist but not falling apart.

Allow the meat to cool together with the juices in the braising pan. Remove the meat and cut away the strings binding it. Discard the trotter pieces and pass the sugo through a sieve over a bowl or large glass measuring cup (glass will allow you to see the fat more clearly as it separates from the clear juice below) to capture the vegetables. Skim away any fat that has accumulated at the surface of the sugo; you should end up with as much liquid as you added, if not slightly more. Return the sugo to the pot and cook over medium heat until reduced by one third to one half to a slightly thickened consistency. Grind in fresh black pepper to taste. When the meat is cool, cut it evenly into thin slices about ¼ inch thick.

To serve, transfer the slices to a large sauté pan that holds them comfortably with minimal overlapping. Pour the sugo over all. Warm the meat gently in the sugo and at the same time allow it to further reduce around the meat to an intense yet still pourable consistency. Serve on individual plates with buttery mashed potatoes and more of the wine you used to make the marinade.

Aromatic Focus

Another method of altering and enhancing the fundamental flavor of a braise and its sugo is to proportion the aromatic addition, or base it entirely, on a complementary flavor so that *it*, rather than the flavor of the meat rendering, stands in relief. Sturdy varieties of wild mushrooms are delicious with just about any meat or poultry. Fennel, particularly the wild variety, shares a strong affinity with fish, as does the aromatic rind of citrus fruit. In the height of summer, when multiple varieties of peppers and onions hit their peak, I always think of braises of pork, which welcome the sweet mellowness of stewed sweet peppers or new onion.

Gelatinous cuts of meat such as lamb shanks, oxtails, or pork shoulder hocks that transform to a melting texture with slow cooking and leave the impression of richness are greatly enhanced and offset by the sharpness of vinegar. Because

of its pungency, vinegar is first reduced to focus its flavor in the base, and then combined with meat broth. Pork shoulder hocks are more often available smoked than fresh and are undervalued as meat that can stand on its own. The hock is a cut just below the shoulder to a point just above the upper knee joint of the foreleg.

Pork Hocks Agrodolce

Because bone-in pork hocks make an unwieldy portion, I prefer to bone and tie them before braising. Bone-in hocks weigh about 1¼ pounds apiece. Removing the bone is a simple matter that leaves ¾ pound of meat. Cut along one side of the short and very visible bone that runs through the hock, then the other, to remove the meat (save the bones for future meat broth). Season the hock meat on the side you cut away from the bone and roll it up into a rough heart-shaped form. Tie the meat to secure it firmly.

Choose a heavy-bottomed pot capable of containing 6 hocks comfortably side by side. (I use a pot that is 12 inches in diameter.) Salt and pepper the outside of the shanks and brown them slowly over moderate heat in 4 tablespoons of olive oil, turning the shanks to expose the raw surfaces to the bottom of the pot. Adjust the flame to encourage even browning and the buildup of residues on the bottom. This process will take about 30 minutes. Remove the hocks from the pot and transfer them to a platter. Pour off any excess rendered fat and oil, leaving a thin film.

Add 2 red onions and 2 medium-size carrots, all cut into ¼-inch dice, plus 6 sliced cloves of garlic, a small sprig of rosemary, and a few crushed juniper berries. Stew the vegetables for 10 minutes until softened, then add 3 tablespoons tomato Conserva (page 46) or good tomato paste and cook for an additional 5 minutes. Stir the vegetables often with a wooden spoon. Because of the water content in the vegetables, the residues will release easily with the stirring. Raise the heat and add ½ cup of condiment-grade balsamico and ¼ cup vin cotto. Cook until reduced by half. Add the browned hocks to the pot, and then add 4½ cups hot Meat Broth (page 135). Bring the liquid slowly to the boil, reduce to a simmer and transfer the pot to a 325°F. oven. Braise for 2½ hours, or until tender. Turn the hocks every 30 minutes so that their exposed sides are fully bathed in the braising liquid (open cooking requires that the hocks be turned so that the exposed surfaces do not dry out). Turning also allows the hocks and the juices, tomato Conserva, and vin cotto that cling to the meat to continue to reduce and caramelize. The turning under of these caramelized surfaces contributes to the depth of color and added flavor in the finished dish.

Transfer the hocks to warm plates or to a platter. Pass the braising liquid and vegetables through the fine sieve of a food mill and return to the pot. Reduce the sugo by about half to a viscous consistency over high heat. While the sugo is reducing, remove the strings binding the hocks. Season the sugo with ½ teaspoon of finely ground black pepper, pour it over the hocks, and serve at once.

Braising without a Residue

Certain cuts of meat and poultry are better suited to bottom-up braising with minimal or no residue formation. In the case of meat like veal, young spring lamb, or rabbit, gentle browning or no browning at all yields a sugo that is more in keeping with the nature of the meat. With braising cuts of duck or chicken (the legs and wings), it is virtually impossible to develop a residue from browning the skin side because of its high fat content. While the skin caramelizes, it protects the flesh from direct exposure to the heat and prevents it from giving up its flavorful juices. What is rendered in the pan is largely fat. In the case of legs cut free from the carcass, browning them on their flesh side

inevitably results in the formation of a crust that only makes for dry, tough eating. My method instead is to render as much as possible of the skin-side fat, discard it so that the sugo is not greasy, and then cook the legs flesh side down in the braising liquid in an open pan. In order to ensure that the skin remains crisp and the flesh becomes fully tender, it is important to choose a pan that fits however many legs you wish to cook side by side with a small amount of separation, and to bring the level of the braising liquid to the point where the skin meets the flesh. This way, the meat renders directly into the braising liquid.

Duck Legs Braised in Red Wine

Salt and pepper six fresh duck legs (2½ pounds). If you divide the legs from whole birds yourself, press the leg of the bird against its breast so that the skin is not tensioned before you release it with the knife. Make a cut that guarantees the skin is fully covering the knee joint, trace around the inner thigh to the back of the bird, and cut under the "oyster." Trace a line through the flesh down the center backbone. Free the hipbone from its joint and cut the leg free from the back of the bird.

Brown the legs, skin side down, over moderate heat in a small amount of olive oil. As the fat renders from the skin, pour it off. Over the course of the 20 minutes it takes to brown the skin, it will be necessary to pour off the fat 2 to 3 times. Remove the legs from the pan and transfer them to a platter. Add 6 medium-size shallots, peeled and diced (6 ounces), and a few sprigs of fresh thyme. Stir the shallots and thyme together and cook them over medium heat for 5 minutes. Add 1½ cups of good, fruity red dry wine and 2 cups of poultry or meat broth (see Meat Broth, page 135) and bring to a boil. Arrange the legs in a baking dish or casserole skin side up so that they fit comfortably side by side. Add the wine and broth, shallots, and herbs. Brush any herbs and shallots on the skin into the liquid so that it is fully exposed to the heat.

Braise the legs uncovered in a moderate oven (350°F.) for 1¼ hours, or until they yield easily to the point of a knife. The point of open braising is to keep the skin crisp and to allow for concentration of sauce as the duck cooks.

Remove the legs from the liquid, spooning away any excess fat at the surface, and pass the braising juices through the finest plate of a food mill, scraping in as much of the shallots as possible. If the sugo is suitably thickened and its flavor has a fulfilling intensity, simply warm the legs, skin side up, in the passed sugo. Otherwise, reduce the sugo further, together with the legs, until you are satisfied with its flavor.

Rabbit in Bianco

Rabbit is the most delicate in flavor of all game and is virtually without fat. In order to preserve its muted character I prefer to stew it in a mixture of olive oil and water with minimal aromatics and no preliminary browning.

If you find rabbit to be too bland or lean to your taste, you may consider adding to the finished sugo a little mustard, capers or olives, softened spring garlic, your favorite fresh herb, or a good viscous condiment-grade balsamico. In a richer version that preserves the subtle taste of rabbit, a little cream, egg yolk, lemon juice, and grated Parmigiano can be added and very gently warmed with the sugo just prior to serving. Stewed young artichokes make a superb accompaniment.

Sectioning the rabbit

Purchase a nice plump rabbit weighing about 3½ pounds. Turn the rabbit on its back. Remove the back legs by making a perpendicular cut through the backbone at the very top of the legs. Open the two attached legs and split them apart by making a cut down the center vertebrae.

Then cut each thigh away from the leg, 1 inch above the knee joint.

Make another cut across the length of the rabbit at the beginning of the rib cage to remove the saddle (loin) and split it along the backbone. Make a perpendicular cut in each half to yield 4 pieces that include the belly flaps and kidneys, if attached.

Cut the rib cage and shoulder section in half along the backbone and through the neck. Separate each half at the shoulder to yield 4 pieces, 2 from the rib section and 2 shoulders with forelegs.

Return to the saddle sections. Wrap the belly flaps extending from the loin muscles around the meat and bone and secure with twine.

Braising

Place the rabbit in a deep skillet (approximately 11 inches wide by 4 inches deep) that will hold it snugly in a single layer. Pour 3 ounces of extra-virgin olive oil and 1 cup of cold water over the rabbit. Season the rabbit well with salt only. Quarter and slice thin the white of 1 medium leek, plus 1 large garlic clove. Scatter the leeks and garlic and 3 or 4 sprigs of thyme over the rabbit. The oil and water mixture should come about halfway up the sides of the rabbit pieces. Bring to a simmer over moderate heat, then stir the aromatics into the rabbit pieces and reduce the flame as low as it will go. Cover with a tight-fitting lid.

Simmer the rabbit, turning the pieces over every 30 minutes, for 1½ hours, or until the leg muscle (the densest muscle and therefore the bellwether of the process) yields easily to the point of a knife. Transfer the rabbit to a warm platter, reduce the sugo until you are happy with its flavor, and spoon a little over each piece.

Warm Salad of Atlantic Cod
with Tomatoes, Fish Essence,
and Olive Oil

Fresh tomatoes give focus to bottom-up fish extractions perfumed with olive oil in a loose emulsion. The following sauce is particularly delicious with Atlantic cod, the bones and heads of which make a refined essence without a forceful, fishy flavor. Atlantic cod is perhaps the most delicate fish available these days in both texture and flavor. It is also very lean, but if cooked carefully it can be quite moist, retaining its silken texture. The tomatoes cut into a small dice, in combination with the fish essence, lend a soft acidity. This is boosted by the vinaigrette used to warm the blanched curly endive or frisée on which the fish sits.

To make 4 portions, request from your fishmonger a fresh, 12- to 14-ounce fillet of Atlantic cod and with it the bones from which it was removed. Ask for a piece of the head if available. Cut up the bones and head into rough 3-inch pieces, cut away any pieces of the gills, and wash the bones well to remove any bits of the liver. To portion the fillet, first remove the pin bones in the thickest portion with fish pliers. Next, locate the row of bones running vertically down the middle of the fillet by running your finger down the middle length of the fillet. Use a sharp knife to cut on either side of the bones and remove and reserve the strip containing them. Beginning at the thick end, cut the fillet on the bias into slices about ¼ inch thick.

To a heavy pot that will accommodate the bones in a single layer, add enough olive oil to coat the bottom of the pot, and warm it over medium heat. Add the fish bones to the pot. Slice a small piece of celery, a small carrot, and the white of 1 small leek and add them to the pot, as well as a bay leaf, a little fresh thyme, and sprigs of flat-leaf parsley. Cover the pot and allow the bones to sweat over moderate heat, stirring every so often to prevent them from sticking to the bottom. Add a small amount of water to bring the level of liquid to about half that of the solids, bring to a gentle boil, then remove the pot from the heat. Let stand for 5 minutes, then strain this broth through a fine conical sieve. Return the broth to a clean, wide sauté pan and reduce it rapidly by half to two thirds; it will appear foamy and emulsified. Taste it for intensity and texture. It should be slightly thickened and will have a subtle but persistent fish flavor. While the sauce is reducing, peel, seed, and finely dice a few ripe tomatoes. Add the tomato dice directly to the warm fish essence, add salt and pepper to taste, and set it aside. Next make a vinaigrette with finely minced shallots, a suggestion of garlic, champagne vinegar, olive oil, salt, and pepper.

To cook the fish, salt the fish slices, warm a sauté pan, add a little olive oil, and place the slices in the pan. A nonstick pan is most reliable for cod, as this fish tends to break very easily. Cook the fish over a very gentle heat, as though you were pan-poaching it (this will help to preserve its texture and moisture). It shouldn't take but a few minutes. Turn off the heat when the fish is nearly fully cooked and let it rest in the pan.

Warm the vinaigrette in a sauté pan set over very moderate heat so as not to brown the shallots. Add 4 small handfuls of curly endive or frisée, turn off the heat, and toss the lettuce together quickly. Arrange the lettuces onto individual warm plates, carefully place a few slices of fish on top of the wilted salad, and spoon the sauce over and around the fish.

Pan-Roasting

Pan roasting is an extended browning process that takes place in an open pan with little or no fat. Unlike roasting in the oven or before a live fire, only the pan bottom becomes dry and hot. As such, pan roasting is another kind of bottom-up cooking that coaxes the slow formation of residues on the floor of the pan. Since meats best suited to the process are cut thick, it also cooks them through very gradually, using heat transferred from the bottom of the pan alone. This method allows for better control of browning and of the internal temperature and produces a very moist, succulent quality in the finished meat. Cuts of meat and poultry suited to pan roasting contain either bones or connective tissue, and are moderately tough or dense in their raw state. Lamb and pork shoulder blade chops or shoulder-end loin chops; sectioned joints of chicken, pigeon, duck, and rabbit; skirt and flank of beef; and meaty pork ribs are ideal. Thick fillet cuts of large fish that have high oil content such as large salmon, swordfish, and snapper are also good candidates for pan roasting.

Pan-Roasted Chicken

Short of turning chicken on a spit over live wood embers, I know of no better process for cooking chicken, nor one that delivers more satisfying or true flavors. Sectioned, pan-roasted chicken takes no more time to make overall than one roasted whole in the oven. It does however require more attention to the flame and a patient and repeated return to the pan to adjust the position of the meat. I like to make this dish when I am not distracted or in a hurry to get lunch or dinner on the table. I make it for my family or occasions with good friends who particularly appreciate the taste and aroma of home cooking. Since it takes an hour or slightly more and is best eaten at once, it is unlikely that you would ever find this dish in a restaurant. I have eaten many dishes made by this process in Italian households—chicken of course, but also guinea fowl and pheasant, wild hare, duck, and shoulder of lamb. It is the very manifestation of the common exclamation *saporito,* meaning richly flavored and justly seasoned.

Sectioning the bird

Purchase a plump whole roasting hen weighing 4 to 5 pounds or meaty, bone-in, presectioned chicken. Bone-in chicken helps to conduct heat slowly to the flesh in pan roasting. It goes without saying that meat is always moister and more succulent cooked on the bone. It is important when sectioning a whole chicken to do so in such a way as to maintain coverage of the skin on the individual pieces and to plan your cuts to yield pieces that are as flat as possible. This enables even browning and less turning of the pieces in the pan. Obviously this is not possible with rounded sections such as the leg and the head-end section of the breast.

Cut away the feet if still attached. Lift the flap of skin at the neck cavity and sever the entire neck at the point at which it attaches to the carcass. Cut both wings at the second elbow joint, leaving the drumette attached to the breast. Turn the chicken breast-side down. Using a sharp chef's knife and starting from the tail of the bird angled up toward your knife, cut a straight line through the center of the backbone through the neck end of the bird using a deliberate forward motion of the heavy end of the knife. Open the bird and cut directly through the center of the breastbone to divide it in two. Next cut the thigh and leg away from the breast, taking care to leave the skin intact on all surfaces. Find the knee joint—bend the leg away from then toward the thigh and you will see the joint easily—and cut the leg free from the thigh. Divide the thigh into 3 pieces. The easiest way to accomplish this is by smoothing the skin over the entire thigh, turning it skin side down, and delivering a sharp and decisive chop through the flesh and bone. Divide the breast in three pieces similarly; smooth the skin on the breast and turn it skin side down. Chop roughly parallel to the shoulder joint, yielding a meaty piece that includes the breast and drumette. Then turn the breast and chop it in half perpendicular to its length. Do the same with the other half of the bird.

Cooking the bird

In order to contain the chicken pieces you will need a wide, heavy-bottomed sauté pan or two smaller ones. Roasting hens generally contain enough fat so that it is not necessary to add oil or any other fat to the pan. Bear in mind that not having oil between the skin and pan bottom from the start means that the chicken will tend to stick as juices under the skin run free and begin to caramelize. The addition of oil would help to prevent this but would also reduce the residue formation. For this reason, I prefer not to use it. One trick to keep the skin from entirely sticking is to lift the pieces several times in the early stages of browning, each time gently detaching them from the pan bottom. Some of the fat released when the skin comes into contact with the hot pan then runs under the pieces to lubricate them. But this is not a critical step. Remember that it is flavor you are after and not perfectly intact skin. The browned skin that stubbornly adheres when you are ready to transfer the chicken to a platter for service is stirred up in the final deglazing and inevitably ends up on the chicken in the *jus*. Ugly but delicious!

Warm the pan over moderately high heat. Salt and pepper both sides of the chicken. Arrange the chicken pieces skin side down in the dry pan. Sprinkle the picked leaves of one sprig of fresh rosemary over the chicken. Adjust the heat so that you hear a consistent sizzling. The temperature of the pan should be high enough to encourage progressive browning but not so high that the residues or the skin burns.

Adjust the pan relative to the heat source if you notice any unevenness in the browning. Using a pair of tongs, turn the pieces to expose all sides that have skin attached to the pan bottom. Pay particular attention to the breast pieces, which take less overall time to cook relative to the leg and thigh sections. When the skin sides of the breasts are nicely browned, "park" them on top of the other joints until you are ready to turn all pieces at once onto their second sides. Parking the breast pieces stops the cooking on the second side and assures that they will be as moist as the leg and thigh pieces.

When the thigh and leg sections are nicely browned, lower the heat and turn them over to finish the cooking. Distribute the breast sections similarly. Browning on the skin side takes approximately 40 minutes. Allow another 20 to 25 minutes to complete the cooking on the second side.

Serving

Transfer the chicken to a warm platter. Raise the heat to high and deglaze the pan with 1 cup of hot water. Use a wooden spoon to scrape up the residues and reduce by half or until the sugo has the intensity you like. Spoon the sugo directly over the chicken pieces, making sure to bathe them evenly. Serve at once with lemon slices.

Saltimbocca of Chicken

I've always liked the whimsical suggestion that a food would be so appetizing that it would jump directly from the plate to my mouth. This is the promise of saltimbocca, in its classic Roman rendition, a tender scaloppine of veal layered with prosciutto and sage and quickly sautéed in butter. Sometimes cheese such as mozzarella or fontina is melted over the top and a pan sauce is made by simply loosening any residues in the pan with wine or meat broth, creating a delicate brown emulsion as it joins with the previously added butter.

Chicken saltimbocca is my own spin-off of the classic version. It is reminiscent of the original in both flavor and savor although, in preparation, it more closely resembles chicken Kiev: rather than applying the prosciutto, sage, and cheese to the outside, they are placed in the interior of the butterflied breast.

Purchase 2 boneless chicken breasts. Or, if you prefer to buy a whole bird and use the remaining joints and carcass for other purposes, remove the breasts of one chicken so that each breast is entirely covered with skin. Set the bird breast side up and make an incision on either side of the breast bone. Position your knife close to the rib cage and collarbones. Cut and pull the breast gently away from the carcass. Do not include the wing joint. When most of the meat is drawn away from the bones, cut the skin between the leg and breast so that all of the breast meat is covered with the skin. Free the breast from the bones. Turn the breast on the skin side and remove and reserve the small tapering muscle (this muscle is responsible for raising the wing) sometimes called the fillet. Next, butterfly the breast meat: Beginning at the center line of the chicken breast, make a lateral cut nearly to the edge of the breast so as to open an attached flap on one side. Do the same on the other side. Salt and pepper the butterflied breast lightly on this cut side.

Place a small sage leaf and a small slice of fontina cheese wrapped in prosciutto in the pocket between the flaps. Using a meat hammer or rolling pin, flatten the fillet referred to above to a shape that will cover the pocket. Cover the prosciutto and cheese with the pounded fillet, close the flaps over the filling, and secure the closure with toothpicks from flap to flap. Turn the breasts on their skin side and season them with salt and pepper.

The goal in cooking Saltimbocca of Chicken is to have crisp, rendered skin and moist meat underneath. To this end, most of the cooking takes place on the skin side. Bear in mind that, once the chicken is turned, heat will transfer very quickly through the unprotected flesh.

Warm a heavy-bottomed pan that will contain the breasts with minimal space around the edges. Add a very small amount of olive oil. When the oil is hot, place the breasts skin side down in the pan. Adjust the heat after a few minutes so that the breasts sizzle consistently, and maintain this heat throughout the cooking. When the breasts are thoroughly browned (the time will vary according to how large the breasts are and how much fat is in the skin), carefully remove them from the pan. Discard any excess rendered fat, return the pan to the flame, raise the heat, and deglaze with Meat Broth (page 135) or water to create a little sugo. Reduce the liquid in the pan slightly and arrange the chicken breasts back in the pan skin side up. Cooking the cut side of the breasts in the sugo both protects this tender side of the chicken from toughening and allows for the release of its juices, enabling them to mingle with the sugo. When the chicken breasts are firm to the touch, transfer them to a warm platter or to individual plates and spoon a little sugo over each. Remove the toothpicks from each breast and serve.

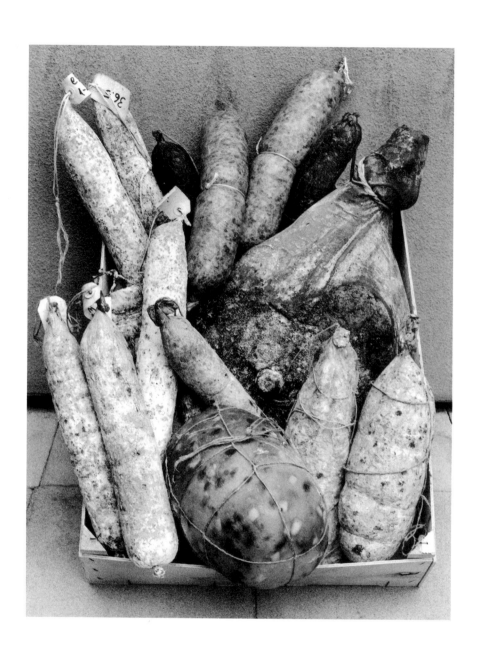

The Whole Hog

Introduction

My brother saw a pig root in a field,
And saw too its whole lovely body yield
To this desire which deepened out of need
So that in wriggling through the mud and weed
To eat and dig were one athletic joy.
When we who are the overlords destroy our
Ranging vassals, we can therefore taste
The muscle of delighted interest
We make into ourselves. . . .
                    – Thom Gunn

Some of the most unforgettable experiences of my life have had to do, in one way or another, with pigs. I remember the enormous box our family would receive each year from my emigrant Italian grandparents. They had settled in Chicago in the first quarter of the century and had purchased a building with adjacent storefronts on the South Side. One was dedicated to clothes for everyday use and was managed by my grandmother; the other was an Italian grocery that specialized in cured meats made by my grandfather, Giovanni. His prosciutto and salame were legendary in the neighborhood, where a primarily Italian clientele with nostalgia for the flavors of the old country prized the pungent smells of aging cheese and dried wild mushrooms and the down-home aroma of house-cured meats. Each year around Christmastime the box would arrive. Opening it would reveal bulk packs of tube socks, skirts, blouses, and underwear for our family, still growing in number after five children. Digging farther down, the smell of fabric sizing was upstaged by a funky animal aroma. There, loosely wrapped in butcher paper, was a fully ripened salame, at least two feet long and four inches in diameter, its carefully spaced trusses slackened from the drying and with the cellar mold still clinging to it.

Because of this annual arrival I have always had a special fondness for *soppressata,* as my grandfather called it, though none since has rivaled it. It was a mosaic of rose-colored pork, coarse-textured but seamlessly bound, rustic in appearance but silky on the tongue. Nearly eight months of aging in a chilly basement cellar left a patina of flavor, not so much faded as grown rich through my grandfather's benign neglect. If I tried hard, I could pick up hints of what it might contain, but the overall effect resisted scrutiny, married as it was to a complex of yeasted fruitiness, subtle spices, and the gaminess of an old sock. The salame was mildly salty and its mellow, garlicky flavors were underscored by a noticeable tang that made my lips smack.

Years later, I asked my grandmother for the recipe. But to my remembered taste it was so much more than her description of its simple elements. It occurred to me then, as it does now, that with foods like grapes and milk that transform to wine and cheese through human intervention, the effects of time and nature are a kind of miracle. Through the bright novelty of the first taste we sense the delicious whole; familiarity enlightens the first impression that nevertheless remains undeducible. Whatever my grandfather did, and knew to leave to be done, amounted to a similar alchemy. Salame, at first "made," then left to ripen on its own, is transubstantiation. I have always been drawn to making food that requires my intervention but where other more obscure forces are also at work. Some element of the process or its outcome always keeps me wondering. Under such circumstances, to arrive at something delicious is both an exciting discovery and an accomplishment, a fitting blend of intuition and grace.

With my ravenous sisters after it, my grandfather's soppressata disappeared quickly and my appetite for salame grew accordingly. Fortunately, our family kept credit with Mario's corner grocery very near our home, and Mario's offered a cold case of various cured meats. Under the guise of an errand for my mother I would regularly scribble in the debit book for a half pound or so of "Genoa," my favorite. Then I'd consume all traces of the purchase, on my way home from school, neat, no condiment required, between the crusty enclosure of dark-bake San Francisco sourdough. During the long afternoon hours of junior high, my appetite, piqued almost painfully by the anticipation of the salty tang and the winy appeal of salame, would literally drive me to distraction. If it weren't for salame, I would probably now be better at algebra.

My romance with salame continued through high school. Through a family friend, I landed my first serious job at Maison Gourmet in San Francisco, a fabulous Italian delicatessen that packed one 30-foot counter with cured sausages of wide provenance. On one side were German Thuringer, teewurst, metwurst, and pale fleischwurst; on the other were cervelat, Krakow, Lebanon bologna, and various smoked sausages. Liver sausages in sewn hog bungs and fresh coarse-ground *luganega* sausage kept company with naked-looking wieners of every dimension—beef franks, bratwurst, garlic sausage, and skinny veal sausage bound in sheep casing. There was an entire section devoted to hams and whole cuts, boiled, roasted, smoked, glazed, and dry-cured. Westphalian ham was ingeniously shipped in a long narrow can and various types of prosciutto, more or less salty, were stacked next to hot and "sweet" coppa, pancetta, and American salted pork belly. Dry-cured and cooked sausages sold the best, and the most popular of these were presliced and piled in mountainous display for more ready sale. Apart from long oblong slices of local dry salame, there was *galantina*, a very coarse, wide-diameter sausage whose predominant component was beef heart; *zampino*, ground pork shanks and head trimmings boiled in a thin pig skin surround; and gloriously Rubenesque mortadella. In the corners of the case were the odd specialties with evocative names: *Landjäger*, a dry, pressed sausage sold in pairs traditionally designed to be looped around the belt of a soldier and eaten as field rations; *Biroldo*, a marvelous spiced blood sausage from Lucca, studded with raisins and pine nuts; and "hot hog head cheese," the favorite of southerners.

Next to this counter and constituting a separate department was the grandest fresh meat display that I have ever known, manned by a cast of butchers whose humor was as raw as the meats they sold. "How do you cook kidneys?" a customer might call out. "Boil the piss out of 'em" was the response. Butchers, I observed, tend to resemble what they do and are in general of two visual types: lean, muscular, and well trimmed like the elegant steaks they lay out, or pale, plump, and as lumbering as a fatted sow. I was also riveted by the stark, snow-white beauty of split pork carcasses, and by the lithe contours of whole suckling pigs, like so many nudes hanging in the dim light of a meat locker.

All of us who worked in the delicatessen and butcher shop were required to pay dues to the meat-cutter's union. Primed on my grandfather's soppressata and Mario's salame, I was more than pleased to join a trade that offered such accessibility and by age sixteen, I had made journeyman status. I spent nearly every weekend throughout high school peddling sausage and honing my knife skills. In large part it is to this early experience of food, and pork flesh in particular (as well as the characters with whom I kept company), that I attribute my continued fascination with pig in every form.

Later, as part of an early trip I made to Italy with the idea of understanding Italian cooking, I had the opportunity to take part in the annual farm tradition of slaughtering a pig in late December. A waiter with whom I worked at a restaurant in the country south of Florence arranged for me to use my knife skills in assisting the *norcino*, a kind of roaming pork specialist who goes from farm to farm to carry out the slaughter and to supervise the making of the cured meats that stock the family larder for the coming year. I arrived at the farm just after sunup and was introduced to a stocky man with close-set eyes and a severe expression who nodded but did not return my *"buon giorno."* Together we walked in silence to the pigpen, where the enormous boar that he had castrated months earlier and that now weighed at least 350 pounds was nosing a scattering of grain. Immediately, the manner of the norcino softened to the tenor of an affectionate pet owner; he began to coo at the pig, which responded at first with a long, reticent gaze, then returned to the business of munching. With measured steps around the pen and the promise of a further bucket of treats, the norcino singsonged the pig to the adjacent barn's stone floor, which had been scrubbed clean. In the corner of the barn with an opening to the sky, an enormous cauldron of water had been put to the boil over a wood fire. He poured down the bucket of corn, stroked the head of the pig affectionately as it drooped toward the feed, and softly uttered the first human words of the day, *"La ringrazio"*—a formal thank you. With that, he drew a small revolver from his pocket and calmly shot the pig just above the eyes. Stunned at first by the sharp crack of the shot, the pig then reacted to the leaden reality, slumped heavily on its side, and squealed mournfully. The norcino now moved slowly but deliberately and with the help of two others beside myself moved the twitching animal to the edge of the barn opening a few feet away. With the head of the pig now positioned over a low stone drop-off, the norcino plunged a knife to the throat and with a deft turn to the jugular allowed the blood, a shocking opaque cranberry, to pour out rhythmically into a white porcelain basin set beneath, steam rising. The pig lurched and heaved, all its involuntary power now seemingly intent on empty-ing itself. The pig fell after just a few minutes, although to me it seemed an impossibly long time. We transferred the bled pig in one coordinated heaving motion to a ladder-like bier made of stout chestnut boughs and carried it to the cauldron. My job was to douse the pig continually with hot water while three others worked furiously to scrape the pig free of the hair using small paddles to which inverted bottle caps had been nailed. In a half hour's time, the pig was as clean as a newborn. We then raised one end of the support and the norcino opened the belly of the pig. He removed the liver, heart, spleen, lungs, stomach, and kidneys, and sent sec-tions of the intestine to be flushed. He severed the head, rinsed it, and instructed me to submerge it and the fore trotters in what remained of the boiling water. Later he tossed in numerous hand-fuls of salt, whole dried peperoncino, peppercorns, and a mixture of crushed spices. Standing over the open carcass, he used a very sharp, long-handled axe to split the pig lengthwise in two. The pig was then flushed with cold water and hung from a rafter to dry in the cold air. We calmed ourselves with espresso, my own corrected with a strong splash of grappa.

Afterward, the norcino set about preparing the seasonings for the various cuts. While I boned and skinned the loins and shoul-ders, he sculpted the massive legs, cut high above the waist of the pig. He first freed the aitchbone, cleaned the cut side of silverskin,

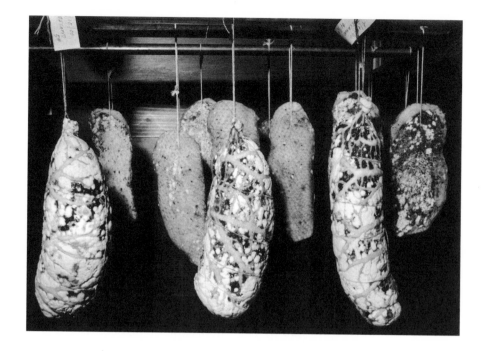

glands, and extra skin, and with two deft semi-circular cuts, beveled the inch and a half of fat around the top of the legs to create the classic drumstick form of prosciutto. He massaged each leg with a mixture of salt, saltpeter, ground black pepper, and chopped garlic, measured entirely by eye. The legs were then transferred to a slanted wooden rack in a cold corner of the barn, a metal pan set beneath, and the salt cure was reapplied so that it covered the cut face. Here the prosciutti would sit for 40 to 45 days to take the salt and to drip. Every so often, the prosciutti would be shifted so that gravity would pull salt into the muscles positioned lowest on the slant boards. If the salt appeared like the bald places on a mountain undergoing snowmelt, the norcino would dust the leg with a little more. It was through a combination of these adjustments, and his skill in "reading" the ham—noticing visually and through a gradual firming of its various muscles—that the norcino would judge the prosciutto ready to be hung to dry.

With the precious hams disposed of, we all then went swiftly to work, separating the lean from the fat, the bellies from the shoulder trim, leaving it to the norcino to proportion the meat and fat for various salame. We finely ground pieces of belly, neck trim, back fat, and shoulder to make *salsiccia fresca*, short links simply seasoned with salt and pepper. These everyday sausages were meant to be eaten cold and half-cured on bread, grilled over wood coals, or turned on a spit with little birds, chunks of bread, and sage leaves. Next came came *finnochiona,* a coarse-ground salame spiced prominently with wild fennel seeds and packed in a wide intestine. Typical Toscano salame was chopped coarse and entirely by hand, its color already deep from the use of the leanest meat from the top loin and shoulder mingled with ivory-white cubes of back fat. The salami were tightly bound with twine and hung from a floor joist near the prosciutti. Because it was such a damp and chilly day, the norcino brought in a can of live embers to warm and dry the room. The most bizarre preparation, and one I was wholly unprepared for, consisted of the whole head of the pig, additional skin trimming, and the fore trotters, left to boil in the cauldron and picked clean, mixed with a liberal amount of *spezie*—a spice mix that included clove, nutmeg, cinnamon, ground ginger, and hot pepper along with shredded lemon peel and parsley. The seasoned meats were packed hot into a jute bag and hung from a tree outside in the cold to stiffen up overnight.

All this work took the better part of the day and it wasn't until nearly four in the afternoon that we sat down to a late lunch in the comforting warmth of the farm kitchen upstairs. By this time I had had my fill of the rich smell of pork. Nevertheless, it would have been rude not to try *migliaccio,* a kind of ill-formed cake made of this morning's pork blood mixed with pork trimmings that was redolent of ground clove and rosemary and fried in olive oil— shocking in its jet-black appearance. After that came *rosticciani,* the most delicious pork ribs I have ever eaten, served directly from the fireplace with an unidentifiable tangle of spiky green leaves gathered in the field beyond the farmhouse window.

It wasn't until I was working in restaurants that I began to make my own sausage. My first efforts were an attempt to make fresh pork sausages on the model of those I had sold in the delicatessen, commonly called luganega. To their peppery, clove-scented taste and coarse texture, I melded my vivid recollection of the aromas and flavors of the simple salt-and-pepper sausages I had made on the farm in Italy. While I liked the flavor of my sausages, there were some enviable differences between commercially made sausages and mine. It soon became evident that the only thing I was really controlling was the seasoning. Commercial sausages could be ground coarse or fine, yet had a firm, bound texture that was also tender; they seemed to retain their moisture without splitting. My own were inconsistent and noticeably less juicy unless I ground them very coarse. They were often but not always crumbly in texture and tended to explode unless I cooked them on the lowest of fires. While the commercially available sausages seemed to lack the rustic charm and authentic flavors of the farm version, I clearly had something to learn about the science of sausage making.

Once I gained some confidence in making fresh sausages I also experimented with more extended curing, and I also started making dry, fermented sausage. In years subsequent to my apprenticeship in Florence, I have repeatedly returned to the Emilia-Romagna, the center of cured meat production, to visit pork butchers and salame and ham makers and to study firsthand the traditions still alive in the foggy plains of the region. The art of producing cured pork meat has deep roots in Italian history and a long continuity particularly in this region. Many types of cured meats, each with a special link to place, enjoy their own DOP or IGP (protected geographical designations). Parma and San Daniele have their own hams, Varzi, its salame, Zibello its culatello, Modena its stuffed pig trotters. I know of no other place that has so glorified the pig in such a range of cured meats or with as much accumulated skill. It was through tasting prosciutti with six different levels of salt, each one *piu dolce*—"sweeter"—with less salt; the myriad variations on salami; mortadella that melts in your mouth; *zampone, cotechino,* pancetta, galantina, and culatello, the summit of cured pork, that I felt the imperative to build my own curing cellar below the basement of my home.

The celebration of the pig has also become a yearly winter tradition at Oliveto. This culminating event, a weeklong series of dinners entitled The Whole Hog, features a menu that utilizes the pig from head to tail. The high point of the menu, and one that we as well as our patrons anticipate each year, is The Grand Salumi platter. Salumi is the encompassing term for salted, cured meats, and our array includes 12 to 15 different cured meats, prosciutto aged 12 and 18 months, culatello, coppa, and 4 or 5 types of fermented sausages whose ripening times span the previous year. There are also fresh sausages made up to 3 days in advance: spiced head cheese sprinkled with minced, vinegared shallots; cooked salame; blood pudding; and *ciccioli,* a suave pâté perfumed with dried thyme and a liberal amount of cracked black pepper.

We pair various pasta types and shapes with sauces made from different cuts of fresh pork. *Gobbetti*, small hump-backed semolina noodles, are dressed in an intense sugo perfumed with rosemary and made entirely from pork bones, meaty scraps, and end-trimmings. We fold thin ribbons of lean pork loin into tagliatelle and toss them both in brown butter with sage and sea salt. Bucatini all'Amatriciana, the famous *primo piatto* from the town outside of Rome whose name it bears, includes a Conserva of tomatoes from last season's crop, new onions, and our own house-cured guanciale (cured pig's jowls). Coarse-ground sausages laced with hot peperoncino makes a spicy al diavolo sauce for penne. We combine the flavorful meat from the neck, bits of trotter, belly, and the ends of mortadella with grated Parmigiano to form a filling for tortellini served in a golden turkey broth.

Pork suggests hearty main dishes and is suitable for braising, boiling, grilling, and spit roasting. Fig wood makes a particularly fragrant fuel for the grill and the spit, its smoke mingling agreeably with the flavor of pork. (Luckily one of our farmers can provide us with an ample supply.) Throughout the evening, country-style pork ribs with a salty rub of fennel seed spin on the spit next to *arista*, the most flavorful top end of the pork loin, their drippings basting the plump Luganega sausages and slabs of polenta below on the grill.

This year, a month before the dinners began, we made a large batch of sauerkraut to accompany slabs of fresh-brined ham and perched thick slices of cotechino on a bed of wilted endives napped with a fonduta of Parmigiano. We offered two braises, pork hocks simmered in a deep burgundy sauce made of concentrated grape juice (saba), and vinegar, and fresh coppa, a superb braising and curing cut within the shoulder that is tender enough to eat with a spoon. With these dishes, we recommended the weightier wines from a list dedicated to the all-pork menu—sturdy Piemontese Nebbiolo, tart Barbera, spicy Rieslings, and Syrah-based wines from the Rhône.

These menus also highlight pork variety meats and end trimmings. Pork tripe figures in a hearty soup with borlotti beans, dry tomatoes, and Lacinato kale. Such soups scream for the wines of the southern Rhône and everyone's favorite last year was a bantamweight 1999 Gigondas from Château du Trignon, a primarily grenache-based wine seemingly made to order for pork and beans. In comparison to beef, lamb, and veal, pork variety meats are milder and less visceral tasting. Pork kidneys are as refined as foie gras in texture and flavor when halved lengthwise, trimmed of all connective tissue and blood vessels, and purged in numerous changes of cold water. I like to slice them thin on the bias, dip the slices in boiling water—all they need to cook—and serve them tossed in creamy mustard vinaigrette with watercress and walnuts. When I first began offering The Whole Hog dinners, most people would shy away from the thought of ordering pig ears and feet. This year it was difficult to keep up with the demand for shredded pig ear salad, leading me to believe that we have a brave band of new converts. The appeal of pig ear salad is in the play of texture with its other bright components. Fresh pig ears are first brined (an optional step) and then boiled in lightly salted water, sliced thin, and left to marinate with lemon peel, champagne vinegar, minced green onion, fine diced carrot, celery hearts, parsley, capers, red pepper flakes, and olive oil. Serving this salad very cold accentuates its appealing crunch and the refreshing pickly mix of vegetables and herbs.

The rich taste and voluptuous texture of pork come forward in forcemeats that include the fore trotters and hind feet of pig. Simmered slowly to tenderness and picked free of their bones, these end trimmings are an overlooked resource. This mixture can be used in stuffing or in filling for pasta and makes a superb stand-alone fritter as well. We chop the mixture coarse, add whole egg, mustard, finely minced sautéed onions splashed with vinegar, a generous amount of fresh ground pepper, and parsley, then re-form it into a rough rectangular shape, bread it, and fry it crisp in olive oil. Pork-feet fritters are delicious with capers or cornichons, or a slice of lemon and a bitter salad such as young dandelion or radicchio.

If you tire of the taste of smoked bacon you may wish to make your own fresh-cured belly of pork (see page 202). Cured belly is a standard item in the Oliveto larder, used to bard lean roasts, as a soup and pasta sauce base component, in stuffing and hors d'oeuvre toppings where it adds richness and savor, and in warm salads.

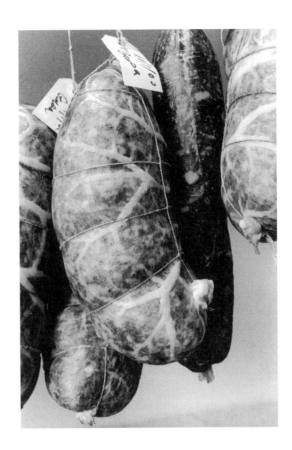

Sausage Making and Meat Curing

If you take pleasure in making your food from scratch, trying your own fresh sausages and cured meats will reward you with entirely unique and delicious products. Farming and home-curing pork is a dying craft and curing your own meat amounts to an act of restoration. It was the emigrant *salumaii* of Italy, Germany's *wurstmachers* and the *charcutiers* of France, among others, who introduced the old traditions to this country. Families too handed down their particular recipes over generations and across nations. Industry, unfortunately, has largely taken over what once was an artisan craft. Cured meats issuing from large-scale manufacture, factory-farmed animals, and the latest technology, delivered in presliced and vacuum-sealed packages, betray a uniformity of

taste primarily driven by additives. Gone for the most part are the use of natural casings, the genuine taste of pork, the influence of the cellar, and other distinctive differences that were once the personal pride of small producers. One has to return to the back roads of Italy, France, Germany, and Spain or know someone who has kept the tradition alive here to find cured meats with any genuine character.

Curing meat is a commitment. It takes time and space and there is some expense involved in setting up your own sausage kitchen. If you intend only to make fresh sausage for immediate consumption, however, a few tools and an afternoon are all it takes. If you decide to delve deeper, you may find your interest grow, as I have, to a consuming pastime. What follows is

The Source of Your Pork

a description of the general principles of making cured meat; the equipment, tools, and materials needed to begin; information you will find useful in understanding why you perform certain steps; and important techniques that directly affect the flavor, texture, and appearance of your cured meats. It is not meant to be exhaustive of all curing techniques or types of sausages, or complete in the treatment of subjects. This would require a separate dedicated volume. Rather, I have included information that will guide you in understanding the important basic principles as they apply to the recipes given below.

The first and most important place to begin in curing your own meat is to line up a good source of pork. Old World sausage makers knew their meat because they both raised and slaughtered it themselves or proximity to the farm source was immediate. You may need to go farther afield. Please see Sources and Resources (page 261) for a superior source of pork that you can buy direct.

Healthy, flavorful pork is raised outdoors year-round, fed well, and managed under the watch of a farmer who cares. It is properly handled from farm to harvest and impeccably fresh. I prefer to purchase fully mature pork or primal cuts that come from animals that have achieved around 250 pounds dressed weight. The pork that I purchase comes from Niman Ranch, a local meat company that has established a partnership with midwestern farmers who raise their hogs on open pasture and deeply bedded barn enclosures into which they are free to come and go. Sows that are farrowing nurture their young in bedded pens in the winter or in barrel-shaped "nests" in the cool grass of an open pasture in more clement weather. Piglets are weaned no earlier than 5 weeks of age so that natural antibodies in the mother's milk can give the pigs the strong start they need to thrive. Most of these farms cultivate not only pork but also the grains that sustain them. When crops are rotated, overhauled bedding mixed with manure is spread on fallow fields to replenish critical soil nutrients. This traditional inter-dependent system requires more intensity, arranged as it is to sustain an ecological cycle, to preserve water supplies, air quality, and the communities it neighbors. By contrast, factory farms exhibit another kind of intensity having more to do with overcrowding, unused concen-trations of waste, and speeding lean meat to market. Factory farms owned by large corporate meatpackers have amputated vital connections to the land, made isolated prisons for one of the most social of animals, and eliminated the need for farmers.

On the small farm, the freedom of space and close interaction with the farmers allow the pigs to live out their natural instincts. Small farmers are more likely to husband older heirloom breeds or hybrids that they have selected for superior quality and adaptability to their farm. The first time I saw these animals in the middle of winter, I was surprised to see how frisky they were romp-ing around in 8° weather on four feet of dried corn stalks. Hogs capable of living outdoors year-round must carry ample fat to insulate them against the cold and heat. They do not rely upon regimens of medications to keep them healthy; they are naturally so.

Short Cures and Long Cures

An essential ingredient of curing any meat is time, more or less of it depending upon what is needed for maturation and drying. These in turn are dependent on the ambient conditions in the cellar, the grind of the meat or size of the whole cut, the process, and the type of casing used. In my own repertoire of cured meats, short cures apply to fresh and cooked sausages such as mortadella, *cotechino*, Luganega, *coppa di testa* (head cheese), cooked salame, and thin whole cuts of pork like salted and spiced belly bacon as well as brined hams and other parts of the pig that are eaten soon after they are made. In the case of fresh or cooked sausages, I have found that while most of the effect of curing takes place quickly, time is necessary for the aromas of the seasonings to blend harmo-niously with the meat.

Long cures apply to large whole cuts of pork such as prosciutto, coppa, rolled pancetta, or culatello that undergo an initial salt and curing process followed by extended cellar aging. Dry-cured salame follows a similar course after a controlled period of fermentation. The length of the aging and ripening phase is directly related to the thickness of the cut or the diame-ter of the salame. In my cellar, prosciutto takes about 14 to 18 months to mature fully. Fermented sausages of 4- to 5-inch diameter stuffed into beef bungs take 100 to 125 days, while finer grind salame in small- to medium-diameter casings require just 20 to 60 days.

Basic Techniques

Weighing and Measuring

You will notice that the recipes in this chapter list salt, curing salt, and spices in gram weights. Standard U.S. weights and measures are not minute enough to measure curing salt, which must be used in precisely limited amounts. Furthermore, the right quantities of ground or powdered spices, whose weights are variable, often do not fit neatly in standard spoon measures. Weighing
is simply a more accurate way to ensure the correct quantities of any additives. For this reason it is important to be able to calibrate the quantity.

In addition to my pound/ounce scale, I use a small electronic scale (see Sources and Resources, page 263) that can be calibrated and that has a "tare" function, meaning that the scale will account for any container weight placed upon it and read zero in the display. My scale toggles handily between ounces and grams and has a limit of 80 ounces (2,000 grams). It is simple to use and ideal for putting a number to pinches of this or that. With it, I also feel secure that I am adding no more and no less curing salt in the recipe batch.

Cold Temperatures, Sharp Blades

The firm, uncrumbly texture and succulent quality of the best fresh and dry-cured sausages are due to three fundamental factors: the temperature of the meat prior to grinding, the use of sharp tools, and extracting the soluble proteins from the meat by the addition of salt and by mixing. I had always heard that it was very important to grind fresh meat at temperatures very close to freezing, which for meat is 28 to 29°F. This also validated the timing and season of the pork rituals in the Old World, where the frigid last days of December have traditionally

been the time to "put up the pig." While we don't have to rely upon the climate to supply our refrigeration, it is still important that the meat remain in the temperature safety zone. The other important reason for the low temperature is to prevent "smear," the degraded condition of the fat in a sausage mixture. Smear is due to meat and fat that are too warm as they pass through the grinder, or it can also be caused by a dull grinder knife and plate. Smear can also result from overmixing. The result is that the fat cells are broken to a pasty purée, leaving their contents to spill out when heated. Since there is no force strong enough to bind smeared fat, it readily exits the casing, causing the sausages to go dry.

Varying the Grind

In order to make sausages that have a lively texture and are visually appealing when sliced, it is important to vary the size of the grind, especially in larger sausages. Too much uniformity in the grind looks and tastes monotonous. For this reason, you will notice my recipes call for the use of grinding plates of various sizes to make a single sausage mixture. I think of the lean portion of the mixture differently from the fat. While it is possible to maintain a range of grinding sizes for the lean in the recipe, fat should not exceed sizes that would make it stand out too prominently.

As a general principle, in all ground sausages, the size of the sausage casing should dictate the grind of the meat and fat, as well as the ratio of lean meat to fat. The smaller the diameter of the casing, the finer the grind. As casing diameters increase, the size of the grind can also increase but only to a point; large chunks of fat are not very appetizing or palatable. Larger pieces of meat and fat also need more adjacent surfaces to form a nexus with one another. If a coarse mix is stuffed into a small-diameter casing, the sausage runs the risk of a crumbly texture and poor distribution of fat to lean. There simply isn't enough room for large pieces to be distributed comfortably side by side. It is also important to remember that in dry sausages there is considerable shrinkage (30 percent on average). Since fat contains less water than the lean meat, shrinkage can further exaggerate the size of the fat particles in the sausage.

Mixing

In order to make sausage with an even distribution of curing salt and seasoning, or other finely dosed ingredients such as water, dextrose, and starter culture, it is important to combine the mixture thoroughly. Mixing is also critical to achieving a good bind—the seamless joining of meat and fat due to protein extraction—that determines any sausage's final texture. Mixing works synergistically with salt and temperature to create bind. Cold temperatures (32 to 35°F.) enhance protein extraction and prevent fat smear that causes fat loss later in cooking and a dry crumbly texture. When mixing by hand, use a stainless-steel bowl large enough to hold the mixture with ample head space and a fairly stiff rubber spatula. After sprinkling the seasonings or other additions over the surface, use a cutting and folding motion to combine the mixture. Then, use the flat side of the spatula to compress the meat and fat while dragging the spatula across the surface of the mixture. The goal is to rub meat particles together in order to extract protein. Alternate cutting and folding with pressing and dragging. Work quickly and vigorously. The meat should feel cold throughout the mixing process. If it is a very hot day, work the mixture over bowl of ice. After 4 to 5 minutes of mixing you will notice that the meat will stiffen considerably and become sticky. You will also observe that the meat leaves a whitish film where it contacts the bowl. At this point, stop mixing. Excessive mixing causes excessive protein extraction and a rubbery texture. It is

important to observe the appearance and feel of the meat mixture and later, the sausage's final texture. Making this connection will enable you to alter the texture of your sausages to a fine and varied degree. If you plan to make sausages regularly or if you make batches larger than 10 pounds in quantity, you may wish to purchase a manual, stainless-steel sausage mixer with rotating blades that takes most of the sweat out of the job (See Sources and Resources, page 263).

Preparing the Casings

As a general rule, all casings, no matter how they are packed, should be rinsed and flushed prior to loading them on the stuffing tube. The first step, however, it to unravel the casings from the their bundles. Casings are tied together with twine. First cut the twine to release the casings, then separate their lengths into smaller bundles. Determine how much casing you need as described below (see page 179). Transfer the casings to a bowl half filled with water and set them in a sink that is likewise partially filled with water. Take a single length of casing and open it at one end. Place the casing under the faucet and allow water to course through and out the other end. If the casing is particularly stiff, repeat this process. Transfer the flushed casing to a small bucket or plastic container with a cover and allow one end to hang over the top rim; this will make it easy to find the end when you are ready to stuff the sausage. Repeat with the remaining casings. Add a small amount of water to the container. If the size of the casings permits, gently place the cover over the trailing ends and store them in the refrigerator until you are ready to use them.

Taking the pH of Fermented Sausage

The goal of fermentation is to lower the acid strength of the meat to pH 5 or less within 48 hours. The pH of fermented sausage should be measured at least three times during the fermentation period: when the meat mixture is stuffed into casing, 24 hours later, and then 8 or more hours afterward or until the goal of pH 5 or less is reached. The second reading at the 24-hour mark will give you some indication of the rate at which pH is dropping. Make sure the pH meter is calibrated before taking the first reading. (Simple instructions for calibration come with the instrument.) To accomplish this you will need two standard buffers (pH 4 and 7)—solutions that maintain a constant pH and act as a calibration reference for the meter.

To take the pH measurement you will need to retain a small amount of the meat mixture (there is always a small amount left over in the stuffing canister after the sausages have been cased). Chop 50 grams of the meat mixture as fine as possible. If you have a mortar and pestle, pound it to a purée. Mix the meat with an equal weight of distilled water (50 grams) to create a slurry. Submerge the electrode of the calibrated pH meter into the slurry and wait for the reading to stabilize. Meanwhile, wrap the remainder of the meat mixture (ground but not chopped to a purée) in plastic wrap in the form of a small sausage and tension it by twisting the excess wrap at either end of the sausage in opposite directions; tie it off with at loop at one end and a knot at the other. Hang this "control" sausage with those that have been stuffed and cased. To take a second and third reading, create a slurry as above with water and meat from the control sausage. Rewrap the control sausage between readings.

Handling Starter Cultures

Starter cultures are recommended for the making of fermented, dry-cured sausage. In combination with a small amount of added sugar (dextrose), time, and the right temperature, it is the culture that causes the critical pH drop in the meat, thereby causing the proteins in the meat to be altered so that they more readily give up water. Cultures also contribute the tang and some of the unique aroma of fermented sausages. For maximum stability, keep dry starter cultures frozen. Measure the amount called for in the recipe, close the storage pouch tightly, and return the remainder to the freezer. Prior to use, disperse the culture in the amount of water given in the recipe. Let the culture stand for 10 minutes. *After* all other ingredients have been blended into the meat mixture, add the diluted culture and mix very thoroughly. Good distribution is essential to even fermentation throughout the meat mixture. Do not allow the culture to contact the other ingredients prior to mixing it with the meat.

Stuffing Sausage

Sausage stuffing machines are simple to use and self-explanatory. Once the stuffer is filled and the stuffing tube is screwed in place, it is important to advance the sausage to the end of the tube before placing the casing on it. This ensures that you will not pump any air into the casing, only meat. While most stuffers are fitted with an air bleed on top, tamping the meat with a tool such as a wooden spoon prevents back pressure from building up and air pockets from forming in the casing.

Casings that are properly flushed should be moist enough to slip on the stuffing tube with ease. If your casings are a little dry, splash water on the stuffing tube to lubricate it before slipping on the casing. Place the casing over the end of the tube and work it to the back of the tube until the entire length of the casing is inserted.

Given the variable length of stuffing tubes and different lengths of casing, you may need to trim the casing if it does not fit entirely.

During the course of stuffing, three movements should occur simultaneously and it takes some coordination to attend to them all. While it is possible to accomplish this alone, I prefer to work with another person when I am making sausage; it is much easier for two people to manage the simultaneous duties with one person operating the machine and managing the flow of sausage to the casing while the other is on the receiving end to organize the output.

Sausage exits the stuffing tube when you operate the crank and the meat is pushed through the cylinder. As it enters the casing, the slack end, pushed to the back of the tube, must be moved smoothly forward so that casing is consistently provided as the meat is extruded. At the same time, the encased sausage must be moved away from the stuffer. Depending on the durability of the casing, the person operating the crank must also judge how tight the sausage should be packed into its casing. Small sausages receive further tensioning when they are tied or twirled into separate links and you must allow for this when judging the tension of the sausage as it leaves the tube. Larger-diameter sausages that are tied into single salame or those that have casing that are closed on one end, such as mortadella, should be filled as completely and firmly as the casing permits. More specific directions for stuffing tension are given in the individual recipes.

Linking Sausage

Making individual sausages from a long, small- or medium-diameter strand is called linking. The "alternate twist" method works well for separating the links. Start by closing one end of the sausage strand with a knot. Next, decide how long you would like your portion to be, and then mark the table on which you are working or use a knife blade as rule to measure the length before you make the twist. Pinch the casing at the designated length between the thumb and forefinger of one hand and twist the sausage away from your body four or five times with the other hand. Repeat the twist in the opposite direction the same distance away from the first sausage to form another. Continue along the length of the casing, alternating the twists until you reach the end of the sausage strand. Tie a second knot in the end to close the strand. Hang the sausages to dry on a dowel in a cool, airy place.

Releasing Air Pockets

Even with careful stuffing and tensioning, it is likely your sausages will have small areas where air pockets have formed between pieces of meat or against the casing. In the case of fresh sausages, air pockets can cause the casing to burst as rendered fat accumulates in the space and creates hot spots when the sausage comes into direct contact with heat. In dry-cured sausages, air pockets can lead to spoilage in the early stages of drying and unevenness in the shape. For these reasons, it is important to examine your linked sausages, one by one, and larger salame for these vulnerable areas. Use a sausage pricker to puncture the air pockets. The casing will shrink immediately against the meat inside.

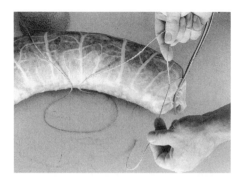

Fig. 1

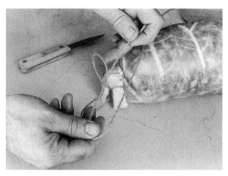

Fig. 2

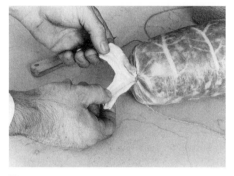

Fig. 3

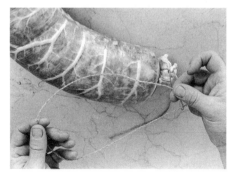

Fig. 4

Butterfly Knot and Hanging Loop

It is very helpful to purchase forceps (see page 262) to hold the tension of the sausage as you tie it (fig. 1). In scissor fashion, the forceps clamp down on the casing and against the stuffing, holding them tight. Sausages have a tendency to plummet to the ground once they are hung unless precautions are taken. Simple square knots are not sufficient to hold the slippery ends against the tension caused by fermentation or in the beginning stages of drying. And after the sausage begins to dry, the casing shrinks with it, which can also result in the sausage slipping through its knot. A simple trick to prevent this is to make a butterfly knot before stuffing the casing. Spread one end of the casing on the table and make a small cut in the center of the casing, parallel to its sides. Separate the two strands (fig. 2). Make a tight square knot just above the cut you made, leaving enough twine on the loose end to tie another similar knot (fig. 3). Next, bring the loose end of the twine under and around the separated strands of casing and tie another knot in crisscross fashion across the first. This guarantees that the sausage cannot slip through the casing. If the casing has two open ends, do the same thing on the other end of the sausage once it is stuffed. Enough string must be allowed to form a loop for hanging the sausage. Six inches is adequate. Form a knot by making two underhand loops with the two strands.

Tensioning and Trussing

The purpose and goal of all tying is to close the ends of the sausage and to encourage the binding of meat within the casing by compaction. Generally speaking, all fresh and dry-cured sausages should be nearly as tight as their casing permits without bursting. Adjusting the tension takes a little practice.

If you find that a sausage you have stuffed and

tied still sits a little slack in its casing, the simplest way to firm it up is to make an extra tie in the middle of the sausage. This compresses both the sausage and the casing and is generally enough to increase the tension. The sausage should feel firm in its casing.

Trussing is necessary for large heavy sausages such as salame stuffed into wide beef bungs, mortadella, or any sausage 3 inches or more in diameter that are longer than 12 inches. I use a continuous half-hitch knot, the hitches an inch apart, that terminates in a loop that I use to hang the sausage. This way the weight of the sausage and its casing are supported by an integrated series of hitches that hold it all together firmly in place.

Orient the sausage on the work surface roughly perpendicular to your body. Place a spool of twine to the side of your more coordinated hand and about 15 inches away from the sausage. If the casing has two open ends, secure the first end tightly with a butterfly knot. Cut the loose end and the end still attached to the spool about 1 inch from the knot. Secure the other end of the sausage in a similar manner. Allow 6 inches of twine on the loose end for the hanging loop that you will later form. Do not cut the end still attached to the spool.

To make hitches, form a full-circle loop by crossing the knot end of the twine over the spool end (fig. 4). Using both hands, slip the loop under the far end of the sausage and pull the loop back to about 1 inch from the knotted end. Tighten the hitch by lifting the slack under the sausage and by simultaneously pulling on the spool end of the twine. Repeat the process along the length of the sausage, creating a series of hitches 1 inch apart and in a line (fig. 5). Maintain tension on the spool end as you proceed so that the sausage becomes snugly bound. When you reach the far end, wrap the twine around the end and turn the sausage 180 degrees (figs. 5 and 6). Draw the twine out 8 inches beyond the knotted end of the sausage and cut it free from the spool. Make a series of hitches on

Fig. 5

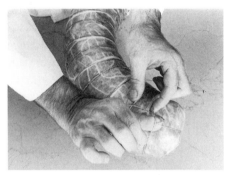

Fig. 6

Fig. 7

Fig. 8

the second side by tucking the twine under the loops with your thumb (fig. 6). Tighten each hitch by pulling on the loose end of the twine. Join the remaining twine in a tight square knot to the 6 inches left at the knotted end (fig. 7). Finally, make two underhand loops with the two strands to form a hanging loop (fig. 8).

Brining

Brine, also called "pickle," is a solution of salt and water. While many people use the terms interchangeably, pickle is used to designate a salt-and-water solution that also contains nitrite or cure. Brine or pickle may also contain other seasonings such as dry spices, herbs, or aromatic vegetables that add appealing background flavors. In Italy brine is called *salamoia* and in some Italian salumerie, meats, particularly beef or veal tongue, can be seen floating in large earthenware crocks in a spicy brine that includes juniper, peppercorns, allspice berries, bay leaf, garlic, and thin-sliced carrots, celery, and onion. Brined meats are typically boiled and served either cold as an antipasto or hot as a secondo, following soup or pasta. Apart from the enhancement the meat receives through its absorption of salt and seasonings, brining also has a tenderizing and moistening effect. Brining requires more or less time depending upon the thickness and density of the cut of meat. As long as the meat remains submerged in brine, the brine is absorbed and diffused it slowly throughout the meat. I don't recommend brining very thick cuts of meat as those thicker than 3 inches may spoil at the center before the salt penetrates.

I use straight immersion brines primarily for pickling tongues and ears destined for cold antipasti, and for other trim cuts used in special cooked sausages that benefit from the additional seasoning, cured flavor, and color they pick up. Thin cuts of pork, such as boneless loin and tenderloin, as well as cubed meats from the

leg or shoulder require a matter of 3 to 5 days to drink up the brine and are delicious skewered and grilled on a wood fire.

If you wish to make your own fresh ham or brine denser cuts such as shoulders or heavy loins, it is wise to inject them first with brine using a brine pump, before immersing them in brine. This is the surest and fastest way to introduce salt to the center of a dense cut of meat, where it is most vulnerable to spoilage. Submerging the meat afterward in the brine allows the brine ingredients to diffuse and equalize throughout the meat.

The basic procedure for brining follows. I include this procedure in the event that the weights of the meat you wish to brine do not correspond to the recipes below. In such a case, it is important when working with percentages of salt or parts per million (ppm) of nitrite to understand the reasoning behind the recipes as the brine elements are based on the weight of the meat and the water it contains.

When formulating your brine there are two calculations to make, the first to assure a minimum "brine strength" or saline concentration, and sugar content, the second for the nitrite addition. Water content varies in raw meat between 60 and 70 percent. When making brine, the amount of salt is measured not only for its concentration in the water of the brine, but also in the water of the meat as well. If the amount of salt added to the brine were based on a percentage by weight of the water in the brine alone, the meat would, in effect, dilute it. In order to season the meat fully and to discourage the growth of bacteria, the brine strength should range between 3 to 5 percent salt in water. I use the average of 65 percent when considering the water-in-meat portion and, because I prefer more lightly salted meats, I add the minimum amount of salt to yield equilibrium brine strength of 3 percent. Sugar is added purely for its flavor-balancing effect on the salt at 2 percent and is calculated similarly.

For safety purposes it is important to make

sure the meat is well chilled. The same applies to the water you use to make your brine, and the conditions of the refrigerator or cold room in which you are storing the meat. Ideally, meat, pickle, and refrigeration temperatures should not exceed 34 to 38°F. at any point during the process.

I also observe the standard for nitrite addition, which is calculated in parts per million. The federal guidelines suggest an addition of 200 ppm for "immersion" cured meats. This level is based on the calculation for nitrite in the brine and in the meat at total equilibrium. This means that the quantity of nitrite is based on the total weight of the meat and the water in the brine.

For the sake of example, let's say you want to brine-cure 5 pounds of boneless pork loin. Place the meat in a clean, nonreactive container large enough to hold it entirely submerged. Five-gallon plastic buckets are very handy for brining, as are square food-grade plastic Lexan containers available in restaurant supply stores. Determine how much water you must add to cover the meat by 3 inches by placing the meat in the container and pouring cold water over it, measuring as you go. For this example, 3 gallons of cover brine should be sufficient to fully immerse the meat. You would then calculate the amount of salt to add (the brine strength) as follows:

1 gallon of water weighs 8.33 pounds
Water weight of loins = 5 pounds × .65 =
   3.25 pounds water
3 gallons water = 25 pounds (rounded)
Weight of water + water in meat = 25 + 3.25 =
   28.25 pounds
28.25 pounds × .03 = .84 pound salt
28.25 pounds × .02 = .56 pound sugar

Once you know the weight of the meat and the weight of the brine, use this simple formula to arrive at the amount of curing salt needed.

Raw weight of the meat = 5 pounds
Weight of the water in the brine =

	25.00 pounds water
	.84 pound salt
	.56 pound sugar
Total brine weight =	26.40 pounds

$$\text{Pounds Nitrite} = \frac{200\ \text{ppm} \times (\text{total brine weight} + \text{raw weight of the meat})}{1,000,000}$$

$$\text{Pounds Nitrite} = \frac{200 \times (26.4\ \text{pounds} + 5\ \text{pounds})}{1,000,000}$$

$$\text{Pounds Nitrite} = \frac{200 \times 31.4}{1,000,000}$$

Pounds Nitrite = .006 pure nitrite

As noted above, sodium nitrite is commonly sold as a curing mix, a blend of common salt and nitrite. The nitrite content must be listed on the package; the curing mix I recommend (see page 263) is 6.25 percent pure nitrite. Because the formula above gives the result in pure nitrite you will have to divide the amount of pure nitrite by the percentage of nitrite in your curing mix. To do this, express the percentage of nitrite in the cure mix as a decimal (move the decimal two places to the left) and divide the amount of pure nitrite needed by the percentage of nitrite in the cure mix:

.006 / .0625 = .096 pounds curing mix

With such a small amount, it will be necessary to convert to grams. There are 16 ounces in a pound and 28 grams in an ounce, so:

.096 pounds curing mix × 16 ounces × 28 grams =
   43 grams of curing mix

For the sake of accuracy, I convert the salt and sugar to grams as well:

.84 pounds salt = .84 × 16 ounces × 28 grams = 376 grams salt

.56 pounds sugar = .56 × 16 ounces × 28 grams = 251 grams sugar

However, because a significant amount of salt comes along with the nitrite in your curing mix, you must deduct the amount from the total quantity called for. Again, assuming a curing mix that is 6.25 percent nitrite (and therefore 93.75 percent salt), calculate as follows:

43 grams of curing mix (6.25 percent nitrite)
　− 3 grams of pure nitrite (rounded)
　= 40 grams of salt
376 grams salt − 40 grams
　= 336 grams additional salt

You are now ready to assemble the brine:

3 gallons ice-cold water
336 grams salt
251 grams sugar
43 grams curing mix
5 pounds boneless pork loin

You can also make a spicy version of this brine for use in curing tongues, ears, and small cuts of meat. The percentages of salt and sugar are the same.

Cuts of Pork for Sausage

My own repertoire of cured meats has developed directly out of the use of the entire animal, but this is not practical for most home sausage makers. While it is possible to turn any cut of pork into the raw material for fresh sausage or dry-cured salame, it is most practical and economical to use meat from the shoulder and leg. Shoulder of pork is divided into two retail cuts called Boston Butt and Picnic. These cuts, plus the interior trimmings from the neck, are the most flavorful part of the pig. The cost of skinless, boneless leg or skinless, blade-out butt is roughly equivalent. The recipes that follow call for a certain percentage of lean meat to fat in the form of back fat, the firmest fat running along the top length of the pig from the end of the shoulder to the beginning of the legs. In order to prepare either shoulder or leg for sausage, I separate the lean from the fat, connective tissue, silverskin, and glands. To determine how much untrimmed meat to buy, assume that the proportion of lean after trimming for both leg and shoulder cuts varies on average between 55 and 65 percent. Variation in yield depends upon the breed and feeding regimen of the animal. The addition of belly meat for fresh sausage is also an asset to the final flavor and texture of coarse-ground sausage and certain cooked sausages. Belly is a softer cut and its fatty portion bears a more pronounced aroma of pork than backfat. Pork belly varies widely with respect to the proportion of lean to fat it contains. Belly that contains 35 to 45 percent lean is ideal for fresh sausage, an amount that you determine roughly by looking at the striping of lean in the belly viewed in cross section. Note that when using belly in any sausage, you should adjust the amount of fat to lean to account for the fat the belly contributes.

Tools and Equipment

In order to make your own fresh sausage and to cure your own meat you will need a stable work surface on which to cut meat and rest a few essential tools. Maple butcher block is ideal, but any solid countertop or table fitted with a cutting board works fine. SHARP KNIVES make the job of skinning, boning, separating fat from lean, and cubing meat an easy task. I use two different knives with a similar scimitar profile, one 6 inches long that is ideal for boning and cutting up small pieces of meat, the other 12 inches long for slicing through larger cuts. The curved form of a scimitar blade mimics the most common action of cutting, a semicircular backward motion toward the body and through the meat. Sharp knife blades and the right form of tool also reduce the repetitive stress of cutting on your arm muscles, tendons, and joints, as less pressure is necessary to accomplish the task. Keep a honing steel handy to maintain the edge of the blade.

The other important cutting tool is the MEAT GRINDER. A grinder functions in a similar manner whether manual or motor-driven. Chunks of meat are driven to the headpiece of the tool by an auger and forced through a round, perforated plate against which a three- or four-sided blade circulates. Both the blade and the holes in the plate have sharp edges that readily reduce the cubes of meat to the size of the holes as they pass through. Most grinders come with at least two plates. Standard dimensions of the holes for small commercial grinders are 1/8 inch, 3/16 inch and 3/8 inch. These sizes are ideal for the small sausage kitchen. Options for larger and middling-size plates are also available and their circumferences are sized according to those of the meat grinder. Motor-driven home grinders or attachments to mixers offer similar, if not identical, sizes and options.

A standard FOOD PROCESSOR is needed to make smooth emulsion sausages such as mortadella and frankfurter-type batters. The larger the bowl, the fewer number of batches you will have to run through it. It is very important that the blade be as sharp as possible so as not to overwork and thereby raise the temperature of the meat. The smooth, bound texture of emulsion sausages is dependent upon the lean and fat reaching a specific temperature. A sharp blade ensures that the meat is chopped to the right consistency before it moves beyond this point. Provided the blades are very sharp, food processors may also be used to make coarse-ground sausage and salame. Its advantage over the grinder is that it produces less heat while cutting. Sausages made in a food processor also display a pleasingly irregular matrix of lean and fat.

A SAUSAGE-STUFFING MACHINE with a variety of attachable stuffing tubes suited to the diameters of different casings is indispensable. A sausage stuffer is a stainless-steel metal cylinder with an opening at the bottom where the stuffing tube is screwed in place with a large nut. The sausage mixture is pushed through the cylinder by the action of a crank. Cylindrical sausage stuffers are fitted with a rubber gasket or bleed hole that allows air to escape as the meat packed beneath it compresses. Stuffers come in a variety of sizes for home or small-production kitchens. The piston-type stuffers described above are best. Always avoid using stuffing tubes adapted to the meat grinder. The turning action of the auger can smash or overheat the meat and fat, creating an undesirable dry texture in the finished sausage.

Commercial sausage makers use a MIXER with a series of rotating stainless-steel blades that gently circulate throughout the sausage batter, adding a minimum amount of heat in the process. A small, stainless-steel manual mixer that works on the same principle and can handle 20 pounds comfortably is available for this purpose (see Sources and Resources, page 260).

You will need CONTAINERS FOR MIXING AND STORING your meat mixtures. Square stainless-steel pans or food-grade plastic are ideal. If you plan to do your own brining of hams or other cuts of pork, you will need a 5- to 10-gallon bucket. Containers should be sized to your means of refrigeration as well as the size of the batches you anticipate making. It is important that your refrigerator maintain temperatures below 40°F., the safety zone for the storage of all food.

Small Tools

A RAPID-RESPONSE THERMOMETER that can be calibrated is useful for checking the temperature of meat before and after you grind it, as well as for cooked sausage, brines, and emulsions.

If you want to make fresh ham, you will need a MANUAL MEAT PUMP, an inexpensive tool that looks like a large syringe. Brine is delivered to a probe at the end of the pump through a perforated needle that sends a spray of brine in all directions to the muscles of the ham.

A SPICE GRINDER such as one sold for the grinding of coffee is essential for reducing whole spices to ground powders.

A HOUSEHOLD MEAT SAW is a valuable tool if you plan to buy whole cuts or sides of pork or are in a position to deal with the entire carcass.

BUTCHER'S TWINE is used for tying and trussing cured meat. The sturdiest twine is made from flax and has an appealing brown color (see Sources and Resources, pages 260-261) that will lend your sausages an Old World look. However, it is somewhat hard on the hand if you are tying a lot of sausages. A more comfortable alternative is made from synthetic fiber; it is very strong, and somewhat elastic, which allows it to be cinched tight. It is also very soft and leaves none of the small annoying cuts that straight cotton or flax twine leave on your hands after a day of sausage making.

SURGICAL FORCEPS are indispensable for holding the tension of sausages while securing the ends of casing with twine. Without them you will have to work with a partner or your sausages will not be tensioned properly and are likely to suffer from air pockets within. Forceps operate like scissors but have blunt, curved ends that clamp and hold the casing tightly. I use two sizes and types, a 5-inch, curved artery forceps for small, thin casings, and a 10-inch, curved dressing forceps for all larger, thicker casings. See page 262 for a source.

Since sausage stuffers and the manual process of filling casings often leave small air pockets between the skin of the casing and the sausage meat inside, it is very important to have a SAUSAGE PRICKER to release the trapped air. A sausage pricker is a small tool with sharp needles protruding from the end. Before using a sausage pricker, it is advisable to sterilize the points of the needles against a hot flame so as not to introduce unwanted bacteria to the meat.

Lengths of WOODEN DOWELS are necessary for hanging your sausage to dry or ripen.

A small PH METER will verify the rapid drop in acidity necessary for the safety of fermented sausage. The meters are available in a wide range of prices and you needn't buy the most expensive. Along with the meter, it is important to also purchase buffers for calibrating the meter before each use. I prefer to purchase powdered encapsulated buffers (pH 4 and pH 7) that can be reconstituted in distilled water. Premade bottled buffers deteriorate over time; powdered buffers can be made fresh each time you wish to use them.

A HYGROMETER is necessary to measure relative humidity in the fermentation and aging stage of dry-cured sausage. You may also need a humidifier or dehumidifier to control humidity in the fermentation area and some high-wattage lights to increase the amount of heat in the area where you hang the sausages (for further explanation, see Environment for Fermentation, page 187).

For access to sources for small tools and equipment, see pages 262-263.

Sausage Casings

Sausage casings fall into two categories, natural and artificial. Artificial casings are designed to be used on machines that are impractical for the home or small-scale sausage maker. With the exception of an artificial collagen casing that I use merely as a uniform cylindrical container for head cheese, I prefer to use natural casings derived from the intestines of hogs, sheep, and beef. Natural casings enhance the aroma of dry-cured sausages and have a pleasingly irregular and authentic appearance. There are also practical advantages in using them. Natural casings are elastic, have good tensile strength, and fit snugly on the stuffing tubes. At the same time, they demand attention on the part of the sausage maker in determining the right degree of packing pressure relative to the strength of the casing. Only the small-diameter casings, those from sheep, hogs, and beef, are edible with the sausage filling itself. Large casings such as beef middles and beef bungs serve only as containers for cooked sausage meat as they are too tough to actually be edible.

In the case of aged, fermented sausage, the casing is a crucial partner in the ripening, drying, and maturation process. In the early stages of drying, the casing acts as the permeable skin through which moisture migrates to the outside of the sausage. The casing plays a role (along with the degree of humidity and air movement in the cellar) in regulating the speed at which the sausage dries. Maturation is assisted by yeast and mold that populate the irregular surfaces of the casing, suppressing undesirable bacteria and protecting the sausage from light and oxygen. Molds eventually reach beyond the casing surface to deep inside the sausage to further condition it. As the sausage meat dries and shrinks, so does the casing, eventually creating a nearly impermeable barrier to moisture.

All casings, whether natural or artificial, are sold in standard units of measure depending on their size and type. Casings are sold individually or in bundles and hanks (used interchangeably) or sets that correspond to a fixed length. Casings are measured in meters as well as a useful measurement called green weight that refers to a casing's approximate capacity after stuffing and prior to cooking or smoking. You can use this information to determine how much casing will be required to hold the amount of sausage you intend to make. Bear in mind, however, that the casing capacity is approximate; yields are based on commercial production where machines can carefully regulate packing pressure. It is wise to order a little more casing than you calculate you will need. For approximate stuffing capacities and other useful information on natural casings, refer to the International Natural Sausage Casing Association's (INSCA) website on page 260.

Natural Casings

SHEEP CASING is tender and edible and ideal for smooth, frankfurter-type emulsions or small, coarse-ground sausages. They are the smallest natural casings available, with diameters ranging from 16 to 28 millimeters or larger. Sheep casing comes in 91-meter bundles (also called hanks) that go a long way. Loading sheep casing on a stuffing tube can be frustrating because the end openings are difficult to detect and to separate.

When purchasing sheep casing, particularly in a small diameter, specify that you would like it shirred if possible. Shirred casings are preapplied to a flexible plastic sheath that makes its transfer to the stuffing tube much simpler.

HOG CASING is taken from the longest intestine (there are approximately 20 meters of it) and extends from the stomach of the pig to the bung cap. It is a smooth, tubular intestine and comes in a range of diameters depending on the size of the pig from which it is taken. Like sheep casings, hog casings are sold in hanks or bundles 91 meters in length and are also sold in 1- to 2-meter lengths called shorts. A bundle, the minimum unit of purchase, may seem like a huge amount, but if stored properly it will keep for several months.

Regular intact HOG BUNGS, also called fat ends as well as sewn hog bungs, are sold as individual pieces and are a special-order item. Regular hog bungs, tied on one end, make a very distinctive-looking sausage with a flare at the bottom. Tied hog bungs are superb for dry-cured salame. They are thicker along their length and dry more slowly than beef middle casing, the more common choice for dry-fermented salame. With them I have made some of the most appealing sausages, fully cured and ripened evenly from the center out with a soft, refined texture. Hog middle casings are problematic for other than cooked salame or liver sausage as they have overlapping, curly edges that resist drying and as such are prone to unevenness or exaggerated mold buildup at the folds.

Natural BEEF CASINGS offer the most useful sizes for medium- and large-diameter cooked and dry-cured sausages. They are strong and elastic and provide the durable skin needed to hold the weight of a sausage mixture over time. All casings, but particularly those from beef, have a rather strong, visceral odor. This should not be mistaken for spoilage. The odor washes away for the most part when the casing is flushed. Later, when the sausage is hung to dry, it is hardly noticeable.

The most common beef casings are middle casings that range in diameter between 45 and 65 millimeters and up, and rounds that are taken from the long runner intestine corresponding to the middle intestine of the hog. Beef rounds are so named for their characteristic ring shape; when stuffed, they coil naturally. Beef middles and rounds are commonly sold in sets, consisting of 9 to 18 meters and 18 to 30 meters, respectively. Bung caps are also sold in sets and are taken from the section of the beef intestine between the runner and the middle. I use 4- to 5-inch-wide bung caps to make my largest salame, such as Genoa and Toscano. Bladders, the traditional casing for mortadella, are the widest of the natural casings and come salted or dried in sizes that hold from 5 to 14 pounds of meat. They are sold by the piece. Bladders have an appealing pear-shaped form and are particularly rugged.

All casings are graded for quality. In sheep, an A-quality casing has no holes or weaknesses and is best for smooth, emulsion-type sausage wherein flaws are detectable. B-quality casings are of acceptable strength and are best used for more coarse-ground sausage. There is a single quality standard for hog casings. Hog casings vary primarily according to the species of pork, the climate in which they were raised, and their diet. Some casings will be white, grayish white, or clear; others will have a darker color and more visible veining. With beef casing, look or ask for export quality, which refers to casings free of nodules or windows, thinner spots that make the casing prone to splitting. Casings are generally packed in one of two ways: salted or preflushed and salted. Depending on the type, preflushed casings are sent out in a salty slush, in a wet pack with less salt, or a in a brine solution.

Once you have determined how much casing you will need by referring to the tables for capacity per casing limit to "green weights" (see INSCA, page 260), cut the casing to length. Rinse salted or slush-packed casings with fresh water to remove the surface salt, and then soften them by soaking them in fresh water at room temperature for about 30 minutes. It is not necessary to rinse wet-pack casings or those that have been stored in brine solution. Regardless of the type, you should next flush the casings with cold water, allowing it to run from one end to the other (the exception to this is shirred sheep casing that is preflushed and loaded on its sheath). Finally, take the casing to the stuffing table and place it in a bowl of warm water. This will soften a little of the natural fat in the casing and allow it to slide on and off the stuffing tube easily. Before placing the casing on the stuffing tube, expel the excess water by stripping it between your fingers.

Salted casings should be stored in a cool environment (38°F.) or refrigerated. When removing a portion of the casings for use, re-salt the unused portion heavily and keep them in a tightly closed plastic bag. Sheep and hog casings that arrive in wet pack, preflushed in slush, or in brine solution may also be re-salted should you have excess. Drain those casings of any water or brine, and then mix in enough salt to cover. Store the casings in a sealed plastic container for later use.

Salt, Sugar, Curing Salt, and Seasonings

When applied to meat, curing is a broad term that describes the transformation of flavor, color, texture, aroma, and the chemical composition of meat brought about principally by its interaction with salt, curing salt, seasonings, and other additives. In the case of fermented sausages, beneficial microorganisms are invited to proliferate naturally or are purposely added to transform the flavor, texture, and fundamental physical properties of meat. Curing as applied to fermented meats encompasses a process influenced by time, temperature, and humidity; by molds and yeasts; and by the nature of the physical environment where cured meats are left to mature. The original purpose of curing meat was to prevent it from spoiling and to preserve it for future use. Ready accessibility of fresh food and the convenience of refrigeration would seem to make the need for cured meat obsolete or at least more of a pleasure than a necessity. But the momentum that cured meats have gained over the centuries of their evolution and their prominent position in many traditional cuisines still drive the imaginations of sausage makers and the appetites of consumers.

Like yeasted bread, cured meat is a complex of balanced ingredients that act synergistically. The modern meat industry has developed a lengthy list of "non-meat" ingredients that play functional roles in cured meats. These fall under the general headings of salts, sugars, seasonings, cure accelerators, antioxidants, binders, and extenders, the greater portion of which are not necessary for home or small-scale cured meat production. My own approach is to use five basic additives and to limit their quantities to levels that support the fundamental flavor of the most important ingredient, the meat itself. It is imperative to emphasize again that the limited use of additives in meat curing is predicated upon the availability of very high-quality, fresh meat. At the same time, it is very important to be vigilant about cleanliness and about accurate measurement of ingredients in a recipe; to maintain control of the temperature of the meat before, during, and after you have done your work on it; and to follow the guidelines in the recipes that follow.

Salt

The most fundamental ingredient in the curing of meat has always been, and remains, salt, or sodium chloride. Salt is an excellent preservative because it acts to speed up the dehydration of meat. In so doing, it decreases the possibility of spoilage by limiting the amount of water available for the growth of certain bacteria. Together with the reduction of water within the meat and in synergy with nitrite (see below), salt is very effective in reducing the potential for organisms that can cause food poisoning. Its addition, in fact, entirely changes the types of microbes present in the meat, a phenomena called floral inversion.

Meat is made up of 60 to 70 percent water, various forms of protein, and fat. When combined with the water in meat, salt forms brine. Brine strength, a measurement of the amount of salt in water that is added to it in a recipe, determines the extent to which salt-soluble proteins in the meat are extracted. Protein extraction directly affects the finished texture, moisture retention, succulence, and slicing characteristics of many types of sausage. The chloride ion of salt contributes another important function, helping it retain moisture, which improves the texture and palatability of cured meat. Salt also enhances the flavor of meat. Almost any form of food-grade salt can be used in curing; however, salt with additives such as iodine or anti-caking agents should be avoided. I use high-purity salt (see Sources and Resources, page 260) because it is the best guarantee against impurities in salt in the form of metal ions that can lead to rancidity and loss of color in cured meat.

It is important not to alter the amount of salt in the recipes that follow for reasons of flavor and safety. The quantities are calibrated both for flavor and in order to discourage growth of unwanted organisms.

Water

Water is a very effective carrier of salt and other elements of the cure. Salt readily dissolves in water to form the pickle, also called brine, that is used for the curing of hams and whole cuts. Water also assists as a dispersing medium for the seasonings in the curing mix, and particularly curing salt that is added in very small quantities. Added water is vital in the formation of meat emulsions (see Mortadella, page 191) and gels, the water–protein matrix in sausages that sets upon heating. In modern commercial production, a whole range of "water-added" or "enhanced" meats has been developed as a response to the use of much leaner pork. Added water mimics the moist effect of fat although with an entirely different mouth feel and flavor result. Such products are also highly manipulated to enable this substitution. The use of water in the recipes below is minimal and is never intended as a fat replacement but rather to enhance the texture of sausage or provide what is needed to bring about a meat emulsion. If you know that your water is hard, use distilled water.

Nitrate and Nitrite

Nitrate, and the compound to which it is converted in meat called nitrite, has been used for centuries in curing. Historical summaries on food preservation attribute the original source of nitrate, also known as saltpeter, to crude salt gathered by the first food preservers. Nitrate is a naturally occurring chemical compound found

in water, soil, rocks, plants, and even in the human body. It is difficult to trace where or when the use of salt containing this substance first began in the curing of meat. Nevertheless, there is a persistent belief that changes in meat color and flavor due to the use of salt containing crude nitrate were observed to be beneficial and desirable long ago. And as cured meats have evolved, the use of curing salt and the changes in color and flavor they effect have distinguished them from meat in any other form. Without the addition of nitrite (or nitrate), cured meats as we know them would not exist. One need only taste the difference between an uncured roast leg of pork and a rosy ham to understand its role. By the late 1800s the use of saltpeter was recommended to promote cured-meat color and later it was discovered to be a very effective inhibitor of some bacteria and in particular of the microorganism that causes botulism. (The word *botulism*, by the way, derives from the Latin word for sausage: *botulus*. Sickness related to the eating of sausage must, therefore, have been very commonplace.) Around the same time, experiments confirmed that *nitrite* is the active curing agent. *Nitrate* serves as a reservoir for the production of nitrite through a conversion process by microorganisms in the meat. Nitrite, once converted to nitric oxide, reacts with the red pigment myoglobin in meat. It is this reaction that is ultimately responsible for cured meat's color.

Today the use of nitrate and nitrite is still widely considered to be an essential element of the curing process for aesthetic reasons, for safety, and for its functional effectiveness. Nitrite is a very potent antioxidant and assists in keeping the flavors of cured meat fresh and free from the off flavors that inevitably develop when meat is held without it for an extended period of time. But the levels of use of nitrite are closely defined and limited for particular cured meats. Nitrate and nitrite first came under close scrutiny following the bacon controversy of the early 1970s. Trace amounts of nitrosamines, known carcinogens directly related to the use of nitrite, were detected in samples of bacon fried at high temperatures. The findings stimulated a great deal of research on nitrite in cured meats and their safety as a food.

Defining the health risk of a very low level of a chemical in foods is problematic for regulatory officials and in the case of nitrite remains inconclusive. But rather than banning nitrite, scientists and the regulatory agencies adopted a reasonable and balanced response based on the risk versus benefit question. The National Academy of Sciences/National Research Council noted that "for the average U.S. citizen 87 percent of nitrate ingested comes from vegetables and when the conversion of nitrate to nitrite in the human body is considered, most of the nitrite to which the average U.S. citizen is exposed actually comes from vegetables (72 percent) and less than 10 percent comes from cured meat" (*The Health Effects of Nitrate, Nitrite, and N-Nitroso Compounds, Washington, D.C.*, National Academy Press, 1–3 and 1–4, 1982).

Although the contribution of nitrite was considered to be small, the committee nevertheless recommended that the amounts added to cured meats be reduced in light of overall exposure from other sources but not eliminated, because of the recognition of the protections it afforded against botulism.

The current thinking that is reflected in the code of federal regulations administered by the U.S. Department of Agriculture indicates that the important benefits of the controlled use of nitrite and nitrite in cured meats outweigh the potential carcinogenic risk to humans. I accept this position with the added proviso that, as with all foods, moderate consumption is the best practice.

Through my trials, I have found that I can, in fact, employ less than the allowable limits of nitrite and still retain the most important characteristics of curing. Research on reduced amounts confirms my approach on the safety side. Notwithstanding these considerations, the use of nitrate and nitrite in curing must be for-

mulated with great caution. When consumed at levels higher than allowed in cured meat products, nitrate and nitrite are toxic. It is particularly important when scaling a recipe up or down to weigh and measure carefully. It is also wise to purchase nitrite and nitrate in cure mixes that are added in fixed quantities to a salt carrier. Most of these cure mixes (see Sources and Resources, page 262) are tinted pink so that there is no mistaking them.

Protection against spoilage or food poisoning in cured meat is not dependent upon the use of nitrite alone. Nitrite has proven to be an effective inhibitor but is no singular guarantee; its combined effect with salt is noted above. The safe practice of curing meat is also ensured by using high-quality meat and by refrigerating it properly, processing it cold, and controlling its temperature at vulnerable stages. Under these circumstances, I feel very comfortable with my "less is better" approach, which is reflected in the recipes below.

Sugar

Sugar is used in cured-meat seasoning mixtures primarily to balance flavor and salt intensity. It also plays a critical role in providing a nutrient source for lactic-acid-producing organisms in fermented sausages. Standard sucrose, from cane or beet sugar, is used to balance flavor. Dextrose, a simple sugar derived from corn, is most commonly used as a nutrient source for lactic-acid bacteria in fermented sausages. Other common sweeteners include corn syrup and corn syrup solids.

Spices and Fresh Seasonings

Spices and fresh herbs or vegetables such as garlic give cured meats their distinctive flavor personality. It is critical that you use only very fresh spices. Whenever possible, grind your own.

Fermented Dry-Cured Sausage

I often meet with a surprised or wary response when I tell people that the cured meat they are eating has been fermented. Apart from foods or beverages whose character and flavor depend on it, like wine, cheese, yogurt, and sauerkraut, to name a few, fermentation is often associated with spoilage. The idea of fermentation of dense muscle is an obscure idea. And, since meat is valued primarily in its fresh state, the invitation of bacteria necessary to bring fermentation about may seem undesirable. Yet it is fermentation that gives traditional dry-cured sausage its complex flavor and savory tang and contributes to its firm, bound texture. Since dry-cured sausages are never cooked, fermentation also provides at least one critical assurance of the stability and safety of the meat.

Traditional fermented sausages relied upon natural fermentation much as some winemakers rely upon native vineyard yeasts to transform grape juice to wine. Sausage makers trusted fermentation to chance microorganisms that originated in the meat itself, in their cellars or in their work environments. Implicit in the old methods was a reassuring knowledge of the source of the meat, the natural environment, and tried-and-true methods validated by years of trial and error and repetition. In small manufactures these natural meat fermentations were often perpetuated by a method similar to that used by bread bakers called "backslopping," whereby a small quantity of one day's production is set aside in order to inoculate the next. Modern starter cultures accomplish the same task much more quickly, immediately inoculating the meat with millions of cells that take precedence over competing organisms. Today, backslopping and wild fermentation are considered risky from the standpoint of safety and consistency. Furthermore, backslopping may introduce extraneous microorganisms with the potential to impart strange flavors in successive batches. Sausages left on their own may ferment only partially or not at all, spoilage organisms may outcompete beneficial ones, or a superb batch may result. Having myself experienced all of these results, I've settled on the use of starter cultures.

Starter Cultures

Fermentation in meat, in the most basic terms, is the conversion of sugar to lactic acid by lactic-acid-producing bacteria. In order for fermentation to occur, the bacteria must have food to grow. This is why dextrose (corn sugar), a simple sugar, is a common ingredient in dry-cured sausage recipes. Typically, dry-cured recipes contain .5 to 1 percent dextrose. Varying the amount yields a more or less tangy sausage.

Since the late 1950s, prepared starter cultures have been the favored means of initiating lactic-acid fermentation in meat. Starter cultures for the traditional dry-cured sausages also include benign species of another bacteria, staphylococcus, that produces no acid but enhances color and flavor development. Commercial starter cultures that perform very effectively are available to the home sausage maker in freeze-dried form (see Sources and Resources, page 263) and are simple to use. A measured amount of the culture proportional to the batch weight of the sausage is rehydrated in distilled water and added to the sausage mixture after all other salts and seasonings have been mixed in. Thorough mixing is important to fully distribute the culture throughout the mixture.

Meat fermentation must be carried out within the temperature zone where bacteria grow rapidly. The optimal range of your particular culture will be specified in the protocol by the vendor. For home or small production, it is more practical to use the lower-temperature cultures, which perform at warm room temperature.

Successful fermentation hinges on the simultaneous lowering of the meat's pH as its temperature rises. The pH scale runs from 0 to 14. The neutral point is 7. Reading acid on the pH scale is counterintuitive. Below the neutral point, acidity actually *increases*; above 7 the alkalinity increases, in both cases rising at an exponential rate. So, a pH reading of 6 is 10 times more acidic than a reading of 7 and a pH reading of 5 is 100 times more acidic than a reading of 7, and so forth.

Troublesome microorganisms are pH sensitive, and a timely fermentation that yields a safe, low pH creates an environment in which they are inhibited or cannot grow. Meat fermentation is a kind of balancing act, the goal of which is to lower the pH quickly enough as the temperature rises in the meat mixture so that potential spoilage organisms cannot get started. In addition to the use of starter cultures, the direct addition of organic acids also provides an acid tang to sausages and reduces pH to safe levels without fermentation. But sausages made with these chemical acidulants do not have the chance to develop the more mellow flavors of fermented meat, and using them is more like concocting an imitation rather than letting nature run its course.

Generally speaking, meat that has been properly handled and chilled has a pH of 5.6 to 5.9, though it may reach as high as 6.4. The goal of fermentation is to achieve a pH of less than 5.3 within 48 hours. The proper use of starter cultures, the right environmental conditions, and a pH meter make this easily possible and verifiable.

The formation of lactic acid and the corresponding drop in pH during the course of fermentation have other beneficial effects on the development of dry-cured sausage. The acid denatures the proteins much as a fried egg protein is denatured by heat to produce a firm, bound texture. You will notice your sausages tighten in their skins considerably after fermentation. Reducing the pH also brings the proteins in the meat to the point where they most readily give up water. Not only does this promote even drying, it reduces the time necessary to bring it about. The giving up of water also decreases "water activity," a measurement used to determine the amount of available water to sustain microbial growth. This decreased potential for unwanted microorganisms further contributes to the safety of the sausage.

The final flavor effect of fermented sausages depends upon the quality and flavor of the pork and the complex flavors that develop during the ripening and maturation process. My own process with fermented sausage is to continually experiment with cultures, levels of salt, seasoning, and aging periods. You also may wish to experiment with different cultures and the variables over time. If you do so, be sure to keep precise and thorough records of what you've done. You will want to repeat that which is successful and avoid that which is not. The goal is to optimize the culture with the process and the seasonings to get the flavors you most desire.

Environment for Fermentation

Sausage makers rely upon temperature- and humidity-controlled environments to ferment and age their dry-cured products, which permit them to make sausages of all types year-round.

Dry-cured sausage manufacturers have special holding areas called drip rooms where temperature, humidity, and the air movement can be controlled during fermentation. Knowledge of the ambient parameters for fermentation makes it possible to replicate similar conditions in the corner of a home kitchen or clean basement area.

It is simplest to set up a fermentation space in an insulated room whose temperature and humidity can be maintained within the range called for by the culture you are using. For the purposes of the cultures recommended in the recipes below, warm room temperature (70 to 80°F.) is sufficient. If a space with these ambient conditions is unavailable, you can create a tented or curtained enclosure using thick plastic sheeting secured to the walls and ceiling of the area and use heat lamps directed around the enclosure, to warm it. Plastic sheeting also acts as a vapor barrier and if the area is small enough and the ambient humidity is sufficiently high, the enclosure is all you will need. I have successfully fermented small batches of salami in a 33-gallon plastic bag fixed to either end of a dowel on which the salami hung, the center of the bag pulled away from contact with the sausage on either side. If you need to increase humidity because you live in a dry place, an inexpensive vaporizer quickly adds moisture to the enclosure. Control of relative humidity is important during fermentation to keep the exterior of the sausage moist and supple. Proper relative humidity also prevents a condition called case hardening, a drying and sealing-off of the surface of the sausage that prevents moisture from migrating out. Case hardening eventually leads to spoilage in the center of the sausage.

The general rule for fermentations at lower temperatures is to maintain relative humidity in the fermentation area between 5 and 10 percent lower than that in the sausage itself (approximately 90 percent). Dry sausage, then, is typically fermented at a relative humidity of 80 to 85 percent with slow, steady movement of air until the pH drops to the desired level.

Curing Cellar

The cellar is as much an ingredient in sausage making as the cave is for cheese, or the vat for wine. In a natural cellar, meat ripens in a particular quality of air and is affected by air movement, humidity, and shifts in temperature. The physical environment of the cellar also harbors microorganisms such as yeasts and molds that become part of the skin and flavor fabric of maturing meat. Having visited such cellars throughout Italy with the idea of building my own, I returned less enlightened about a fixed technique for drying and ripening sausage than made aware of the interesting complexities involved in carrying it out in a natural environment.

Modern sausage makers use environment-controlled rooms to dry sausages predictably year-round. Thanks to both examples, I have learned what to aim for; based on the experience of my own cellar over time, I now know what conditions favor the best results. But developing a cellar for ripening and drying sausage that is not altogether conditioned through artificial means is a matter of discovery rather than control, which is both the fun and fascination of it. Obviously, I cannot provide a recipe for a curing cellar that incorporates the same natural influences present in my own. But, by describing it, I hope to make you aware of the basic principles involved.

I begin curing and ripening meats just outside the curing cellar in a workspace that maintains a temperature of about 65°F. Above the workspace are rails attached to the ceiling for hanging sausage and I am able to close a plastic curtain around this area during fermentation. Within this curtain I place a warm steam humidifier to bring temperature and humidity into the optimal range.

Once my sausage has fermented and achieved the necessary drop in pH, I move it to the cellar to dry and mature. The time necessary for drying and maturation of dry sausage is dependent upon the diameter of the sausage, the casing thickness and type, and the temperature, relative humidity, and air movement in the cellar. There are many opinions and little agreement about the most effective blend of the last three variables. Nevertheless, the fundamental principle in the control of drying is to assure that as moisture migrates outward from the sausage interior, it is moved away from the surface of the sausage at the same, or at a slightly greater, rate.

My sausage cellar is 10 feet beneath the ground at the base of a north-facing hillside. It is a rectangular room bounded on all sides by thick concrete walls and maintains a constant temperature of about 50°F. My cellar is impermeable to water but its relative humidity fluctuates in the wet season and with the degree of saturation in the deep soil surrounding it.

Prosciutto, coppa, culatello, and other whole cuts begin in a closed, refrigerated salting case that measures 8 feet high by 8 feet wide by 4 feet deep. I built the case by first insulating the north-facing wall with thick foam board and covering it with 4-inch-wide, smoothly sanded redwood that is tightly lapped together. I chose redwood for its good resistance to deterioration in moist environments and because it looks stunning. Three tall insulated glass doors, also made of redwood and fitted with rubber seals, shut tight against the face frame. This case offers the option of refrigeration for one important reason: Whole cured cuts such as prosciutto or coppa are vulnerable to spoilage in the initial period of salting, and neither my cellar temperature nor the seasonal temperatures in the San Francisco Bay Area drops to points low enough to prevent spoilage.

There is no installed control for humidity or air movement in my case since its limited size allows me to use the existing refrigerator fan and heat from a track of lights to regulate the moisture and air movement within. The added heat causes the evaporator in the refrigeration system to kick on, which pulls moistures out of the air within and directs it to a small copper pipe to the outside. My lights are on a dimmer that allows me to control the amount of heat I introduce and the corresponding humidity. On the center wall I have mounted a thermometer and hygrometer that measures temperature and relative humidity. Humidity in my curing case fluctuates with the amount of cured meat I have hanging there and its degree of freshness. Whole cuts of meat contain as much as 70 percent water when they first enter. I know that when I have added newly cured meat to the case, I need to adjust the humidity by means of turning up the lights. Throughout the drying process I keep a regular eye on the humidity reading and how it is affecting the appearance and feel of the meat. If molds are growing prodigiously, or the meat feels a little tacky, I know I need to either increase air movement or decrease humidity or both. When the case is fully loaded, I have found it necessary to place a small fan on the floor of the case in one corner to increase airflow. If the meat looks and feels a little dry, off goes the small fan and down go the lights.

My cellar has two access doors. One is an entry passage from the adjoining garage; the other swings wide to a drafty passageway to the garden. The garden door is important because it allows me to open the room wide to permit the entry of fresh air from the outside. As meat ripens, strong aromatic compounds can develop and it is necessary to refresh the air in the cellar. Access to good clean air has always been an essential ingredient in traditional aging rooms. I don't generally open the cellar to hot days, because doing so would push the temperature above 60°F. and would invite flying insects that are more readily attracted to the smell of ripening meat in warm air. In the summer months I open the doors of the refrigerated case to the surrounding cellar alone. I try to exchange the air once a day and when there is no wind to carry the current, I set a small fan to blow in the corner of the room facing the case. The sausages appear to thrive in these circumstances and maintain a wholesome aroma during the course of drying.

Recipes

☙

Fresh Italian Sausage
Makes 45 sausages weighing just under
3.5 ounces each

The roots of this highly seasoned pork sausage are ancient. "Lucanica" sausage, named after Lucania, the Roman name for the southern Italian region today known as Basilicata, was widely praised by Roman writers. Nevertheless, the northern regions of Lombardy (where it is called Luganega, perhaps after the lakeside town of Lugano) and the Veneto also claim it jealously as their own. All over Italy I have encountered different forms of Lucanica that vary in their proportion of lean to fat and the composition of the spices used to season it. They nonetheless share a common shape, size, and casing. Lucanica is a plump, juicy sausage, highly seasoned with salt and pepper and a range of spices that often includes fennel, aniseeds, or clove. My own rendition includes a small percentage of boiled pork skin that enhances both the texture and the flavor. Lucanica is stuffed into standard natural hog casings about 1¼ inches in diameter and is eaten fresh. It is no better than when simply slowly browned in a pan over low heat for 4 to 5 minutes per side, then finished in a preheated 375°F. oven for an additional 3 to 4 minutes and serve with wilted greens dressed with minced shallots, lemon or vinegar, and olive oil. In the fall, I make a sauce with the last of the fresh tomatoes, onions, and garlic, then combine the sauce with grilled sliced sausages and layers of polenta sprinkled with Parmigiano. This sausage is delicious cooked on skewers next to boneless pieces of poultry marinated with herbs and olive oil or whole small sections of birds such as quail or pigeon alternating with olive oil-doused chunks of bread and sage leaves. These can be broiled in the oven, spit roasted, or placed on the charcoal grill. Often, these sausages figure in the Oliveto menu in a mixed grill of pork, in which pieces of roasted loin and leg are laid out next to ribs and shoulder chops. If you are going to eat the sausages right away, no curing salt is necessary. If you wish to hold them for up to a week or longer, use the quantity listed below.

7 pounds lean pork, preferably from the shoulder
2 pounds 5 ounces fresh back fat
1 pound fresh pork skin to yield 13 ounces after cooking
80 grams salt
6 grams Instacure No. 1 (see Sources and Resources, page 262)
14 grams freshly ground black pepper
3 grams dry sage
1 gram powdered cayenne
14 grams fresh garlic, smashed to a paste in a mortar
8 grams sweet aniseeds
14 grams dextrose (corn sugar)
138 grams ice-cold water

Grinding the lean

Cut the pork and pork fat into rough 1-inch chunks and lay the pieces out on a sheet tray. Cover the tray with foil and place it in the freezer. Make sure the meat and fat are very cold before grinding (32°F. is ideal; the meat will feel nearly frozen). In the meantime, cut the pork skin into 2-inch pieces. Cook the pork skin in boiling water for 40 minutes, or until it offers little resistance to the point of a knife. Refresh the pork skin under cold water, and then grind it through a 3/16-inch plate. Re-weigh the pork skin (you will have something less than you started with due to shrinkage during cooking and remnants left behind in the grinder shaft); if you are short of 13 ounces, open the grinder plate, remove the skin, and chop it fine by hand. Lay the skin on a plate and refrigerate it.

Grinding the lean and the fat with the skin

When the meat and fat are very well chilled, transfer the pieces to a mixing bowl. The skin will have congealed. Cut or break it into small pieces and add it to the bowl along with the salt, curing salt, and seasonings. Mix quickly with a spatula to distribute the ingredients and seasonings. Grind the mixture once through a 1/4-inch plate into a large chilled bowl; if it is warm in your kitchen, place ice under the bowl. Add the cold water and mix vigorously for about 5 minutes with a large spatula, alternately cutting through the mixture with the edge of the spatula and turning it over to blend all of the ingredients. As you mix you will notice the meat grow firm and compact. When the mixture is thoroughly combined and feels quite sticky, stop mixing.

Immediately stuff the sausage into standard hog casing and twirl the sausages off to roughly 4 1/2-inch lengths. Hang to dry in warm, dry air until the sausages lose their surface moisture, then refrigerate. The sausages may be frozen and will keep well for several months if well wrapped.

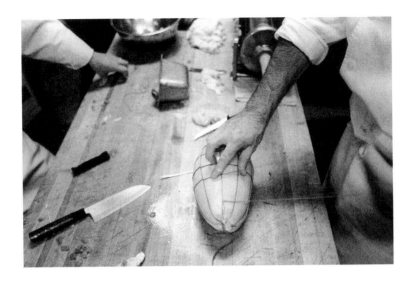

Mortadella

The Italian city of Bologna and the surrounding region has long been the renowned center of pork curing. Oddly enough, its name has become synonymous with that uniformly ground, monotonously textured log with a strange, cooked-earth color we all remember from childhood. The irony is that American bologna is a direct descendant of what is considered by some to be the noblest of all pork products. In Italy, mortadella is made in enormous casings that match its monumental reputation. It is common to walk into delicatessens throughout Emilia-Romagna and meet with mortadelle that weigh 100 kilos, the market weight of an entire pig!

Mortadella is a sausage with a seamless frankfurter-like texture, spiced liberally with cracked and whole black peppercorns, a scattering of pistachio nuts, and pearly white jowl fat. Mechanical cutting tools have supplanted the mortar and pestle of the past. At Oliveto, I use a bowl chopper. At home, you can make a very fine mortadella using a food processor. It nevertheless remains a labor of love. Mortadella is demanding in terms of time and process. But, should you decide to take it on, you will be rewarded with something sublime to eat, impressive to share, and fascinating to learn about.

Making mortadella involves making a meat emulsion or "batter" much as one would a mayonnaise, although the ingredients bound together are assuredly more solid. The miracle of mortadella's texture and silky mouth feel is the joining of elements—water and fat, like water and oil in mayonnaise, that ordinarily do not mix. A meat emulsion is made up of three fundamental parts: water, fat, and an emulsifier. The water in meat, as well as that which is added in the recipe, combines with salt-soluble proteins to form a matrix called the "liquid phase" of a meat emulsion. This matrix also contains other cellular components of the meat, spices, and seasonings. The so-called "solid phase" is made up of fat, reduced to tiny particles by the action of continuous chopping. Water and fat do not separate because of the third and perhaps most important element, the emulsifying agent that acts as a barrier between the two but is mixable with both. Meat contains an abundant form of protein that unfolds to offer "water-hating" portions of its molecules toward the fat phase and "water-loving" portions toward the liquid phase. In so doing, it provides a coating or membrane around the fat droplets. At the same time the proteins bind water and the two opposing phases are held in suspension.

Temperature is important in the making of mortadella both in the cutting stage and later when the sausage is cooked. Chopping increases the temperature of the fat through the friction of the blades. As it heats up, the fat softens and chopping enables the reduction of the fat particles to a very small size. In the case of pork, chopping should continue until a temperature of 60 to 62°F. is reached. Upon heating, the meat proteins entrap fat and water, which contributes to mortadella's moist, refined texture.

Mortadella
Makes one 3¾-pound mortadella

This recipe can be made in one batch in a 3-quart food processor. Make sure the blades are very sharp. If your machine is smaller than 3 quarts, determine how much of the meat and fat will fit in the bowl (leave about 2½ inches of head space) and divide it into batches along with the salt, cure, and seasonings. Mortadella is traditionally encased in a bladder, a hard-to-come-by item, which provides a sturdy container that can withstand poaching without splitting and lends this sausage its teardrop shape. If bladders are not available to you, substitute a 4½-inch beef bung cap or roll the raw batter in several layers of plastic wrap to form a neat cylinder and secure it as tightly as possible with string at either end.

1¾ pounds lean shoulder of pork
1 pound back fat
34 grams salt
3 grams Instacure No. 1 (See Sources and
     Resources, page 262)
312 grams ice, crushed in the food processor
9 grams fresh garlic, crushed to a paste in a
     mortar
15 grams dextrose
2 grams mace
1 gram ground coriander
1 gram ground cinnamon
1 gram powdered cayenne
75 grams fresh pork jowl or back fat, cut into
     rough ⅜-inch dice, cooked for 3 minutes in
     boiling water, refreshed in cold water
31 grams whole, fresh, shelled pistachio nuts
2 grams coarsely cracked black peppercorns

Grinding meat and fat

Before grinding, make sure the meat and fat are well chilled (32°F. is ideal). If necessary, place both meat and fat on separate covered trays and place them in the freezer to bring the temperature down. First, grind the lean pork shoulder through a 3/16-inch plate. Transfer the meat directly to the food processor bowl. Without cleaning the grinder, grind the fat similarly into a bowl and refrigerate it.

Cutting the meat, taking the temperature

Add all of the salt, curing salt, half of the ice, and the garlic, dextrose, mace, coriander, cinnamon, and cayenne to the ground meat. Cut the meat in a food processor to a very smooth, pale pink paste with a temperature of 42 to 45°F. If you notice that some of the meat is climbing up the side of the bowl during the chopping and escaping the blade, stop the machine and use a spatula to reincorporate it into the mixture before continuing.

Emulsifying the meat and fat

When you have finished chopping all of the lean meat, add the chilled fat and the remaining ice. Process the mixture again to a consistently smooth paste. Turn the machine off every so often and use a spatula to fold the paste gathering at the top of the machine to the bottom. Stop the machine when the temperature of the paste reaches 62°F. Transfer the paste to a bowl.

Folding in the cubed fat, pistachios and pepper

Using a stiff spatula, fold in the cubed, cooked pork jowl, the pistachio nuts, and the pepper so that it is evenly distributed.

Casing and Cooking

Stuff the mortadella into a large, flushed beef bladder or beef bung casing (see Sources and Resources, pages 260-261). Secure the end with a butterfly knot and create a loop to hang the mortadella afterward. Place the mortadella in a deep pot and pour over cold water to cover it. Place a plate and pan lid on the mortadella to keep it submerged. Heat the water to 160°F. and hold it there over a low flame for the duration of the cooking. Cook to an internal temperature of 155°F. If the mortadella is cased in a bladder, it will take 3½ to 4 hours to reach the finished temperature; 4- to 5-inch beef bungs will take about half this time. In either event, take the temperature regularly to monitor the cooking. Immediately plunge the mortadella into an ice bath to bring the temperature down. Store for several days before eating. Mortadella is best sliced paper-thin.

Coppa di Testa

My Italian friend from Modena finds it amusing and ironic that the most humble foods born of less fortunate times should be so clamored after in the upscale delicatessens and restaurants of modern Italian cities. Coppa di testa, a magnificent "head cheese," *ciccioli,* and cotechino are the legacy of farming people whose efforts under a landlord meant that their share of the bounty required making the most of slender means and unredeemable scraps. Coppa di testa and cotechino have been improved for modern times by the inclusion of leaner meats, fine seasoning, and a less rustic appearance. My own versions follow suit. The modern version of head cheese from Siena, delicately laced with the warm spices found likewise in the celebrated sweetmeat confection called *pan forte di Siena,* and the more plainly seasoned mosaic of meats that goes by the name coppa di testa in Bologna's overflowing delicatessens, is one of the most exalted products of the pig. My version is a combination of the two, a blend of meat and a small amount of skin from the fore trotters; a good quantity of pork tongues, which lend refinement of both flavor and texture; and selected portions of the head cooked together in a spicy broth. After the meats cool, I pick the meat from the trotters and head, peel the tongues, and slice them into varying sizes. The unique texture of coppa di testa is dependent upon the dimensions and shapes of its elements. It should look like a sort of crazy quilt of meats. Unlike other sausages that rely upon protein binding and heat to set them to a firm texture, coppa di testa is held together by the release of gelatin from collagen in the skin and connective tissues of the fore trotters and head (with a safe assist from some added powdered gelatin) that stiffens when cooled.

Coppa di Testa
Makes 4½ to 5 pounds picked meat,
enough to fill a 24-inch length of 100-millimeter
collagen casing

You will need a large pot with 20-quart capacity to contain the meats and particularly the head and fore trotters, which take up a lot of room. The spicing of coppa di testa takes place in two stages. Whole and cracked spices and salt are added to perfume the water in which the meats are simmered. Picked free of the bones, the meat is combined with some of the gelatin-rich cooking broth and its spices. Afterward, additional spices are added before encasing the meat to punch up its flavor.

9 pounds pork head
5¾ pounds pork fore trotters
4 pounds fresh pork tongues
3 gallons water, or as needed

Spices and aromatics for the broth
175 grams salt
4 grams whole cinnamon stick
2 grams whole cloves
4 grams whole coriander seed
6 whole dry bay leaves
2 grams whole nutmeg, smashed coarsely
   in a mortar
15 grams whole peppercorns
5 grams cracked allspice berries
1 medium onion, quartered
1 large carrot, peeled and cut in chunks
1 celery stalk, cut in chunks

Place the head in a deep pot, then add the fore trotters. Add the tongues last. It's a good idea to count the number of tongues you place in the pot since they cook before the heads and trotters and must be fished out first. Cover the meats with the water and bring them to the boil. Skim away the white froth that rises to the surface, reduce to a simmer, and add the salt, spices, and vegetables. After 1 hour and 20 minutes, remove the tongues from the pot and transfer them to a bowl. Cover the tongues with a little of the broth as they will be much easier to peel if they remain warm. Continue to cook the meats for an additional 25 minutes, then transfer them a sheet pan to cool. Reserve the cooking broth.

Use a small paring knife to peel and cut away the skin from the tongues and cut them into uneven pieces ½ inch to ¾ inch thick. When the fore trotters cool, separate the joints and pull the meat from the bones, separating the meat from the skin. Do the same with the head. Slice the ears as thin as possible. Discard the bones. Sort through the meat from the trotters and head a second time and cut away obvious fat or gristle. The picked meat should be as lean as possible.

Coppa di testa has the most interesting texture when the meat is cut to various sizes. To this end, chop some of the meat fine; leave other pieces large (approximately 1 inch in overall size), and other pieces middling in size.

Assembly and final seasoning
1 quart plus 1 cup broth from the cooking
½ gram ground cloves (¼ teaspoon)
1 gram ground cinnamon
½ gram freshly grated nutmeg (¼ teaspoon)
11 grams salt
40 grams powdered gelatin

Pour 1 quart plus 1 cup of warm broth over the picked and chopped meats. Add the spices and salt, sprinkle the gelatin over the top, and let it stand for 5 minutes, then stir the mixture well. Check the salt. The mixture should have a little more salt than your taste tells you is just right—the impression of salt diminishes in cold foods.

Soak a 24-inch length of collagen casing 100 millimeters in diameter in warm water for ten minutes. Drain the casing and tie a tight butterfly knot in one end. Fill the casing as you would a pastry bag: Stand the casing in a deep pot to steady it as you fill it, invert the open end, and use a ladle or large spoon to transfer the coppa di testa mixture to the casing. Twist the casing

end to tension the sausage. Use forceps to hold it tight while you tie it snugly. Chill the coppa di testa, preferably standing on end in the pot, overnight.

Slice the coppa a little more thickly than salame with a thin, sharp knife or meat slicer and arrange it on a platter. Serve it by itself, with mustard, or with a scattering of minced shallots doused in white wine vinegar and fresh chopped parsley.

Cotechino

Makes 8 cotechini, 20 ounces each

Cotechino, the celebrated boiling sausage of the Emilia-Romagna, is eaten by itself with beans, lentils, mashed potatoes, or sauerkraut. In other northern regions it is part of the grand dinner of boiled meats called bollito misto, served with an array of vegetables and condiments, most typically green herb sauce, fresh horseradish, and fruit mustard. It is one of the most luxurious of cooked sausages. Cotechino derives its marvelous, slightly sticky texture and also its name (*cotica* means "skin") from the inclusion of precooked pork skin.

5 pounds lean pork shoulder, cut into 1-inch cubes

1 pound 11 ounces fresh back fat, cut into 1-inch cubes

3 pounds 5 ounces fresh de-fatted pork skin, preferably from the belly

80 grams salt

7 grams Instacure No. 1 curing salt (see Sources and Resources, page 262)

9 grams finely ground black pepper

1 gram ground coriander

1 gram ground cloves

1 gram powdered cayenne

1 gram ground cinnamon

18 grams dextrose

½ gram mace (scant ¼ teaspoon)

½ gram freshly ground or grated nutmeg (⅛ teaspoon)

Hog middles or beef wide middle casings, (approximately 60 millimeters in diameter)

Make certain the meat is well chilled (32°F. is ideal) before grinding. If necessary, lay the meat on a baking sheet, cover it with plastic wrap, and chill it in the freezer. Cut the pork skin into 2-inch pieces, place them in a pot, cover with water, and bring to the boil. Skim any white froth that rises to the surface, reduce the heat to a gentle boil, and cook for 40 minutes to 1 hour, or until the skin is very tender to the point of a knife. Drain the skin in a colander; scrape away any fat adhering to the underside of the skin, lay onto a baking sheet, and chill.

Grind the skin through a ³⁄₁₆-inch plate. Combine the meat, fat, and skin in a bowl and mix them together. Grind the mixture once through a ³⁄₈-inch plate. Add the salt, curing salt, and seasonings and mix with a heavy-duty spatula until slightly stiff and sticky to the touch.

Pack in tied hog middles or wide beef middle casings. Tie tightly. Poach the cotechini in 170°F. water for 1 hour. Carve the sausage on a large platter or cutting board with a trough to catch the juices that run. Add the juices to the garnish (lentils or beans are particularly flattered) or use them to baste the slices you lay on the platter.

Ciccioli

Makes two 9-inch standard loaves

Ciccioli in the region of Emilia-Romagna refers to a savory pressed cake made from the renderings of lard. Traditional ciccioli has a caramelized color and crackling-like texture from the frying of the fatty scraps and skin. My own rendition is altogether different from the Italian model with a softer, more voluptuous texture that comes from rendering pork trimmings over a low flame until they are very tender. If you make fresh or dry-cured sausages from whole cuts such as shoulders or legs, you will be left with fat and meat scraps after separating lean from fat. What looks like discard can be transformed into a sublime pâté reminiscent of French rillettes. Ciccioli is a rich treat and a little goes a long way. I like to serve ciccioli as an appetizer with grilled slices of sourdough that have been rubbed with garlic and a tart salad of spicy greens such as arugula. Set out ciccioli as part of a party buffet with little pickles or olives and crostini and you will very likely see the whole loaf disappear.

3½ pounds fatty pork trimmings

1½ pounds leg or shoulder fat, cut into rough 1-inch pieces

27 grams salt

3 grams Instacure No. 1 (see Sources and Resources, page 262)

2 bay leaves

2 cups water

5 grams freshly ground black pepper

½ grams dried thyme (½ teaspoon)

Combine the pork trimmings, fat, salt, curing salt, and bay leaves, add water in a 6-quart sauce or braising pot. Bring to a boil, then reduce the heat slightly. When you see the fat run from cloudy to clear, reduce the heat to a very gentle simmer, cover the pot, and cook for 50 minutes more. Pour the contents of the pot into a colander set over a bowl to catch the rendered fat. Turn the meat onto a cutting board and chop it very coarse, then add it back to the fat in the bowl. Add the pepper and thyme and mix well. Line two 9-inch standard loaf pans with plastic wrap. Spoon an equal amount of the meat and fat into each pan. Cover with plastic wrap and chill overnight. Refrigerated, ciccioli will last well for several weeks.

⟳
Pork Liver Pâté
Makes one 2-quart pâté

This pâté has the smooth, spreadable texture of a mousse with subtle background flavors from warm spices. In order to achieve an emulsion, it is important to bring *all* ingredients to cool room temperature (62 to 65°F.) before blending them. This temperature makes it possible to reduce the fat to very fine particles: Higher temperatures cause the fat to melt and the batter to separate, and lower temperatures do not permit the fat to be cut fine enough to achieve the right texture. This pâté is simple to prepare and makes an ideal antipasto spread on toast and with a glass of off-dry vin santo, vintage Madeira, or Oloroso Sherry.

1 pound 7 ounces fresh pork liver, veins removed

1 pound 11 ounces fresh pork leg fat (substitute back fat if unavailable)

1¼ cups Meat Broth (see page 135)

1¼ cups heavy cream

15 grams shallots, finely diced

10 grams fresh flat-leaf parsley, chopped

5 egg yolks, at room temperature

¼ cup vin santo or Madeira

2 grams Instacure No. 1 (see Sources and Resources, page 262)

21 grams salt

6 grams dextrose

9 grams finely ground black pepper

3 grams freshly grated or ground nutmeg

4 grams ground coriander

1 gram ground cloves

1 gram ground cinnamon

1 gram sweet paprika

21 grams dried (powdered) milk

Preheat the oven to 300° F.

Cut the pork liver and the pork fat into 1-inch pieces. Cook the fat in boiling water for 5 minutes, drain it, then let it cool to room temperature. Combine the broth and cream in a sauce pot, add the shallots and parsley, and heat the mixture to a simmer. Remove from the heat and let the mixture cool to room temperature.

Line a 2-quart pâté or terrine mold with plastic wrap.

When the fat and the broth and cream mixture are cool, place them and the remaining ingredients in a blender and allow the machine to run at medium speed until the mixture is very smooth. Pour the mixture into the pâté mold. Set a piece of oiled parchment paper on top, and then cover tightly with foil. Set the mold in a deep pan and pour hot water around it to reach the level of the mixture. Bake for 30 minutes at 300°F. Reduce to 250°F. and cook for 1½ hours more, or until the temperature in the center of the pâté reaches 160°F. Cool at room temperature. Store for at least a day in the refrigerator before serving. Pork liver pâté will hold well for up to a week.

⟲
Pâté Campagnola
Makes one 2-quart pâté

This rustic pâté made of coarse ground pork belly, pork jowls, and liver is equally at home on a picnic blanket or at an elegant table. When you purchase fresh pork belly, ask for the leaner end. If pork jowls are unavailable, substitute the fatter end of the belly. Because the spices are added in minute quantities, I prepare a mixture that I call "five-spice blend" (not to be confused with Chinese five-spice powder). Cane fat, the lacy stomach membrane of a pig or lamb, is used to line the pâté mold and both bastes and protects the exposed top of the pâté as it cooks. For a source refer to the Niman Ranch online market (see page 261).

1 pound 2 ounces fresh pork belly
15 ounces fresh pork jowls, skinned
1 pound 2 ounces fresh pork liver
⅜ cup dry red wine
1 cup whole milk
3 large eggs, beaten
7 grams Instacure No. 1 (see Sources and
    Resources, page 262)
26 grams salt
5 grams dextrose
2 grams five-spice blend (see Note opposite)
4 grams finely ground black pepper
83 grams minced yellow onion
10 grams finely minced garlic
30 grams finely chopped fresh flat-leaf parsley
130 grams caul fat

Preheat the oven to 350°F.

Cut the belly, jowls, and liver into 1-inch pieces. Pour the wine over the mixture, mix, and then chill the meat thoroughly (30 to 32°F. is ideal) before grinding.

Grind half of the belly and the jowls and all of the liver through a 3/16-inch plate. Grind the remaining belly and jowls through a 3/8-inch plate. Add the milk and the remaining ingredients except the caul fat and combine well.

Line a 2-quart pâté mold with caul fat so that it overhangs the top by about 2 inches. Spoon the mixture into the mold, tamp it on a hard surface to settle the ingredients, and fold the caul fat over the meat mixture to completely cover it. Place the pâté, uncovered, in a deep pan and pour hot water around the mold to the level of the mixture.

Bake for 1 hour, or until the top of the pâté is well browned. Reduce the heat to 250°F. and cook for 1 hour more, or until the temperature reads 155°F. in the center. Cool at room temperature. Store in the refrigerator for at least a day before serving. Pâté Campagnola will keep for 10 days if well refrigerated. Serve sliced with a crusty, slightly sour loaf and your favorite pickles.

Note
To make five-spice blend, combine 25 grams whole nutmeg, 15 grams cinnamon stick, 4 grams whole cloves, 50 grams black peppercorns, and 15 grams coriander seeds. Grind the spices to a fine powder in a spice grinder. Reserve what you don't use for later use.

Oliveto House-Cured Ham

One of the high points of our Oliveto menu in celebration of pork is this simple ham. For most people, ham is synonymous with smoked flavor and they are taken by surprise when they taste pure pork enhanced only with salt, a little sugar, curing salt, and background spices. This ham is moist and pink-complexioned and notably delicate in flavor. It is delicious sliced thin with a stew of white beans or little peas, herb-scented mashed potatoes, braised cabbage, or sauerkraut.

The goal in curing a fresh ham is to deliver the salt and curing salt to the center of the ham as fast as possible to prevent it from souring. Using a meat pump fitted with a spray needle is far more effective and speedy than simply immersing the ham in brine.

The ideal size for a home-cured ham is 13 pounds or so, skin, leg bones, and aitchbone (pelvic bone) included. It is important to purchase a very fresh leg of pork and to cure it immediately after. If this size and quantity of meat is more than you want to tackle, you can also make a superb ham from the boneless shoulder-end loin of pork. Ask for boneless loin of pork cut 8 ribs from the shoulder end. This cut weighs about 8 pounds. Whichever cut you choose, make sure that the meat is well chilled prior to curing; 32 to 35°F. is ideal. You will need two different containers — a large, deep pan to contain the ham while you inject it and a 5-gallon bucket to immerse the ham afterward.

There is no precise method for injecting the leg or loin with the brine. The goal is to introduce the brine to all of the muscles of the leg and particularly, deep against the shin and thigh and pelvic bones. The brine pump (see Sources and Resources, page 260) is like a giant hypodermic needle. The needle is perforated so that brine sprays in all directions when inserted in muscle. Make certain the pump is very clean before use. To load brine in the pump, hold the needle fully submerged in the brine and draw the pump handle back. Plunge the needle into muscle slightly above the perforations and press on the handle to inject the brine.

The loin, which has an even thickness and no bones, is simple to inject. As a general guideline, space the pattern of injection 1½ inches apart and insert the needle to half of the width of the muscle. Clearly, some muscles of the leg are thicker and denser than others and toward the top of the ham you will encounter the structure of the aitchbone. When you are in the area of any bone, direct the needle toward it. In the case of the heaviest muscle, the butt, it may be necessary to inject it from various angles. Likewise, probe at various points around the aitchbone and the top of the leg to distribute the brine evenly. The surest indication that you are reaching all muscles of the leg is the gradual swelling and stiffening of the muscles.

⌾
Oliveto House-Cured Ham
For 12

For the fresh pork leg
3 gallons water
454 grams salt
300 grams sugar
10 grams allspice berries
20 grams black peppercorns
5 grams whole cloves
10 grams whole juniper berries
2 onions (1 pound), sliced thin
2 carrots, peeled and sliced thin
2 celery stalks, sliced thin
Small bunch of fresh flat-leaf parsley
Small bunch of fresh thyme
8 bay leaves
57 grams Instacure No. 1 (see Sources and
    Resources, page 262)
1 very fresh leg of pork (13 pounds), skin on,
    aitchbone attached, trotter removed 1 inch
    above the hock joint

For the shoulder-end loin
2 gallons water
295 grams salt
195 grams sugar
6 grams allspice berries
13 grams black peppercorns
1 large onion, sliced thin
1 large carrot, sliced thin
1 large celery stalk
Small bunch of fresh flat-leaf parsley
Small bunch of fresh thyme
5 bay leaves
44 grams Instacure No. 1
8 pounds boneless shoulder-end loin of pork

To prepare the brine solution, put the water in a large pot. Add the salt and sugar. Crack the whole spices coarse in a mortar and add them to the brine along with the sliced vegetables and herbs. Warm the brine to 160°F. to release the spice and vegetable aromas and to dissolve the salt and sugar. Chill the brine to 34°F., stir in the curing salt, and dissolve it thoroughly.

While the brine cooks, prepare the pork leg. Cut away the tailbone and trim away the skin and fat and any glands on the flank side. Remove any excess fat around the skinless area of the aitchbone. Turn the leg aitchbone down and cut away the skin approximately two thirds of the distance from the top to the shank end. Trim the fat to an even layer about ¼ inch thick. Square off the top of the ham. If you are using a loin cut, simply trim the cover fat to about ⅛ inch.

Place the ham inside a deep pan with the shank end facing you. First, inject brine directly through the base of the foot, three or four times, adjusting the position of the needle so that the entire shank section receives the brine. Next, turn the ham aitchbone up so that the shank end is facing away from you. Beginning at one edge just above the skin, plunge the needle deep into the heavy muscle of the lower leg, directing the needle toward the bone. Continue injecting brine at 1½-inch intervals across the leg. You will notice the various muscles of the leg swelling as you pump the brine. Once you have reached the edge of the leg, return to the starting point and make a second row of injections 1½ inches behind the first. Continue, altering the angle of the needle around the bone, until you have injected the entire leg. In all, it should take 15 to 16 injections.

If injecting a loin, simply space the injections 1½ inches apart. Direct the pump through the ends of the loin and at points along either side.

Not all of the brine you inject will remain inside the leg or loin. As one muscle fills with brine it exerts pressure on those adjacent to it and brine will trickle or flow out into the pan. Next, place the leg or loin into a bucket and pour any of the brine left in the pan over the ham. Place a clean ceramic plate on top of the meat to keep it submerged and cover the bucket. Refrigerate at 32 to 38°F. for 5 to 6 days. The ham is now ready to roast.

Remove the ham from the brine and pat it dry. Remove the aitchbone, which will make it easier to carve into neat slices, and tie the ham tightly every inch until you reach the hock. Tie the loin similarly at 1-inch intervals. Preheat the oven to 375°F.

Roast the ham to an internal temperature of 140°F., about 3 hours. Allow 1 hour and 20 minutes and 140°F. for the loin. Let the meat rest for 15 minutes before carving.

Italian Bacon

Almost all cured Italian bacon, with the exception of that made in the northern provinces, is unsmoked and goes by the name of pancetta. Pancetta (from *pancia*) is an anatomical term meaning pork belly and the name for one of the most utilized cured meats in the Italian repertory. Unlike American bacon, pancetta is tightly rolled and tied and hung to cure like salame. Regional differences in curing mixes, the ratio of lean to fat, and levels of dryness and aging account for a great deal of variation from one pancetta to the next. Tuscan *rigatino* is cured flat and resembles American salt pork, although rigatino it is much less salty. Rigatino (from *riga*, meaning "stripe") takes its name from the ample lean meat that streaks through it. It is often eaten in long thin slices with bread. In and around Rome a type of bacon is made from a triangular cut of the whole pork cheek and jowl; it goes by the name of guanciale. Guanciale has a more pronounced pork flavor and tends to have a greater proportion of fat to lean. Guanciale is the distinctive ingredient in the celebrated pasta dish bucatini all'amatriciana. The most common form of flat cured belly is Tesa. Tesa means "extended," and its name refers to the long stretch of the pork belly and the habit of curing it flat. Unlike the furled pancetta that requires a relatively longer time to mature, Tesa is ready to eat in a matter of 8 to 15 days, depending upon its thickness. Tesa is a staple of the Oliveto kitchen, indispensable to the foundation of stuffings for pasta, meat, and poultry; it adds richness to ragùs and is useful for barding lean meats for the spit or winding around skewers of grilled variety meats such as sweetbreads or livers. Roasted whole or cut into slices and grilled, it is the savory component of Oliveto's most popular salad, a warm mix of bitter greens, walnuts, and shards of Parmigiano-Reggiano cheese dressed with aceto balsamico and olive oil.

Tesa

Makes 12 pounds

28 grams whole black peppercorns

¼ gram whole cloves (15 cloves)

¼ gram allspice berries (5 allspice berries)

1 gram freshly grated nutmeg

7 grams red pepper flakes

½ gram juniper berries (about 15 small juniper berries)

168 grams salt

9 grams Instacure No. 1 (see Sources and Resources, page 262)

12½ pounds skin-on very fresh pork belly, approximately 40 percent lean

67 grams garlic, chopped coarse

100 grams red wine

Combine the peppercorns, cloves, allspice berries, nutmeg, red pepper flakes, and juniper berries in a spice grinder and grind them coarse. Add the spices to the salt and the curing salt.

Place the pork belly in a large square pan and rub the spice mixture liberally and evenly into the meat. Use all of the seasoning salt. Combine the garlic and the wine and sprinkle it lightly over both sides of the meat so as not to wash away the spicing. Set the Tesa to cure in the refrigerator at below 40°F. for 8 to 15 days.

Tesa is ready when the salt and curing salt have penetrated to the center of the width of the belly. Taste-test it by cutting a thin slice. (If you'd rather not eat it raw, crisp it first in a sauté pan.) Tesa will keep well for up to 30 days if well refrigerated and may be frozen as well. If you decide to freeze it, wrap it well in freezer paper and store in a plastic bag.

Dry-Cured Salame

Throughout the year I make many types of salame which vary one from the next in the cut of pork used, the size of the fat and grind, lean to fat ratio, salt and spicing, degree of tang, and the size and type of the casing. I try to have sausages ready to eat at all times, and the casing type and size as well as the degree of coarseness of the grind of the meat determine the length of the drying period, ranging from 20 to 120 days. Recipes for four of these sausages follow. If you wish to experiment or develop your own dry-cured salame, observe the limits with respect to salt, curing salt, and the use of cultures in the guidelines given below. These are the structural elements of dry sausage that ensure the safety, stability, and texture of the sausage. Spices and other seasoning primarily affect flavor and can be altered according to your taste.

• For purposes of safety and taste, salt should be added at the rate of 2.8 to 3 percent of the raw weight of the meat and fat.

• Salame combines lean meat with fat from the back of the pig that is firmest and of the best quality. In order to obtain an accurate ratio of lean to fat, no matter what cut you use, if necessary pork meat should be "leaned out" (separated from any fat, tendons, or connective tissue it contains) before being combined with the back fat called for in the recipe.

• In general, ground, dry-cured sausage that has a smooth texture and a moist, savory flavor and is easily sliceable contains fat in the range of 25 to 30 percent of the total of lean meat and fat combined, though there are no hard and fast rules. Decreasing fat will yield a drier, tougher salame, which may or may not be desirable. You may wish to experiment not only with the amount of fat your salame contains but also with cutting it by hand rather than putting it through the grinder. Hand-cutting fat in irregularly sized pieces makes for a less uniform appearance in the cut slices as well as very distinct separation of fat and lean. When sizing the fat, consider the diameter of the casing. As the casing diameter decreases, so should the size of the fat pieces.

• Follow the protocol for rehydrating the starter culture in distilled water (see page 204) and observe the optimal temperature range for the particular culture during fermentation.

• Dextrose is a nutrient necessary for fermentation in dry-cured sausage. For the starter cultures referred to in the recipes below and sourced on page 260, the amount of dextrose necessary for fermentation should not fall below .5 percent of the raw weight of the meat and fat. For example, let's say you want to ferment a sausage mixture made up of 18 pounds of lean and 7 pounds of fat. The total raw weight of these two elements is 25 pounds. First convert the raw weight to grams:

25 pounds × 16 ounces × 28 grams = 11,200 grams. Then multiply this product by .005 (.5%) = 56 grams dextrose

The amount of dextrose you add is directly related to how much lactic acid is produced in the sausage. If you want a sausage with more tang, add a bit more dextrose in your next trial.

• Use Instacure No. 2 for fermented, dry-cured sausage. In addition to nitrite, this curing salt contains a small amount of nitrate, which ensures the safety of the sausage and helps to retain color and prevent rancidity during maturation.

• Whenever you are experimenting, keep accurate records of the additions and changes you make so that you can compare your new and old results. First record what you sense the sausage is lacking or contains too much of; also, write down the ways in which the finished sausage meets your taste expectations. Your first impression of the sausage is usually the best one. Use this description to adjust the amounts of salt, dextrose (within the limits), and seasonings. Such a description might read like this: "The sausage is a little too salty and needs more

Use of Starter Cultures

Starter cultures are dosed to the batch according to how much sausage mixture one package will ferment. This amount is listed on the front of the package, for example, "One package, 42 grams, is enough to ferment 500 pounds of meat." To calculate how much you will need for the smaller batch you intend to make, first determine the amount of culture to be added to a pound of meat:

42 grams culture/500 pounds meat = .084 grams

Then, multiply this product by the raw weight of the meat and fat in the batch you are making, for example:

25 pounds meat and fat × .084 =
 2.1 grams culture

Disperse the measured amount of the culture in an amount of water equal to .5 percent of the batch weight of sausage. For example: 25 pounds × 16 ounces × 28 grams × .005 = 56 grams of distilled water. Distilled water is preferred, although tap water is generally sufficient if it is not heavily chlorinated or does not contains heavy metals (hard water) that might prove detrimental to the live microorganisms. After all other ingredients have been blended into the meat mix, add the diluted culture and mix very well. *Good distribution is essential.* Do not allow the culture to directly contact the other ingredients prior to mixing with meat.

coarsely ground black pepper. The sausage has a nice tang—acid balance is fine. Garlic could be increased. There is too much clove."

• Adding spice and seasoning is where you can feel most free in designing the flavor of your own sausage. While it may be difficult at first to forecast the flavor effects of altered amounts of seasoning, it is wise to err on the side of less rather than more, as the drying process concentrates flavors. I find it helpful to think in terms of percentages. With experience, you will find that you will be able to foretaste that a particular sausage needs to be 10 percent more tangy or 20 percent less spicy. Once you make these decisions, calculate the adjustments accordingly.

• Most sausage is ready to eat when it has lost 30 to 35 percent of its weight. You may wish to leave your sausage in the cellar longer for more concentrated flavor or a drier texture.

Spicy Soppressata

*Makes 9 sausages weighing approximately
2¼ pounds each*

Stuff this salame in a wide beef middle approximately 65 millimeters in diameter. Beef middle
casings are measured in sets or bundles of 9 and
18 meters (approximately 30 and 60 feet) each.

14½ pounds lean meat from the leg of pork
5 pounds back fat
250 grams salt
43 grams dextrose
15 grams red pepper flakes
30 grams cracked black pepper
1 gram dried thyme
30 grams fresh garlic, crushed in a mortar
1 gram ground cloves
1 gram ground ginger
1 gram freshly grated nutmeg
22 grams Instacure No. 2 (see Sources and
    Resources, page 262)
Starter culture (see Use of Starter Cultures, left)
Distilled water

Chill the meat and the fat. When it is very cold,
grind the lean meat through a ⅜-inch plate.
Cut the fat by hand with a sharp knife into thin
strips and then uneven pieces about 1/8 to
¼ inch wide. Add the salt, dextrose, and seasonings to the meat. Dissolve the curing salt in
½ cup of water, pour it over the meat, and mix
to distribute with a stiff spatula. Dissolve the
starter culture by stirring it into the distilled
water. Pour the culture over the meat and mix
again very thoroughly and until the mixture
feels sticky.

Pack the meat tightly in wide beef middle
casings (approximately 65 millimeters in diameter) and tie them at 10- to 12-inch lengths. Tag
the sausage with its finished weight and the
date. Prick the sausages all over to release any
air between meat and casing. Wrap a small
amount (about 4 ounces) of sausage mixture
(use what is left over in the stuffing canister)
in plastic wrap and tie it at both ends. This will
be used to check the pH before, during, and at
the end of fermentation. Hang it with the
sausages. Ferment according to the desired temperature range for the culture you are using and
at 80 to 90 percent relative humidity until the
pH drops to 5 or less. This usually takes 36 to
48 hours. Check the pH at the beginning, after
24 hours, and then again at the end of the
fermentation.

Transfer the sausages to the aging cellar and
hang them there at 50°F. with 70 to 75 percent
relative humidity for 50 to 60 days, or until the
sausages have lost about a third of their initial
weight.

Genoa-Style Salame

Makes 6 salami

Genoa salame is a fine-textured sausage with small bits of fat and a sour tang accented by the flavor of white pepper. Traditionally, Genoa salame is cased in 4- to 4½-inch-wide beef bungs (width specification for beef bungs always falls in a marginal range of ½ inch). You will need 3 whole bung caps to case these salami; one bung cap makes two sausages approximately 12 inches long.

When purchasing shoulder of pork, bear in mind that you will need enough to yield the amount given below *after* you have "leaned out" the shoulder (removed as much fat and connective tissue as possible). Pork shoulder yields approximately 60 percent lean meat.

18½ pounds leaned-out shoulder of pork
6½ pounds fresh back fat
336 grams salt
75 grams dextrose
25 grams sugar
35 grams white pepper
28 grams Instacure No. 2 (see Sources and
    Resources, page 262)
75 grams red wine
8 grams fresh garlic, pounded in a mortar
Starter culture (see Use of Starter Cultures,
    page 204)
Distilled water

Make certain the lean meat and fat are very cold. Grind all of the lean and the fat through a 3/16-inch plate. Add the salt, dextrose, sugar, and white pepper. Dissolve the curing salt in ½ cup of water. Pour the red wine over the garlic and then add it to the meat mixture along with the dissolved curing salt. Mix to distribute with a stiff spatula. Dissolve the starter culture in the distilled water; let it stand for 5 minutes, then add it to the sausage mix. Mix very thoroughly again and until the meat feels sticky.

Bung caps are open on one end and closed on the other. Open the casing and fill it under the tap with lukewarm water. Overturn the casing and let the water out. You will notice that the casing has a round hole about 4 inches from the open end. Cut the casing just below this hole and discard the short piece to which it attaches. Repeat the process of filling and emptying the casing several more times until it feels soft and supple, then cut it in two equal lengths. One bung cap will yield two casings, the first with one end closed, the other with both ends open. Tie a butterfly knot on the end of the piece that is open at both ends. Pack the sausage mixture in a stuffing machine fitted with the largest stuffing horn. Load the casing and pack it as tight as possible. Tie off the sausage with another butterfly knot and hanging loop and secure the sausage with half-hitches every inch along its length. Tag the sausage with its finished weight and the date. Prick the sausage all over to release any air between meat and casing. Wrap a small amount (about 4 ounces) of sausage mixture, left over in the stuffing canister or stuffing horn, in plastic wrap, tie it at both ends (this will be used to check the pH before, during, and at the end of fermentation), and hang it with the sausages. Ferment according to the temperature range for the culture you are using and at 80 to 90 percent relative humidity until the pH drops to 5 or less. This should take 36 to 48 hours. Check the pH at the beginning, after 24 hours, and then again at the end of the fermentation.

Hang in a 50°F. cellar with 70 to 75 percent relative humidity. The sausages are ready to eat after about 90 to 120 days, or when they have lost about one third of their initial weight.

Hunter's Loop

Makes 10 sausages

Hunter's loop is a fine-ground salame perfumed with wild fennel seed and cased in beef round that naturally coils into a loop when stuffed. Given the diameter of the casing, the aging time is relatively short. Hunter's loop is a handy size for carrying on picnics or, as its name suggests, to accompany walks in the wild.

15 pounds lean pork shoulder

5 pounds back fat, cut into 1-inch pieces

22 grams Instacure No. 2 (see Sources and Resources, page 260)

250 grams salt

45 grams dextrose

15 grams wild fennel pollen (see Sources and Resources page 262)

30 grams whole black peppercorns, roughly cracked in a mortar

40 grams fresh garlic, crushed to a paste in a mortar

Starter culture (see Use of Starter Cultures, page 204)

Distilled water

Chill the meat and fat until very cold. Mix the meat and fat together and grind through a ⅛-inch plate into a mixing pan. Dissolve the curing salt in 1/2 cup water. Add the salt, dextrose, the seasonings, and dissolved curing salt and mix to distribute with a stiff spatula. Dissolve the starter culture in the water and mix into the meat very thoroughly and until the mixture feels sticky.

Stuff the sausage tightly into 46-millimeter beef round casings. Tie off one end of the casing with a butterfly knot, leaving 6 inches of twine. These casings naturally loop, and when the sausage makes nearly a full circle, tie the other end similarly with a separate piece of twine. The sausage should weigh approximately 2 pounds. Proceed in the same manner with the remaining meat, tying off the end, stuffing, and then clos-ing the other end. Join the sausages at the nodal points by tying the separate strands of twine at either end together to form a ring.

Tag each sausage with its finished weight and the date. Prick the sausage all over to release any air between meat and casing. Wrap a small amount (about 4 ounces) of sausage mixture, left over in the stuffing canister, in plastic wrap, tie it at both ends (this will be used to check the pH before, during, and at the end of fermentation), and hang it with the sausages. Ferment according to the temperature range for the culture you are using and at 80 to 90 percent relative humidity until the pH drops to 5 or less. This takes 36 to 48 hours. Check the pH at the beginning, after 24 hours, and then again at the end of the fermentation. Hang in a 50°F. cellar with 70 to 75 percent relative humidity. The sausages are ready to eat after about 45 days, or when they have lost about one third of their initial weight.

Toscano-Style Salame
Makes a 20-pound batch

Toscano is a distinctively lean salame with relatively large hand-cut fat pieces, a deep red color, and a chewy texture. Its seasoning consists simply of salt, pepper, and garlic.

18¼ pounds lean pork from the leg
1¾ pound back fat
22 grams Instacure No. 2 (see Sources and
     Resources, page 262)
8 ounces red wine
28 grams fresh garlic, pounded to a paste in a
     mortar
270 grams salt
36 grams whole black peppercorns roughly
     cracked in a mortar
45 grams dextrose
Starter culture (See Use of Starter Cultures,
     page 204)
Distilled water

Cut the lean pork into rough 1-inch pieces and chill it thoroughly. Grind the lean meat through a ⅜-inch plate. Cut the back fat by hand into small uneven pieces no larger than 1/4 inch and combine it with the ground meat. Transfer the lean and the fat to a tub for mixing. Dissolve the curing salt in ½ cup of water. Pour the red wine over the garlic and add it along with the salt, pepper, dextrose, and dissolved curing salt to the meat. Mix well with a stiff spatula. Dissolve the starter culture in distilled water; pour it over the meat and mix again very thoroughly to distribute the culture and until the mixture feels sticky. Stuff the sausage mixture into 4- to 4½-inch beef bungs. Tie off the sausage with a butterfly knot and hanging loop and secure the sausage with half-hitches every inch along its length. Tag the sausage with its finished weight and the date. Prick the sausage all over to release any air between meat and casing. Wrap a small amount (about 4 ounces) of sausage mixture, leftover in the stuffing canister, in plastic wrap,

tie it at both ends (this will be used to check the pH before, during, and at the end of fermentation), and hang it with the sausages.

Ferment at the optimal temperature range for the culture you are using and until the pH drops to 5 or less. Check the pH at the beginning, after 24 hours, and then again at the end of the fermentation. Hang in a 50°F. cellar with 70 to 75 percent relative humidity. The sausages are ready to eat after about 75 to 90 days, or when they have lost about one third of their initial weight.

Prosciutto

My yearly curing cycle spans 14 months and begins and ends with prosciutto. Of all the cured meats I make, prosciutto takes the longest. Over the course of nearly 400 days, prosciutto undergoes a maturation process that comes to fullness in the remarkable bloom of aroma when the ham is later opened. That moment each year is like a birth, a long season's waiting for the revelation of what can only be imagined by looking from the outside. Prosciutto is an act of patience and a stunning transformation, raw flesh to rose-colored, mildly salted delicacy that nearly melts on the tongue. Your own prosciutto is likely to taste like none you have ever tasted before.

Traditionally pigs were slaughtered in Europe in November and December for want of winter fodder. The onset of the cold season was also advantageous to the curing process, bringing the cool temperatures necessary for preservation in a natural environment. While refrigeration makes it possible for me to make prosciutto at any time of the year, I nevertheless maintain the seasonal tradition as I observed it in Italy and put up two dozen or so legs in late December and early January and another dozen in the early spring.

Perhaps the most challenging part of making prosciutto is finding a suitable leg of pork. To make prosciutto you will need the entire hind leg of pork, including the trotter, from a large, fat animal. Unfortunately, most butchers will not know what you are talking about if you ask them to prepare a leg for prosciutto. There is no such specification listed among standard American meat cuts. Pork legs for prosciutto weigh in at 30 to 35 pounds before trimming and are cut free from the carcass perpendicular to its length at a point 3½ inches above the tip of the aitchbone, the S-shaped bone that protrudes from the center of the inside of the leg. This allows for enough of the muscle on the top of the leg to be included so that the ham can be sculpted in the traditional rounded chicken-leg form. The leg should have ample fat cover—about 1½ inches—and all of the skin. Removal of the trotter, tail bone, pelvic bone, sirloin, and flank-side fat yield a leg ready for salting in the ideal range of 25 to 28 pounds. It is critical that the leg of pork be as fresh as possible and be kept cold prior to trimming and salting. The leg should also be free of any skin lacerations or gashes that might invite bacteria during the course of curing and aging.

If you decide to make prosciutto, I would recommend you do so with a friend to assist, preferably one with some practiced knife skills if you do not possess them yourself or who can help you with the instructions as you work. Boning and trimming the leg is not difficult once you familiarize yourself with its bone structure and have had the chance to try it a few times. The key steps in making prosciutto are:

- Boning and trimming the leg
- Salting
- Resting
- Cleaning
- Initial aging
- Sealing and final aging

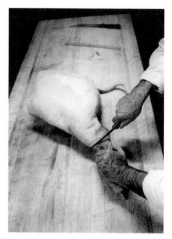
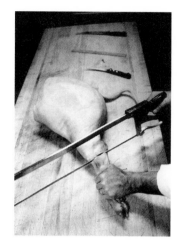
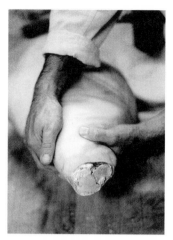

Fig. 1   Fig 2   Fig. 3

Boning and Trimming the Leg

Freeing the Foot and Securing the Shank with a Loop for Hanging the Ham

Place the leg on a wooden worktable or ample counter space fitted with a large cutting board. Remove the foot just below the lower knuckle joint. Removing the foot at this juncture is very important since the hard shank-end bones act as a barrier to spoilage at the foot; cutting higher exposes the bone marrow that could cause the ham to spoil from the inside out. To free the foot from the leg, locate the bulging tarsal bone that protrudes from the back of the foot (fig. 1). Using a knife, score directly across the skin of the foot (figs. 2 and 3) 1 inch below the bulge in the direction of the bottom of the foot. Use a saw to cut straight across the shinbones and finish the cut with your knife to free the foot.

Holding several overlapping courses of heavy-duty twine in both hands with about 8 inches of slack, tie a tight knot just above the bulging bone (fig. 4). This handy bulge acts as a stop on the knot, absorbs the tension of the hanging ham,

and keeps it from plunging groundward over the long course of aging. Now bring the strands of twine in each hand around the other side of the bulge, crossing over those already wound around it, and tie another tight knot so that the shank is secured in two places. Tag the ham with the date and its raw weight. Knot the ends of the strands into a loop that extends beyond the bottom of the foot about 3 inches so that the ham can hang free (fig. 5).

Fig. 4

Fig. 5

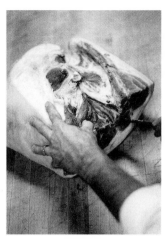

Fig. 6

Removing the Tailbone, Pelvic Bone, and Aitchbone

Place the ham skin side down and with the shank end facing away from you. If the leg of pork you purchase includes the tailbone, cut it away along with any vertebrae still attached at the side of the leg (fig. 6). Looking at the top end of the leg in cross section, you will notice the severed end of the pelvic bone. The pelvic bone is in one piece; however, for the purposes of boning, I think of it in two parts—the portion of the bone that runs to the top of the leg bone (femur) and its continuation, called the aitchbone. The pelvic bone contains the "socket" that covers the "ball" portion (rump knucklebone) of the femur. The aitchbone veers off at a near right angle deep into the butt of the ham.

Start by getting a feel for the placement and direction of the top pelvic bone. Cut on top and all around it closely with your boning knife to free it from the flesh. Next, with your knife held nearly vertically on the foot side of the aitch-

bone, cut down and close against it (fig. 7). As you cut, pull the aitchbone back toward the top of the ham to reveal the joint where the socket meets the top of the femur. Cut the cartilage around the socket to release the pelvic bone from the round rump knucklebone.

It is important to sever the aitchbone above the point where it plunges into the heavy butt muscle; otherwise, you will leave a deep hole in the side of the ham that could invite bacterial problems during aging. This is the trickiest part of boning the leg. Pull the aitchbone by the socket back away from the butt of the ham. You will notice a spur of bone that remains attached to the butt. Use a saw to sever that bone as close to the socket as possible without cutting into the flesh of the ham. You may need to insert the blade tip of a cleaver in the cut in order to finish the job. Cut away any flesh still adhering to the pelvic and aitchbone and remove it in one piece.

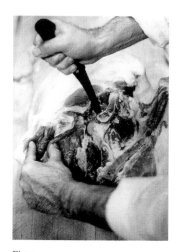

Fig. 7

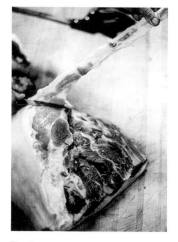

Fig. 8

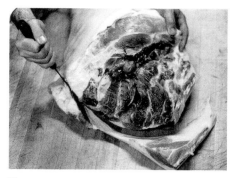

Fig. 9

Fig. 10

Fig. 11

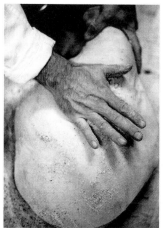

Fig. 12

Fig. 13

Fig. 14

Trimming and Sculpting the Ham

With the ham still lying skin side down, turn the ham 180 degrees so that the shank end is now closest to you. Cut away the skin, heavy fat, and lymph glands on the flank side (fig. 8). Cut away the excess flesh to the side of the rump knucklebone, trim the silverskin and any soft fat covering the exposed muscles, and trim the skin at the midsection of the ham so that it traces a smooth arc from one side to the other. To sculpt the traditional "chicken-leg" form of the top leg, cut away fat and skin to an evenly rounded shape (fig. 9). Last, make several more passes with your knife to smooth the contour of the face of the ham.

Massaging

In order to make the dense muscles of the leg suppler for salting, particularly the buttock muscle, use a rolling pin without handles or similar wooden dowel to beat on the skin side of the ham. Give the leg forty to fifty firm whacks, paying particular attention to the heavy butt portion, until you feel the muscles of the ham soften and loosen slightly. Then turn the ham flesh side up and, using both thumbs, exert a downward pressure 3 inches back from the rump knucklebone and forward toward it (fig. 10). The point of this is to massage out any blood remaining in the femoral artery, which could increase the potential for spoilage.

Salting

Since leg sizes are variable and the amount of salt and other elements of the cure are fixed, you will need to make a simple calculation based on the weight of the raw trimmed ham. Once you know how much it weighs, measure out an amount of salt equal to 6 percent of the weight of the ham. To this salt add Instacure No. 2 (see Sources and Resources, page 260) in the proportion of 28 grams for each 25 pounds of meat.

Salt
  28-pound leg × .06 = 1.68 pounds salt = 752 grams salt

Instacure No. 2
  Since the rate for curing salt is based on 25 pounds, divide 28 by 25 = 1.12 and multiply by 1 ounce = 1.12 ounces or 31 grams Instacure No. 2

Mix the salt and curing salt in a bowl. Add to it about ½ cup of water, which will help the salt to adhere and to more readily be absorbed by the meat. Place the ham on a table and massage in small handfuls of salt first at the foot (fig. 11), then all over the skin side, and finally on the face of the ham (figs. 12 and 13). Then, starting with the top end of the ham, pack salt evenly about ¼ inch thick on the surface, patting it down firmly with your hands. When you reach the rump knucklebone, pack salt heavily all around it. Pack a heavier ½-inch layer of salt on the butt end up to the point where the skin begins. Gather up any salt left over on the table and unused salt and reserve it for later use (fig. 14). Carefully place the ham on a nonreactive rack (I fashioned my own out of wooden dowels) with a catch pan underneath to capture the water the ham will release; or use a perforated, square plastic food container called a Lexan set over a solid Lexan (available at most restaurant supply stores). Orient the ham roughly from corner to corner. Wrap a piece of kitchen parchment under the foot and entirely cover the foot with the salt cure. Move the ham to the cold room or refrigerator. The ideal conditions for storing the ham while it is being salted are 34 to 38°F. and 75 to 80 percent relative humidity with minimal air movement. The initial salting takes approximately 40 days.

Place a clean block of wood under the bottom of the pan at the ham's rounded end so that it rests at any angle of about 30 degrees. This will help the butt end sit as low as possible and let gravity assist in the movement of salt to the heavy muscles of the leg and shank. Keep the unused salt nearby and store it next to the ham. Over the course of this period it is important to look in on the ham every 2 to 3 days, to drain the water it releases and to observe how the ham is taking the salt. "Reading" the ham during this initial salting period is part of the skill of making prosciutto. Since you can only watch from the outside, your best indication that the ham is absorbing the salt is to examine the surface and to probe the various muscles with your fingers. Areas where the salt has penetrated will appear bald and the muscles will have stiffened. The top end of the ham will be the first area to drink up the salt and the ¼-inch layer you packed on should be sufficient to season this part of the ham. However, if you sense by feeling the muscles from side to side in front of the rump knucklebone that any are still soft, add a little more salt. As the salt disappears from the heavier muscles behind the rump knucklebone, reapply salt until you have used all of it. After 40 days the ham should feel firm all over and have taken in all or nearly all of the salt. If any remains, massage it into the heavier muscles. The ham should also have lost approximately 3½ to 4 pounds of water or about 15 percent of its initial weight.

First Aging and Cleaning

Hang the ham in a cool place (less than 40°F.) for about 6 months with a relative humidity of 70 to 75 percent and slow air movement. It is important for changes of fresh air to enter the curing cellar. During the cool season, I open the back door of my cellar to let the natural breeze blow in. No doubt this also introduces irregularities in temperature and humidity, a condition that enhances water loss in the hams in their first aging period. Because of the resident mold spores within my cellar, the ham becomes populated by a white mold over the course of this period. When it covers the cut face of the ham and portions of the skin and foot, I take it down and dust the mold away with a coarse towel or brush. I repeat this process at least once before moving the ham into the main body of the cellar, where the temperature is 50 to 52°F. and the humidity fluctuates between 55 and 75 percent. At this point, the surface of the ham has darkened considerably and is noticeably drier; however, the mold has kept it from becoming leathery. The skin too has transformed from its pale pink beginnings to a tawny brown. When the ham has lost 25 percent of its initial raw weight, it is time to seal it and to move it out of refrigeration.

Sealing and Final Aging

Because final aging of the ham takes place in drier ambient conditions, it is necessary to seal the exposed surface to help slow the rate of moisture loss and to prevent the surface from toughening. Prosciutto is sealed with a mixture of pork leaf fat (kidney fat) and rice flour called *sugna* in Italian. Kidney fat is a very hard fat with a higher melting point than fat from other parts of the pig and is the only fat from the pig that is suitable for sealing a ham. First, scrape or use a moist towel to remove bits of mold on the inside surface of the ham as well as on the skin side of the leg. For one ham, combine 4 ounces of leaf fat with 15 grams rice flour. Using your thumb, smear the fat in an even layer around the rump knucklebone and the entire cut surface of the ham. Hang the ham in the cellar at 50°F. for about 6 months, until it feels quite firm at its thickest points and has lost at least one third of its original trimmed weight. It is now ready to eat.

Cooking Backward

The Place of Dessert in a Menu

Introduction

A menu succeeds or fails for a variety of reasons, not the least of which is how it makes one feel physically afterward. Like the acts of a play, or the movements of a symphony, the courses of a menu define the form and feeling of eating. Dessert is the "finale" and as such, occupies a special, if no more important, place in a menu. Dessert can push a meal over the top, let it down with a heavy thud, or thwart the expectations set up by the previous courses. It determines if we leave the table feeling a little too enriched, overstuffed, or deprived. In the best of circumstances, dessert is a dénouement in which the logic of the menu unfolds in sweet fulfillment of what has come before. This of course presumes that the menu, whether ordered or planned, has been a conscious consideration rather than a matter of impulse. Unfortunately, the intoxication of sweetness is often more compelling than the art of eating or the better instincts of those who dine; dessert is often little more than the opportunity to satisfy a craving, mollify the "sweet tooth," or indulge in the guilty pleasures of chocolate, ice cream, or caramel bliss. In this case, dessert no longer belongs to the menu as a whole; it is merely tagged on as an afterthought.

This chapter considers dessert as the starting point in the creation of a menu. Admittedly, this is an unusual perspective. Chefs don't generally begin thoughts of a menu with the course that falls at the end. But looking backward to what precedes dessert is a way of ensuring its pleasure and purpose in the entirety of a meal. I am fortunate enough to have the confidence of regular customers as well as newcomers to Oliveto who are happy to put dinner in my hands. Also, at each week's end, I often plan a four- to five-course prix-fixe menu within the format of the larger à la carte offering. These menus are conceived to celebrate peak-of-the-day seasonal produce or are unified by a theme—the arrival of spring, wild mushrooms and truffles in late autumn, or newly pressed olive oil. Sometimes it is the interplay of texture or color that dictates the menu's direction or the quartet of sensations—sweet, salty, bitter, sour—that define taste. Dessert may also be organized around a particular flavor that creates continuity with elements of dishes that come before. Or it is some irresistible fruit or aroma that displays most characteristically the mark of its season. The art of making a menu, or of eating, for that matter, rests in the particular combination of elements, the progression, transitions, and proportions that make for a balanced whole. Beginning with dessert, I find myself returning to the simple principle that variety and contrast are the keys to sustaining interest in the forward-moving events of a meal. The challenge and the fun are in imagining the path that makes this important arrival both graceful and fitting.

Dessert First

Often, in walking through our local farmers' market, I am so riveted by the appearance and flavor of some fruit at its peak that an idea for dessert takes precedence over the savory dishes. Such was the case recently with the arrival of the first Gravenstein apples from nearby Sebastopol. Gravensteins, the earliest good baking apple to appear on the market, enjoy a short season and are one of the first harbingers of fall. They ripen in late August to mid-September, typically the hottest and driest of our local summer months, when fall seems more than a season away. Few apples can compare in overall balance to Gravensteins; they are as delicious eaten out of hand as they are in baked desserts. Ripe Gravensteins tend to be small but are at once sweet, tart, and snappy-crisp, with a pronounced cidery aroma that satisfies what seems to be lacking in the complement of characteristics of most other varieties. Like the ripest and best examples of any fruit, Gravensteins have deep, generous flavors. Biting into one is like biting into a roomful of apples.

A Menu of Roasted Courses

Salad of Parched Summer Vegetables
1999 Rosé Gris de Gris, Fonsainte

~

Sea Scallops Gremolata
1999 Sauvignon Blanc, Petrucco

~

Timballo of Risotto with Quail and Chanterelles
1998 Pinot Noir, Navarro

~

Roast Leg and Loin of Lamb with Cranberry Beans
1997 Chianti Classico Riserva, Monsanto

~

Warm Yeasted Apple Pudding
1997 Sauternes, Château Roumieu-Lacoste

Yeasted apple pudding comes out of the oven deeply browned on the top and with the bready aroma of yeast. To complete this backward-looking menu, spit-roasted lamb seemed the ideal main course, not only for this meat's compatibility with fruit but because it referred to the roasted quality of dessert. I decided to carry the theme further with the first course, a salad of summer vegetables whose separate components—eggplant, tomatoes, tromboncino and costata romana squashes, onions, and sweet peppers—were concentrated and caramelized through browning in a hot oven or frying in olive oil or browning in a hot oven, sliced and served at room temperature in a raisin vinaigrette. Giant sea scallops are no better than when seared to a crusty brown in clarified butter and showered with gremolata. Pan-roasted quail and summer chanterelles were joined to Canaroli rice cooked al dente with saffron, and served with the residues from the roasting pan.

Warm Yeasted Apple Pudding
For 6 to 8

I cannot take total credit for this dessert as I first had a version of it in a roadside trattoria in Panzano in Chianti, where it was called *torta di mele*. It is nevertheless re-created from memory and I believe improved if only on account of the marvelous qualities of the Gravenstein. If you cannot find Gravenstein apples, Sierra Beauty and Cox Orange Pippin will also produce wonderful results. But any of your favorite regional baking apples will do.

The baking time for this pudding can vary depending on the variety of apple used. Gravensteins cook quickly. If you use a drier apple such as Sierra Beauty, it may take as long as 1½ hours. In any event, the pudding should be soft to its center with a deeply browned surface.

3 pounds Gravenstein apples
½ cup whole milk
1¼ teaspoons dry yeast
5 tablespoons melted butter
2 tablespoons all-purpose flour
1 whole egg
⅓ cup sugar
⅛ teaspoon salt

Preheat the oven to 375°F. Butter a 9-inch round baking pan.

Peel, halve, and core the apples. Using a mandoline, slice the apples ⅛ inch thick and place them in a large bowl. Pour the milk into a small sauce pot and bring to a lukewarm temperature over low heat. Sprinkle the yeast over the milk and allow it to proof. When the yeast is proofed, whisk the melted butter, flour, egg, sugar, and salt into the milk. The mixture will resemble a thin batter. Pour this batter over the sliced apples and mix thoroughly, turning the apple slices so that they are covered in batter. Turn the apples into the prepared pan and smooth the top with a spatula. Set the pudding aside to rise at warm room temperature for 1 hour, or until you notice that the batter has swelled slightly and appears puffy.

Bake the pudding on the middle rack of the oven for 1 hour and 10 minutes, or until it is tender when probed in the middle and deeply browned all over its top surface. Allow the pudding to cool for at least 20 minutes before cutting. Serve warm with vanilla ice cream or crème fraîche.

Associating Flavors

Cold Antipasto of Clams, Mussels, and Oysters
with Green Herb Sauce
1998 Gavi, San Bartolomeo

~

Vellutata of Cauliflower
1998 Vernaccia, Terre di Tufi, Teruzzi & Puthod

~

Spit-roasted Pork Shoulder with Sweet Anise
Braised fennel
1998 Syrah "Offerus," JL Chave

~

Bitter Orange Cake with Compote of Blood Oranges
1998 Monastrell Dulce, Olivares

Citrus fruits come fully into season in the months of December, January, and February. Tangerines and mandarin oranges arrive first. Meyer lemons, a sweet, soft-skinned California variety, soon develop such a depth of color and become so sweet they can almost be eaten out of hand. Grapefruits swell with juice and pomelos the size of soccer balls overwhelm their bins in the market. Citron, sweet limes, and bergamot are latecomers, and while blood oranges make an early appearance, they seem to come into their own only late in the season. Of all the citrus, blood oranges are the most visually striking. In full season their skins are blushed a deep crimson and the flesh, particularly of the Moro variety, is nearly black. The skins of blood oranges also contain pungent oil, more pleasantly bitter and spicy than that of other varieties, that lends its distinct perfume to cakes, creams, and sauces both savory and sweet. In drafting the menu above, my guiding principle was to associate the flavor of blood orange with ingredients of the other courses with which it might be matched harmoniously. The flavor associations are implied rather than explicit.

Planning courses to precede this dessert, I could have chosen duck, which has a time-tested association with orange. Lamb and pork share a similar richness of flavor, and the character of each is counterbalanced by the acidic partnership and sharp aroma of orange. I decided on pork because it pairs so well with fennel and its aromatic cousin, sweet anise, both of which agree with the flavor of orange. Fennel and oranges figure commonly in the cooking of Provence and southern Italy, and I was further reminded of wild fennel flowers and fennel seeds, the singular aroma in the seasoning mix of *porchetta*—the marvelous whole roast pig found in outdoor marketplaces throughout Tuscany. For the middle course I remembered that a Sicilian friend had once served me a salad of steamed cauliflower with a tart olive oil dressing that included blood orange juice, grated orange peel, chopped anchovies, and black olives. While the anchovy and briny olives offset the muted flavor of cauliflower, it was the flavor of orange that made it really come alive. Since then I have often used orange to accent dishes based on cauliflower, a vegetable that always needs some form of improvement. Hence the orange-scented cauliflower soup.

At this point, considering the whole menu for balance, it seemed appropriate to begin with a bright, lean course. Both the roast pork and the butter-cake dessert are rich in effect. And even though the soup was made with water only, blended cauliflower is seemingly creamy. Lightly steamed clams and mussels, along with raw oysters (which likewise welcome the flavor of orange), dabbed with olive oil, minced shallot, lemon, and chopped green herbs (tarragon, chives, parsley, chervil), provided just the right contrast. I also decided to serve this dish well chilled to counter the hot soup.

Bitter Orange Cake
with Compote of Blood Oranges
For 8

2 blood oranges
½ pound (2 sticks) unsalted butter,
 at room temperature
2 cups sugar
2 egg yolks
2¼ cups all-purpose flour
2 teaspoons baking powder
½ teaspoon salt
½ cup finely chopped walnuts

Preheat the oven to 350°F. Grease a 9-inch tube pan with butter and dust it with flour. Cut off the stem ends of the oranges and quarter them. Purée the oranges whole (skin and pulp) to a smooth consistency in a food processor. Measure 1½ cups the purée and set aside (discard any extra). Set the purée aside. Cream the butter and sugar on medium-high speed in the bowl of a free-standing electric mixer until light, white, and fluffy, approximately 5 minutes. Add the egg yolks and mix until smooth, then add the orange purée and continue to mix to incorporate it fully. Sift together the flour, baking powder, and salt. Add these ingredients to the bowl and mix until well combined. Mix in the walnuts on low speed. Scrape down the sides of the bowl and mix the batter briefly with a spatula. Smooth the batter into the tube pan. Bake until a skewer inserted into the middle of the cake comes out clean, approximately 40 minutes. Turn the cake out onto a rack to cool.

Compote of Blood Oranges

8 blood oranges
2 cups water
1 cup sugar

Wash the fruit and remove the peel from 3 of the oranges using a vegetable peeler. Take only the peel and none of the white pith. Cut the peel into very fine strips about 1/16 inch wide. Put the peel in a nonreactive saucepan, cover with the water and sugar, and bring to a boil. Reduce to a simmer and cook the peel for about 20 minutes, or until a thin syrup forms when you spoon a little onto a cold plate.

In the meantime, using a very sharp, thin blade, slice off all of the peel and the pith of the oranges. Then cut sections from the oranges free from the membranes. When you have sectioned all of the oranges, gently mix them with the blood orange syrup.

To serve the cake, place a slice on each plate and spoon some of the syrup and orange segments around it.

Weight

Carpaccio of Local Halibut, agrumato
1991 Pas Opere Gran Cuvée, Franciacorta

~

Risotto of Asparagus
1999 Arneis, Giacosa

~

Roast Spring Lamb
Cipolline Onions and New Potatoes
with Green Garlic
1996 Nebbiolo-Barbera, "Bricco Manzoni,"
Rocche dei Manzoni

~

Strawberry Millefoglie with Whipped Cream
1996 Brachetto d'Acqui Pineto, Marenco

The experience of weight in food is both a matter of its actual mass and an expression of the intensity of flavor, the degree of richness, and the feel of the food in the mouth. It is not difficult to imagine foods that might be characterized as weighty in the obvious sense. Few people would argue against the way a porterhouse steak with baked potato or braised pork shoulder with beans tips the scale. Weight as applied to flavor, richness, and mouth feel is more subjective. Such impressions are more apparent when foods are put side by side in a menu. A succession of courses that leaves the good feeling of fullness without torpor balances both of these kinds of weight. And a dessert that ends on a light note is a good way of bringing previously more weighty courses into equilibrium.

When the first strawberries appear, it is a welcome sign that a major change in complexion is ahead in the parade of bright fruit that finally emerges from winter. Few desserts are more appealing than fresh berries and cream, plain and simple, unless you add to it the sweet, sparkling Moscato wine from Asti that seems to be made for just this kind of pairing. Pastry is only in the way unless it is as light as the cream itself. Risotto of asparagus has the most gravity

of all the courses in this menu. Rice that has absorbed nearly four times its weight in broth sits heavy; it is important to remember to offer a moderate portion. But the grassy flavor of asparagus warmed with saffron and the final enrichment of butter and Parmigiano also contribute to the impression of weight, as full flavor is married to richness. The approach to this course, like the finish to the menu, is nearly insubstantial—thin slips of fresh halibut, pounded thin and dressed with sea salt and *agrumato*, lemon-scented olive oil. Spring lamb is perhaps the most delicate of meats and its accompaniments of small new potatoes and the flat Italian onions called cipolline provide a more moderately weighty bridge to dessert.

❧

Strawberry Millefoglie
For 8

Puff pastry is made up of hundreds of very thin layers of dough and butter. These layers cause the dough to rise when baked, and give it its wonderful flakiness. As you're making this dough, bear in mind that overworking it or allowing it to become warm will cause the flour and butter to mix together and you won't get discrete layers. Keep the dough cold at all times. On a hot day, make the dough early in the morning, freeze the flour first, or wait until it cools off.

For the rough puff pastry
½ **pound (1½ cups plus 3 tablespoons)**
 all-purpose flour
¼ **teaspoon salt**
½ **pound (2 sticks) unsalted butter**
About ⅓ **cup ice water**
Granulated sugar, for sprinkling on the dough

Put the flour and salt into a large bowl. Cut the butter into ½-inch cubes. Add the cubes to the flour, and toss them with flour until coated and well distributed. Using your thumbs and first two fingers, break up some of the cubes. This makes the butter more malleable, which will help later when you start rolling the dough. When you have flattened and broken up three fourths of the cubes, begin adding the water, about one fourth at a time. Pour over the surface of the flour in a thin spiral. Using your hands, quickly and lightly toss the mixture two to three times to distribute the water. After about three additions of water, you'll start to see lumps appearing in the bowl. Make one last addition of water, tossing lightly and briefly as before. Look at the dough. If it appears very floury and won't hold together when lightly packed, add a little more ice water. The dough should cohere, but just barely, when you press down on it. It should be evenly moist, without being wet or sticky at all. Pat the dough into a rough rectangular shape against the side of the bowl. Flour your rolling surface generously. Slide the dough out of the bowl and pat it again into a rectangle that measures approximately 5 by 3 inches, and is about 1 inch thick. (If you have no experience with this dough, it will look frightening at this point, a rough, shaggy mass that looks like it could never be converted into a smooth, cohesive dough. Don't be intimidated!) Quickly roll the dough into a larger rectangle measuring approximately 6 by 7 inches. Then fold the dough up for its first "double turn": Imagine a line down the very middle of the dough. Slide your hands under the right edge of the dough, and fold it up onto the dough, so that the right edge meets your imaginary middle line. Don't worry if parts of the dough break and fall off and don't end up on top of the dough as they should; just pick the pieces up and place them where they are supposed to go. Now repeat the lifting and folding process on the left side of the dough. The dough should vaguely resemble an open book. Now close the book by folding one half of the dough up onto the other half. This completes the first turn.

If the dough is still quite cool to the touch after the first turn, make a second turn right away. If it is warm, refrigerate the dough for 15 minutes to firm it. To make the second turn, rotate the dough so that the fold is parallel to your body. Now roll it and fold it exactly as before. Wrap the dough and refrigerate for 15 minutes to rest and chill. Remove it from the refrigerator and give it two more double turns. Then wrap the dough well in plastic wrap and refrigerate it overnight.

Rolling and Cutting the Dough

Remove the dough from the refrigerator. Roll the dough into a rectangle measuring 14 by 16 inches. Sprinkle both sides with sugar. Using an oval cutter 3½ inches wide and 4 inches long, cut out 12 ovals. (You will need 8 ovals. Still, it's good to bake a few extra as one or two may break when they are split in half.) Place the ovals on a parchment-lined baking sheet and freeze until very firm, approximately 20 minutes.

Preheat the oven to 400°F.

Bake the pastry ovals for 20 to 25 minutes. Transfer to a wire rack to cool completely. When cool, use a paring knife to split each oval in half horizontally.

Strawberry Sauce

1 pint sweet, ripe strawberries
Approximately 2 tablespoons sugar

Hull and halve the berries. Sprinkle them with sugar, and purée in a food processor until smooth. Strain the purée through a fine-mesh sieve. Taste the purée for sweetness and add a little more sugar if needed. Set the purée aside.

Sliced Berries
1 pint ripe, sweet strawberries
Approximately 2 tablespoons sugar

Hull the berries and slice thin. Sprinkle them lightly with sugar and mix well. Refrigerate until you're ready to assemble the millefoglie.

Whipped Cream
1 cup heavy cream, preferably not ultra-pasteurized
1 tablespoon sugar
½ teaspoon vanilla extract

Whip the cream with the sugar and vanilla to very stiff peaks. Refrigerate until ready to assemble.

Assembly
Confectioners' sugar, for dusting

Place the bottom half of an oval in the middle of each of 8 dessert plates. Spoon a few berry slices onto each oval. Put a large spoonful of whipped cream on top of the berry slices. Place another layer of berry slices on top of the whipped cream. Sprinkle the remaining eight ovals with confectioners' sugar and place them on top of the berries and whipped cream. Drizzle or pour about 1½ tablespoons of strawberry sauce on each plate, around the millefoglie, and serve at once.

Texture

Salad of Green Beans, Cherry Tomatoes,
and Purple Pearl Onions
2000 Sauvignon Blanc, "Mock," Santa Maddalena

~

Soup of Fresh Cannellini Beans with Farro
and Pigeon
1998 Barbera d'Alba, Cantina del Pino

~

Fritto Misto of Fish, Shellfish, and Vegetables
1999 Chardonnay, "Gail Ann's Vineyard,"
Russian Hill

~

Rose-Scented Panna Cotta with
Compote of White Nectarines
2000 Moscato d'Asti, Soria

The role that the texture of food can play in the fabric of a menu is perhaps the least considered means of providing contrast between courses in Western cooking. In cuisines that exalt texture for its own sake, and not as an incidental characteristic of food, eating becomes an even richer sensory pleasure. I was reminded of this recently while eating at the Japanese restaurant of a fellow chef. I am happiest leaving the menu to him and when I do I am always surprised by his heightened sensitivity to the tactile sensations of food. The menu he prepared left me thinking about the dimension of texture and how it could be used to punctuate a menu.

Panna cotta is Italy's homage to the pure pleasure of cream. It sets with gelatin to a tremulous consistency, and its velvety smoothness dissolves to a sweet grassiness in the aftertaste. The version I chose for this menu also traps the soft perfume of rose petals. As an immediate contrast prior to dessert, I planned fritto misto of fish, shellfish, and summer vegetables, an assortment of textures due not only to the bite of the various elements when fried in oil but also to their surface coating. Eggplant, squash, romano beans, and thin lemon slices softened to various degrees under their crisp shell of leavened batter, along with fresh sardines and little shrimp rolled in egg and bread crumbs, played off tender squid dusted in semolina and flour. A timbale of farro and pigeon followed, its grainy chewiness offset by a smooth sauce of fresh cannellini beans. The menu opened with a trio of salads served cold to accentuate the "squeakiness" of just-picked green beans, the pop of cherry tomatoes, and the layered bite of pearl onions.

Rose-Scented Panna Cotta with Compote of White Nectarines
For 10

When gathering or purchasing roses to infuse this panna cotta, choose the most fragrant and be certain that they have not been sprayed with any sort of insecticide.

6 cups heavy cream, preferably not
    ultra-pasteurized
¾ cup sugar
Pinch of salt
3½ cups coarsely chopped rose petals
6 tablespoons cold water
2 tablespoons powdered gelatin

Place the heavy cream, sugar, and salt in a sauce pot. Warm the cream gently until it is too hot to touch but well below the simmer. Turn off the heat, add the chopped rose petals, stir well, and let steep for 10 minutes. When the flavor is strong enough, strain. If it seems too subtle, continue to steep the petals until you notice their pronounced taste in the cream. Bear in mind that the flavor will not appear as strong when cooled. Set the cream aside.

Place the 6 tablespoons of cold water in a small bowl and sprinkle the gelatin evenly over the water. When the gelatin has softened, about 5 minutes, whisk in some of the warm cream to dissolve it. Whisk this gelatin-cream mixture back into the cream, then pour it through a fine-mesh sieve into a medium-size mixing bowl.

Arrange ten 5-ounce ceramic ramekins on a baking sheet. Set the bowl with the cream in a larger bowl over ice. Stir the cream with a rubber spatula, scraping the bottom of the bowl constantly so that the panna cotta doesn't set where it comes into contact with the ice. When the mixture is very cold and slightly thickened, remove the bowl from the ice and pour the mixture into the ramekins. Refrigerate for 2 hours, or until the panna cotta is set.

White Nectarines

14 small white nectarines
3 tablespoons sugar
1½ cups cold water

Cut 6 of the nectarines into ¼-inch slices, to yield about 2½ cups. Place these in a small sauce pot with the sugar and cold water. Bring to a boil, reduce the heat, and simmer for 45 minutes. Pour the nectarine slices into a strainer and allow the clear liquid to drip into a container beneath. Discard the slices. Taste the clear liquid, add more sugar if necessary, then cover and refrigerate.

Peel, halve, pit, and dice the remaining 8 nectarines into ½-inch pieces, to yield 2 cups of diced nectarines. Add the diced nectarines to the chilled nectarine syrup.

To serve the panna cotta, carefully unmold each by running a paring knife around the edge of the ramekin. Invert the ramekins onto dessert plates and allow the panna cotta to drop out onto the plates. Spoon about 3 tablespoons of the diced nectarines and a little of their syrup around each panna cotta and serve.

Color

Salad of Fresh Porcini Mushrooms, Fennel,
Hearts of Celery, and Parmigiano
1999 Ribolla Gialla, "Vinnae," Jermann

~

Chilled Spinach, Cucumber, and Beet Soup
1999 Tocai Friulano, Petrucco

~

Sautéed Wild Salmon with Crookneck Squash
and Squash-Blossom Sauce
1997 Pinot Noir, "Southeast Block Reserve,"
Bethel Heights

~

Zuccotto of Summer Berries
1997 Passito Bianco, Tenuta Valleselle

As much as a successful menu is a progression of different flavors, textures, and weight, it is also a palette of colors. Although color is one of the most directly appreciable aspects of food, its effect in a menu is more subliminal, working on our sense of surprise over the course of a meal. The color of food inevitably mirrors the season; nevertheless, an all-pastel menu in spring is monotonous, too many dark tones on the winter table feels heavy and ponderous, and a summer menu goes overboard if its dishes are interminably bright.

If food could be said to have mood and tone, then color is the primary means of displaying it. Color evokes a spectrum of impressions, the subtlety, depth, richness, vitality, plainness, or exuberance of food influencing our expectations of what we are about to enjoy. We "eat with our eyes." Thinking about color when making a menu is yet another way to plan for variation that keeps the experience of eating compelling as the menu progresses. Of course, there are as many ways to paint a menu as a canvas. My preference is for clear contrasts that announce what's new in tone and character in the dishes that follow one another.

The idea for this menu began with a variety of summer berries that were at the height of their season. We decided to create a dessert that would capture their mingled flavors in a takeoff on *zuccotto*, a dome-shaped Italian sponge cake brushed with liqueur that is filled with a mixture of sweetened cream, grated chocolate, and hazelnuts. Our version is spiked instead with grappa, a flavor that blends well with summer berries. The cake slices are spread with berry jam and whole berries are folded into layers of sweetened cream and cake. To make the colors dance we pour sauces made from each fruit around each portioned slice. Visually, this dessert is striking, its ruby-, crimson-, and purple-tinted sauces blood-lush and passionate. On the other end of the menu the muted tones of a salad of shaved fresh porcini mushrooms, hearts of celery, thin slices of fennel, and transparent shards of Parmigiano stood in pale contrast to the vibrant solids of a chilled spinach soup stained in its center with a purée of red beets. The sunny colors of salmon and crookneck squash in a vinaigrette thick with their yellow-orange blossoms followed, a middle palette in relation to the colors of the other courses that stood apart, yet prepared the way for dessert.

~

Zuccotto of Summer Berries
Serves 10 to 12

This recipe calls for a variety of summer berries. If all are not available, choose whichever are ripest and most flavorful. In all, you will need 2 pints of strawberries and 1¾ pints of other mixed berries (blackberries, raspberries, ollalieberries). Making zuccotto is time consuming. In order to pace the process you may wish to make the sponge cake, the two sauces, and the jam ahead of time and reserve the making of the filling and frosting for the final assembly.

Sponge Cake

Melted butter, for the pans
1¼ cups all-purpose flour, plus more for dusting the pans
1¾ cups plus 1 teaspoon sugar
½ teaspoon salt
½ teaspoon baking powder
¾ cup egg yolks (from about 10–12 large eggs)
¼ cup plus 2 tablespoons orange juice
1½ teaspoons vanilla extract
1 tablespoon grated and finely chopped orange zest
¾ cup egg whites (from about 5–6 large eggs)

Preheat the oven to 350°F. Line two 12 by 17-inch sheet pans, with 1-inch sides, with parchment paper. Brush the sides and the lining with melted butter. Dust the sides and lining with flour, knocking out any excess.

Sift the flour, 1¼ cups plus 1 tablespoon of the sugar, the salt, and the baking powder into a large mixing bowl. In another mixing bowl whisk together the egg yolks, orange juice, and vanilla. Pour the yolk mixture into the sifted flour, scraping the bowl with a rubber spatula to transfer all of the yolk. With a sturdy wire whisk, whisk together the yolks and the flour mixture until smooth. Mix in the orange zest.

Place the egg whites in the bowl of a standing mixer fitted with the whisk attachment. Whip the egg whites until they hold a soft peak. Reduce the machine's speed to medium, and begin to add the remaining sugar, 2 tablespoons at a time. Add the sugar slowly but before the egg whites begin to look dry and overwhipped. This slow addition of the sugar will allow the egg whites to expand to their full volume, resulting in a nice fluffy cake with a tender texture. When all the sugar has been added, continue to whip the whites on medium speed only until all the sugar is dissolved and the whites are very stiff. Remove the bowl from the machine, and add half of the yolk and flour batter to the egg whites. Fold the batter into the whites until almost completely combined. Pour the rest of the batter into the whites and fold it into the whites completely. I prefer to use a handheld plastic dough scraper curved on one side for folding, as I feel it gives me more control and a better feel for the batter. If you don't have one of these, a rubber spatula also works well.

Divide the batter between the two pans and spread as evenly as possible. The best tool to use for this is an offset cake spatula. Bake for about 20 minutes, or until the cakes are firm in the middle and spring back when lightly pressed.

Summer Berry Jam
2½ cups strawberries
1½ cups blackberries or boysenberries
1½ cups raspberries
¼ cup sugar

Wash and hull the strawberries. Cut them into ½-inch pieces. Then put all of the berries and the sugar into a wide saucepan. Bring the jam to a boil, and boil rapidly, stirring constantly, until very thick, 10 to 12 minutes. Pour into a storage container and refrigerate until needed.

Assembly
For Soaking the Sponge Sheets
⅓ cup grappa
3 tablespoons sugar

Filling
1½ cups heavy cream, preferably not
    ultra-pasteurized
2 tablespoons sugar
2 tablespoons grappa
½ teaspoon vanilla extract
½ cup hulled and diced strawberries, cut into
    ½-inch pieces
1½ cups assorted berries, such as raspberries,
    blackberries, boysenberries, or olallieberries

Line a 1½-quart dome-shaped bowl with plastic wrap. Cut a 12-inch circle of sponge cake, then remove a wedge-shaped piece that is slightly more than one quarter of the circle so it will conform to the shape of the bowl. Cut another circle out of the other sheet of sponge cake that is the same diameter as the top of the bowl. Cut a third circle that is 2 inches smaller in diameter than the top of the bowl. Combine the grappa and the 3 tablespoons of sugar and stir until the sugar is dissolved. Fit the partial circle into the bowl and join the edges together to fully line the bowl. Brush this cake with some of the sweetened grappa. Spread about ½ cup of the summer berry jam onto the entire surface of the sponge circle in the bowl.

To make the filling, whip the heavy cream with the sugar, grappa, and vanilla until very stiff. Fold in all the berries. Fill the cake-lined bowl about one third full with some of the cream and berries and smooth the surface. Brush the smaller cake circle with more of the sweetened grappa, and place it, brushed side down, on top of the cream. Brush the top of this cake with grappa and then spread 2 tablespoons of the jam on it. Fill the bowl up, right to the top, with another layer of the berry-cream filling. Brush one side of the remaining cake circle with grappa and spread it with ¼ cup of the jam. Flip it, jam side down, onto the filling. Brush the other side with grappa. Cover the zuccotto with plastic wrap and refrigerate until completely chilled, at least 4 hours.

The Sauces
Strawberry Sauce
1½ cups hulled, halved strawberries
1 tablespoon sugar

Place the berries in a food processor with the sugar. Blend to a smooth purée. Pass the purée through a sieve to catch the seeds and refrigerate.

Berry Sauce
1½ cups mixed berries such as raspberries, boysenberries, blackberries or olallieberries
2 tablespoons sugar

Warm the berries and the sugar briefly in a sauce pot, then purée them in a food processor. Strain and refrigerate.

Frosting
½ cup heavy cream, preferably not ultra-pasteurized
1 teaspoon sugar
1 teaspoon grappa
⅛ teaspoon vanilla extract

Shortly before serving, unmold the zuccotto by inverting it onto a plate and removing the plastic wrap. Whip the heavy cream with the sugar, grappa, and vanilla until it just barely holds a stiff peak. It should still look smooth and shiny. Spoon the cream onto the top of the zuccotto, and frost it with a metal cake spatula. Cut into wedges using a very sharp knife. Lay the wedges flat on the plates, and drizzle about 1 tablespoon of both sauces around each wedge.

Singular Flavors

Salad of Artichokes Braised in Olive Oil
2000 Rosé di Saignée, Bergerie de l'Hortus

~

Ravioli of Early Peas
1999 Pinot Blanc, WillaKenzie Estate

~

Pan-Roasted Mackerel
New Potatoes
1999 Primofiore, Quintarelli

~

Raspberry Meringue Soufflé
1990 Vouvray Moelleux, Fontainerie

Food that speaks convincingly of itself without the crutch of added enhancements has as much to do with the quality of the prime ingredients as it does the cooking method. At Oliveto, we are always working on new ideas for dishes, not so much for the sake of novelty as to develop a fresh or more evolved view of seasonal food and to critique our own attempts. The logic for this menu emerged from a conversation shared among the heads of the Oliveto kitchen around the idea of raspberries and how to best capture their unique flavor and perfume. It seemed fitting to continue the theme of singular flavors throughout the menu.

We were only partly pleased with a soufflé built on the customary base of flour, milk, and whole eggs. Unmistakably raspberry, the flavor was nevertheless compromised by the richness of the base. We opted instead for the Italian meringue method that likewise owes its structure to beaten egg white but eliminates the need for flour, yolks, or milk. This yolkless architecture is a more transparent medium for conveying the flavors of fragile fruits. To compensate for the leanness of the soufflé, we offered a thin custard sauce on the side.

There is nothing simpler and more simply good than artichokes slow-braised in olive oil. This method allows for the pure flavor of artichoke to come forth. New peas need next to nothing to bring their flavor out and into focus. These we cooked briefly in a minimum of water and a little salt, mashed them fine, then used this purée as a filling for ravioli tossed in sweet butter. Mackerel has an assertive flavor all its own. Rich in oil content particularly under the skin, it needs a bare stream of olive oil, a little sea salt, and a moderately hot pan to deliver all it has. To this end we removed backbones and pin bones and cooked the butterflied fillets under a light weight to crisp the skin.

⌔

Raspberry Meringue Soufflé
For 8
Italian meringue soufflés can be prepared 4 hours ahead of baking, a real advantage if you want to make soufflés for a dinner party (or your own busy restaurant). They also take far less time in the oven (10 to 12 minutes to full set) and they hold their lift longer than richer soufflé mixtures.

4 cups (approximately 2½ half-pint baskets) raspberries
¾ cup plus 1 tablespoon granulated sugar, plus more for dusting the ramekins
¼ cup plus 2 tablespoons water
½ cup plus 1 tablespoon egg whites (from about 4 large eggs)
3 tablespoons confectioners' sugar, plus more for sprinkling the soufflés
Melted butter, for brushing the ramekins

Place 2½ cups of the raspberries and ¾ cup of the granulated sugar and the water in a small sauce pot. Bring to a boil, reduce to a simmer, and cook for 10 minutes. Strain the raspberries through a sieve and return the syrup to the pot. Whip the egg whites in the bowl of a standing mixer with the whisk attachment until soft peaks form. Add the confectioners' sugar slowly and continue whipping until stiff. Bring the raspberry syrup back to a boil again and attach

a candy thermometer. When the syrup reaches 242°F., pour it slowly into the beaten egg whites with the machine running. When all the syrup has been added, continue to beat the meringue until it comes to room temperature. While the meringue is cooling and beating, toss the remaining 1½ cups of raspberries with the remaining tablespoon of sugar in a small bowl. Brush eight 5-ounce ceramic ramekins with melted butter, and dust each ramekin with sugar.

When the meringue mixture is cooled to room temperature and quite stiff, transfer it to a large pastry bag fitted with a ½-inch plain round tip. Fill each ramekin one third full with meringue. Place 3 or 4 of the sugared raspberries in each ramekin. Pipe another layer of meringue into each ramekin so that each is now two thirds full. Place 3 or 4 sugared raspberries on this second layer of meringue. Cover with the remaining meringue. It will come approximately ¼ to ½ inch over the top of each ramekin. Refrigerate the soufflés until you are ready to bake and serve them.

Custard Sauce
2 cups half-and-half (or 1 cup of heavy cream and 1 cup whole milk)
½-inch piece of vanilla bean, split in half lengthwise
5 tablespoons sugar
¼ cup egg yolks (from 3 to 4 large eggs)

Place the half-and-half, vanilla bean, and 3 tablespoons of the sugar in a sauce pot. Bring it to a boil. As it heats, whisk together the egg yolks and the remaining 2 tablespoons of granulated sugar in a stainless-steel bowl. When the half-and-half comes to a boil, immediately remove it from the heat. While whisking the egg yolks, ladle about one fourth of the hot half-and-half into the yolks. When well combined, pour the tempered yolks back into the hot half-and-half in the pot and return the pot to the burner. Cook the custard over low heat, whisking constantly, just until you see and feel it thicken slightly. Immediately remove it from the heat and pour it through a fine-mesh strainer into a storage container. Chill the custard, covered, in the refrigerator.

Baking and Serving

Preheat the oven to 400°F. Bake the soufflés for 9 to 10 minutes, or until they are puffed, brown on top, and just cooked through. Remove the souffles from the oven, sprinkle the tops with confectioners' sugar, carefully place the hot ramekins on plates, and serve at once. Serve the custard sauce on the side in a pitcher.

Rich and Lean

Cold and Spicy Broccolini Salad
1998 Gavi, "Capello del Diavolo," San Bartolomeo

~

Black Sea Bass with Citrus Sauce
1998 Vernaccia, Terre di Tufi, Teruzzi & Puthod

~

Rotolo of Chicken with Prosciutto and Sage,
Salsa Pevra
1993 Valpolicella, Quintarelli

~

Hazelnut Meringata with Chocolate
and Espresso Sauce
1982 Vintage Port, "Madalena," Smith Woodhouse

Both richness and leanness are relative qualities that exist across a continuum in cooking. While I can imagine a far richer possibility for dessert and its preceding course in a menu such as the one above, the logic of this particular menu is determined by the effect of its courses in direct relation to one another. This menu is composed of two complementary parts—one lean, one rich.

The middle of winter poses limited options for desserts with seasonal fruit other than citrus. At such times, we often turn to the use of nuts, chocolate, dried fruit, and other reliable staples of the pastry kitchen. Because we often have an abundance of egg whites on hand left over from pasta making, pastry creams, citrus curds, soufflés, and meringues are a logical choice for the dessert menu. Meringues by themselves are too sweet for my taste. But mixing their sugar and egg white base with hazelnuts or almonds, piping it into flat disks, and layering these with lightly sweetened whipped cream tones down the cloying aspect of a meringue, making of it more of a texture than a toothache. Hazelnut *meringata* is rich from the cream and flecks of chocolate in its layers but is so light and airy it hardly seems so. The delight in eating it is the high degree of contrast between its elements: The nut meringue is crunchy while the whipped cream between its layers is the opposite extreme of almost insubstantial softness. Both carry bits of nuts and chocolate that dissolve on the tongue but are then carried further in a sauce combining melted chocolate and espresso. This dessert is a good example of the way in which extremes of color, texture, and flavor can meet to modulate each other.

Looking for a harmonious course to precede the meringata, I decided against fish since it more readily suggests a clean, fruit-based dessert such as an ice or tart. Given the forceful flavor of chocolate and espresso, I also steered away from braised red meat dishes that have sauces equally intense and brooding in mood. In order to provide some difference in texture and tone between the two, I felt that the preceding course should best be soft and somewhat subdued in character. I planned a boneless chicken leg rolled with prosciutto and sage and poached in a rich chicken broth. Because black pepper and chocolate are compatible, I made salsa pevra, a bread sauce liberally spiked with pepper, and a stew of buttered leeks.

Since the effect of the meringata and the chicken was decidedly soft and rich, it seemed right to provide a lean contrast in the preceding courses. Sautéed fillet of black sea bass with a tangy sauce made from blood orange juice, zest, and fruity olive oil and herbs took the menu in a fresh direction with a different food group and accents of tarragon and chervil. Broccolini is a variant of heading broccoli that sends out small florets on thin, succulent shoots. Looking over the entire menu, the obvious options for variation in the first course were temperature and seasoning. Broccoli invites strong seasoning such as hot pepper, garlic, and anchovy and is enlivened with lemon and olive oil. It is also most appetizing served chilled when high-pitched seasoning and the cold temperature join forces to issue a wake-up call to the appetite.

Chocolate Hazelnut Meringata

For 8

⅓ cup hazelnuts
½ cup egg whites (from 3 to 4 large eggs)
¾ cup plus 2 tablespoons granulated sugar
½ teaspoon vanilla extract
2 pinches salt

Confectioners' sugar, for sprinkling

Preheat the oven to 350°F. Place the hazelnuts on a sheet pan and toast for 12 to 15 minutes, until browned and fragrant. Cool the nuts completely, then grind them fine in a food processor. Reduce the oven heat to 300°F. In the bowl of a standing electric mixer fitted with the whisk attachment, whip the egg whites to soft peaks at high speed. Reduce the speed to medium, and gradually add the granulated sugar, 2 tablespoons at a time. Wait approximately 1 minute between each addition of sugar. When all the sugar has been added, add the vanilla extract and the salt, and whip only until the meringue holds very small straight peaks. Fold in the ground hazelnuts with a rubber spatula. Cut out 2 pieces of parchment paper to fit 2 half sheet pans. On each sheet, trace 12 circles, each with a diameter of 2¾ inches. Line the sheet pans with the tracing facing down.

Spoon the meringue into a pastry bag fitted with a plain ½-inch tip. Pipe the meringue out onto the parchment from the center of each circle outward. Bake the meringues for approximately 1½ hours, or until crisp. Cool the meringues completely and store them in an airtight container if you are not going to use them right away.

Chocolate Sauce
4 ounces chopped semi-sweet chocolate
1 cup heavy cream

Place the chopped chocolate in a medium-size heatproof bowl. Bring the cream just to a boil and pour it over the chocolate. Stir until smooth. Pour it into a storage container, cover, and set aside.

Espresso Sauce
1 cup heavy cream
5 tablespoons granulated sugar
$\frac{1}{4}$ cup egg yolks (from 3 to 4 large eggs)
2 tablespoons cold espresso

Place the cream and 3 tablespoons of the sugar in a medium saucepan. Whisk the egg yolks and the remaining 2 tablespoons of sugar together, and place them in a heat-proof bowl. Bring the cream to a boil and immediately remove it from the heat. While whisking the egg yolks, ladle about one fourth of the hot cream into the yolks. When they're smooth, pour the yolks back into the hot cream in the saucepan. Return the cream to the burner. Cook the custard, whisking constantly, until you see and feel it thicken slightly. Immediately remove it from the heat and pour it through a fine-mesh strainer into a storage container. Cover the custard, and put it in the refrigerator to chill. When the custard is cold, whisk in the espresso.

Filling
$\frac{2}{3}$ cup heavy cream
1 teaspoon granulated sugar
$\frac{1}{3}$ teaspoon vanilla extract
$\frac{1}{2}$ cup finely chopped semi-sweet chocolate

Whip the cream with the sugar and vanilla until very stiff. Fold in the chopped chocolate and refrigerate, covered, until needed.

Assembly
Place a dot of filling in the middle of each of eight dessert plates; this will anchor the meringata. Spread 2 tablespoons of filling on 8 meringue circles and place on the plates. Top with another meringue circle, and spread it with another 2 tablespoons of filling. Sprinkle the remaining 8 circles with confectioners' sugar, and place one atop each meringata. Spoon 1 tablespoon of each sauce around the meringatas and serve.

Salty, Bitter, Sour, Sweet

Oysters Baked on Rock Salt
2000 Sauvignon Blanc, Cain Musque

~

Artichoke and Cardoon Soup
2001 Rosé, Château la Conorgne

~

Charcoal-Grilled Pigeon with Vinegar Sauce, Rapini
Greens
2000 Nero d'Avola "Benuara," Cusumano

~

Tart of Dried Plums and Walnut Frangipane
10-year-old tawny port, Niepoort

Planning for contrast in a menu is most often a matter of introducing variety in the details from course to course. Changing the food group or its texture, temperature, or color; changing the weight of the dish; moving from lean to rich or vice versa; and altering the cooking method are all ways to achieve the contrast that gives a menu momentum. Contrast can also work on a more basic level if it is oriented to the primary sensations of taste: sweet, sour, bitter, or salty.

The structure of this menu emerged in the process of planning dishes to precede a tart of dried plums and walnut frangipane. Baked dried plums have a rich mouth feel and persistent sweetness that is offset by a buttery surround of walnut frangipane. The pairing of tawny port accentuated the nutty component in both the wine and the tart and amplified the concentrated sweetness of the dried plums. Pigeon is known for the "sweet" quality of its flesh and succulent skin, which invites an acidic counterpoint such as that lent by a vinegar-based sauce.

With two courses decided—one sweet, one acidic, and both rich in character—it was time for a transition. As it was a chilly, drizzly day in early spring, I settled on a hot soup of the artichokes and tender cardoons that had just made their first spring appearance. Both cardoon stalks and the leaves of young artichokes leave a pleasing bitter aftertaste and provided the right

foil to the courses that followed. It was not difficult to think of something salty and piquant as a first course; a carpaccio of tuna with capers, crostini of briny olives chopped into tapenade, or a chicory salad draped with prosciutto and shards of Parmigiano could easily have fit the bill. In the interest of making the underlying theme of the menu as clear as possible, I chose oysters, which announce the taste of salt more clearly than any other food I know.

⟳

Tart of Dried Plums and Walnut Frangipane

For 8 to 10 (Makes one 9-inch tart)

Dried Italian prune plums make a tart with a meaty bite. They enjoy a short, early summer season and are easily dried in a very low convection oven for several hours. However, if these are not available to you, choose large, moist prunes with a soft interior.

You will need a 9-inch tart pan with removable bottom.

Tart Dough

2¼ cups all-purpose flour
¼ cup sugar
¼ teaspoon salt
8 ounces (1 stick) unsalted butter, cool,
    cut in 1-inch cubes
1 egg yolk

Place the flour, sugar, and salt in the bowl of an electric mixer fitted with a paddle. Mix in the butter on the lowest speed until the dough barely starts to come together in the middle of the bowl. Stop the mixer, add the yolk, and continue to mix until the dough is uniformly mixed. Divide the dough into 2 equal pieces. Wrap the pieces in plastic and refrigerate for a minimum of 4 hours. You will need only one of the packages to make this tart; the other may be frozen for later use.

Preheat the oven to 350°F.

Roll out the tart dough into a 10-inch circle (1 inch larger in diameter than the 9-inch tart pan). Fit the tart dough circle into the pan, pushing it all the way into the pan where the bottom meets the rim. Trim off the excess. Refrigerate the crust until completely cold. Bake the crust until it is well browned, about 30 minutes. Remove the crust from the oven and set it aside to cool. Keep the oven at 350°F.

Plum Filling
20 dried plums (prunes), pitted
2 cups red wine
½ cup sugar

Combine the dried plums, red wine, and sugar in a small pot. Bring them to a boil, reduce to a simmer, and cook for approximately 5 minutes, until the dried plums are tender but still hold their shape. Remove from the heat and let the dried plums cool in their liquid.

Frangipane Filling
1¼ cups walnuts, lightly toasted and ground
½ cup sugar
Pinch of salt
6 tablespoons unsalted butter, melted
1 large egg
2 tablespoons heavy cream

Place the ground walnuts, sugar, and salt in a large bowl and stir to mix with a rubber spatula. In a smaller bowl, whisk together the melted butter, egg, and cream. Pour the wet ingredients into the dry, and stir with a rubber spatula just until the filling is combined and smooth.

Assembly
Remove the dried plums from the poaching liquid and place them on paper towels to drain. Pour the frangipane filling into the baked tart shell. Place the dried plums in the filling, spacing them evenly. The tart shell should be quite full. (As it bakes, the filling will rise up around the dried plums, partially covering them and keeping them from drying out too much in the oven during baking.) Bake the tart for approximately 30 minutes, until the edges of the frangipane feel set and the center is firm on top and soft underneath. Remove the tart from the oven and allow it to cool. While the tart is cooling, reduce the red wine in which the plums were poached to a thick glaze, about ½ cup. Just before serving, brush this glaze on the face of the tart.

Serve the tart warm with vanilla ice cream and a drizzle of the red wine glaze.

Spring Is Here

Green Garlic Crostone
2000 Greco di Tufo, Feudi di San Gregorio

~

Minestra of Carrot and Celery Root
1999 Tocai Friulano, Bastianich

~

Spiedino of Rabbit
Braised Artichokes
1996 Chardonnay "l'Angelica," Manzoni

~

Chestnut-Flour Crepes with Ricotta and
Chestnut Honey Sauce
1990 Vin Santo, Avignonesi

The scent of early spring in my neighborhood hangs like soft perfume in the morning air. The scent lasts as long as the sun is low, then returns again for a longer stay, particularly after a warm dusk. All things fresh and uncloying seem to be wrapped up in it. As the season warms and progresses, blossoms get down to business, spreading their petals wide and thrusting out their stamens for every bee to buzz. The transition of the scent of spring from sweet, come-hither to raw and unabashed is like new love after the blush of seduction. That scents, both pretty and wild, should attract bees to the undergarments of flowers and us to the fragrant air of this communion is only half the ecstasy of spring. We also get honey as a result. The flavor of honey can be mild and indistinguishable, like that bees transform from clover or linden, or it can return the direct scent of the plant, as does honey from sage, lavender, or eucalyptus. But only chestnut honey seems to seal within it the primal aroma of bees and blossoms and the heavy sweetness they make together.

Chestnut honey (see page 260 for source) is pungent and unmistakable. A little bit goes a long way. Its aftertaste is reminiscent of the bitter almond taste in the kernels of stone fruits. Chestnut flour crepes with ricotta and chestnut honey sauce was designed to feature this

remarkable taste. It seemed fitting to precede dessert with other springs dishes: We chose grilled tender chunks of rabbit wrapped in pancetta and skewered with sage leaves, with the season's first artichokes. New, sweet carrots made a delicately creamy soup accented with chopped chervil leaves. Spring garlic the size and shape of young leeks, sliced and briefly softened in olive oil, mixed with arugula vinaigrette and the minced green tops, and piled on toasted slices of sourdough, made a vivacious appetizer.

The taste logic of this menu had much to do with presenting the new and muted flavors of spring side by side. As one of our chefs put it, the menu was "a piece of a cloth. You could eat it all together." Unlike the workings of other menus that rely upon a progression of flavors, textures, colors, weight, and different cooking methods to sustain forward momentum, this menu was more homogenous in its taste effects. It nevertheless played on the contrast between the warm richness of honey and butter in the dessert echoed by a similar sweet smoothness in the soup, the comparatively lean, grassy taste of spring garlic and arugula in vinaigrette, and later the smoke-roasted flavors of the rabbit and the mildly bitter taste of artichokes.

Chestnut-Flour Crepes with Ricotta and Chestnut Honey Sauce

For 8 (16 crepes)

For the crepe batter
1 cup whole milk
⅛ teaspoon salt
¼ teaspoon sugar
2 tablespoons unsalted butter
¼ cup chestnut flour (see Sources and Resources, page 260)
¼ cup plus 2 tablespoons all-purpose flour
1 tablespoon plus 1 teaspoon peanut oil
1½ large eggs
¼ cup beer

Place the milk, salt, sugar, and butter in a small saucepan and heat, stirring, just until the butter has melted. Put the flours in a large bowl, and add the oil and the eggs. Mix slightly with a wire whisk, whisking in a little of the flour. Gradually add the warm milk, whisking all the while. When all the milk has been added and the mixture is smooth, mix in the beer. Strain the batter into a container and refrigerate, covered, for at least 2 hours and preferably overnight. Bring to room temperature before using.

Heat a 6-inch black steel crepe pan or a 6-inch nonstick sauté pan until hot. Rub the pan with a little peanut oil to prevent the first crepe from sticking. Take the pan off the heat, ladle in about 1½ tablespoons of batter, and quickly tilt the pan so that the batter covers the bottom evenly. Return the pan to the heat and cook the crepe until little holes form on its surface and its edges begin to brown. Lift the edge of the crepe with the tip of a bamboo skewer, grab it with your fingers, and flip it over. Cook the other side for approximately 30 seconds. To remove from the pan, simply invert the pan. Stack the crepes on a plate. When cool, wrap the crepes in plastic wrap to keep them soft and flexible.

Ricotta Filling
1 cup ricotta cheese (preferably sheep's milk)
2 tablespoons sugar

Beat the ricotta and sugar together until smooth. Cover and refrigerate until needed.

Chestnut Honey Sauce
¼ cup mild honey
¼ cup chestnut honey
8 tablespoons (1 stick) unsalted butter

Heat the honeys in a small saucepan until bubbles appear at the edges of the pan. Turn off the heat, add the butter 2 tablespoons at a time, and whisk until the butter is melted and the sauce is smooth.

Assembling and Serving
Preheat the oven to 375°F. Fold the crepes in half, then in half again and place them on a baking sheet. Open each crepe so that 3 of the 4 layers are on the bottom, and 1 is on the top. Place 1 tablespoon of ricotta filling in each crepe. Put the crepes in the oven and heat until they are crisp and the filling is warmed, approximately 2 minutes. Place 2 crepes on each plate and drizzle them with 2 tablespoons of the chestnut honey sauce. Serve warm.

Intensity

*Salad of Marinated Chanterelles and
Radicchio di Campo*
1999 Pinot Gris, "Carabella Vineyard," La Bête

~

Spiced Gnocchi alla Romana
*2000 Soave Classico Superiore,
"San Vincenzo," Anselmi*

~

*Grilled Spiedino of Quail with Wine Grapes,
Olives, and Walnuts*
2000 Sangiovese di Romagna, "Ceregio," Zerbina

~

Torta of Raisins Cooked in Grape Must
Tokáji Aszú, "6 Puttonyos," Gabor

Intensity in dessert can manifest as richness, as assertive sweetness, as flavor concentration, or as complexity. Unless the courses that lead up to such a finish are calculated, dessert can leave guests with the blunt feeling of having eaten too much, too richly, or without relief. The dessert that completes this menu is both very sweet and intensely focused in fruit flavor; the butter crust that seals the filling enhances it rich effect. Torta of Raisins Cooked in Grape Must paired with the extraordinary Hungarian wine Tokáji Aszu epitomizes the end of the harvest season—autumn's withered fruit pushed beyond ripeness by the final blaze of summer, its honey-colored light, and the intimation of winter darkness. Raisins steeped in saba (concentrated grape juice) make a nearly black filling for the pastry, but its taste conjures the opposite, a saturation of light. So too for the wine, its deep amber color with a golden glint at its edge only hinting at its surprising concentration of sugar, sappy extract, "noble rot," and warm sherry-like aromas.

To set the stage for the torta and wine, I looked for possibilities that were dissimilar in intensity. I ruled out roast pork in favor of a less weighty approach even though its proven affinity for dried fruit such as prunes suggested a possible association. Instead, I chose quail grilled over a fruitwood fire, sectioned and skewered with slices of pancetta and sage leaves. The smokiness from the fire and the accompaniment of oil-cured olives, nuts, and grapes (this last element providing a fresh hint of what was to come) and the salt-blistered skin of the bird provided a savory counterpoint to the final course without heaviness. Since sour is the opposite of sweet, I planned a dish with acidic elements to open the menu, steamed chanterelles tossed with sherry vinaigrette in a salad of burgundy-to-faded-yellow field radicchio that resembled fallen leaves. A middle course of semolina gnocchi provided the most marked diversion from dessert. Both mild in flavor and texturally smooth, it was a calming prelude to this bold ending. Despite the due consideration of the courses leading to dessert, we were careful to offer a moderate portion of the torta so as not to push a good thing too far.

Torta of Raisins Cooked in Grape Must
For 10

Pastry
2¼ cups all-purpose flour
¼ cup granulated sugar
¼ teaspoon salt
½ pound (2 sticks) unsalted butter, cool,
    cut in 1-inch cubes
1 egg yolk

Place the flour, sugar, and salt in the bowl of standing mixer fitted with a paddle. Mix in the butter on lowest speed just until the dough barely starts to come together in the middle of the bowl. Add the yolk and continue to mix until the dough is uniformly mixed. Divide the dough into 2 pieces, one approximately 12 ounces to form the bottom and the other 9 ounces to form the top. Wrap the 2 dough pieces in plastic and refrigerate them for a minimum of 4 hours before rolling.

Raisin Filling
2½ cups mixed raisins in equal quantities
    (dark seedless, golden or muscat, currants)
1 cup saba (see Sources and Resources,
    page 260)
½ cup plus 1 tablespoon water
1 cup sugar
5 tablespoons condiment-grade balsamico
Pinch of salt
1 tablespoon potato starch

Combine the raisins, saba, ½ cup of the water, the sugar, balsamico, and salt in a large sauce pan. Bring to a boil, lower the heat, and simmer until the raisins are tender, about 10 minutes. Mix the remaining 1 tablespoon of water with the potato starch in a small bowl and add it to the raisin mixture. Cook for 1 minute more, stirring constantly. Set the filling aside to cool.

Assembly and Baking
1 egg
1 tablespoon heavy cream
Sugar

Preheat the oven to 350°F. Remove the tart dough from the refrigerator and let it warm up slightly. Roll the larger piece into a circle 11 inches in diameter. Fit the circle carefully into a 9-inch tart pan with a removable bottom, pressing well into the corner where the sides meet the base. Place in the refrigerator to relax and chill. Roll the smaller piece of dough into a 10-inch circle and place in the refrigerator to chill. When the tart shell is completely chilled, place it in the oven and bake it only until golden brown, approximately 15 minutes. Remove it from the oven and set it aside to cool.

Fill the tart shell with the raisin mixture, place the 10-inch crust on top, and press to close. Trim the edges, then make a few thin slashes in the top center of the tart. Mix the egg and cream and brush it all over the top of the dough. Sprinkle liberally with sugar. Raise the oven temperature to 375°F. Bake the torta for 20 to 25 minutes, or until the top is evenly and thoroughly brown. Serve slightly warm.

Autumn

Dungeness Crab and Mussel Salad
1996 Silex, Dageneau

~

Soup of Autumn Squashes, Crostino of Parmigiano
1997 "Batar," Querciabella

~

Guinea Fowl Braised in Vinegar Lees
Swiss Chard
1995 Gattinara, Villa Claudia

~

Muscat Grape Ice with Shriveled Grapes
1995 Moscato, Loazzolo

Autumn brings wine grapes whose varietal character can be captured in the form of smooth ices or granita. The most recognizable of these is muscat, a tawny, gold-colored grape with an effusive perfume that evokes orange flower, ripe melon, and a gentle spiciness. Just as the wine of muscat, unlike almost all other wine varieties, retains the perfume of the fresh grape, so does the flavor of its ice remain true even though the juice is cooked. In keeping with the seasonally evocative flavor of this dessert, I chose dishes to precede it that have a strong locus in our autumn season. In early November, small mussels that are full and sweet come on the market. These became the basis of a salad of cos lettuces dressed with meyer lemon, new oil from a local press, and an accent sauce made from a quick reduction of the mussel's steaming liquor bound with a splash of cream. Squashes and pumpkins of all types, colors and sizes are also superabundant. I find that I can get the right complement of flavors only by using a mixture of them to make soup and settle on delicata for its refined flavor, acorn for the starch it provides, and sugar pumpkin that contributes sweetness. It seems fitting to pull out the braising pot since the weather has turned cold and foggy and I have just drawn vinegar from my balsamico casks, which leaves me with several quarts of lees, the flavorful sediments that precipitate in the cool season when the vinegar goes dormant following its warm weather fermentation. The sharpness of the lees in the braising liquid provides a bright counterpart to the mellow richness of the guinea fowl and the whole plate, a deep purple from the mingling of vinegar lees, pheasant rendering, and red chard, is reminiscent of the recent grape harvest.

While the substance of this dessert is the ice itself, it actually has two additional takes on the muscat flavor: So as to refer directly to the grape itself, we present the dessert with a small bunch shriveled in a very slow oven to concentrate its perfume and drizzle the ice with late-harvest Moscato wine.

Muscat Grape Ice with Shriveled Grapes
For 8

4 pounds ripe muscat grapes
½ cup sugar
¼ to ½ cup sweet Moscato wine

Set aside 8 little clusters of grapes, each holding 3 to 5 fruit. Remove the rest of the grapes from the stems and place the grapes in a large pot. Squeeze them with your hands so that they release some of their juice (this will prevent the grapes from sticking and burning), then add ¼ cup of the sugar. Bring the grapes to a boil, reduce the heat, and simmer for 5 minutes. Remove the grapes from the heat and purée them in batches in a food processor. Pass the purée through a fine-mesh strainer into a mixing bowl and stir in ¼ cup of the Moscato wine. Taste the purée for sweetness; if you find it too tart, add a little more of the sugar. If it needs a stronger muscat flavor, add up to another ¼ cup Moscato wine. When the purée is flavored to your liking, pour it into a large, flat-bottomed glass baking dish and place it in the freezer. Stir the ice every 20 minutes until it is frozen, approximately 1½ to 2 hours.

Preheat the oven to 300°F. To shrivel the grapes, put a rack on a sheet pan. Arrange the reserved clusters on top. Bake for 45 minutes to 1 hour, or until the grapes are slightly shriveled. Remove them from the oven to cool. Serve the ice in chilled cups with a cluster of grapes to the side.

The Shape of a Menu

Four Types of House-Cured Sausages (Salame Toscano, Genovese, Mortadella, Coppa di Testa)
Bitter Lettuces
N. V. Lambrusco, Barbolini

~

Maccheroni al Sugo di Carne
1999 La Sagreta Rosso, Sicilia

~

Halibut with Fresh Porcini Mushrooms
1997 "Batar," Querciabella

~

Fricasee of Rabbit
1998 Chardonnay, "Kleinstein," Santa Maddalena

~

Budino of Pears with Almonds
1997 Orvieto, "Calcaia," Barberani

Sometimes I think of a menu as having a graphic shape. This menu might look like this:

To my mind the most gentle and soothing of fruits is the pear, particularly when baked or poached or used as the central ingredient in cakes or puddings. In this menu, its simple uncomplicated taste is the opposite of the first course. Paired with a late-harvest wine slightly sweeter than the fruit and almond custard surround, this fruit dessert follows the motif established by the preceding courses and their wines: a gradual diminishment of flavor intensity and concentrated flavors that open out to progressively softer and more calming ones.

Cured sausages have a strong and complex focus that results from the intensification of flavor of the meat through the curing process. Compared to other means of concentrating flavor, curing represents a different kind of reduction, one that takes place through the gradual evaporation of the water in the meat, the stiffening of its texture, and, with these changes, the greater assertion of its spices and seasonings. Cured sausages are nothing less than exciting to eat at the beginning of a menu, a riot of taste sensations that are at once salty, tangy, and peppery, leaving the impression of sweetness from the marriage of meat and spice.

Maccheroni with meat sugo is similarly intense in savor but already more mellow in effect. Rendered of various meats that have been browned, repeatedly deglazed, and simmered in a small amount of meat broth, the sugo is then passed through a sieve to extract its essence.

Halibut, particularly the type that arrives from northern Pacific waters, is an especially moist and delicate fish, here paired with the earthy taste of fresh porcini mushrooms. Rather than browning the mushrooms, I sliced the caps thin, chopped the stems fine, and stewed them in butter, parsley, and a little fruity olive oil. The juice of fresh porcini mushrooms is naturally thick as though they contained a bare amount of clear starch. The texture of the cooked fish and mushrooms is one of the most harmonious I know and its more subtle taste takes the flavor level down from the previous course. Perhaps one of the most muted and delicate of meats is rabbit, here gently braised with fennel, cream, and lemon and served with a stew of young leeks and new potatoes, a soft bridge to an even more yielding sweet course.

Pear and Almond Budino
For 8

2 large ripe pears
4 tablespoons unsalted butter
⅓ cup almond paste
½ cup plus 1 tablespoon granulated sugar
Six ⅓-inch slices of Italian sourdough bread, crusts removed
2 cups whole milk
½ cup heavy cream
2 whole eggs
3 egg yolks
Pinch of salt

Peel, halve, and core the pears. Cut them lengthwise into ¼-inch-thick slices. Melt 2 tablespoons of the butter in a large sauté pan. Add the pear slices and sauté them for approximately 5 minutes, or until tender. Transfer the pears from the sauté pan to several paper towels to cool and drain. Mix the almond paste and 1 tablespoon of the sugar until smooth in the bowl of a freestanding electric mixer. Add the other 2 tablespoons of the butter and mix until smooth. Spread this mixture onto the 6 slices of bread.

Place the milk and cream in a small saucepan and heat it until it steams. Whisk together the eggs, egg yolks, and the ½ cup of sugar in a medium mixing bowl. While whisking, pour the hot milk into the egg mixture. Pour the mixture through a fine mesh strainer. Stir in the salt.

Preheat the oven to 350°F.

Place half of the sautéed pears in the bottom of a 1½ quart baking dish. Put 3 of the bread slices on top of the pears. Distribute the rest of the pear slices on top of the bread. Place the last 3 bread slices on top of the second layer of pears. Pour the custard mixture into the baking dish. Now place the baking dish in a larger dish, such as a roasting pan. Pour enough hot water into the roasting pan to reach halfway up the sides of the baking dish. Place the budino in the oven and bake for approximately 1 hour and 10 minutes, until a paring knife inserted into the middle comes out clean. Serve warm.

Summer Peaches

Aperitivo: Peach leaf wine

~

Babcock Peach with Old Balsamico

~

Summer Lady Peach Soup with Almonds
1999 Estate Viognier, Alban Vineyards

~

Roast Pigeon
Spiedini of Pigeon Livers, Sun Crest Peaches,
and Pancetta with Young Dandelion
1998 Cabernet Sauvignon, "Hidden Vineyard," Topel

~

Semifreddo of Peaches and Mascarpone
1995 Delice du Semillon, Joseph Phelps

To my taste, the quintessential fruit of summer is the peach, and this menu celebrates this luscious fruit throughout. The challenge in creating an entire meal around peaches lies in modulating its sweet presence and integrating its flavor so that the courses are neither repetitively sweet nor redundant in taste. Part of the solution is to offer different varieties of peaches (those presented here all ripen together in July). The menu opens simply with an aperitivo of chilled rosé, barely sweetened and left to infuse with peach leaves for several weeks. The wine picks up the soft fragrance of the peach as well as the faint suggestion of bitter almond (reminiscent of the kernel inside the pit) in the aftertaste. In a prime state of ripeness, the white Babcock peach is unsurpassed perhaps by any other fruit. The Comice pear may rival Babcock's delicacy but cannot approach its refinement. Its exquisite perfume evokes the light scent of pale roses, its skin, complexion, and fragile flesh, the innocence of a newborn. Ripe Babcock peaches need no completion; nonetheless, a small pool of old balsamico poured into its pitted well is pure ambrosia. In order to translate the peach to the savory side, I blended Summer Lady peaches, a large, meaty variety, with delicata squash to make a barely sweetened, pale ochre soup with a garnish of toasted almonds. Roast pigeon followed, served with peaches skewered and wrapped in pancetta that acted as a condiment to this sweet-fleshed bird.

The semifreddo returned the fresh flavor of peaches. Its layers of orange-scented sponge cake suffused with peach syrup, diced ripe peaches, and sweetened mascarpone amplified the flavor of peach carried even further by the sauce.

For a source for the peaches mentioned here and many other varieties, see page 262.

⟋

Semifreddo of Peaches and Mascarpone
For 8

Sponge cake
Melted butter, for the pan
1/2 cup plus 1/3 cup all-purpose flour
3/4 cup plus 2 tablespoons and 1/3 cup sugar
1/3 teaspoon salt
1/3 teaspoon baking powder
Scant 1/2 cup egg yolks (about 4 eggs)
1/4 cup orange juice
1/4 teaspoon vanilla extract
2 teaspoons finely chopped orange zest
Scant 1/2 cup egg whites (about 4 eggs)

Preheat the oven to 350°F. Line a 12 by 17-inch half sheet pan, with 1-inch sides, with parchment paper. Brush the sides of the pan and the paper lining with melted butter. Dust the sides and lining with flour and knock out any excess.

Sift the all-purpose flour, 3/4 cup plus 2 tablespoons of the sugar, the salt, and the baking powder into a large mixing bowl. In another mixing bowl, whisk together the egg yolks, orange juice, and vanilla extract. Pour the yolk mixture into the sifted flour mixture, scraping the bowl with a rubber spatula to remove all the yolk. With a sturdy wire whisk, whisk together

the yolks and the flour mixture until smooth. Mix in the orange zest.

Place the egg whites in the bowl of an electric mixer. Fit the machine with the whisk attachment. Whip the egg whites until they hold a soft peak. Reduce the machine's speed to medium and begin to add the remaining 1/3 cup sugar, 2 tablespoons at a time. Add the sugar slowly, waiting at least 30 seconds before making the next addition. By adding the sugar slowly you'll increase the volume of the egg whites as much as possible, resulting in a nice fluffy cake with a tender texture. When all the sugar has been added, continue to whip it on medium speed only until all the sugar is dissolved and the egg whites are very stiffly whipped. Remove the bowl from the machine, and add half of the yolk and flour batter to the egg whites. Fold the batter into the whites until almost completely combined. Pour the rest of the batter into the whites and fold it in completely.

Pour the finished batter into the prepared pan, and spread it evenly. The best tool to use for this is an offset cake spatula, which really makes the job easier. But even with the proper spatula, this is still a difficult job. Don't expect that you'll be able to spread the batter completely evenly in the pan. Put the pan in the oven and bake until the cake is firm in the middle and springs back when lightly pressed, about 20 minutes. When the cake has cooled completely, run a butter knife around the edges to release it from the sides of the pans. Flip the cake out onto a flat surface, and peel the parchment paper off. Cut the cake in half crosswise. Put the cake back on a clean sheet pan, with a sheet of parchment between the pieces. Cover tightly with plastic wrap and set aside until needed.

Peach Sauce

5 ripe peaches
¼ cup plus 2 tablespoons sugar
½ cup water

Slice the peaches roughly, skin and all. Put them in a pot with the sugar and water and simmer them until the peaches are cooked through, approximately 10 minutes. This prevents the peaches from oxidizing. Purée the peaches and their liquid in a food processor while still hot, then put them through a fine-mesh sieve. Taste, and add more sugar if necessary. Cover and refrigerate until needed.

Peach Syrup

2 peaches
¼ cup sugar
1¼ cups water

Cut up peaches roughly, skin and all. Place in a pot with the sugar and water. Bring to a boil, reduce to a simmer, and cook for 30 minutes. Pour the peaches into a strainer and allow the clear liquid to drip through into a storage container. Discard the peach pulp. Taste for sweetness and add a little more sugar if necessary. Cover and refrigerate until cold.

Assembly

3 cups peeled and diced ripe peaches
⅔ cup heavy cream, preferably not
    ultra-pasteurized
2 tablespoons sugar
1 teaspoon vanilla extract
3 cups mascarpone

Trim the 2 halves of sponge cake so that they will fit snugly one atop the other into a 3-quart rectangular glass baking dish. Peel and dice the peaches. To peel the peaches, plunge them into boiling water for 10 to 15 seconds, then remove them quickly and put them into ice water. The skins will slip off easily. Cut into ½-inch dice.

Whip the heavy cream with the sugar and vanilla extract until stiff. Fold the whipped cream into the mascarpone. (Commercially available mascarpone is often very thick. If you purchase mascarpone with this quality, stir in a small amount of liquid cream to soften and loosen it before folding in the whipped cream.) The mixture should be very stiff.

Fit one of the pieces of sponge cake into the bottom of the baking dish. Brush the sponge with some of the peach syrup. Now spread half of the diced peaches in an even layer over the sponge cake. Spoon half of the mascarpone mixture onto the peaches, and spread in an even layer.

Brush the other sponge sheet with peach syrup, and flip it, brushed side down, into the baking dish. Brush the other side with more peach syrup. Spread the rest of the diced peaches on the second piece of sponge. Spoon the remaining mascarpone atop the peaches and smooth into an even layer. Cover the semifreddo tightly with plastic wrap, and refrigerate until completely chilled, at least 4 hours.

To serve, place each piece on a plate and drizzle about 2 tablespoons of peach sauce around it.

Refreshment

The good effect of eating a meal, particularly when appealing flavors tend to induce people to eat heartily, depends upon planning for refreshment within the menu and at its close. I think of refreshment as both relief and stimulation— relief from richness, from the strength of certain flavors, or when the feeling of weight or the overall combination begs a simple, clean contrast; and when the edge is taken off the appetite near the end of a meal, the stimulating effect of the right sweet course can rescue a meal from the feeling of satiety. Pomegranate granita did just that in this autumn menu. Its frozen temperature, the granularity of its texture, and its sweet/astringent flavor immediately provided the respite needed after the richness of sea scallops, buttery tortelli enriched with beef marrow, then the fire-roasted flavors of duck and wild mushrooms.

Pomegranate Granita
Makes about 1 quart

**10 to 12 large, ripe pomegranates to yield
 1 quart juice**
⅔ cup fresh-squeezed orange juice
1 tablespoon fresh-squeezed lemon juice
½ cup sugar

It is very important that you use large, very ripe pomegranates with large, deep-red seeds. It is wise to wear latex gloves when handling pomegranates because their juice is acidic and stains the skin.

Cut the pomegranate's broad side and gently press them over an electric juicer to about two thirds of the depth of the cut fruit (aggressive use of the juicer will yield a bitter juice). Remove the remaining seeds, put them in a large strainer, and squeeze them by hand. Pass the juice through a fine sieve. Let the juice settle for 4 hours or overnight in the refrigerator. You will notice a dense sediment on the bottom of the container with a clear, darker layer on top. Pour the clear, darker layer into a container and discard the sediment. You should have about 3 cups.

Combine the pomegranate juice with all the other ingredients and whisk to combine well. Pour the juice into a shallow, noncorroding baking pan, cover with plastic wrap, and place in the freezer. When the juice is fully frozen, take it out and drag the tines of a fork over the surface of the ice to reduce it to granules. Return to the freezer for several hours before serving.

Conversation with
a Glass of Wine

Among wine drinkers, there are those who relish it for its own sake and others for whom wine is justified by food. For the passionate aficionado, the build of a wine, the intricacies of its aroma, nuance of color, vintage, and varietal expression, not to mention its warm intoxicating effects, can easily overtake considerations of its relation to food. I have sat around more than one table where the meal was little more than a garnish to wine-speak and liquid abandon. For me, wine is fundamentally a beverage, although a special one, that can only be fully appreciated in the context of eating. These camps are not mutually exclusive, of course. It is possible to both be captivated by wine and find it most fulfilling when partnered with food. To discover what wine is meant for is an adventure and a pursuit, a pleasure that lies in the promise of a fine meal.

As the new century progresses, it is increasingly rare to experience the traditional nexus of food, wine, and place. Wineries everywhere now contend with the economic realities of a widely expanded market, the pressure toward uniformity, and long-distance expectations of taste. Much wine is falling into the new vats of the "international style," well made but with blurred edges, no longer for the village but for the world. Grapes that traditionally flourished in specific regions have found new homes thousands of miles away, stretching the boundaries of what constitutes the classic taste of, say, San Giovese, Nebbiolo, or Tocai Friulano. At the same time, inward-looking New World vintners, well versed in the old traditions of winemaking and with many seasons of experience of their own, have discovered terroir—the unique influences of soil and microclimate, the grape *and* its habitat, that inform the humbling Old World notion that "wine makes itself." In the large picture, then, wine that reveals its tradition or terroir appears more distinctly localized than ever while that made to appeal to the global citizen with a taste for fusion or a comforting uniformity is less expressive of any place in particular.

Wine has never been more abundantly available or diverse. But how are we to know wine removed from its place of origin and the native food with which it belongs, or when it is blended into the vast geography of a hybrid international style? And among the sea of choices in any well-stocked cellar, wine list, or broker's bin, how does one marry it to a meal? This is a question that has continued to absorb my interest not only because I am regularly called upon to make wine recommendations for my customers or because I feel it is important as a restaurant owner to assist servers in arriving at some basic consensus about the wine list and the menu. I am also constantly surprised, intrigued, and challenged by what I discover. I have learned as much from pairings that failed as from those that hit the mark. Such experiments have left me skeptical of "expert" advice, of "classic matches," of rating systems that reduce wine to a number, and of the reliability of particular vintages and famous estates.

It is a pity that much of the advice on the subject, however well meaning, tends to treat wine and food as static and predictable. It doesn't take long for even the novice taster to realize the wide differences that can manifest in, say, pinot noir grown in different locations, or the same species of oysters from a different sea.

Wine and food matches, other than those already proven through trial or familiarity, are difficult at best to preconceive. The successful marriage of food and wine is something that happens in a live moment. Wine is ever evolving, and food, no matter how well known or rehearsed, is subject to wide variation given the state of the raw ingredients and the manipulations of the cook. Add to this the myriad conditions that influence our experience of wine and food—our level of appetite, the mood of the table, the weather, the trappings of a meal—and the likelihood is much stronger that what happened last time will not necessarily happen again. This suggests is that there is a lot of fun to be had in negotiating the shifting ground of pairing food with wine.

My own criterion for harmonious food and wine pairing is reciprocity: Is the food enhanced by the wine and vice versa? Still, this leaves much to be desired by way of explanation. What does it mean to say that a particular food and wine are made for each other? This is a rich question, and the answer is not reducible to generalities. In my experience, a match works *because* it is unique. Nevertheless, since there are common physical sensations associated with taste and a language to describe what wine and food share or hold away, it is at least possible to point in the right direction.

It is no coincidence that the words used to describe wine's fundamental characteristics are borrowed largely from the vocabulary of the human body; what is sensed directly via the flesh cannot otherwise be described in more meaningful terms. Wine is said to have "body" that is "fleshy" or "thin," a "nose," "legs" (also called "tears"), and "backbone." Tannin in wine is its soft "muscle" or firm "grip"; acid its "nerve." The weight of a wine ranges from the "lean" to the "brawny," an attribute that is also related to texture registered by "mouth feel"; a "plump" roundness in wine is charming while a wine that has fallen out of shape is "flabby."

When it comes to the aroma of a young wine or the bouquet that only age confers, the wine lexicon expands into nature to encompass the elusive trail of scent. Wine runs the gamut from roses to skunk, geranium flower to wet dog, orange blossom to tar; it binds the subterranean scent of mushroom and truffle and the airy scent of grass.

Wine finds its red robe perfumed with blackberry, currant, and spice; or its green to golden transparency scented with lemon, honey, and green olive. There is no end to what one can find in even the quickest sniff of a wine when it mixes with memory and imagination. These revelations are often fleeting, made as they are of the same stuff as dreams. As soon as you wake to what wine has summoned up, and return to pull it closer into memory, it once again slips beneath the surface.

There is a strong element of mystery as well. When transformed to wine, the straightforward juice of the grape can conjure scents that, however congruous with it, are essentially foreign. How does the aroma of raspberry, leather, cat pee, kerosene, rocks, lychee, or clove find its way into a glass of wine? Whether actual or imagined, the scents attributed to wine seem to be drawn from thin air. Food, no less evocative, is grounded in the earth and expresses the taste and scent of itself. It may not be too wild a conceit to compare wine to spirit and food to matter. Wine animates food. Food gives wine form and directs it to a purpose. I cannot otherwise explain the rare synergies or the altered dimensions of taste that occur when the two are put together.

In the protocol of tasting, the aromas in wine are usually considered first then judged in relation to how they are held within the whole. Such orderly scrutiny is not usually applied to food. We tend to concentrate primarily on the way food tastes, period. But guessing at a match of food and wine is more than a one-sided affair and necessitates paying closer attention to the nature of food on the plate.

By looking at food we can usually make a quick and fair assessment of what we are about to eat. Aroma tells us more. But it isn't until we actually taste food that we have the complete story. Food varies from rich to lean, can be subtle or complex in flavor with every grading in between. In its range of texture, it surpasses the possibilities of wine. Food that mirrors the season bears its mark. Weather affects its mood. The weight of food relates to its mass: There is no doubt, for example, that braised lamb shank sits heavier than fillet of sole. Weight also represents the intensity of food's flavor—its feel in the mouth—and corresponds to levels of leanness or richness. In every way that wine is rustic, simple, elegant, or faceted, food can follow suit.

Wine works with food by providing either contrast or complement. Wine's structural components, tannin and acid, work underneath flavor, compensating for the richness or intensity of food by offering a cleansing or refreshing effect. In the case of tannin, the pleasantly dry, constricting sensation can be just what is needed to counter the dark intensity of a braise or the marbled richness of roasted meat. Conversely, certain powerful cheeses such as Gorgonzola tame the harsh tannins in big red wines so that the flavor of the fruit is not stopped short. Wine can act like a simple season-ing or condiment, enlivening food with a spark of acidity, a breath of spice, the caress of its texture, or the warmth of wood. Wine also behaves like a sauce in the way it can underscore or amplify the flavors in meat, fish, and fowl. Food can likewise draw a wine into the open to reveal what it only intimates on its own. Wine can smooth the passage of cheese, envelope or offset the layered flavors of a braise, or extend the horizon of sweetness in dessert.

Over the years, I have developed my own approach to trying matches. Live conversation is its model, but rather than having people talk, I prompt myself, or others if among a group, to observe and to comment on a dialogue in which food and wine are the primary conversers. Discord is as welcome as agreement and equally valuable since both train the observer to recognize in the sum of a particular food and wine some small aspect of how it all adds up. Rather than coming to the table with a set idea, armed with book knowledge or someone else's best advice, we need little more than awakened senses and an open mind. Responding can-didly and testing one's preconceptions in light of the actual sensual experience is also humbling.

When initiating such a discourse, I begin with the food. On my home turf, I know what to expect; if eating in an unfamiliar setting, the situation is more precarious as even the best-intended descrip-tion of a dish can be misleading. The first question I ask of the food is what is its character and mood: Is it lean, rich, subtle, or pro-nounced in taste? What is its weight? Are its flavors simple or lay-ered? Is it formal or homey? Are there any elements in the food that might compete with the wine, like vinegar or other strong sea-soning? Next, I ask what the food might beg for by way of contrast or complement. Then I try to associate the food with a place and within a tradition in order to narrow the field of choice. Food doesn't always have a particular locus or it may not traditionally have been conceived in tandem with wine, as is true of certain ethnic cuisines. In such cases, matching can be challenging.

Once I have identified several wines to which the food most clearly refers, or I have made my best guess, the stage is set. I make my choice, put myself in the observer's seat, and let the conversa-tion happen. By way of example, here's how I recently began and what I overheard:

I was really very hungry. A morning spent forging cramped sentences at my writing desk followed by a long, purgative bike ride into the spacious outlooks of the Berkeley hills had left my mind clear and my stomach growling. In anticipation of an early dinner on my own, I called my favorite restaurant to ask about the evening's offerings as there were a number of bottles in my cellar that were ready to drink. Since I was planning to eat my meal in solitude and I enjoy allowing a single wine to cavort with different foods, I decided to opt for one bottle throughout the meal. The front desk kindly faxed me a "rough" of the menu to help me gauge my choice. Scanning the à la carte menu for possible connections, I found a clear reference to Provence in the succession of Crostone of Salt Cod with Gypsy Peppers and Capers followed by Minestrone of Summer Vegetables with Pesto (*soupe au pistou* moved across the Italian border), Roast Lamb with Artichokes, Garlic, and Wild Fennel, and a refreshing Peach Sorbetto. I could easily imagine this meal with a 1985 Bandol I was holding that might very well have reached its peak. But this was a meal made to be enjoyed on a balmy summer evening under the plane trees, I decided, and here I was in sweater weather with the wind pulling a chilly blanket of fog from San Francisco Bay. What's more, the salt cod seemed to cry out for a splash of cold rosé (brrr, no thanks!). I moved on. Another clear theme was the flavors of Piemonte. In the appetizer section I found warm Treviso radicchio salad with anchovy and grana reminiscent of *cardoni* (cardoons) and the hot bath of anchovies—Piemonte's *bagna cauda*. Among the pastas, classic tajarin, the celebrated hand-cut egg noodles with brown butter and sage, and afterward, boneless spit-roasted pigeon stuffed with prosciutto, fontina, and sage. My stomach began to sound off again. With the promise of comfort images of dark-breasted birds turning in front of a wood fire, I could already feel my bones warming. Menu resolved, I sorted through my cellar bins for Piemontese wines. I passed over Dolcetto and Freisa, which had too little weight to cover all the bases of the courses I'd planned. My Barbarescos were too young to tap and the Barbera d'Asti I had tasted recently had more acerbic force than I was willing to reckon with on an easy Sunday evening. If I were to stay in Piemonte, it seemed, it would have to be Barolo, certainly no lightweight in any respect. But I hoped to find in the dusty bottle of 1989 Cannubi from Scavino I settled upon, a wine whose structural power might have ceded to the buried elegance it had only intimated when I first tasted it some years back.

I arrived at my table, a quiet corner at the end of a long banquette. As I was studying the menu for any last-minute changes my waiter arrived to let me know that pasta with braised oxtails had been added late in the day. Barolo with buttered Tajarin or pappardelle with oxtails? Okay, but what about the preparation? He explained that the oxtails had been deeply browned, onions and fresh tomatoes had been added along with a small amount of diced carrot and celery; the residues were deglazed with meat broth, then sweetened with a tint of tomato paste and sent to mellow in a slow oven. Some 3½ hours later the meat was picked from the bones and tossed with wide egg noodles and the reduced braising juices. I was reminded of Stracotto al Barolo, Piemonte's marvelous mar-

riage of beef and wine. I asked my waiter to open the wine and let *it* decide. "Shall I decant?" he asked. I explained that I prefer to sample the wine before aerating it. What a pity this ritual of uncorking wine hours before or dumping it into the odorless air of outsized glass. We wait for years for wine to mature, then let the first reward of such patience evaporate on the side table, or dissolve in the stream of a speedy vortex, or, however solemn, in the trickle against a candle flame. The first scent may not be pleasant, but to let it stray or blow it away is to miss the opportunity of knowing a wine from the moment of its entrance. The opening of wine and the arrival of food in the context of a meal are like a curtain rising on a play, the acts of which are suggested by the courses of the menu. If food and wine could be imagined to converse, then each becomes a character actor that shapes and is shaped by the interactions of a meal. Considered in this light, any meal can become theater, an occasion for observance and reflection that reveals food and wine on the stage.

Principal Voices

BAROLO: The so-called "King of Wines and Wine of Kings," made from the Nebbiolo grape, said to be named after the foggy mists of Piemonte

TREVISO: A bitter red radicchio that takes its name from the town in the Veneto region in and around which it is grown

OXTAILS: Actually the tail of a cow

PIGEON: Descendant of the wild blue rock dove

PANNA COTTA (PC): A formed cream-based dessert that originated in Piemonte

Minor Voices

CARDONI: A bitter plant in the artichoke family whose leafy stalks resemble celery

FONTINA: A pungent cheese from the Valle d'Aosta used to make the Piemontese melted cheese sauce called Fonduta

With a clean pop of a long cork, Scavino's Barolo escapes like a genie from its bottle, hovers from eighteen inches, moves in to fill the atmosphere of my small table, then vanishes to collect some higher wish. The first pour is cloudy and littered with sediment.
(The wine begins to speak . . .)

BAROLO: *I've been a long time on my side. It would have been kind of you to stand me up next time to let my floccules drop rather than sully my first impression. Grazie alla Madonna, Scavino kept me free from the tight squeeze of that filter. I asked him, dare you force a king to strip? Don't worry, it's all in my neck.*

Sure enough, I pour another glass and it runs clear. Angled against the white purity of the tablecloth, the wine is a transparent garnet, its rim the tawny brown of onion skin. Rather than the powerhouse I expect to see evidenced in a depth of color, this Barolo appears to be a medium-bodied wine, even fragile, showing like the faded plum that tells of wine that's past its prime. I swirl Barolo and when it returns to its former level, long "tears" run languidly down the inner face of the glass. There they settle and remain in a bead at its glinted edge. I swirl again, take several quick sniffs, and lower the glass. Its aroma is reclusive, secretive, and indistinct like the misted patch of blue I catch momentarily in the shifting grayness of the sky from my window-gazing seat.

BAROLO: *What do you expect? Before joining the family of Barolo my name was Nebbiolo. I spent my first year with my head in a fog, afterward locked tight in a barrel, and then corked under the green obscurity of this bottle. Give me time to sort myself out.*

I hope that tasting will reveal something more. Taking the wine in and chewing it hard, I search for descriptors. But before I can put words to my first impressions, tannin ambushes the wine surrounding it in its constricting grip. It now resembles over-stewed tea trailing bitterness in a thin wake of flavor. Swallowing, I feel a prickly acidity, then a low burn in my throat that tracks all the way to my chest. It's so harsh that I start to worry that I have overestimated the readiness of this wine and I consider changing course altogether, as it is difficult to imagine any food that would find its match in this monster. In my mind, I imagine radicchio turned caustic, tajarin obliterated, pigeon pummeled, sour grapes . . .

BAROLO: *Per l'amor di Dio, stop spinning. Give me time to breathe!*

With the jury still out, I ask my waiter to stall my food. I call the maître d' to decant the wine, then give it a vigorous swirl. I clean my mouth with bread and butter, chat with the couple seated beside me, and wait. Twenty minutes later, the wine has undergone a miraculous transformation. What was before a faint scattering of scents is now collected in a bouquet, too various to disassemble at once, better to be discerned in time as its separate flowers open. Also, in what appears a near complete reversal, the hard tannin that previously snuffed the possibility of finding any fruit seems to have fallen into the greater composite of the wine. Fully present but shifted to a position farther back, it now permits the bouquet to surface and sustains its length. There is more dried fruit than fresh— cherry, fig, raisin, and the withered plum its color suggests. Then faded Rose rides up on a leather saddle with licorice on her breath. I am momentarily confused by the suggestion of smoke coming not from the hearth around the corner but smoldering quietly in the low ground of the wine.

BAROLO: *If I were you, I'd change track on the tajarin. There's a train approaching. Would you try to stop it with a toothpick?*

This is for sure a massive wine and the beefy weight of braised oxtails seems a better fit. I hail my waiter, change my order, and moments later the meal begins.

TREVISO: *Scavino, you flatter me. I don't usually find myself in such lofty company. Most wine turns away when I appear, if not for my acid tongue then perhaps for the bitterness in my heart.*

BAROLO: *Eh Treviso, we Piemontese are not as haughty as we might appear. You remind me of another friend, Cardoni, who has a bitter streak as well. In my region they dip him raw in a hot bath of olive oil, anchovies, and garlic and knock back hardball wines like there was no domani. Here bitterness is a virtue, you see. Good for the blood, we say, and the promise of longevity.*

I lift a forkful of salad (uh-oh, lemon in the dressing), then take a sip of wine. Like milk after artichokes, the wine makes the salad taste almost sweet at first, then compounds its astringency in the finish. Anchovies blend beautifully. Shards of Parmigiano smoothe the tannic edge.

TREVISO: *Long live the King! And thanks for the positive reinforcement. But I'm not certain we're to our host's taste. It's really rather shocking . . .*

BAROLO: *There you go again, lamenting yourself. You don't see me losing my nerve, do you? Sometimes a mild assault on the taste buds is just what is needed in the front of a meal. Think of the way the pickly and the salty meet the high pitch of hunger or a sleepy appetite. We're just the flip side of the same coin. The bitter can breed a craving or clear the path for more.*

Like my first take on the wine, the pappardelle does not possess the dark intensity I had envisioned. Yet its down-home aroma fills my head, like those in my grandmother's small kitchen did on holiday mornings. The sauce is both rustic and refined, with a clarity that fathoms the middle depths of beef's flavor. Together, meat and sauce have a slippery richness that wraps its silky coat around the tangle of noodles. I can hardly stay my fork.

BAROLO: *A moment of your time . . .*

The wine has further rounded, but it is also stretching a taut line of acidity. Its bouquet is even more effusive, but taking another bite of oxtail and a swallow of wine, I meet with a refusal to merge.

BAROLO: *You're too soft for me.*

OXTAILS: *Any meat* would *be.*

BAROLO: *To stand my strength you should have been drowned in wine instead of broth; take a tip from stracotto al* you-know-who *next time.*

OXTAILS: *I'm perfectly content to sit you out.*

BAROLO: *You're starting to sound like Treviso.*

OXTAILS: *You can lead a cow to water but you can't make him . . .*

BAROLO: *. . . drink me, drink water, let's just get on with it.*

Before I was old enough to take wine neat my mother diluted it to childhood strength with water. Now its cold purity flushes the heat in my chest, dissolves all differences in taste, and keeps tipsiness in check. Ten minutes later I'm ready for what's next. Roast pigeon arrives hot from the spit, exhaling the sappy aroma of burning fig wood. Browned fingerling potatoes flank the bird that leans on a mahogany pool of sauce flecked with bits of chopped giblets.

PIGEON: *I'd prefer to fly above your quarrel with that cow. Before we begin, you should know the chef cut out my breastbones. If my flesh is not to your liking, at least you'll find companionship with your paesana Fontina tucked inside.*

BAROLO: *At least* you *can't complain of a bitter heart.*

Cutting into the bird, its crimson juice erupts, then trickles down to stain the sauce. Its flesh is lean and livery but between the salty blister of skin and meat, there is a soft sumptuousness, fat that has the smooth tenor of foie gras. The wine embraces the bird and its own smoky overtones like a new lover. I carve again, and this time Fontina binds with the slice, slowing Barolo's penetrating force, then both rush to a height of flavor neither has known before.

PIGEON: *In me you've found your perfect match?*

BAROLO: *You're quite a pretty little catch.*

PIGEON: *Our host is nearly out of breath, let's fly away before he finishes the rest.*

Nearing the end of my meal with this wine, this food, I feel ravenous all over again. I chew the wing and leg bones clean, smash potatoes into the remaining sauce, then mop the plate clean. Against a competing voice that warns me to let perfection rest, I decide to try a final sweet course with the inch of wine that remains in my glass. I recall its suggestions of fruit but find no candidates that correspond on the dessert menu. Sorbet is out of the question, chocolate too much, and warm apple tart seems the wrong direction. I throw caution to the wind and order Rose Geranium Panna Cotta. It arrives with an unexpected corona of blackberry sauce twenty times darker than Barolo. This version falls between barely-set custard and flan but is richer than both. I spoon into it and it trembles. In my mouth it melts effortlessly, then is joined by rose geranium's faint sachet of spice and flower. Blackberry is only distracting.

PC: *I shudder to think what you might do to me.*

BAROLO: *I'm hardly sure myself.*

PC: *To thrash delicacy would be a crime. How could one as tough as you possibly make me shine? How about an espresso instead and call it a night?*

BAROLO: *I'm determined to last this out. Our host has held me through my youth and here I am in middle age, with more to add and still engaged. Take heart and stay awhile, if not to shine at least to smile.*

Much to my surprise, like mild cheese and wine, Barolo and panna cotta walk the line together, trading spice and faded rose in a strange symmetry that neither would have chosen. Nothing risked, nothing gained, I tell myself as I finish my glass and pay the bill. As I walk into the night, I think of the lucky luxury I've enjoyed but also the fleeting irony of eating. For in the short space of several hours, I've drained twelve years of waiting, consumed the long-practiced artistry of chefs, felt the mysterious congruity of new, now old moments in time. It will never be quite the same, the small table, the mood, the night, this food with this wine. All will now be sentenced to the vapor of memory. But for the moment the meal remains in my pores. I can still taste it as it travels with me through the foggy distance home.

Sources and Resources

Aceto Balsamico and Saba

• www.oliveto.com
Italian aceto balsamico tradizionale and condimento balsamico are available online.

• Corti Brothers in Sacramento carries rare and limited aceto balsamico from the Modena and Reggio Emilia Consortia, as well as condimento balsamico and excellent saba from the Azienda Agricola San Geminiano.
Phone orders only: (916) 736-3800; fax:(916) 736-3807.

• www.manicaretti.com
Aceto balsamico tradizionale and various condimento vinegars from the Leonardi acetaia are available (see their store locator for a local source). Manicaretti is a wholesaler, but individual bottles can be purchased direct from the Pasta Shop, Rockridge Market Hall, Oakland, CA; (888) 952-4005.

• Stephen Singer, Olio
Traditional and condiment-grade balsamico from the acetaia of PierLuigi Sereni.
Inquiries and sales: ssingerolio@earthlink.net

• Agrodolce, Inc.
For information on balsamic vinegar production, barrels, and supplies, contact agdol@earthlink.net.

Anchovies

• www.agferrari.com
Rizzoli Acciughe Salate are whole anchovies preserved in rock salt, available online in a 850-gram tin (30 ounces). After opening the anchovies, transfer the unused portion to a storage container with a top that fits them tightly and cover with sea salt. Stored in this manner, the anchovies will last 4 to 6 months.

Chestnut Flour

• www.agferrari.com or www.chefshop.com
Available in the late autumn and early winter months. Enter "chestnut flour" at the search prompt.

Chestnut Honey

• www.manicaretti.com
Offers very good Italian chestnut honey by mail order; (888) 952-4005.

Grain and Flour

• www.oliveto.com
For specific flour and grains referred to in the recipes in "Pasta Primer."

• Giusto's Specialty Food Company
344 Littlefield Avenue South, San Francisco,
CA 94080 (650) 873-6566; fax (650) 873-2826
Giusto's, established in 1940, is a mill offering a wide spectrum of excellent whole-grain and refined flour, cereals, and dry legumes, many of which are organically farmed.

• www.diamondorganics.com
A large selection of organic grains and flour.

Farro

• Available in 500-gram (1.1-pound) and 5-kilogram (11-pound) from Rustichella d'Abruzzo. Mail order direct from the Pasta Shop, Rockridge Market Hall, Oakland, CA; (888) 952-4005.

Fennel Pollen

• www.fennelpollen.com/order.htm
Available in 15 gram tins (approximately ½ ounce) or in bulk from Sugar Ranch.

• www.manicaretti.com
Manicaretti offers fennel pollen in 200 gram (7.1 ounce) bags.

Fish

• www.mbayaq.org
For an annotated listing of "best choices," go to the Seafood Watch Chart. A "best choice" is defined as a wild population that's abundant enough to sustain fishing, low levels of wasted catch, and fish caught or farmed in ways that protect the environment. Lists type of fish, provenance, level of fishing, and specific information

related to the health and regulatory status of fisheries, fishing methods, and exploitation of certain species. Updated frequently. Has many links to articles and to other organizations. Drawbacks: Lists value-added items such as canned and frozen food, can err on a local level, and offers no opinion on the flavor and texture of certain fish (i.e., farmed fish).

• www.seafoodchoices.com
Seafood Choices Alliance "brings ocean conservation to the table by providing chefs, fishermen, and other seafood purveyors with the information they need to make sound choices about seafood." Offers "Seasense Database," a tool for making sustainable seafood choices. The database features a brief description of 20 common fish with recommendations by the National Audubon Society, Monterey Bay Aquarium, and Environmental Defense. Like other sites, this one favors environmentally safe farmed fish such as catfish without regard to flavor and texture.

Flour Mill

• www.2-life.com/gmform.htm
Online ordering of SAMAP hand-driven and electric stone grain mills.

Extra-Virgin Olive Oil and Citrus Oil (Agrumato)

• www.oliveto.com
Cold-pressed extra-virgin olive oil from California and Italian olive varieties.

• www.mcevoyranch.com
McEvoy Ranch, Petaluma, California
Grower and producer of some of the finest olive oil from Italian varieties planted in 1991. McEvoy Ranch has its own olive mill and olive plant nursery. Offers newly pressed oil December through March.
For direct sales from the ranch, call (707) 769-4122. See the website for a list of local distributors near you.

• www.manicaretti.com
Manicaretti offers a selection of very good oil from Tenuta di Capezzana, Castello di Volpaia, and Frescobaldi "Laudemio" as well as agrumato (citrus oil). Agrumato lemon and orange are highly recommended. Mail order through the Pasta Shop, Rockridge Market Hall, Oakland, CA; (888) 952-4005.

Meat

• www.nimanranch.com
E-market offers numerous cuts of beef, pork, and lamb. Ships fresh (not frozen), every day. Unusual products: commercial sheep casing, commercial hog casing, pig feet (front), pork back fat, pork caul fat (frozen), pork belly (skinless), pig tails.

• www.eatwild.com
Includes a short essay on the value of grass-fed versus conventionally raised animals. Under "Suppliers" lists grass-fed farms by state with a description of the farm and feeding regimens, along with web links and postal and e-mail addresses. The majority of the people listed on the site have small, family-owned operations and sell their meat directly from the farm or at local farmers' markets. Some of the larger farms have retail outlets and can ship to any state of the country.

• www.morrisgrassfed.com
Joe and Julie Morris
500 Mission Vineyard Rd.
San Juan Bautista, CA 95045
jmorris900@earthlink.net

• www.greatbeef.com
The mission of this site is to "introduce consumers of clean, healthy, humanely raised meats to independent family farmers and ranchers who produce them." Has 18 member listings. Each farm is different from the next, offering various other animals (pork, goats, poultry) as well as fruits, vegetables, grain, and dairy products. All "naturally" raised (see their definition). Each must be contacted to determine availability and shipping.

Organic Produce

• www.purefood.org/purelink.html
Organic Consumers Association. An extremely useful site. Offers National Directory of Farmers Markets' by state. Lists 348 co-ops and natural food stores by state (and city), including some foreign. Links educational organizations and articles.

• www.caff.org/farmfresh
California Association of Family Farmers. If you live in California, this is a wonderful source for farmers' markets, U-picks, farm stands, and dairy, egg, and meats from family farmers. Listed by crops, by area, and even by zip code.

• www.farmersmarket.ucdavis.edu
Another site for farmers' markets with lists by California county. Most listings have a partial roster of produce by season. California Federation of Certified Farmers' (CAFF) Markets site. Regional information on what is grown where. Also links with CAFF.

• www.ccof.org
Lists farmers' markets, produce stands, U-picks by state. Lists phone number, fax number, address, certification status, and products. Many states have no listings, however.

• www.csacenter.org
Website for Community Supported Agriculture and the Robyn van En Center. The directory lists member farms by state alphabetically, with their addresses and phone, fax, e-mail, or web addresses. Resources, referrals, and links to national, state, and regional organizations related to community-supported agriculture.

• www.diamondorganics.com
Based in Freedom, California. Mail-order organic produce. Profiles eleven local organic farmers. Uses FedEx. Ships year-round. Bread, groceries, eggs, grains, organic samplers of vegetables, seasonal fruit, garden salads, fruits, citrus, and flowers.

Peaches

• www.froghollow.com
Frog Hollow Farm in Brentwood, California, offers a superb selection of tree-ripened peaches (16 varieties) and nectarines (11 varieties). Consult the "crop timetable" for a seasonal schedule of available fruit. Frog Hollow ships anywhere in the country.

Polenta (Whole Grist)

• Anson Mills specializes in "artisan-quality" fresh, cold-milled products from certified organic and heirloom seed corn, wheat, and Carolina gold rice.
2013 Green St., Columbia, SC 29205
Available by mail order online at www.ansonmills.com.

Bulk 25-pound bags or 12-ounce bags (minimum purchase is 4 bags).

Pasta Machines

• www.surlatable.com
Pasta machines by Atlas. Chitarra tool with rolling pin for cutting fresh pasta sheets. Microplane cheese graters.

• www.cooking.com
Offers pasta machines made by Imperia and electric extruders by SIMAC as well as some small tools for cutting and shaping pasta.

Sausage Making Tools, Equipment and Supplies

• Butcher and Packer Supply Company
1468 Gratiot Avenue, Detroit, MI 48207; 800-521-3188
Offers a wide range of products from casing to cutlery, grinders, brine pumps, mixers, and starter culture for dry-fermented sausage. Online ordering at www.butcher-packer.com

• The Sausage Maker
A reliable source for casing and meat-curing supplies. I use this source for curing salt. Sausage Maker sells two types. Instacure No. 1 contains 6.25 percent sodium nitrite on a salt carrier. It is used for all meats that require cooking. Instacure No. 2 is formulated for dry-cured meats and contains both sodium nitrite (6.25 percent) and sodium nitrate (1 percent). Sausage Maker also sells powdered dextrose and purified salt.
Toll-free ordering at 1-888-490-8525 or online at www.sausagemaker.com.

Forceps for Use in Tying Casings

• See Global Trade Alliance, surgical instruments division. (602) 803-8303, or online at www.gtamart.com/mart/products/surginst/. Look for "dressing forceps."

• Also, Spectrum surgical instruments (800) 444-5644 or (330) 686-4550.

• INSCA-International Natural Sausage Casing Association is an excellent source for information on all types of natural casings and stuffing capacities. Go to www.insca.org, scoll to "casing info," and follow the prompts.

Digital Ounce/Gram Scales

• www.aweighscales.com
A number of scales to choose from at reasonable prices.

• www.scalesgalore.com/tmulti.htm
Offers a range of digital kitchen scales including solar powered.

• www.pastryitems.com/digital_scales.htm
Model E-80 (80 ounce/2000 Portion × 1-ounce/ 1-gram) battery or AC powered AC adapter is included. Very durable and suited to frequent use.

Sausage Stuffers, Grinders, and Mixer

• www.butcher-packer.com/c_sausagestuffers.htm
Offers a water-powered stuffer, the smallest (5-pound) of the "Tre Spade" line and Frederich Dick stuffers. Also carries the "Tre Spade" hand mixer, 44-pound capacity.

• www.amer-rest-equip.com
Offers the excellent Italian-made "Tre Spade" horizontal sausage stuffer in all of the available sizes. Scroll to "Food Processing," then to "Alfa," then to "Sausage Stuffer."

• www.alliedkenco.com
The Torrey company makes excellent grinders in various sizes for the passionate home sausage maker and for small commercial production.

pH Meter and Buffers

• www.pollardwater.com
Look for the "pH testr 2" by Oakton, a very good pocket-sized digital pH meter. Also purchase pH buffer tablets. Search under pH buffers.

Meat Cultures for Fermented Dry-Cured Sausages

• Meat cultures are supplied by chr.-Hansen company. Read about them at www.chr-hansen.com. Click on "Products," then enter "Cured Meat Cultures" in the product search prompt.

• www.butcher-packer.com
Cultures are sold online by Butcher and Packer. Search under Starter Cultures on the home page. Cultures arrive in cold-packed pouches, enough to ferment hundreds of pounds of sausage. When you receive the package, and after removing the culture, close it tight, place it in a resealable freezer bag, and store it in the freezer.

Squid Ink

• www.markys.com/squidink.htm

Tomato Seeds and Plants

• www.seedsavers.org
This is the Internet site for the Seed Savers Exchange in Decorah, Iowa. Seed savers sells online both seed packets and organically grown transplants (available for sale in April and May) of many heirloom tomatoes as well as other vegetables. The primary focus of Seed Savers Exchange is traditional varieties grown by Native Americans, Amish and Mennonite communities, and farmers and gardeners who have perpetuated the heirloom varieties of their immigrant ancestors. Visit their website for a current seed catalogue and plant listing with full-color photographs of available varieties.

Tomatine

• Tomato leaves, often thought to be poisonous, are in fact harmless and perhaps even beneficial. According to a study by the Agricultural Research Service, USDA (*Food and Chemical Toxicology*, July 2000, v.38, no.7, pp. 549–553), the alkaloid tomatine is not absorbed from the digestive tract into the blood stream because it binds to cholesterol, which also passes unabsorbed. In addition to the flavor that tomato leaves contribute, they may also contribute to lower cholesterol.

Truffles

• www.chef-ready.com
A reliable mail-order supplier of fresh white and black truffles. Order toll free at (888) 737-5151; call beginning late October for white and autumn black truffles and December for black winter truffles.

Index

Conversion Chart
Equivalent Imperial and Metric Measurements

American cooks use standard containers, the 8-ounce cup and a tablespoon that takes exactly 16 level fillings to fill that cup level. Measuring by cup makes it very difficult to give weight equivalents, as a cup of densely packed butter will weigh considerably more than a cup of flour. The easiest way therefore to deal with cup measurements in recipes is to take the amount by volume rather than by weight. Thus the equation reads:

1 cup = 240 ml = 8 fl. oz.   ½ cup = 120 ml = 4 fl. oz.

It is possible to buy a set of American cup measures in major stores around the world.

In the States, butter is often measured in sticks. One stick is the equivalent of 8 tablespoons. One tablespoon of butter is therefore the equivalent to ½ ounce/15 grams.

LIQUID MEASURES

Fluid Ounces	U.S.	Imperial	Milliliters
	1 teaspoon	1 teaspoon	5
¼	2 teaspoons	1 dessertspoon	10
½	1 tablespoon	1 tablespoon	14
1	2 tablespoons	2 tablespoons	28
2	¼ cup	4 tablespoons	56
4	½ cup		110
5		¼ pint or 1 gill	140
6	¾ cup		170
8	1 cup		225
9			250, ¼ liter
10	1¼ cups	½ pint	280
12	1½ cups		340
15		¾ pint	420
16	2 cups		450
18	2¼ cups		500, ½ liter
20	2½ cups	1 pint	560
24	3 cups		675
25		1¼ pints	700
27	3½ cups		750
30	3¾ cups	1½ pints	840
32	4 cups or 1 quart		900
35		1¾ pints	980
36	4½ cups		1000, 1 liter
40	5 cups	2 pints or 1 quart	1120

SOLID MEASURES

U.S. and Imperial Measures		Metric Measures	
Ounces	Pounds	Grams	Kilos
1		28	
2		56	
3½		100	
4	¼	112	
5		140	
6		168	
8	½	225	
9		250	¼
12	¾	340	
16	1	450	
18		500	½
20	1¼	560	
24	1½	675	
27		750	¾
28	1¾	780	
32	2	900	
36	2¼	1000	1
40	2½	1100	
48	3	1350	
54		1500	1½

OVEN TEMPERATURE EQUIVALENTS

Fahrenheit	Celsius	Gas Mark	Description
225	110	¼	Cool
250	130	½	
275	140	1	Very Slow
300	150	2	
325	170	3	Slow
350	180	4	Moderate
375	190	5	
400	200	6	Moderately Hot
425	220	7	Fairly Hot
450	230	8	Hot
475	240	9	Very Hot
500	250	10	Extremely Hot

Any broiling recipes can be used with the grill of the oven, but beware of high-temperature grills.

EQUIVALENTS FOR INGREDIENTS

- all-purpose flour = plain flour
- coarse salt = kitchen salt
- cornstarch = cornflour
- eggplant = aubergine
- half and half = 12% fat milk
- heavy cream = double cream
- light cream = single cream
- lima beans = broad beans
- scallion = spring onion
- unbleached flour = strong, white flour
- zest = rind
- zucchini = courgettes or marrow